THE GOSPEL OF
JESUS CHRIST IN THE
OLD
TESTAMENT

THE GOSPEL OF JESUS CHRIST IN THE OLD TESTAMENT

edited by
D. Kelly Ogden, Jared W. Ludlow,
and Kerry Muhlestein

THE 38TH ANNUAL
BRIGHAM YOUNG UNIVERSITY
SIDNEY B. SPERRY SYMPOSIUM

RSC
BYU

DESERET
BOOK

The Sperry Symposium is sponsored annually by Brigham Young University and the Church Educational System in honor of Sidney B. Sperry. In the course of his forty-five years as a religious educator, Dr. Sperry earned a reputation for outstanding teaching and scholarship. The symposium seeks to perpetuate his memory by fostering continuing research on gospel topics.

Copublished by the Religious Studies Center, Brigham Young University, Provo, Utah, and Deseret Book Company, Salt Lake City, Utah.

http://rsc.byu.edu/rsc_rec_pub.php

Library of Congress Cataloging-in-Publication Data

Sperry Symposium (38th : 2009 : Brigham Young University)
    The gospel of Jesus Christ in the Old Testament : the 38th Annual Brigham Young University Sidney B. Sperry Symposium / edited by D. Kelly Ogden ... [et al.]
        p.   cm.
    Includes bibliographical references and index.
    ISBN 978-1-60641-138-4 (hardbound : alk. paper)
    1. Bible. O.T.—Criticism, interpretation, etc.—Congresses.   2. Jesus Christ—History of doctrines—Congresses.   3. Church of Jesus Christ of Latter-day Saints—Doctrines—Congresses.
4. Mormon Church—Doctrines—Congresses.   I. Ogden, D. Kelly (Daniel Kelly), 1947–
    BS1171.3.S635 2009
    221.6—dc22

                                                                        2009014042

Printed in the United States of America
Sheridan Books, Chelsea, MI

10   9   8   7   6   5   4   3   2   1

CONTENTS

PREFACE

The Old Testament is foundational scripture. Understanding its contents will help us to understand other scripture, for the New Testament, the Book of Mormon, the Pearl of Great Price, and the Doctrine and Covenants contain numerous passages from the Old Testament and presuppose that the reader is familiar with the first testament of Jesus Christ. Often students of the gospel fail to see the Old Testament as a witness of Christ and his gospel, yet this book of scripture not only guided the children of Israel but became the scripture for early Christians and Book of Mormon peoples. The frequent quotations and allusions to the Old Testament by later writers in the New Testament and Book of Mormon certainly demonstrate its applicability to their understanding of the gospel and the plan of our Heavenly Father.

The gospel of Jesus Christ has been needed since the inception of human residence on planet earth, and we know that his gospel has indeed been on the earth from the beginning. The book of Moses records, "And thus the Gospel began to be preached, from the beginning, being declared by holy angels sent forth from the presence of God, and by his own voice, and by the gift of the Holy Ghost. And thus all things were confirmed unto Adam, by an holy ordinance, and the Gospel preached" (Moses 5:58–59).

The Prophet Joseph Smith further declared:

Perhaps our friends will say that the Gospel and its ordinances were not known till the days of John, the son of Zacharias. . . . For our own part we cannot believe that the ancients in all ages were so ignorant of the system of heaven as many suppose, since all that were ever saved, were saved through the power of this great plan of redemption, as much before the coming of Christ as since. . . . We conclude that whenever the Lord revealed Himself to men in ancient days, and commanded them to offer sacrifice to Him, that it was done that they might look forward in faith to the time of His coming, and rely upon the power of that atonement for a remission of their sins.[1]

President Brigham Young likewise attested the presence of the Savior's truths throughout the Bible: "In all my teachings, I have taught the Gospel from the Old and New Testaments. *I found therein every doctrine, and the proof of every doctrine, the Latter-day Saints believe in, as far as I know.* . . . There may be some doctrines about which little is said in the Bible, but they are all couched therein, and I believe the doctrines because they are true, and I have taught them because they are calculated to save the children of men."[2]

We cannot be true students of the Book of Mormon or Doctrine and Covenants without also being students of the Old Testament, for Jesus himself declared the Old Testament scriptures "are they which testify of me" (John 5:39). We would expect to find Old Testament teachings and language in all other, later scripture because they are all from the same Source. "Know ye not that the testimony of two nations is a witness unto you that I am God, that I remember one nation like unto another? Wherefore, I speak the same words unto one nation like unto another. And when the two nations shall run together, the testimony of the two nations shall run together also. And I do this that I may prove unto many that I am the same yesterday, today, and forever. . . . For I command all men, both in the east and in the west, . . . that they shall write the words which I speak unto them" (2 Nephi 29:8–9, 11).

It should not surprise us, then, that the doctrines of the gospel of Jesus Christ were taught and practiced in the time frame of the Old Testament: the first principles and ordinances of the gospel; the pillars of the Creation, Fall, and Atonement; the ordinance of celestial marriage and subsequent importance of children, posterity, and family history work; the covenant and the mission of holy and chosen people; the sacrament; tithes and offerings; patriarchs and patriarchal blessings; names and titles of God, Jehovah, Jesus Christ; the appearance of God and angels; the role of prophets and prophecy, including messianic prophecies; revelation, dreams, and visions; premortal life; the spirit world; worship practices; record keeping; miracles; observance of holy days and Sabbaths; priesthood functions and administrations; Temples and Temple worship, clothing, and sealing power; laws of health; scattering and gathering of Israel; apostasy and restoration; missionary work, or raising the warning voice to individuals and nations; human deification (*theosis*, or the doctrine of humans' potential to become like Heavenly Father); signs of the last days; the Second Coming; the Millennium; and Zion. All these things were known and taught during Old Testament times.

Great doctrines of the kingdom were known, taught, and practiced, including sacrifice, moral cleanliness, forgiveness, consecration, deliverance, service, scripture study, prayer, obedience, love, mercy, fasting, spiritual rebirth, gratitude, perfection, reverence, happiness, good works, integrity, praise for the Lord, humility, foreordination, accountability, and more.

This volume, *The Gospel of Jesus Christ in the Old Testament*, features papers delivered at the 38th annual Sidney B. Sperry Symposium (2009) on a variety of vital subjects. Elder F. Melvin Hammond, emeritus member of the Seventy, introduces this volume with a look at the remarkable contributions of the Prophet Joseph Smith in understanding the Old Testament. Other writers illuminate such diverse subjects as eternal marriage, family, and motherhood in the Old Testament; the plan of salvation in early Old Testament writings; the roles of vicarious sacrifice, Temple worship, covenant making, and angels in the salvation of God's people; the significance of the Lord's loving-kindness; vivid gospel teachings from the books of Ruth, Isaiah, and Hosea; the functions of the Holy Spirit in Old Testament times; and an examination of how Christian writers in the post–New Testament era saw Christ and his gospel throughout the Old Testament.

> D. Kelly Ogden
> Kerry M. Muhlestein
> Jared W. Ludlow
> Thomas R. Valletta
> Patty A. Smith

NOTES

1. Joseph Smith, *Teachings of the Prophet Joseph Smith*, comp. Joseph Fielding Smith (Salt Lake City, 1976), 59–61.

2. Brigham Young, in *Journal of Discourses* (London: Latter-day Saints' Book Depot, 1854–86), 16:73–74; emphasis added.

THE GOSPEL OF JESUS CHRIST IN THE OLD TESTAMENT

Elder F. Melvin Hammond

I n considering the theme "The Gospel of Jesus Christ in the Old Testament," I feel "like a droplet of spray proudly poised for a moment on the crest of a wave, undertaking to analyze the sea."[1] Or, as Moses said after seeing God and His innumerable creations, "Now, for this cause I know that man is nothing, which thing I never had supposed" (Moses 1:10).

"A Bible! A Bible! We have got a Bible, and there cannot be any more Bible" (2 Nephi 29:3). This prophetic description of biblical convictions as they would exist today was given by the Lord to Nephi in about 550 BC. For thousands of years, Jews and Gentiles alike have made this same narrow, restrictive declaration concerning the Old and New Testaments.

Such were existing conditions in 1820 when Joseph Smith Jr., a young farm boy, began a search for truth. The religious sects of the day, using the Bible, were vigorously proselyting for new converts. There was great "confusion and strife among the different denominations" (Joseph Smith— History 1:8). Young Joseph said: "My mind at times was greatly excited,

Elder F. Melvin Hammond is an emeritus Seventy.

the cry and tumult were so great and incessant. The Presbyterians were most decided against the Baptists and Methodists, and used all the powers of both reason and sophistry to prove their errors, or, at least, to make the people think they were in error. On the other hand, the Baptists and Methodists in their turn were equally zealous in endeavoring to establish their own tenets and disprove all others" (Joseph Smith—History 1:9).

Lamenting the apparent differences between the local religious leaders, Joseph said, "The teachers of religion of the different sects understood the same passages of scripture so differently as to destroy all confidence in settling the question by an appeal to the Bible" (Joseph Smith—History 1:12). In his confusion, he turned to the admonition of James in the New Testament: "If any of you lack wisdom, let him ask of God, that giveth to all men liberally, and upbraided not; and it shall be given him" (James 1:5). With innocence and pure faith, the boy followed the admonition and appealed in secret prayer to the only perfect source of truth, his Heavenly Father. Then in a moment unique in all of history, God the Father and His Beloved Son, Jesus Christ, appeared in glory to Joseph Smith. From that moment on, knowledge and understanding began to cover the earth and illuminate the minds of men.

Praise be to God for a modern-day prophet! Were it not for Joseph Smith, we would still be mired down in the black tar of ignorance, "ever learning, and never able to come to the knowledge of the truth" (2 Timothy 3:7). Until Joseph Smith came on the scene, no one had understood many of the truths found in the Old Testament for over a thousand years.

The Jews still conformed to the Mosaic covenant, completely unaware that Israel had broken the "everlasting covenant" (Isaiah 24:5). Christianity's use of the Old Testament had been relegated to a carefully selected menu of character-building stories. As light and knowledge burst forth, the old Mosaic covenant was replaced with the new and everlasting covenant! The everlasting covenant given anew in every dispensation was appropriately called the new and everlasting covenant in this, the last dispensation.

Clearly the world had misinterpreted, misconstrued, and misunderstood the divine message of the Bible, namely that Jehovah was none other than Jesus Christ, the Son of the Everlasting Father; that the gospel of salvation was given in the beginning to Adam and Eve and was ever-lasting; and that all the prophets had declared these same eternal truths.

The remarkable visit of the Father and the Son to Joseph in 1820 was only the prelude to many extraordinary events that gradually led to a further understanding of truth restored to the earth. The following events in the life of Joseph Smith will lead us to a better grasp of our theme, the gospel of Jesus Christ in the Old Testament.

1. In 1823, three years after the glorious visitation of God the Father and His Beloved Son, Jesus Christ, to the boy Joseph Smith Jr., an angel calling himself Moroni made an appearance to Joseph and informed him of golden plates that were buried in a hill not far from his home. He was told that, using an instrument called the Urim and Thummim, he was to translate the writings engraved on the plates. The plates contained a sacred record of an ancient people who had inhabited the American continent. Joseph was told that after visiting the site every year for four years he was to obtain possession of the plates and commence an interpretation.

2. On September 22, 1827, the plates were obtained by Joseph, and by the spring of 1829, the translation was completed. Although there were many impediments to the printing, the work continued and in the early spring of 1830, the first editions of the Book of Mormon were ready for distribution.

3. During his work on the Book of Mormon, Joseph Smith was commanded to commence a translation of the Bible relying on revelation. In June of 1830, with Oliver Cowdery acting as scribe, the work began in earnest. He started with the book of Genesis. It is interesting to note that the Prophet was only twenty-four years old and Oliver but twenty-three years old at the time.

It seems important at this point to emphasize the respect that Joseph had for the Bible—both the Old and New Testaments. He said that those who read the Bible can "see God's own handwriting in the sacred volume: and he who reads it oftenest will like it best, and he who is acquainted with it, will know the hand [of God] wherever he can see it."[2] However, he recognized that there were many omissions and "many plain and precious things" had been lost. Said he, "I believe the Bible as it read when it came from the pen of the original writers. Ignorant translators, careless transcribers, or designing and corrupt priests have committed many errors."[3]

As the Prophet Joseph Smith began to translate the Bible, truths so long hidden from the world came to light. Keys to understanding the scriptures were revealed. The gospel of Jesus Christ, with the priesthood and all the ordinances necessary for salvation, had been given to man from the beginning. Suddenly, the Creation of the earth, the Fall of man, the Atonement of Jesus Christ, and the holy priesthood all began to make sense. And the new knowledge gave a clear pattern to follow in order to obtain eternal life.

Adam, Enoch, Abraham, Isaiah, and others have become heroes in my eyes. There was great purpose in their lives. I see them as real people—yet spiritual giants—prophesying, performing miracles, struggling to bless their people, defending the truth, and preaching the gospel of Jesus Christ.

Adam and Eve

Adam and Eve were cast out of the Garden of Eden because they transgressed a law given to them by God. They ate the forbidden fruit of the tree of knowledge of good and evil and in so doing became mortal—knowing good from evil, enduring pain (physical and emotional), having natural feelings of sadness and happiness, and being subject to Satan's temptations. Children were born to them. In their need, Adam and Eve called out to the Lord and heard His voice, "and they saw him not; for they were shut out from his presence" (Moses 5:4). They were commanded to worship the Lord their God and make a sacrificial offering of a firstborn lamb from their flock. "And Adam was obedient unto the commandments of the Lord" (Moses 5:5).

After many days, an angel of the Lord appeared to Adam and Eve and taught them the purpose for sacrifice, saying, "This thing is a similitude of the sacrifice of the Only Begotten of the Father, which is full of grace and truth" (Moses 5:7). The angel further taught them that they should do all things in the name of the Son, that they should repent, and that they should call upon God in the name of the Son forevermore. The Holy Ghost fell upon Adam and taught him that even though "thou hast fallen thou mayest be redeemed, and all mankind, even as many as will" (Moses 5:9).

Can you imagine the joy they felt as the gospel was given to them? Is there any way to express the happiness that entered into their hearts? They responded to their newfound knowledge just as any of us would: "they made all things known unto their sons and their daughters" (Moses 5:12). But some of their children did not accept the truth, and the scripture sadly states that "they loved Satan more than God" (Moses 5:13). Still, the plan of happiness was in place—Jesus Christ was the Redeemer, and all men could be redeemed through obedience to the laws and ordinances He prescribed, including baptism and receiving the gift of the Holy Ghost.

No one is nor can be exempt from these basic ordinances; hence Adam "was caught away by the Spirit of the Lord, and was carried down into the water, and was laid under the water, and was brought forth out of the water. And thus he was baptized, and the Spirit of God descended upon him, and thus he was born of the Spirit, and became quickened in the inner man. And he heard a voice out of heaven, saying: Thou art baptized with fire, and with the Holy Ghost" (Moses 6:64–66).

Adam lived to be 930 years old. He preached the plan of salvation to his children and grandchildren. As has been stated, some rejected the word of their first father; others listened, believed, and acted on his teachings. Abel, Seth, Enos, Cainan, Mahalaleel, Jared, and Enoch—one righteous son after another came forth, "and they were preachers of righteousness, and spake and prophesied, and called upon all men, everywhere, to repent; and faith was taught unto the children of men" (Moses 6:23).

The prophet Daniel in the Old Testament refers to Adam as the Ancient of Days (see Daniel 7:9). We know him as Michael, who helped Jehovah form the earth and is the mortal father of all men. The Prophet Joseph Smith declared, "He (Adam) is the father of the human family, and presides over the spirits of all men."[4] Further Joseph stated, "Christ is the Great High Priest; Adam next."[5]

ENOCH

Enoch, the seventh patriarch from Adam, is another of my scriptural heroes. He is hardly mentioned in the Old Testament. After the "begats" and "all the days of," we read, "And Enoch walked with God: and he was not; for God took him" (Genesis 5:24). We shall look further at this scripture in a moment, for it has a thrilling ending. Enoch was well acquainted with Father Adam. According to the order of the priesthood, which came through Adam to his sons and grandsons, "Enoch was twenty-five years old when he was ordained under the hand of Adam; and he was sixty-five and Adam blessed him" (D&C 107:48).

While Enoch was journeying among his people, the voice of the Lord came to him. He was commanded to preach repentance to the people, and if they would not repent, they would incur the wrath of the Lord: "They have brought upon themselves death; and a hell I have prepared for them, if they repent not" (Moses 6:29). Enoch was humbled by this command, and he asked the Lord, "Why is it that I have found favor in thy sight, and am but a lad, and all the people hate me; for I am slow of speech; wherefore am I thy servant?" (Moses 6:31). The Lord comforted Enoch, assuring him that His Spirit was upon him, and the Lord gave a most remarkable promise to him: "All thy words will I justify; and the mountains shall flee before you, and the rivers shall turn from their course; and thou shalt abide in me, and I in you; therefore walk with me" (Moses 6:34). Following this wonderful blessing of comfort, the eyes of Enoch were opened, and he saw "the spirits that God had created; and he beheld also things which were not visible to the natural eye" (Moses 6:36). From that moment, the people referred to him as a seer, and they gathered to hear him and said, "A wild man hath come among us" (Moses 6:38).

Enoch led his people into battle against their enemies, and so great was his faith that he "spake the word of the Lord, and the earth trembled, and the mountains fled, even according to his command; and the rivers of water were turned out of their course; and the roar of the lions was heard out of the wilderness; and all nations feared greatly, so powerful was the word of Enoch, and so great was the power of the language which God had given him" (Moses 7:13). "And it came to pass in his days, that he built a city that was called the City of Holiness, even Zion" (Moses 7:19).

I get chills when I read these powerful words about this unique prophet of God. Enoch was so great that the people believed his message, and they lived together in righteousness. "And the Lord called his people Zion, because they were of one heart and one mind, and dwelt in righteousness; and there was no poor among them" (Moses 7:18).

Now I refer back to the biblical scripture found in Genesis 5:24: "And Enoch walked with God: and he was not; for God took him." To this day, no one has understood this passage of scripture except those who have read and believed the inspired translation of the Bible by Joseph Smith.

As for Enoch, he was blessed to see the day that God took the righteous into heaven: "And lo, Zion, in process of time, was taken up into heaven" (Moses 7:21).

An amazing vision showing all the nations of the earth passed before the eyes of Enoch. He saw the wickedness of the people and the eventual destruction that awaited them. He beheld the Crucifixion of the Son of Man, even Jesus Christ, "and the earth groaned; and the rocks were rent" (Moses 7:56). And Enoch wept! But despair and sorrow vanished, for the Lord said, "And righteousness will I send down out of heaven; and truth will I send forth out of the earth, to bear testimony of mine Only Begotten; his resurrection from the dead; yea, and also the resurrection of all men; and righteousness and truth will I cause to sweep the earth as with a flood, to gather out mine elect from the four quarters of the earth, unto a place which I shall prepare, an Holy City, that my people may gird up their loins, and be looking forth for the time of my coming; for there shall be my tabernacle, and it shall be called Zion, a New Jerusalem" (Moses 7:62).

This prophetic vision was shown thousands of years before the coming of Jesus Christ to the earth. Enoch saw the truth that would come out of the earth—the Book of Mormon—and the Restoration of the fulness of the gospel, which would gather the elect into a Holy City—Zion, the New Jerusalem.

There have been very few prophets so great as Enoch. I admire him for his humility, his courage, his righteousness, and his special ability to see and talk with God. He will always be a favorite of mine.

ABRAHAM

In the early days of July 1835, the Prophet Joseph Smith obtained several Egyptian mummies along with two or more papyrus scrolls. After beginning a translation of the scrolls, Joseph wrote in his journal, "I commenced the translation of some of the characters or hieroglyphics, and much to our joy found that one of the rolls contained the writings of Abraham, another the writings of Joseph of Egypt, etc.—a more full account of which will appear in its place, as I proceed to examine or unfold them. Truly we can say, the Lord is beginning to reveal the abundance of peace and truth."[6]

Every soul who claims lineage in the house of Israel looks back to Abraham as their father. Little is known about his early life. We do know that at some point he married a woman named Sarai. It is also documented by Paul in his letter to the Galatians that the gospel was preached to Abraham—"first, Faith in the Lord, Jesus Christ; second, Repentance; third, Baptism by immersion for the remission of sins; fourth, Laying on of hands for the gift of the Holy Ghost" (Articles of Faith 1:4; see Galatians 3:8).

In his own words Abraham described his remarkable search for the blessings of the fathers:

> And finding there was greater happiness and peace and rest for me, I sought for the blessings of the fathers, and the right whereunto I should be ordained to administer the same; having been myself a follower of righteousness, desiring also to be one who possessed great knowledge, and to be a greater follower of righteousness, and to possess a greater knowledge, and to be a father of many nations, a prince of peace, and desiring to receive instructions, and to keep the commandments of God, I became a rightful heir, a High Priest, holding the right belonging to the fathers. It was conferred upon me from the fathers; it came down from the fathers, from the beginning of time, yea, even from the beginning, or before the foundation of the earth, down to the present time, even the right of the firstborn, or the first man, who is Adam, or first father, through the fathers unto me. I sought for mine appointment unto the Priesthood according to the appointment of God unto the fathers concerning the seed. (Abraham 1:2–4)

Abraham's search for the blessings of the fathers was not an occurrence of chance; he was chosen before coming to earth. Abraham said, "Now the Lord had shown unto me, Abraham, the intelligences that were organized before the world was; and among all these there were many of the noble and great ones; and God saw these souls that they were good, and he stood in the midst of them, and he said: These I will make my rulers; for he stood among those that were spirits, and he saw that they were good; and he said unto me: Abraham, thou art one of them; thou wast chosen before thou wast born" (Abraham 3:22–23). This foreordination of righteous priests was explained further by Alma, the great Nephite prophet, "And this is the manner after which they were ordained—being called and prepared from the foundation of the world according to the foreknowledge of God, on account of their exceeding faith and good works; in the first place being left to choose good or evil; therefore they having chosen good, and exercising exceedingly great faith, are called with a holy calling, yea, with that holy calling which was prepared with, and according to, a preparatory redemption for such" (Alma 13:3).

What a heartache it must have been for Abraham to see the wickedness of his father's family, for he was raised in Ur of the Chaldees by a family that had left the faith of their fathers and practiced idolatry. According to the book of Abraham, Terah, the father of Abraham, actually attempted to offer up his righteous son as a sacrifice to pagan gods (see Abraham 1:12–15, 30). Only through the intervention of Jehovah was Abraham's life preserved and the wicked priests destroyed (see Abraham 1:20).

Following this harrowing experience, Abraham was commanded to leave Ur and go to the land of Canaan. He was obedient to the Lord, took Sarai and a nephew named Lot, and journeyed to a land which was called Haran. It is interesting to note that Terah had repented of his attempt to sacrifice Abraham and followed him to Haran. Later Terah reverted back to his idolatrous ways, died, and was buried in Haran.

While Abraham lived in Haran, the Lord appeared to Abraham and commanded him, saying, "Arise, and take Lot with thee; for I have purposed . . . to make of thee a minister to my name in a strange land which I will give unto thy seed after thee for an everlasting possession, when they hearken to my voice" (Abraham 2:6). Then a most remarkable blessing was pronounced upon Abraham. The Lord said:

I will make of thee a great nation, and I will bless thee above measure, and make thy name great among all nations, and thou shalt be a blessing unto thy seed after thee, that in their hands they shall bear this ministry and Priesthood unto all nations;

And I will bless them through thy name; for as many as receive this Gospel shall be called after thy name, and shall be accounted thy seed, and shall rise up and bless thee, as their father;

And I will bless them that bless thee, and curse them that curse thee; and in thee (that is, in thy Priesthood) and in thy seed (that is, thy Priesthood), for I give unto thee a promise that this right shall continue in thee, and in thy seed after thee (that is to say, the literal seed, or the seed of the body) shall all the families of the earth be blessed, even with the blessings of the Gospel, which are the blessings of salvation, even of life eternal. (Abraham 2:9–11)

Being obedient, they left Haran and journeyed to the land of Canaan. As they traveled, they came to the land of Jershon. There Abraham built an altar and offered a sacrifice to the Lord. As mentioned, sacrifice had been a required offering since the beginning and was done in similitude of the sacrifice of the Holy Messiah, who would sacrifice His own life to atone for the sins of all men (see 2 Nephi 2:6–7).

Late in their lives, Abraham and Sarai, now called Sarah, were told that they would have a son. She was skeptical because of her advanced age; however, in due course a son was born to them and they named him Isaac. Paul, in his letter to the Hebrews, gave an interesting commentary on this extraordinary birth: "Through faith also Sara herself received strength to conceive seed, and was delivered of a child when she was past age, because she judged him faithful who had promised. Therefore sprang there even of one, and him as good as dead, so many as the stars of the sky in multitude, and as the sand which is by the sea shore innumerable" (Hebrews 11:11–12).

Then an awful command came to Abraham from God: "Take now thy son, thine only son Isaac, whom thou lovest, and get thee into the land of Moriah; and offer him there for a burnt offering upon one of the mountains which I will tell thee of" (Genesis 22:2). How could this possibly be? Abraham did love his son, his only son through Sarah. But even more, how could the covenant of God be fulfilled—the promise of innumerable seed, the blessing of his descendants holding the priesthood, the continuation of his ministry to take the gospel to all the inhabitants of the earth and to ensure that the families of the earth would have an opportunity of life eternal? We can be certain that he also remembered very well the idolatry of his father and himself being laid on an altar as a sacrifice to pagan gods.

With the trial of his faith looming before him, Abraham took his beloved son Isaac on a three-day journey to the place of sacrifice. The trusting son said to his father, "My father: and he said, Here am I, my son. And he said, Behold the fire and the wood: but where is the lamb for a burnt offering?" Abraham replied, "My son, God will provide himself a lamb for a burnt offering: so they went both of them together" (Genesis 22:7–8). There Isaac was bound and placed on an altar, and Abraham took the knife in his hand to slay his son. In this critical moment, the angel of the Lord called out and said, "Lay not thine hand upon the lad, neither do thou any thing unto him: for now I know that thou fearest God, seeing thou hast not withheld thy son, thine only son from me" (Genesis 22:12).

The test was passed. Abraham had given up his own will to that of the Lord. A ram caught in a thicket was offered up as the sacrifice, and the covenant of God with Abraham was kept, "Look now toward heaven, and tell the stars, if thou be able to number them: and he said unto him, So shall thy seed be" (Genesis 15:5).

The great Book of Mormon prophet Jacob correlated the sacrifice of Isaac with that of the Nephites keeping the law of Moses to remind them of Christ in these words, "And for this intent we keep the law of Moses, it pointing our souls to him; and for this cause it is sanctified unto us for righteousness, even as it was accounted unto Abraham in the wilderness to be obedient unto the commands of God in offering up his son Isaac, which is a similitude of God and his Only Begotten Son" (Jacob 4:5). Even our Heavenly Father was willing to offer up His own Son as a sacrifice so that all His children could have access to salvation; however, in His case there was no ram in the thicket, and the life of His Son, Jesus Christ, was taken.

From Abraham to Isaac, to Jacob, to Joseph, to Ephraim and Manasseh, and to other noble prophets down to the meridian of time, the gospel was taught and obeyed with its saving principles and ordinances.

True, the children of Israel rejected God during the time of Moses and consequently were left with the "preparatory gospel, which gospel is the gospel of repentance and of baptism, and the remission of sins, and the law of carnal commandments" (D&C 84:26–27). Still, Moses held the keys of the priesthood and presided over his people as a living prophet. Joseph Smith declared, "Some say the kingdom of God was not set up on the earth until the day of Pentecost, and that John did not preach the baptism of repentance for the remission of sins; but I say, in the name of the Lord, that the kingdom of God was set up on the earth from the days of Adam to the present time. Whenever there has been a righteous man on earth unto whom God revealed His word and gave power and authority to administer in His name, and where there is a priest of God—a minister who has power and authority from God to administer in the ordinances of the gospel and officiate in the priesthood of God, there is the kingdom of God."[7]

For nearly two millennia following the death, Resurrection, and Ascension of Christ and the subsequent killing of the Apostles, the world began a spiritual decline into darkness. With the Restoration of the gospel and the priesthood through Joseph Smith the Prophet, the words of Parley P. Pratt ring in our ears, "The morning breaks, the shadows flee; lo, Zion's standard is unfurled! The dawning of a brighter day majestic rises on the world."[8] The so-called "dark ages" of despair were replaced with hope and joy. A new day had dawned! The stone cut out of the mountain without hands, as described by Daniel, began to roll forth and become a great mountain to fill the earth (see Daniel 2:34, 45). The kingdom of God had been reestablished on the earth, and the seed of Abraham had begun to proclaim the reality of Jesus Christ and His everlasting gospel to all the world.

Isaiah gave a prophetic description of the life of the Savior, including His sorrows and suffering. Said he, "He was bruised for our iniquities" and "brought as a lamb to the slaughter" (Isaiah 53:5, 7). This wonderful messianic proclamation may be one of the most famous of all the scriptures. The great composer Handel brought the beauty of Isaiah's words to the world in his stunning musical masterpiece, *Messiah*. Isaiah followed with a remarkable question, "And who shall declare his generation?" (Isaiah 53:8).

The Book of Mormon prophet Abinadi stood before his evil accusers and defended his knowledge of the Atonement of Christ by asking, "Even all the prophets who have prophesied ever since the world began—have they not spoken more or less concerning these things?" (Mosiah 13:33). Then after quoting Isaiah chapter 53, Abinadi testified that Christ would soon fulfill the prophecies of his life, death, and Resurrection. Further, he demanded, "And now I say unto you, who shall declare his generation? . . . And who shall be his seed?" (Mosiah 15:10). He answered his own questions in this way:

> Behold I say unto you, that whosoever has heard the words of the prophets, yea, all the holy prophets who have prophesied concerning the coming of the Lord—I say unto you, that all those who have hearkened unto their words, and believed that the Lord would redeem his people, and have looked forward to that day for a remission of their sins, I say unto you, that these are his seed, or they are the heirs of the kingdom of God.
>
> For these are they whose sins he has borne; these are they for whom he has died, to redeem them from their transgressions.
>
> And now, are they not his seed?
>
> Yea, and are not the prophets, every one that has opened his mouth to prophesy, that has not fallen into transgression, I mean all the holy prophets ever since the world began?
>
> I say unto you that they are his seed.
>
> And these are they who have published peace, who have brought good tidings of good, who have published salvation; and said unto Zion: Thy God reigneth! And O how beautiful upon the mountains were their feet! (Mosiah 15:11–15)

This description of the seed of Christ was followed by a lovely pronouncement, "And again, how beautiful upon the mountains are the feet of those that are still publishing peace! And again, how beautiful upon the mountains are the feet of those who shall hereafter publish peace, yea, from this time henceforth and forever!" (Mosiah 15:16–17). And the work goes on as thousands of missionary voices are raised to publish peace, to proclaim the reality of Jesus Christ, and to announce the Restoration of His gospel.

The extraordinary commitment, depth of understanding, and strength of character of these faithful young people is displayed in the following clipping I recently received from the *Signal*, a newspaper in California, of an interview with the top graduate from the local high school, Bryce DeFiguierido. I quote only a portion of the questions and answers from the article:

> *What is the secret to your academic success?*
>
> A long time ago, I decided to work hard and never settle for less than my best.
>
> *What person has been a role model, or has inspired you, during your high school years?*
>
> My family has been a huge influence in my life. We spend a lot of time together, and my parents and siblings are very important to me. They have helped shape me into the person I am. I am very grateful for the relationship we share. I always try to do my best and make them proud of me. . . .
>
> *What are your plans and goals for the future?*
>
> I am enrolling at Brigham Young University this fall. After a year, I will serve a two-year mission for the Church of Jesus Christ of Latter-day Saints. When I return, I will finish my bachelor's degree in mechanical engineering with a minor in music. I then plan to earn a graduate degree in either business or biotechnology. I want to go into neuroprosthetics, designing robotic prostheses that can be controlled by the human nervous system.
>
> Starting a family is also very important to me. I hope to be able to have a close family and raise my children to be people of character.[9]

There was no "maybe I will serve a mission, or perhaps I will get a college education." Bryce knew where he was going and what he intended to do with his life. I am especially proud of this young man, because his mother was one of the amazing missionaries who served with us in the great country of Bolivia. Although Bryce is certainly an outstanding young man, there are tens of thousands who profess the same commitment and aspirations, for they are the seed of Abraham and the seed of

Christ, and "how beautiful upon the mountains are the feet of those that are still publishing peace!" (Mosiah 15:16).

Now I return to Joseph Smith, the Prophet, Seer, and Revelator of the Lord Jesus Christ in this, the last dispensation. All the information given in this brief treatise that might shed some light on the Old Testament must be attributed to Joseph Smith. Brigham Young, a true and loyal friend, said of Joseph, "What is the nature and beauty of Joseph's mission? You know that I am one of his Apostles. When I first heard him preach, he brought heaven and earth together; and all the priests of the day could not tell me anything correct about heaven, hell, God, angels, or devils: they were as blind as Egyptian darkness. When I saw Joseph Smith, he took heaven, figuratively speaking, and brought it down to earth; and he took the earth, brought it up, and opened up, in plainness and simplicity, the things of God; and that is the beauty of his mission."[10]

The impression that Joseph Smith has made on me personally is captured in this short verse that I wrote about him: "With each new birth cast into the sea of men, a gentle ripple is begun. Cause and effect is quite the same for all. For some, the ripple moves for but a moment, then quickly slips and dies. For most, creation's tiny wave leaves little trace of having been. A few move out like tidal waves which never ebb away. They crash upon the human race and mark the life of men—so is Joseph Smith, the Prophet."

So the tidal wave of Joseph Smith rolls forward. We are all products of his eternal vision and of the keys that he received. One day we shall see him. Then we will praise him as the Prophet of the last dispensation, and we will praise him as the one who helped us understand all previous dispensations. We will see that Joseph Smith was the prophet who best showed us the gospel of Jesus Christ in the Old Testament.

————————

NOTES

1. Will Durrant, quoted by Hugh B. Brown, devotional address at Brigham Young University, March 25, 1958.

2. Joseph Smith, *Teachings of the Prophet Joseph Smith*, comp. Joseph Fielding Smith (Salt Lake City: Deseret Book, 1938), 56.

3. Smith, *Teachings*, 327.

4. Smith, *Teachings*, 157.

5. Smith, *Teachings*, 158.

6. Joseph Smith, *History of the Church of Jesus Christ of Latter-day Saints*, ed. B. H. Roberts (Salt Lake City: Deseret Book, 1957), 2:236.

7. Smith, *History of the Church*, 5:256.

8. Parley P. Pratt, "The Morning Breaks," *Hymns* (Salt Lake City: The Church of Jesus Christ of Latter-day Saints, 1985), no. 1.

9. Sharon Cotal, "Canyon Valedictorian Wants to Make Family Proud," *Signal*, June 3, 2008, A3.

10. Brigham Young, in *Journal of Discourses* (London: Latter-day Saints' Book Depot, 1854–86), 5:332.

2

ETERNAL MARRIAGE AND FAMILY IN THE OLD TESTAMENT

Michael A. Goodman

More than the sacred literature of any other people, the Torah is the story of family, of marriages, and not prettied-up versions, either, but the stuff of real marriages—love, romance, anger, deceit, honor, faithfulness, distrust, infidelity, companionship, intimacy. . . . Perhaps that explains why marriage becomes the ultimate paradigm for the relationship between God and the Jewish People.[1]

At first thought, the Old Testament may not come to mind as a rich source from which to study marriage and its centrality to the gospel of Jesus Christ. In fact, the words *marry* and *marriage* appear only six times in the entire volume (see Genesis 38:8; Exodus 21:10; Numbers 36:6; Deuteronomy 25:5; Psalm 78:63; Isaiah 62:5). With such apparent paucity of information on marriage in general, the Old Testament would seem even less likely to reveal much concerning eternal marriage. In fact, one of our faithful scholars commented, "I am not aware of any specific reference to eternal marriage in the Old or the New Testament."[2] However,

---

Michael A. Goodman is an associate professor of Church history and doctrine at Brigham Young University.

what the Old Testament fails to teach didactically, it often illustrates powerfully throughout its narrative.

To understand the sacred literature of the Jews, it is essential to understand that Israel's relationship to their God is seen as a marital relationship.[3] Historically, Judaism, marriage, and the family have been almost inextricably intertwined. In fact, marriage and family have been one of the primary defining institutions of Judaism for millennia.[4] Anciently as well as in modern times, it would be hard to overstate the central role of marriage and family to Judaism.

An informal review of the literature reveals that Latter-day Saint authors most frequently refer to marriage in the Old Testament in the context of plural marriage or levirate marriage. However, the Old Testament contains more about marriage than these two issues. President Brigham Young once stated, "In all my teachings, I have taught the Gospel from the Old and New Testaments. I found therein every doctrine, and the proof of every doctrine, the Latter-day Saints believe in, as far as I know. . . . There may be some doctrines about which little is said in the Bible, but they are all couched therein."[5] Though the Old Testament is not likely to be the first place Latter-day Saints turn for historical and doctrinal explication of eternal marriage, it has much to offer us in our effort to understand this central aspect of the gospel of Jesus Christ.

The Centrality of Marriage in the Gospel Plan

Before beginning a study of eternal marriage in the Old Testament, it is important to understand how eternal marriage is central to the plan of salvation.[6] As the name indicates, eternal marriage had no beginning and will have no end. It is as eternal as the plan itself. As President John Taylor put it, "The principles that we believe in reach back into eternity. They originated with the Gods in the eternal worlds, and they reach forward to the eternities that are to come."[7] There is no shortage of statements by those we sustain as prophets, seers, and revelators pertaining to the divine origin and centrality of marriage and family in the gospel plan. President Joseph Fielding Smith taught that marriage involves "an eternal principle ordained before the foundation of the world and instituted on this earth before death came into it."[8] Elder Bruce R. McConkie taught, "Marriage and the family unit are the central part of the plan of progression and exaltation. All things center in and around the family unit in the eternal perspective."[9] President Young taught that marriage "lays the foundations for worlds, for angels, and for the Gods; for intelligent beings to be crowned with glory, immortality, and eternal lives. In fact, it is the thread which runs from the beginning to the end of the holy Gospel of Salvation."[10] Indeed, President Spencer W. Kimball taught, "Family is the great plan of life as conceived and organized by our Father in heaven."[11] Statements like these and countless others leave little ambiguity as to the importance of marriage in God's plan of happiness.

With an understanding of the eternal nature of marriage and its importance in the plan of salvation, it would seem strange if the Old Testament failed to witness to these truths. Even though the words *marry* and *marriage* appear only six times in the Old Testament, the Old Testament is one of the most powerful witnesses we have of the doctrine of marriage and family. Aspects of this doctrine include the patriarchal order, covenant marriage, the sealing powers, and the gospel of Abraham as the gospel of celestial marriage.

The Patriarchal Order

The narrative in Genesis seems more centered around marriage and family than almost any other book in sacred writ. This is logical when we understand that the Church of God on the earth throughout the duration of Genesis was founded on the patriarchal order. "The patriarchal order," writes Elder Cree-L Kofford, "refers to priesthood government by family organization."[12] Genesis is the only book of scripture where the patriarchal order was the prevailing priesthood organization. This meant that not only families themselves but God's kingdom on the earth was directed by patriarchs. Adam was not just a righteous father to his family; he was the prophet of God on the earth and the one man who held all priesthood keys necessary for exaltation. The *Encyclopedia of Mormonism* states that "from Adam to Jacob, the main office of God's priesthood was that of patriarch. Adam, Enoch, Noah, and Abraham administered the Lord's work, established covenants between God and the faithful, recorded their teachings and prophecies, and gave special priesthood blessings."[13]

Each of these men in the patriarchal office held the high priesthood.[14] Some have mistakenly thought that the patriarchal priesthood is a separate priesthood in and of itself. However, the patriarchal order is a part of the Melchizedek Priesthood because all priesthood is Melchizedek.[15] The patriarchal order is the highest order in the Melchizedek Priesthood.[16] When the Melchizedek Priesthood was withdrawn from ancient Israel, the full measure of the patriarchal order was also withdrawn.[17] Hence, the organization of the Church from the days of Moses onward was no longer patriarchal or centered in the family. As a result, the marriage and family-centered focus of the narrative may seem less central to the story line throughout the remainder of the Bible. This does not diminish the centrality of marriage and family in the gospel or the Old Testament; it simply explains why of all books of scripture, Genesis is so highly focused around marriage and family.

The book of Genesis, however, revolves almost totally around the patriarchal order, or priesthood governance within families. It tells the story of how families, couples as well as children, established their relationship with each other and with God. The saga began with the marriage of the first patriarch, Father Adam, to Mother Eve. Their marriage set the stage for the patriarchal order and, as the patriarchal order itself, was eternal. Elder Henry B. Eyring explained that "the first marriage was performed by God in the garden when Adam and Eve were immortal. He placed in men and women from the beginning a desire to be joined together as man and wife forever to dwell in families in a perfect, righteous union."[18] Thus eternal marriage became a focal point of the creation of man from the beginning of scripture. The scripture record does not detail the eternal nature of the marriages that followed. However, as President Joseph Fielding Smith taught, the plan envisioned eternal marriage as a central tenet of the Lord's plan, not simply marriage till death do us part: "Marriage as established in the beginning was an eternal covenant. The first man and the first woman were not married until death should part them, for at that time death had not come into the world. . . . It is the will of the Lord that all marriages should be of like character, and in becoming 'one flesh' the man and the woman are to continue in the married status, according to the Lord's plan, throughout all eternity as well as in this mortal life."[19]

The first commandment given to Adam and Eve after their eternal marriage centered on their role as husband and wife. They were commanded to "be fruitful, and multiply, and replenish the earth" (Genesis 1:28). This commandment is central to the plan of salvation as well as the patriarchal order. All things in the plan depended on Adam and Eve fulfilling this commandment. In fact, our understanding of the nature of this command is crucial in helping us understand why the Fall is essential to the Lord's plan for mankind. The commandment to multiply and replenish the earth was given before it was even possible to be fulfilled. Until the Fall, Adam and Eve were not capable of having children (see Moses 5:11). President Wilford Woodruff taught that "Adam and Eve came to this world to perform exactly the part that they acted in the Garden of Eden; and I will say, they were ordained of God to do what they did, and it was therefore expected that they would eat of the forbidden fruit in order that man might know both good and evil by passing through this school of experience which this life affords us."[20] To those familiar with the restored gospel, this makes perfect sense. Mankind's salvation is completely dependent on men and women marrying for eternity and inviting children into their homes and hearts whom they will then have the responsibility to lead and guide through eternity. All of this is part and portion of the patriarchal order.

Of course, Adam and Eve were not the only married couple spoken of in the book of Genesis. After Adam and Eve's fall, we watch as they begin their family and try to bind their children not only to themselves but to God. With sadness, we read the story of their children Cain and Abel. Cain becomes a sad example of an unrighteous father as sure as Adam is our first and possibly best example of a righteous patriarch. On the one hand, we see the result of Cain's iniquity through his wife, children, and grandchildren as they are cut off from the Lord. On the other hand, we see the results of Adam and Eve's righteousness in the lives of Seth and his posterity.

Another powerful example of the patriarchal order is Noah. We mourn with Noah and his wife as the posterity of Adam and Eve (and likely most of Noah's posterity) refuse to come unto Jehovah and be saved. Those of Noah's posterity who did hearken to their patriarch entered the ark to escape the coming destruction: Shem and his wife, Japheth and his wife, and Ham and his wife. Interestingly, as soon as these couples disembarked from the ark, they were again commanded to multiply and replenish the earth (see Genesis 9:1). From Noah, the book of Genesis follows the patriarchal line through Shem to Joseph, great-grandson of Abraham. The story of Abraham (whom two-thirds of the world reverences as the prime example of a patriarch) is the story of family. Abraham—whose very name, "father of the faithful," reminds us of God and family—married Sarah, and they built their relationship with each other and with God. We next see Abraham and Sarah guide their birthright son, Isaac, into his own marriage with Rebekah, and the saga continues as we watch Isaac and Rebekah guide their son Jacob into marriage. The remainder of the book of Genesis is dedicated to the story of Jacob's marriages to Leah, Rachel, Bilhah, and Zilpah and the story of their children, the twelve sons (soon-to-be tribes) of Israel. Hence the entire book of Genesis revolves around the patriarchal order and its role in the gospel of Jesus Christ.

It is important to remember that the patriarchal order will continue through all eternity. Though not used as the central organizational order of the Church from the days of Moses onward, it was restored in the last dispensation through the Prophet Joseph Smith (see D&C 110). Elder Kofford taught that "the patriarchal order will be the order of things in the highest degree of the celestial kingdom; thus, without participation in the sealing ordinance, you simply cannot qualify for admission to that high and holy place."[21] No wonder Elder L. Tom Perry taught, "There is then a particular reason why men, women, and children should understand this order and this authority in the households of the people of God, and seek to make it what God intended it to be, a qualification and preparation for the highest exaltation of His children."[22]

COVENANT MARRIAGE

The Old Testament is one of the most powerful sources from which to teach the importance of marriage in the covenant. To many in the world, the Old Testament admonition to marry in the covenant amounts to little other than a cultural issue where the Israelites were encouraged to marry other Israelites. However, those with an understanding of the doctrinal reasons for marrying in the covenant understand there is much more involved than simply marrying within one's own culture and traditions. Marriage within the covenant allowed that covenant to be perpetuated to the next generation. It allowed mothers and fathers to pass on not only cultural traditions but also faith in the God of Israel. Marrying out of the covenant could bring everlasting consequences. Where better to teach that than from the Old Testament?

The events leading up to the Flood are a powerful witness of the dangers of marrying out of the covenant. The book of Genesis tells us that the sons of God were marrying the daughters of men. The book of Moses account of the same story tells us that the sons of men were marrying the daughters of God. What becomes clear from the story is that those who were in the covenant were marrying those who were out of the covenant. President Joseph Fielding Smith explains:

> Because the daughters of Noah married the sons of men contrary to the teachings of the Lord, his anger was kindled, and this offense was one cause that brought to pass the universal flood. You will see that the condition appears reversed in the Book of Moses. It was the daughters of the sons of God who were marrying the sons of men, which was displeasing unto the Lord. The fact was, as we see it revealed, that the daughters who had been born, evidently under the covenant, and were the daughters of the sons of God, that is to say of those who held the priesthood, were transgressing the commandment of the Lord and were marrying *out of the Church.* Thus they were cutting themselves off from the blessings of the priesthood contrary to the teachings of Noah and the will of God.[23]

Because the conditions on the earth were so wicked at that time, the result of marrying out of the covenant created a situation where it was impossible for Heavenly Father to continue sending his children to earth without damning them. It can be argued that these marriages out of the covenant made it impossible to reverse the tide of violence and corruption then sweeping the earth. A righteous home is the greatest bulwark God has on earth to hold back the tide of evil. When those who were born in the covenant married those who were already absorbed in the evil that surrounded them, their children were no longer afforded the opportunity to be raised in a home where they would be taught the gospel and nurtured in the ways of God. The consequence was that "the end of all flesh is come before me, for the earth is filled with violence, and behold I will destroy all flesh from off the earth" (Moses 8:30).

Besides the events leading up to the Flood, the examples of Abraham, Isaac, and Jacob further reinforce the importance of marriage in the covenant. When the time came for Isaac to marry, Abraham made his servant swear that he would not take a wife for Isaac from among the Canaanites but that he would go back to Abraham's kindred and choose a wife from among them (see Genesis 24:1–4). Endogamous marriages, or marriage within one's social or familial group, served many cultural purposes, including easier couple adjustment as well as keeping land, cattle, and other properties within the family.[24] However, as is made clear through the narrative, the servant who was assigned to find Isaac a wife clearly saw his work in religious or spiritual terms. He petitioned God to grant him success, sought miraculous intervention, and received that intervention on behalf of not only Isaac but also Abraham. From Laban and Bethuel's reaction to Abraham's servant's narrative, they clearly saw divine intervention in the process as well. From the gospel's perspective, none of this is surprising because the main purpose of this mission was to find a wife for Isaac, who was a member of the Lord's covenant people.

We see the story repeated with Isaac and Rebekah's concern for Jacob's and Esau's marriages. In Genesis 26, Esau marries Judith and Bashemath, both Hittites. The scriptures state that Esau's marriages out of the covenant "were a grief of mind unto Isaac and to Rebekah" (Genesis 26:35). In Genesis 27:46, Rebekah said to Isaac, "I am weary of my life because of the daughters of Heth: if Jacob take a wife of the daughters of Heth, . . . what good shall my life do me?" In order to make sure his son married in the covenant, Isaac strongly forbade Jacob to take a wife "of the daughters of Canaan" (Genesis 28:1) and commanded him to go to his grandfather's house and take a wife of the daughters of Laban, his uncle.

Throughout the Old Testament, there is a strong witness of the importance of marriage in the covenant and the dangers that follow marrying out of the covenant. In Exodus 34:16, the Lord warns the children of Israel not to intermarry with the inhabitants of the land lest "thou take of their daughters unto thy sons, and their daughters go a whoring after their gods, and make thy sons go a whoring after their gods."

In Deuteronomy 7:3–4, Israel is commanded, "Neither shalt thou make marriages with them; thy daughter thou shalt not give unto his son, nor his daughter shalt thou take unto thy son. For they will turn away thy son from following me, that they may serve other gods." Judges 3:6–7 relates that the Israelites "took their [Canaanite] daughters to be their wives, and gave their daughters to their sons, and served their gods." As a result of these marriages, the Israelites "did evil in the sight of the Lord, and forgat the Lord their God."

Few stories serve as a stronger warning of the dangers of marrying out of the covenant than the saga of Samson. From his first marriage outside the covenant with a Philistine woman to his relationship with Delilah, his relationships paved the way for his downfall. The same lesson continued with Solomon. Like Samson, his beginnings were auspicious. The Lord blessed Solomon with wisdom and understanding, riches and honor, and promised him that if he would "walk in my ways, to keep my statutes and my commandments, . . . then I will lengthen thy days" (1 Kings 3:14). However, as time passed, Solomon "loved many strange women, together with the daughter of Pharaoh, women of the Moabites, Ammonites, Edomites, Zidonians, and Hittites" (1 Kings 11:1). Even though the Lord had commanded Israel not to marry out of the covenant, "for surely they will turn away your heart after their gods," Solomon chose to disobey this counsel. As a result, "his wives turned away his heart after other gods: and his heart was not perfect with the Lord his God" (1 Kings 11:2, 4).

We next see the same lesson in the writings of Ezra. The last two chapters of Ezra tell the sad story of those who were delivered out of bondage in Babylon returning to the practice of marrying out of the covenant. Chapter 9 recounts how Ezra rent his garments and mantle, plucked off the hair of his head and beard, and sat down to mourn over these marriages. He exclaims, "O my God, I am ashamed and blush to lift up my face to thee" (Ezra 9:6), and laments that after all of the blessings the Lord had given Israel, they again began to fall into iniquity through marrying out of the covenant. His impassioned prayer and speech had the temporary result of Israel promising to put away the wives they had married out of the covenant (see Ezra 9–10). However, by the end of Nehemiah, the prophet again had to rebuke the people and the priests for marrying "wives of Ashdod, of Ammon, and of Moab" (Nehemiah 13:23). By the end of the Old Testament, Malachi laments, "Judah hath dealt treacherously, and an abomination is committed in Israel and in Jerusalem; for Judah hath profaned the holiness of the Lord which he loved, and hath married the daughter of a strange god" (Malachi 2:11).

Surely, it would be hard to find a stronger indictment against marrying out of the covenant and a stronger plea to marry in the covenant. Almost every time an individual or the people in general married out of the covenant, the result was the same. Their hearts were turned away from the God of Abraham, the God of Isaac, and the God of Jacob. It is no wonder the prophets mourned so dramatically and condemned so strongly marriage out of the covenant as they tried to keep Israel connected to their covenant with God.

THE SEALING POWERS

No discussion of marriage and family in the Old Testament would be complete without a discussion of the sealing powers. The last two verses in the Old Testament promise: "Behold, I will send you Elijah the prophet before the coming of the great and dreadful day of the Lord: And he shall turn the heart of the fathers to the children, and the heart of the children to their fathers, lest I come and smite the earth with a curse" (Malachi 4:5–6). This promised restoration was of such great importance that if it were not fulfilled, the entire earth would be smitten with a curse, or utterly wasted, as it reads in Joseph Smith—History 1:39 and Doctrine and Covenants 2:3. From latter-day revelation, we know that Elijah was to be sent to restore the sealing powers, the power to bind on heaven what is bound on earth. Though this restoration included the power and authority to "seal and validate *all* ordinances of the priesthood so that ordinances performed on earth are binding in heaven as well," it is best known for conveying the authority to bind and seal families for eternity.[25] In fact, in reference to Malachi 4:5–6, the Prophet Joseph Smith stated that the word *turn* should actually be rendered as "bind" or "seal."[26]

Malachi does not make plain the connection between the Old Testament prophet Elijah and the sealing powers. We gain some insight from a statement by Joseph Smith that "Elijah was the last Prophet that held the keys of the priesthood."[27] We might wonder if the prophets who followed Elijah would have held these keys, including "such men as Elisha, Joel, Hosea, Jonah, Amos, Isaiah, Micah, Nahum, Jeremiah, Zephaniah, Obadiah, Daniel, Habakkuk, Ezekiel."[28] However, from the rest of Joseph Smith's original statement, it is clear he did not mean no man after Elijah held that power on earth. He went on to say that "the Savior [whose birth and mortal life obviously followed Elijah] had authority and power to bestow this blessing" but did not because the house of Israel was not worthy or ready to receive it.[29] Therefore, Elijah was not the last prophet to hold these keys but seems to be the last who exercised them in ancient times and was the one the Lord appointed to bestow those keys on others. Robert L. Millet explained, "The keys of the kingdom of God have always been on earth when the higher priesthood was on earth; there must be order in the house of God. Those keys would have been held by the Lord's anointed after the time of Elijah. Elijah was not the last man to hold keys in the Old Testament period, since many did after him, but he was the last one in the Old Testament commissioned to return in the dispensation of the fulness of times to see to it that 'all the ordinances may be attended to in righteousness.'"[30]

We have further witness of the importance of Elijah's mission because it is one of the few prophesied events mentioned in all of the standard works. We have the fulfillment of the prophecy recorded in Matthew 17 and Mark 9 in the New Testament—the accounts of Moses and Elijah bestowing their priesthood keys on Peter, James, and John. That this was but the first part of the fulfillment is shown by Jesus Christ's repeating the prophecy from Malachi to the Nephites in future tense in 3 Nephi 25. This, of course, occurs after Moses and Elijah had already bestowed their keys on Peter, James, and John in New Testament times. Over a millennium and a half later, Moroni repeated the promise to Joseph Smith as recorded in the Pearl of Great Price (see Joseph Smith—History 1:38–39). Joseph Smith next experienced another fulfillment of this sacred promise when Elijah appeared and bestowed the sealing powers on the Prophet and Oliver Cowdery as recorded in Doctrine and Covenants 110. It has also been suggested that there may yet be another fulfillment of the prophecy based on the words of Joseph Smith given in 1840, four years after Elijah's coming recorded in Doctrine and Covenants 110. Robert L. Millet stated that part of the original prophecy might still be fulfilled in some future time: "Joseph Smith stated that

Elijah 'will, before the last dispensation'—meaning, presumably, at some *future time* before the dispensation is complete—'restore the authority and deliver the keys of the Priesthood, in order that all the ordinances may be attended to in righteousness.'"[31]

THE GOSPEL OF ABRAHAM

One more connection to marriage and family from the Old Testament is referred to in Doctrine and Covenants 110. It teaches that another Old Testament prophet held keys essential to eternal families. Before Elijah came to Joseph and Oliver, a prophet called Elias came "and committed the dispensation of the gospel of Abraham, saying that in us and our seed all generations after us should be blessed" (D&C 110:12). Much has been written regarding who this Old Testament prophet might have been. The name *Elias* may sometimes refer to Elijah, though we would assume this Elias is a different person as he is referred to in the same section of scriptures using the name Elias, not Elijah. *Elias* is often used as a title instead of a proper name, referring to one who comes to prepare the way. Some have concluded that since this prophet was restoring the keys of the gospel of Abraham, he must have lived in the days of Abraham. It has been suggested that one possible candidate is Melchizedek, who ordained Abraham to the higher priesthood. President Joseph Fielding Smith believed that this Elias was Gabriel, whom Joseph Smith taught was Noah. However, even President Joseph Fielding Smith cautioned, "What prophet this Elias is that was sent to restore these keys is not definitely known."[32]

More important than whom this prophet was is what he restored. What is the "dispensation of the gospel of Abraham," and what does it have to do with the keys which Elijah restored? Elder McConkie taught that the gospel of Abraham was

> The commission, the mission, the endowment and power, the message of salvation, given to Abraham. And what was this? It was a divine promise that both in the world and out of the world his seed should continue "as innumerable as the stars; or, if ye were to count the sand upon the seashore ye could not number them."

Thus the gospel of Abraham was one of celestial marriage. . . . This power and commission is what Elias restored, and as a consequence, the righteous among all future generations were assured of the blessings of a continuation of the seeds forever, even as it was with Abraham of old.[33]

The gospel of Abraham included the patriarchal order spoken of above "by which the Abrahamic Covenant is perpetuated from generation to generation among the faithful. Abraham was given a promise of innumerable posterity both in the world and out of the world."[34] In some way which has not been made clear, the sealing powers delivered by Elijah are connected with the keys delivered by Elias that contain the dispensation of the gospel of Abraham.

CONCLUSION

The Old Testament might be more properly called the First Testament. It is the first testament of Jesus Christ and his gospel. Though each of the standard works is often identified with a specific time frame, location, or dispensation of the gospel, each contains sacred and precious truths which are vital to our latter-day understanding of the fulness of the gospel of Jesus Christ. Though in some ways, the Old Testament may be considered the least likely to contribute to our understanding of eternal marriage and its role in the Lord's plan, there are actually several aspects of marriage where it may inform as powerfully as any other source, ancient or modern. When it comes to understanding the patriarchal order, covenant marriage, the sealing powers as well as the gospel of Abraham, the Old Testament becomes a treasure trove of light and knowledge.

NOTES

1. Blu Greenberg, "Marriage in the Jewish Tradition," *Journal of Ecumenical Studies* 22 (1985): 5.

2. Robert L. Millet, *Getting at the Truth: Responding to Difficult Questions about LDS Beliefs* (Salt Lake City: Deseret Book, 2004), 85.

3. Jocelyn Hellig, "A Jewish Woman's Reflections on the Pressure of Secularist and Hedonist Influences on the Traditional Jewish Ideals of Marriage and Family," *Dialogue and Alliance: Journal of the International Religious Foundation* 9, no. 1 (Spring/ Summer 1995): 91.

4. Richard L. Rubenstein, "Marriage and the Family in Jewish Tradition," *Dialogue and Alliance: Journal of the International Religious Foundation* 9, no. 1 (Spring/ Summer 1995): 17.

5. Brigham Young, in *Journal of Discourses* (London: Latter-day Saints' Book Depot, 1874), 16:73.

6. See "The Family: A Proclamation to the World," *Ensign*, November 1995, 102.

7. John Taylor, *The Gospel Kingdom*, ed. G. Homer Durham (Salt Lake City: Bookcraft, 1987), 14.

8. Joseph Fielding Smith, *The Way to Perfection: Short Discourses on Gospel Themes* (Salt Lake City: Genealogical Society of Utah, 1931), 251.

9. Bruce R. McConkie, *Doctrinal New Testament Commentary* (Salt Lake City: Bookcraft, 1977), 1:546.

10. Brigham Young, *Discourses of Brigham Young*, ed. John A. Widtsoe (Salt Lake City: Bookcraft, 1976), 195.

11. Spencer W. Kimball, "The Family Influence," *Ensign*, July 1973, 15.

12. Cree-L Kofford, "Marriage in the Lord's Way, Part One," *Ensign*, June 1998, 12.

13. Victor L. Ludlow, "Priesthood in Biblical Times," in *Encyclopedia of Mormonism*, ed. Daniel H. Ludlow (New York: Macmillan, 1992), 3:1138–39.

14. Joseph Fielding Smith, *Doctrines of Salvation*, comp. Bruce R. McConkie (Salt Lake City: Bookcraft, 1956), 3:104.

15. Joseph Smith, *Teachings of the Prophet Joseph Smith*, ed. Joseph Fielding Smith (Salt Lake City: Deseret Book, 1976), 180.

16. Lynn A. McKinlay, "Patriarchal Order of the Priesthood," in *Encyclopedia of Mormonism*, 3:1067.

17. Joseph Fielding Smith, *Doctrines of Salvation*, 3:104.

18. Henry B. Eyring, "That We May Be One," *Ensign*, May 1998, 66.

19. Joseph Fielding Smith, *Doctrines of Salvation*, 2:71.

20. Wilford Woodruff, *The Discourses of Wilford Woodruff*, ed. G. Homer Durham (Salt Lake City: Bookcraft, 1946), 233.

21. Kofford, "Marriage in the Lord's Way, Part One," 7.

22. L. Tom Perry, "Fatherhood, an Eternal Calling," *Ensign*, May 2004, 72.

23. Joseph Fielding Smith, *Answers to Gospel Questions* (Salt Lake City: Deseret Book, 1957), 1:136–37.

24. Bruce A. Chadwick, Camille Fronk, Ray L. Huntington, Tim B. Heaton, and Brian K. Barber, "Tradition amid Social Upheaval: The Palestinian Muslim Family," *BYU Studies* 40, no. 4 (2001): 154.

25. Kent P. Jackson, *From Apostasy to Restoration* (Salt Lake City: Deseret Book, 1996), 222.

26. Joseph Smith, *Teachings*, 330.

27. Joseph Smith, *Teachings*, 172.

28. Robert L. Millet, *Selected Writings of Robert L. Millet* (Salt Lake City: Deseret Book, 2000), 39.

29. Joseph Smith, *Teachings*, 172.

30. Millet, *Selected Writings*, 42.

31. Millet, *Selected Writings*, 41.

32. Richard O. Cowan, *Answers to Your Questions about the Doctrine and Covenants* (Salt Lake City: Deseret Book, 1996), 128.

33. Bruce R. McConkie, *Mormon Doctrine*, 2nd ed. (Salt Lake City: Bookcraft, 1966), 219–20.

34. Joel A. Flake, "Gospel of Abraham," in *Encyclopedia of Mormonism*, 2:555.

3

MOTHERHOOD IN THE OLD TESTAMENT

John Hilton III and Lani Hilton

Jaroldeen Edwards, a mother of twelve children, had just published a novel and was being interviewed in her home by two female reporters. Although she tried to maintain a professional appearance, her children embarrassed her by continually seeking her attention. As the reporters were leaving, one went to use the telephone, leaving Jaroldeen alone with the senior reporter. Jaroldeen recounts:

> "There's something I want to tell you," [the reporter] said intensely. . . . "I just want you to know that we were sold a lie."
>
> "What do you mean?" I asked, totally puzzled.
>
> "I mean, when I went to college they lied to us. . . . We were told not to throw our lives away on husbands and children, but to go out into the world and to succeed. We were told that only through a professional career could we 'find ourselves' or live a worthwhile life.

John Hilton III is a doctoral student in instructional psychology and technology at Brigham Young University and a part-time instructor of ancient scripture.
Lani Hilton is a wife and mother.

"I just want you to know that this morning I have realized it was all a lie. . . . *I would trade all my so-called worldly success for one day of living your life.*"[1]

Countless people today believe what the reporter was taught, that motherhood is a burden and that there are better areas for women to pursue. But many mothers in the Old Testament would disagree. These women offer several lessons for modern-day matriarchs. In contrast to some current philosophies, the Old Testament teaches the importance of motherhood by establishing the significance of posterity and the influence and blessings that come from raising children. It provides several accounts of sacrifices mothers made and shows how those sacrifices changed history. The Old Testament also teaches of the powerful influence mothers have—not only on their children but on entire nations and future generations.

An Overview of Motherhood in Old Testament Times

The word *mother* or one of its derivatives occurs 232 times in the Old Testament—50 percent more than all of the other standard works combined (see the table below).[2] This figure indicates that the Old Testament teaches significant lessons regarding motherhood.

Times a form of the word "mother" is used	
Old Testament	232
New Testament	96
Book of Mormon	41
Doctrine and Covenants	6
Pearl of Great Price	9
Total	384

Just as modern mothers have a variety of roles and time-consuming responsibilities, so too did ancient mothers. These tasks included "keeping the home in order, caring for small children . . . , tending gardens and small animals, producing textiles, and taking responsibility for food preparation and preservation."[3] These duties were often lengthy and complicated. For example, in order to provide clothes for the family, sheep or other animals had to be sheared. "After shearing, the wool or hair was beaten to free it from embedded dirt or leaves. Then the mother of the family, assisted by her daughters, combed the wool, spun it into thread, wove it on the family loom, and sometimes dyed the cloth in a vat."⁴

Even making bread was a time-consuming process. The cereal crops used by the Israelites would "require a complex series of operations to make them edible. The grains must be processed by soaking, milling, grinding; the flour is then mixed into a dough, set to rise, and baked in order to produce bread. Grain processing alone could easily consume two hours or more per day of a woman's time, not including the procurement of fuel and tending of the oven fires that were the prelude to baking."⁵

In addition to managing the home, mothers in the Old Testament were highly involved in the lives of their posterity. They had a large role in the training and instruction of their children (see Deuteronomy 21:18; Proverbs 1:8; 6:20) and significantly influenced their future (see Genesis 27:1–17). We note that "of the forty-six recorded instances of naming children in the Old Testament, in twenty-eight the name is given by the mother. It is generally accepted that name giving in the Old Testament represented an expression of authority."⁶

Motherhood was perhaps the deepest desire of women in the Old Testament. One scholar wrote, "For ancient Israelites the most important contribution a woman could make to a household was to present her husband with children. . . . Indeed, the noblest contribution a woman could make to a household in general and her husband in particular was to bear a son for him. Through childbearing, a woman earned her place in life and her share in the household. Conversely, failure to deliver on this obligation was viewed as a curse and a shameful disgrace."⁷

Although one might think that women during Old Testament times were less than or subservient to men, their roles were equally important. Many of these mothers were powerful teachers, significantly affecting the nurturing and teaching of their children and generations after them.⁸ Beginning with Eve, Old Testament matriarchs offer several lessons for modern-day mothers.

MOTHERHOOD IN THE GARDEN OF EDEN

A continual pattern throughout the creation concerns the importance of posterity. The first recorded statement that God made after creating male and female was "Be fruitful, and multiply, and replenish the earth" (Genesis 1:28).[9]

The word *Eve* itself is "from the Hebrew root *hyh*, 'to live,'" and means "living, life giver."[10] When Adam called his wife Eve, it emphasized her role in bearing children. "And Adam called his wife's name Eve; because she was the mother of all living" (Genesis 3:20). After Adam and Eve had partaken of the fruit, the Lord spoke to Eve regarding her responsibility for motherhood, saying, "*Thou shalt* bring forth children" (Genesis 3:16; emphasis added). Having children was both a blessing and a commandment—and Adam and Eve fulfilled it. We read, "Adam knew his wife, and she bare unto him sons and daughters, and they began to multiply and to replenish the earth" (Moses 5:2). Having children was a source of joy. Eve "was 'glad' after the Fall, realizing she otherwise 'never should have had seed' (Moses 5:11)."[11]

Although not all women are able to have children, Sheri L. Dew pointed out that mothering is an inherent part of womanhood. She said, "Both God the Father and Adam called Eve 'the mother of all living'— and they did so *before* she ever bore a child (Moses 4:26). . . . Motherhood . . . is the essence of who we are as women."[12] From Eve we learn that from the beginning man and woman were to be married and have children. Motherhood is a vital part of womanhood; it is a role that can bring great joy.

POSTERITY AND THE ABRAHAMIC COVENANT

Having children was also a key part of the Abrahamic covenant. The patriarch Abraham, as well as his descendants, received promises from the Lord that can help us understand Old Testament teachings on the significance and blessings of posterity. The Lord promised Abraham that his wife Sarah would "be a mother of nations; kings of people shall be of her" (Genesis 17:16). Later, the Lord promised, "I will multiply thy seed as the stars of the heaven, and as the sand which is upon the sea shore" (Genesis 22:17).

This same covenant was established with Isaac and, in turn, with Jacob (see Genesis 17:21; 28:1–4). To Jacob the Lord promised, "Thy seed shall be as the dust of the earth, and thou shalt spread abroad to the west, and to the east, and to the north, and to the south: and in thee and in thy seed shall all the families of the earth be blessed" (Genesis 28:14).

Although these promises were given to the patriarchs, the blessings clearly involved both husband and wife. It appears that having an extensive posterity was one of the most sublime blessings that could be offered.

THREE GREAT MATRIARCHS

Although posterity was a key blessing promised to Abraham, Isaac, and Jacob, receiving this blessing was a great challenge for them—and their wives, Sarah, Rebekah, and Rachel.[13] A study of their lives shows how important motherhood was to these noble women.

Sarah is first mentioned in Genesis 11:29. The next verse describes her in relation to motherhood, stating, "But Sarai was barren; she had no child" (Genesis 11:30). Having posterity was so important to her that she gave her maid to Abraham so that he could have seed (see Genesis 16:1–3). This emphasis on Sarah's infertility demonstrates the importance that was placed on motherhood.

The story of Sarah as recorded in the Old Testament is essentially the story of motherhood. When she was ninety and Abraham one hundred years old, "God said unto Abraham, As for Sarai thy wife, . . . I will bless her, and give thee a son also of her: yea, I will bless her, and she shall be a mother of nations; kings of people shall be of her" (Genesis 17:15–16).

Sarah was incredulous that she could bear a child in her old age; nevertheless, "the Lord visited Sarah as he had said, and the Lord did unto Sarah as he had spoken. For Sarah conceived, and bare Abraham a son in his old age, at the set time of which God had spoken to him" (Genesis 21:1–2).

Sarah rejoiced in her motherhood and said, "God hath made me to laugh, so that all that hear will laugh with me" (Genesis 21:6). It certainly was not easy to bear a child in her nineties; however, Sarah focused on the joy that came from motherhood, not the hardships.[14]

Sarah's son Isaac would eventually marry Rebekah. Abraham's needing to sacrifice Isaac is often discussed, but what of the sacrifice that Rebekah and *her* mother made? Rebekah's mother courageously let her daughter make her own choice regarding her marriage to Isaac, and Rebekah boldly declared, "I will go" (Genesis 24:58), and departed to begin a new life. As she left, her family's desires for her centered on her potential for motherhood. They expressed their wishes by saying to her, "Thou art our sister, be thou the mother of thousands of millions" (Genesis 24:60). This farewell, focused on posterity, further helps us understand the high regard in which motherhood was held.

Yet motherhood was not immediately in Rebekah's future. For twenty years she waited for children, but none came. This was a matter of prayer for their family, and ultimately "Isaac intreated the Lord for his wife, because she was barren: and the Lord was intreated of him, and Rebekah his wife conceived" (Genesis 25:21).

Rebekah loved her children. She grieved when they did wrong (see Genesis 26:35) and surely rejoiced when they did well (see Proverbs 23:25). Her son Jacob later traveled to the area where Rebekah had grown up. There he met Rachel and fell in love with her. Through the maneuverings of Laban, her father, Jacob married both Rachel and her older sister Leah. Leah was able to bear children, but Rachel could not. In fact, "when Rachel saw that she bare Jacob no children, Rachel envied her sister; and said unto Jacob, Give me children, or else I die" (Genesis 30:1).

Although Rachel's prayers were not immediately answered, eventually "God remembered Rachel, and God hearkened to her, and opened her womb. And she conceived, and bare a son; and said, God hath taken away my reproach" (Genesis 30:22–23).[15]

Having children *did* take away Rachel's reproach. Her son Joseph became the second in command to Pharaoh and saved his family members from starvation. Rachel also had another son; she made the ultimate sacrifice to become Benjamin's mother. The scriptures state that Rachel was "in hard labour" (Genesis 35:17) and died in the process of giving birth. Her sacrifice stands as a sacred testament to the price of motherhood.

Many people throughout the world today are descendants of these three women—Sarah, Rebekah, and Rachel—each of whom was deeply committed to motherhood. The faith of these great matriarchs is evident in their desire to honor God, be true to their covenants, and raise righteous posterity. Although each struggled to bear children, their consecrated service as mothers has blessed "thousands of millions" (Genesis 24:60).

GOD'S ROLE IN MOTHERHOOD

An interesting facet of motherhood in the Old Testament is its focus on God's role in sending children to earth. Consider the following examples:

"For *the Lord* had fast closed up all the wombs of the house of Abimelech" (Genesis 20:18; emphasis added).

"And when *the Lord* saw that Leah was hated, *he* opened her womb" (Genesis 29:31; emphasis added).

"*The Lord* gave her conception" (Ruth 4:13; emphasis added).

"But *the Lord* had shut up her [Hannah's] womb" (1 Samuel 1:5; emphasis added).

Each of these statements illustrates that God was involved in the timing of childbirth, and people in the Old Testament recognized this. When "the Lord . . . had closed the wombs of the house of Abimelech, Abraham prayed unto God: and God healed Abimelech, and his wife, and his maidservants; and they bare children" (Genesis 20:18, 17).

Similarly, "Isaac intreated the Lord for his wife, because she was barren: and the Lord was intreated of him, and Rebekah his wife conceived" (Genesis 25:21).

At one point it appears that Jacob felt Rachel was blaming him for their lack of children. When she said to Jacob, "Give me children, or else I die," Jacob responded, "Am I in God's stead, who hath withheld from thee the fruit of the womb?" (Genesis 30:1–2).

These examples contrast with what is often taught in today's world. Many in modern society do not acknowledge God's role in the timing of birth and choose not to include him in their decisions about childbearing.[16]

LESSONS FOR OUR DAY

Eighty-four mothers are mentioned by name in the Old Testament (see the appendix for a complete list). Valuable lessons can be learned from these women, as well as the unnamed Old Testament mothers. Consider the following examples:

Hannah. One of the most prominent mothers in the Old Testament is Hannah, the mother of Samuel. Elkanah, her husband, loved her, "but the Lord had shut up her womb" (1 Samuel 1:5). Her inability to have children was a deep source of pain; she fretted and "wept, and did not eat" (I Samuel 1:7). Elkanah did not fault Hannah; rather, he attempted to comfort her, saying, "Hannah, why weepest thou? and why eatest thou not? and why is thy heart grieved? am not I better to thee than ten sons?" (I Samuel 1:8).

The fact that Hannah continued to worry about this matter leads one to believe that Elkanah was *not* better to her than ten sons. Hannah went to the Tabernacle and covenanted with the Lord that if he would give her a child she would dedicate his life to the Lord. After she "poured out [her] soul before the Lord" and returned from the Tabernacle, "the Lord remembered her" (I Samuel 1:15, 19).

Shortly thereafter, she bore a son, Samuel, and rejoiced, saying, *"For this child I prayed*; and the Lord hath given me my petition which I asked of him" (I Samuel 1:27; emphasis added). As she had promised, Hannah delivered him to the Lord by having him serve in the Tabernacle with Eli. But her dedication to nurturing Samuel did not end. She "made him a little coat, and brought it to him from year to year, when she came up with her husband to offer the yearly sacrifice" (I Samuel 2:19).

In addition, "the Lord visited Hannah, so that she conceived, and bare three sons and two daughters" (I Samuel 2:21). Although Hannah is not heard of again in the scriptural account, one can assume that she experienced joy in her posterity. Hannah provides an example of a woman with a "mother heart"[17] who deeply desired children and sacrificed to raise them up to the Lord. Hannah teaches us to pray for posterity and to cherish those children if the Lord sends them. She was blessed "to be a joyful mother of children" (Psalm 113:9).

Jochebed. Jochebed is another who stands out as a faithful mother in the Old Testament, particularly considering the historical context of her motherhood. The Pharaoh had decreed that all male children were to be killed. Yet when Jochebed gave birth to Moses, she was "not afraid of the king's commandment" (Hebrews 11:23). Seeing that her son "was a goodly child, she hid him three months. And when she could not longer hide him, she took for him an ark of bulrushes, and daubed it with slime and with pitch, and put the child therein; and she laid it in the flags by the river's brink" (Exodus 2:2–3).

Jochebed had her daughter Miriam follow Moses, who was discovered by the Pharaoh's daughter. Miriam then arranged for Moses to return to his mother to be nursed. It is not clear how long Moses stayed with Jochebed; three years may be a good estimate.[18] Nothing is mentioned of what Jochebed taught Moses during that brief period, but it must have been powerful—because although Moses became steeped in the "wisdom of the Egyptians" (Acts 7:22), he "forsook Egypt" (Hebrews 11:27). Teachings from his mother in his earliest years likely had a significant influence on his decision to turn his back on the riches and power that could have been his.[19] Jochebed teaches mothers to be courageous in protecting their children. The words of mothers are remembered (see Alma 56:47–48).

The mothers of kings. The phrase "his mother's name was" appears twenty-one times in the books of 1 and 2 Kings and 1 and 2 Chronicles. While recounting the names and deeds of the various kings, the authors of these books consistently recorded the names of the kings' mothers. One commentator asked, "Was the Chronicler, as he analyzed so well the character of the mothers of the kings of Judah, trying to stress that a nation's rise or fall may be determined by its mothers? Does the Chronicler seem to say to us that if you would sway the world in the direction of good, you must begin with its mothers?"[20]

Detailed information is not available about all of these mothers. Although some kings ignored their mothers (see 1 Kings 15:11–13), many followed their precepts. For example, of King Ahaziah we read, "His mother was his counsellor to do wickedly" (2 Chronicles 22:3). One can only imagine how history would have been different if Ahaziah's mother had been his counselor to do good.

From the mothers of the kings, we learn that mothers influence not just children but nations. In this vein, Elder Neal A. Maxwell asked, "When the real history of mankind is fully disclosed, will it feature the echoes of gunfire or the shaping sound of lullabies? The great armistices made by military men or the peacemaking of women in homes and in neighborhoods? Will what happened in cradles and kitchens prove to be more controlling than what happened in congresses?"[21]

Rizpah. Although the name Rizpah is scarcely known, important lessons can be learned from this "mother in Israel" (Judges 5:7). She was one of Saul's concubines and had two sons, Armoni and Mephibosheth (see 2 Samuel 3:7, 21:8). As part of making peace with the Gibeonites,

David delivered seven of Saul's descendants, including Rizpah's sons, to the Gibeonites, who "hanged them" (2 Samuel 21:9). After her sons were slain, "Rizpah the daughter of Aiah took sackcloth, and spread it for her upon the rock, from the beginning of harvest until water dropped upon them out of heaven, and suffered neither the birds of the air to rest on them by day, nor the beasts of the field by night" (2 Samuel 21:10).

It is unusual that Rizpah's sons were not immediately buried. Deuteronomy 21:23 states that those who are hung "shall not remain all night upon the tree, but thou shalt in any wise bury him that day." Perhaps this makes Rizpah's vigil even more significant because she was still willing to protect the bodies of her deceased sons. The text states that Rizpah worked *by day* and *by night*; her tireless efforts likely continued for six months.[22] Elder Charles H. Hart praised Rizpah: "We have a beautiful picture in Holy Writ of the *mother love* of Rizpah. . . . It is an illustration of the *mother love* that she . . . kept this lonely and faithful vigil."[23] Similarly, mothers today must guard their children by day and by night. There are yet "birds of the air" and "beasts of the field" who would seek to do them harm. Like Rizpah, modern-day mothers in Israel demonstrate their *mother love* as they do all in their power to protect their children.

The Shunammite woman. Another lesser-known mother in the Old Testament is the Shunammite woman. She showed great care for the prophet Elisha, yet when he offered to reward her, she asked for nothing. Elisha and his servant Gehazi determined that her reward should be to have a child, even though her husband was old (see 2 Kings 4:14). Then "the woman conceived, and bare a son at that season that Elisha had said unto her" (2 Kings 4:17). She treasured this child, and when he suffered a serious ailment, she exercised great faith in seeking Elisha to heal her son. She would not trust anyone but the prophet to heal him.

Her story is brief and may appear unworthy of attention. Nevertheless, lessons can be learned from the Shunammite woman. Her name is never mentioned in the scriptures—but this does not detract from her value. Many mothers labor in relative anonymity, yet as the Shunammite woman did, they save the lives of their children. Their work matters. In addition, as the Shunammite woman focused on Elisha, modern mothers bless and heal their children as they focus their attention on the counsel of the living prophet.

CONCLUSION

These examples of lessons from Old Testament mothers are only a few among many. Mothers from Abigail to Zipporah have additional lessons to teach. Beginning with "the mother of all living" (Genesis 3:20), mothers held a supremely important role in the Old Testament, and this role continues to the present day. It is interesting to note that the only scripture quoted in "The Family: A Proclamation to the World" comes from the Old Testament and concerns the importance of posterity (see Psalm 127:3).

Indeed, modern prophets have consistently affirmed the importance of motherhood. President Spencer W. Kimball taught, "No matter what you read or hear, no matter what the differences of circumstances you observe in the lives of women about you, it is important for you Latter-day Saint women to understand that the Lord holds motherhood and mothers sacred and in the highest esteem. He has entrusted to his daughters the great responsibility of bearing and nurturing children."[24]

In a tribute to mothers, Elder Russell M. Nelson quoted the First Presidency as saying, "Motherhood . . . is near to divinity. It is the highest, holiest service to be assumed by mankind. It places her who honors its holy calling and service next to the angels."[25]

Although "for some time it has not been vogue for women to extol the virtues of motherhood or for young women to express the desires of their hearts to be mothers,"[26] Old Testament matriarchs reach across the centuries to affirm the value of motherhood. Their sacrifices altered the course of human history. As we read of mothers in the Old Testament and throughout the scriptures, we should contemplate the sacrifices they made. Their lives testify to us of the importance of posterity and the vital role mothers play in shaping the future of the world.

APPENDIX: ALL MOTHERS NAMED IN THE OLD TESTAMENT[27]

Abigail[1]. Mother of Chileab (2 Samuel 2:2–3).
Abigail[2]. Mother of Amasa (2 Samuel 17:25).
Abihail[1]. Mother of Ahban and Molid (1 Chronicles 2:29).
Abihail[2]. Mother of Mahalath (2 Chronicles 11:18).
Abijah[1]. Mother of Ashur (1 Chronicles 2:24).

Abijah². Mother of Hezekiah (2 Chronicles 29:1).

Abital. Mother of Shephatiah (1 Chronicles 3:3).

Adah¹. Mother of Jabal and Jubal (Genesis 4:19–23).

Adah². Mother of Eliphaz (Genesis 36:2–4).

Ahinoam¹. Mother of Jonathan, Ishui, Melchi-shua, Merab, and
    Michal (1 Samuel 14:49–50).

Ahinoam². Mother of Amnon (2 Samuel 3:2).

Aholibamah. Mother of Jeush, Jaalam, and Korah (Genesis 36:5).

Ahlai. Mother of Zabad (1 Chronicles 11:41).

Anah. Mother of Aholibamah (Genesis 36:2).

Asenath. Mother of Manasseh and Ephraim (Genesis 41:50–52).

Atarah. Mother of Onam (1 Chronicles 2:26).

Athaliah. Mother of Ahaziah (2 Kings 8:26).

Azubah¹. Mother of King Jehoshaphat (1 Kings 22:42).

Azubah². Mother of Jesher, Shobab, and Ardon (1 Chronicles 2:18–19).[28]

Basemath. Mother of Reuel (Genesis 36:4).

Bathsheba. Mother of an unnamed child and Solomon
    (1 Samuel 12:15–24).[29]

Bilhah. Mother of Dan and Naphtali (Genesis 30:4–8).

Bithiah. Mother of Miriam, Shammai, and Ishbah
    (1 Chronicles 4:17–18).

Eglah. Mother of Ithream (2 Samuel 3:5).

Elisheba. Mother of Nadab, Abishu, Eleazar, and Ithamar (Exodus 6:23).

Ephah. Mother of Haran, Moza, and Gazez (1 Chronicles 2:46).

Ephratah (Ephrath). Mother of Hur (1 Chronicles 2:19, 50).

Eve. Mother of Cain, Abel, Seth, and other sons and daughters
    (Moses 5:2, 16–17; 6:2).

Gomer. Mother of Jezreel, Lo-ruhamah, and Lo-ammi (Hosea 1:4–6).

Hagar. Mother of Ishmael (Genesis 16:15).

Haggith. Mother of Adonijah (2 Samuel 3:4).

Hammoleketh. Mother of Ishod, Abiezer, and Mahalah
    (1 Chronicles 7:18).

Hamutal. Mother of Jehoahaz and Zedekiah (2 Kings 23:31; 24:18).

Hannah. Mother of Samuel, as well as three more sons and two daughters
    (1 Samuel 1:20; 2:21).

Helah. Mother of Zereth, Jezoar, and Ethnan (1 Chronicles 4:7).

Hephzibah. Mother of Manasseh (2 Kings 21:1).

Hodesh. Mother of Jobab, Zibia, Mesha, Malcham, Jeuz, Shachia, and Mirma (1 Chronicles 8:8–10).

Hushim. Mother of Abitub and Elpaal (1 Chronicles 8:11).

Jecoliah. Mother of Uzziah (2 Chronicles 26:3).

Jedidah. Mother of Josiah (2 Kings 22:1–2).

Jehoaddan. Mother of Amaziah (2 Kings 14:2).

Jehudijah (Hodiah). Mother of Jered, Heber, and Jeduthiel (1 Chronicles 4:18–19).

Jerioth. Mother of Jesher, Shobab, and Ardon (1 Chronicles 2:18).[30]

Jerusha. Mother of Jotham (2 Kings 15:33).

Jezebel. Mother of Ahaziah, Jehoram (Joram), and Athaliah (1 Kings 16:31; 22:53; 2 Kings 3:2, 13; 9:22).[31]

Jochebed. Mother of Miriam, Aaron, and Moses (Numbers 26:59).

Keturah. Mother of Zimran, Jokshan, Medan, Midian, Ishbak, and Shuah (Genesis 25:2).

Leah. Mother of Reuben, Simeon, Levi, Judah, Issachar, Zebulon, and Dinah (Genesis 29:32–35; 30:21).

Maachah[1]. Mother of Absalom (2 Samuel 3:3).

Maachah2 (Michaiah). Mother of Abijam (1 Kings 15:2).

Maachah[3]. Mother of Peresh and Sheresh (1 Chronicles 7:15–16).

Maachah[4]. Mother of Sheber, Tirhanah, Shaaph, Sheva, and probably Achsah (1 Chronicles 2:48–49).

Maachah[5]. Mother of Gibeon, Abdon, Zur, Kish, Baal, Ner, Nadab, Gedor, Ahio, Zechariah, and Mikloth (1 Chronicles 9:35–37).

Mahalath. Mother of Jehush, Shemariah, and Zaham (2 Chronicles 11:18–19).

Matred. Mother of Mehetabel (Genesis 36:39; 1 Chronicles 1:50).

Merab. Mother of five sons (1 Samuel 18:9; 2 Samuel 21:8).

Meshullemeth. Mother of Amon (2 Kings 21:19).

Milcah. Mother of Huz, Buz, Kemuel, Chesed, Hazo, Pildash, Jidlaph, and Bethuel (Genesis 11:29; 22:20).

Naamah. Mother of Rehoboam (1 Kings 14:21, 31; 2 Chronicles 12:13).

Naarah. Mother of Ahuzam, Hepher, Temeni, and Haahashtari (1 Chronicles 4:6).

Naomi. Mother of Mahlon and Chilion (Ruth 1:2, 20–21; 2:1).

Nehushta. Mother of Jehoiachin (2 Kings 24:8).

Peninnah. Mother of an unspecified number of sons and daughters
(1 Samuel 1:2, 4).

Puah. Mother of an unspecified number of children (Exodus 1:15–21).

Rachel. Mother of Joseph and Benjamin (Genesis 30:22–24; 35:18).

Rahab. Mother of Boaz (Joshua 2:1, 3; 6:17–25; Matthew 1:5).

Rebekah. Mother of Esau and Jacob (Genesis 25:24–26).

Reumah. Mother of Tebah, Gaham, Thahash, and Maachah
(Genesis 22:24).

Rizpah. Mother of Armoni and Mephibosheth (2 Samuel 21:8).

Ruth. Mother of Obed (Ruth 4:17).

Sarai (Sarah). Mother of Isaac (Genesis 21:3).

Shelomith. Mother of an unnamed son (Leviticus 24:11).

Shimeath. Mother of Zabad (2 Chronicles 24:26).

Shimrith. Mother of Jehozabad (2 Chronicles 24:26).

Shiphrah. Mother of an unspecified number of children (Exodus 1:15–21).

Tamar. Mother of Pharez and Zerah (1 Chronicles 2:4).

Timna. Mother of Amalek (Genesis 36:12).

Zebudah. Mother of Jehoiakim (2 Kings 23:36).

Zeruah. Mother of Jeroboam (1 Kings 11:26).

Zeruiah. Mother of Abishai, Joab, and Asahel (1 Chronicles 2:16).

Zibiah. Mother of Joash (2 Kings 12:1; 2 Chronicles 24:1).

Zillah. Mother of Tubal-cain and likely Naamah (Genesis 4:19, 22).

Zilpah. Mother of Gad and Asher (Genesis 30:9–13).

Zipporah. Mother of Gershom and Eliezer (Exodus 18:2–4).

NOTES

1. Jaroldeen Edwards, "Following Christ in Service to Others," *Church News*, March 10, 1990, 8; emphasis added.

2. On average, the Old Testament has one reference to mothers every 5.1 pages; the New Testament, one reference every 4.2 pages; the Book of Mormon, one reference every 13 pages; the Doctrine and Covenants, one reference every 49 pages; the Pearl of Great Price, one reference every 6.8 pages.

3. Carol Meyers, "The Family in Ancient Israel," in *Families in Ancient Israel*, ed. Leo Perdue, Joseph Blenkinsopp, John Collins, and Carol Meyers (Louisville, KY: Westminster John Knox Press, 1997), 25. In addition, see Proverbs 31:13–27 for another list of female responsibilities.

4. Edith Deen, *Family Living in the Bible* (New York: Harper and Row, 1963), 177.

5. Meyers, "The Family in Ancient Israel," 25.

6. Daniel L. Block, "Marriage and Family in Ancient Israel," in *Marriage and Family in the Biblical World*, ed. Ken M. Campbell (Downers Grove, IL: InterVarsity Press, 2003), 67 n. 153.

7. Block, "Marriage and Family in Ancient Israel," 72.

8. It is also interesting to note that, although not directly specified in the Old Testament, for millennia, Jewish tradition has held that whether a child is an ethnic Jew depends on the lineage of the mother, not the father.

9. This same commandment was given to Noah after the Flood (see Genesis 9:1, 7) as well as to Jacob (see Genesis 35:11). Modern prophets have further instructed that it remains in force today ("The Family: A Proclamation to the World," *Ensign*, November 1995, 102).

10. Carol Meyers, "Eve," in *Women in Scripture*, ed. Carol Meyers (Boston: Houghton Mifflin, 2000), 79.

11. Sheri L. Dew, "Are We Not All Mothers?" *Ensign*, November 2001, 97.

12. Dew, "Are We Not All Mothers?" 96.

13. Of course, Abraham and Jacob each had another wife and bore children through other women.

14. Although in Genesis 21:6 Sarah states, "God hath made me to laugh," footnote *a* states that the Hebrew root *tzachak* "means both 'to laugh' and 'to rejoice'; thus there is double meaning implied in its use here." This incident appears to be the foundation for Isaac's name, which means "he laugheth" (Francis Brown, S. R. Driver, and Charles A. Briggs, *The Brown-Driver-Briggs Hebrew and English Lexicon* [Peabody, MA: Hendrickson Publishers, 2001], 850).

15. It is interesting to note that in the scriptures many things happen in threes. These three matriarchs giving birth miraculously is another example of this phenomenon.

16. President Gordon B. Hinckley taught, "The Lord has told us to multiply and replenish the earth that we might have joy in our posterity, and there is no greater joy than the joy that comes of happy children in good families. But he did not designate the number, nor has the Church. That is a sacred matter left to the couple *and the Lord*" (*Cornerstones of a Happy Home*, pamphlet [Salt Lake City: The Church of Jesus Christ of Latter-day Saints, 1984], 6; emphasis added).

17. Julie B. Beck, "A 'Mother Heart,'" *Ensign*, May 2004, 75.

18. Children were "nursed for a customary period of three years," so it may be that this is the amount of time Moses spent with Jochebed (Leo G. Perdue, "The Israelite and Early Jewish Family: Summary and Conclusions," in *Families in Ancient Israel*, 171).

19. President Ezra Taft Benson taught, "Mothers, you are your children's best teacher. . . . Teach your children the gospel in your own home, at your own fireside. This is the most effective teaching that your children will ever receive. This is the Lord's way of teaching. The Church cannot teach like you can. The school cannot. The day-care center cannot. But you can, and the Lord will sustain you. Your children will remember your teachings forever, and when they are old, they will not depart from them. They will call you blessed—their truly angel mother" ("To the Mothers

in Zion," fireside address, February 22, 1987, reprinted in *Eternal Marriage Student Manual* [Salt Lake City: The Church of Jesus Christ of Latter-day Saints, 2001], 356).

20. Deen, *Family Living in the Bible*, 80.

21. Neal A. Maxwell, "The Women of God," *Ensign*, May 1978, 10–11.

22. The vigil was kept "until rain fell and ended the drought—from mid-April until October or November" (Diana V. Edelman, "Rizpah," in *Anchor Bible Dictionary*, ed. David Noel Freedman [New York: Doubleday, 1992], 5:776).

23. Elder Charles H. Hart, Conference Report, October 1916, 128; emphasis added. Located online at http://search.ldslibrary.com/article/view/258276 (accessed September 24, 2008).

24. Spencer W. Kimball, "Privileges and Responsibilities of Sisters," *Ensign*, November 1978, 105.

25. Russell M. Nelson, "Our Sacred Duty to Honor Women," *Ensign*, May 1999, 38.

26. Susan W. Tanner, "Strengthening Future Mothers," *Ensign*, June 2005, 25.

27. This information primarily comes from Meyers, *Women in Scripture*. The Web sites www.alabaster-jars.com/womenindex.html and www.christiananswers.net/dictionary/women.html were also consulted, in addition to original research done by the authors.

28. It is not clear whether Azubah[2] or Jerioth is the mother of these sons.

29. It is possible that Bathsheba is an alternate form of Bath-shua, in which case she is also the mother of Shimea, Shobab, and Nathan (see 1 Chronicles 3:5).

30. It is not clear whether Azubah[2] or Jerioth is the mother of these sons.

31. Although it is not specified that Jezebel is the mother of these individuals, contextual evidence makes it appear likely. See also the entry "Athaliah" in the Bible Dictionary.

4

THE PLAN OF SALVATION
IN THE FIRST SIX BOOKS OF
THE OLD TESTAMENT

Paul Y. Hoskisson

I f "all things which have been given of God from the beginning of the world, unto man, are the typifying of" Christ (2 Nephi 11:4), then why do Christ and His mission not seem to be readily apparent in the Old Testament? Part of the answer, of course, is that Christ and His mission *are* apparent to those with eyes to see. For example, only the Old Testament tells the story of the Creation and the Fall, without which there would be no need for Christ's Atonement.[1] Other teachings of the gospel of Jesus Christ are equally plain and clear, such as the Ten Commandments. Also evident are "the first of all the commandments" (Mark 12:29), "Thou shalt love the Lord thy God with all thine heart, and with all thy soul, and with all thy might," a quote from Deuteronomy 6:5, and the second, "Thou shalt love thy neighbor as thyself," found in Leviticus 19:18.

Another part of the answer is that "many parts which are plain and most precious" (1 Nephi 13:26) have been excised from the Bible. For example, the books of Zenos and Zenock, which were no doubt among the books on the brass plates and which spoke plainly and unambiguously of

---

Paul Y. Hoskisson is a professor of ancient scripture at Brigham Young University.

Christ and His mission, were removed from the scriptural record before the Old Testament, as we currently know it, was canonized.

As far as those parts that were changed or taken out of the Old Testament are concerned, there is not much that can be done to recover them at present. With the exception of a few passages that have been preserved in the Book of Mormon and the Joseph Smith Translation, the restoration of the missing and changed parts must await the discovery of more ancient documents that might contain the missing texts, or the reception of more revelation from the Lord.[2]

Not all the plain and precious parts that are now missing were removed by some beady-eyed, nefarious scribe wielding a cleaver, or, in some cases, the ancient equivalent of an X-Acto knife. Indeed, if someone had a mind to, the plain and precious parts could be eliminated without tampering with the text at all. All that was needed was to mystify or to muddle the gospel understanding of the passage. Such obfuscation could produce the same results as excision, making these gospel truths unavailable to the reader of the Old Testament.

Those plain and precious parts of the gospel of Christ in the Old Testament that are missing because of obfuscation can, at least partially, be restored with a little help. As the Apostle Paul said of some of his contemporaries, "Their minds were blinded: for until this day remaineth the same vail untaken away in the reading of the old testament," but a correct understanding can be restored because the "vail is done away in Christ" (2 Corinthians 3:14). That the lenses of Christianity can help to make clear what once had been muddled was recognized fairly early in Christian history. The author of *Recognitions of Clement*, possibly written between AD 200 and 250, opined that even though "things were indeed plainly spoken *by Him*, but are not plainly written" now because "of the sin which has grown up with men," "when they are read, they cannot be understood without an expounder."[3] Nothing much has changed since the third century AD. Iniquity and disbelief continue to obscure the plain words of the prophets, unless an "expounder," most reliably the Holy Ghost, helps to restore the plain and precious parts.

Nevertheless, not all has been lost. Even with limited light, Christians through the ages have long known and taught that the Old Testament teaches about Christ and His work by direct prophecy, and also through history,[4] parable, allegory, metaphor, simile, symbolism, synecdoche, etc.—teaching methods that are not always clear or self-evident. A few examples that are commonly known will suffice.[5] God declared through Isaiah that there would be both a triumphant Savior of the world (see Isaiah 52) and a Suffering Servant who would take upon Himself our "griefs," "sorrows," "transgressions," and "iniquities" (Isaiah 53). The God of the Old Testament spoke of the Messiah as "the stone which the builders refused" but which "is become the head stone of the corner" (Psalm 118:22), the same stone mentioned in Matthew 16:18 and Ephesians 2:20. God also prophesied through the Psalmist, "My God, my God, why hast thou forsaken me?" (Psalm 22:1), the anguished cry of the Savior on the cross (see Matthew 27:46 and Mark 15:34). Indeed, "the Lord God hath sent his holy prophets among all the children of men, to declare [the gospel] to every kindred, nation, and tongue" (Mosiah 3:13).

As beautiful as the Old Testament is as seen through traditional Christian glasses, the lenses of the Restoration provide an even more precise, complete, and detailed witness of Christ and His mission. For Latter-day Saints, the Old Testament is the oldest witness for Jesus Christ. We understand that Christ as a member of the Godhead created this earth, as outlined in Genesis, under the Father's direction. He spoke to the prophets of the Old Testament. He gave the law to Moses. Throughout the Old Testament, His hand was stretched out still for the redemption of Israel and of the whole world because He is the triumphant Messiah and the Suffering Servant. He is the chief cornerstone the builders rejected. Thus much of the obfuscation that has veiled the gospel of Jesus Christ in the Old Testament can be removed. The dusty layers and opaque encrustations covering the Old Testament can become transparent when viewed through the glasses of the Restoration.

Besides excision and obfuscation, a third reason makes it difficult to see Christ in the Old Testament. God Himself explained that He had a hand in making the Old Testament hard to understand. The Book of Mormon prophet Jacob said that all the holy prophets before his time "had a hope of [Christ's] glory" (Jacob 4:4) long before He was born. But Jacob went on to say that those who heard the prophets by and large "were a stiffnecked people; and they despised the words of plainness, and killed the prophets." At the same time that they rejected the plain testimony of the prophets concerning Christ, they also "sought for things that they could not understand." Therefore, "because they desired it," God took "away his plainness from them, and delivered unto them many things which they [could not] understand" (Jacob 4:14). As a result, many parts of the Old Testament contain things that are not clear and plain, because that is what the people wanted. For example, as Nephi said, "Isaiah spake many things which were hard for many of [Nephi's] people to understand; for they know not concerning the manner of prophesying among the Jews" (2 Nephi 25:1).

Nevertheless, it was never the intention of a loving Heavenly Father "that the Gentiles [or anyone else, for that matter] shall forever remain in that awful state of blindness . . . because of the plain and most precious parts of the gospel of the Lamb which have been kept back" (1 Nephi 13:32), especially those parts that God Himself made difficult because of unbelief and wickedness, giving them instead "many things which they cannot understand" (Jacob 4:14). Perhaps when Christ said, "Ask, and it shall be given you; seek, and ye shall find; knock, and it shall be opened unto you" (Matthew 7:7), He intended, at least in part, that His admonition be applied when reading the Old Testament. For those of His children who "behold with [their] eyes, and hear with [their] ears, and set [their] heart upon all that [God] shall shew [them]" (Ezekiel 40:4), "the mysteries of God" will "be unfolded" to them (Mosiah 2:9), including the understanding of the Old Testament as a testament of "the gospel of the Lamb."

Therefore, it seems to me that if God closed the door to understanding the Old Testament for those who "sought for things that they could not understand" (Jacob 4:14), then it seems equally probable that God also left the door open for those who would understand, for those who do ask, who do seek, and who do knock. With them God willingly shares all the knowledge and understanding that they are willing to receive. In the words of Elder James E. Talmage, "Two men may hear the same words; one of them listens in indolence and indifference, the other with active mind intent on learning all that the words can possibly convey. . . . The one is wise, the other foolish; the one has heard to his eternal profit, the other to his everlasting condemnation."[6] Therefore, true believers can exclaim, as Isaiah did, "The Lord God hath opened mine ear, and I was not rebellious, neither turned away back" (Isaiah 50:5).

At the risk of presuming to know what holy writ is trying to convey, the rest of this paper will illustrate one of the ways I believe the Old Testament teaches the gospel of Jesus Christ. To be more precise, I will explain how the first six books of the Old Testament, often called the Hexateuch, provide an outline of the Plan of Salvation through the details of the stories they contain.[7] My explanation consists of two interwoven parts: first, an explanation of the symbols, metaphors, and similes that represent parts of the Plan of Salvation; and second, how knowledge of various parts of the Plan of Salvation as presented in the Hexateuch might apply today.

In my treatment of this material I will use two different methods, eisegesis and exegesis. Though quite different and in some respects almost opposite approaches, both are legitimate avenues of interpretation. Eisegesis means that the reader comes to the text with preconceived ideas and reads into the text those ideas, filling in the holes and reading between the lines according to the reader's presuppositions. This is partially what I mean when I suggest that looking at the Old Testament through the lenses of the Restoration helps to bring clarity to the text. However, the very nature of eisegesis can and has led to strange and even fantastic readings of the scriptures.[8]

Exegesis means reading out of the text. In this method, very little is assumed when approaching the text; instead, the text is examined in every detail, from smaller questions about which copy of the text is the most accurate—through examination of the spelling, syntax, grammar, authorship, and the setting in real life of the passage—to larger questions about parallel and cognate literatures. For example, if I look up the root of a word, either for a King James English word or for a Hebrew word, and then see how the meaning of the root helps to explain the text, then I would be reading out of the text.

Though many of the explanations of symbols and metaphors that I will use are already well known, I will present many original and lesser-known explanations. And there are many more examples that cannot be included here. However, the uniqueness of my approach is not found in pointing out the meanings, whether new or already known, of the types and shadows of the gospel in the Old Testament. Rather, my contribution consists of stitching together a few well-known symbols, a few less well-known ones, and a few hitherto unrecognized or entirely new images. The end result will be a beautiful tapestry, incomplete as it must be because of present constraints, of the Plan of Salvation as presented in the Hexateuch.

Briefly stated, the portrait of the Plan of Salvation in the first six books of the Old Testament begins with the Eisodus, literally the "entering into" Egypt, and ends with the completion of the Exodus, literally "exiting" Egypt and reentering the Promised Land. In the beginning, Jacob and his family lived in the Promised Land, a metaphor for the celestial kingdom, the presence of God, the land that was the ultimate promise to Abraham. But Jacob and his family could not stay there permanently. They had to leave the Promised Land and enter Egypt. In the Old Testament, Egypt symbolized, through a rather compelling synecdoche, the world and its attendant mortality.

In Egypt, over the course of many years, the family of Jacob became acquainted with, accustomed to, and habituated to the world, and they grew into a large family. Then a prophet arrived to lead them back to the Promised Land. Reluctant at first, they finally left Egypt and experienced several consequential and instructive events in their wanderings. In the end, the Israelites crossed the River Jordan and took possession of the land promised them as their inheritance. With this basic outline in mind, it is possible to explore the story of the Eisodus and the Exodus in much greater detail in order to discover the Old Testament teachings concerning "the great plan of happiness" (Alma 42:8).

The Plan of Salvation has its beginnings in the premortal world. There we chose to leave our Heavenly Father's presence in order to continue to make progress toward our eventual return to the celestial Promised Land. However, neither the premortal existence nor the Promised Land of the Eisodus was the ultimate goal, but, rather, both were stages along the path, the one very real and the other highly symbolic of the real. The ultimate goal was to return to God's presence. As Paul so beautifully stated in the New Testament, "by faith Abraham" sought for an inheritance in a city "whose builder and maker is God" (Hebrews 11:8, 10). That is, Abraham's quest was not for a piece of real estate in mortality, but rather he was seeking a celestial inheritance.

The promise of receiving a land, both the symbolic Promised Land and the celestial kingdom, had been given to Abraham and his descendants, but the realization of the promise in both cases could only come after a sojourn in a foreign land. Just after God gave Jacob a new name, Israel, He also promised him that "a nation and a company of nations shall be of thee, and kings shall come out of thy loins; and the land which I gave Abraham and Isaac, to thee I will give it, and to thy seed after thee will I give the land" (Genesis 35:11–12). The realization of Israel's posterity becoming nations and kings could only happen if he left the Promised Land—the presence of God—and descended to Egypt. The need to leave the presence of God was symbolized in Genesis by the famine, a metaphor which made it clear to Jacob and his family that they could not go on in their present circumstances; they had to leave the Promised Land in order to perpetuate life. Therefore, even though the promise of land for Abraham's descendants had been given years earlier to Abraham, the right to permanently dwell in the Promised Land could only come through leaving it for a season and then returning, precisely as we had to leave temporarily the presence of God in order to be able to return one day forever. The promise of being able to inherit the celestial kingdom was also given to us long before we entered mortality.

It is significant that while still in the promised land, Jacob wrestled with God, calling the place where they struggled "Peniel," which means "the Face of God," or, as Jacob himself explained, "I have seen God face to face" (Genesis 32:30). Indeed, we did see God face-to-face in our premortal existence. It was also in the premortal life that a great struggle took place for the hearts and minds of God's family. In light of the possible symbolic meaning of Jacob's struggle, his reception of a new name must also be seen as symbolic.[9] The name Israel can be translated, among other possibilities, as "God has prevailed," meaning that in the epic, premortal struggle, God prevailed among the two-thirds part of the hosts of heaven. Those of us who came to the earth also had "prevailed" in our premortal wrestle with good and evil. As God told Israel, "for as a prince hast thou power with God and with men" (Genesis 32:28). Likewise, after winning the battle in the premortal life, we became heirs of the kingdom, endowed with power, though in mortality "lessened a little from *elohim*," but "wreathed with glory and splendor" (Psalm 8:5; author's translation).

Just as we were foreordained in the premortal life before coming to the earth, so too Jacob received a promise and a blessing from God before leaving for Egypt, "Fear not to go down into Egypt; for I will there make of thee a great nation: I will go down with thee into Egypt; and I will also surely bring thee up again" (Genesis 46:3–4). Notice that leaving the Promised Land is described as a descent, and returning is ascending. Likewise, we also have the promise given of the Father that He will be with us when we come down into this life if we do not reject Him. We have the promise that we can return to His presence again and live with Him throughout eternity if we have been faithful. That is perhaps why, in the beautifully symbolic language of Genesis 50:13, when Jacob died, Joseph and his brothers returned their father's body to the Promised Land for burial. For the same symbolic purpose, the writer of Genesis recorded that Joseph also extracted a promise from his people that after his death, his remains would be transported back to the Promised Land (see Genesis 50:25), home to the God who gave him life. All of God's children in this world will be taken back physically into His presence.[10]

Joseph in many ways is a Christ figure.[11] Already in the Promised Land, he is singled out from among his brothers. He is the oldest son of Jacob's beloved wife, Rachel, whose name means "ewe" and whose son would then be the "lamb." Joseph's father gave him a special piece of clothing, clothing being symbolic of status and position. The symbolism should not be lost on Latter-day Saints. One of Joseph's own brothers, Judah, suggested that he be sold into slavery. Eventually a caravan of Midianites passed by and Joseph was sold to his distant cousins for the price of a slave, as Christ also would be sold by Judas (the name Judas being the Greek form of the Hebrew Judah) for the price of a slave.

Joseph, as a type of Christ, entered Egypt in the lowly status of a slave in order to prepare a place for his family who would unwittingly follow him into Egypt. There in Egypt he suffered the temptations that are the common lot of mortals, yet he did not give in to temptation but maintained his purity and integrity. Using divine inspiration and his own native intelligence, he raised himself up from slavery to wearing the ring of the king. In effect, he became the de facto ruler of the world that was Egypt, second only to Pharaoh, who remained the de jure ruler. So it is also with Christ, who rules and serves under His Father.

As next in command to the king, Joseph could not only plan for and save temporally every soul of Egypt, but he could also prepare for and save his own kindred in Egypt. In like manner, Christ is our Savior, both in the universal sense that He atoned for Adam's transgression for all people of this world, and in the particular sense that He atoned for personal sin for all those who confess, repent, and enter the covenant with Him, becoming "the children of Christ, his sons, and his daughters" (Mosiah 5:7).

While serving as the savior of all the inhabitants of Egypt and of his own kindred, Joseph performed one of the most Christlike acts of any recorded in scripture. He freely forgave his brothers for the wrongs they had committed against him when it was in his power to exact terrible vengeance. His brothers even expected retribution in the manner of the world: "When Joseph's brethren saw that their father was dead, they said, Joseph will peradventure hate us, and will certainly requite us all the evil which we did unto him" (Genesis 50:15). But it was not in Joseph's heart to seek vengeance. Instead, in the manner of Christ and not the world, he taught them that his being sold into Egypt had been fortuitous and, in the grand scheme of things, certainly foreordained: "Be not grieved, nor angry with yourselves, that ye sold me hither: for God did send me before you to preserve life" (Genesis 45:5). In like manner, all the blunders, pettiness, and even sin that people have perpetrated throughout this earth's existence, as symbolized by the evil intentions of Joseph's brothers, God has used for his own purposes, turning them "unto good, to bring to pass, as it is this day, to save much people alive" (Genesis 50:20) for the celestial kingdom. So it was that Jacob, his twelve sons, and their families, altogether seventy souls (see Genesis 46:27),[12] a wonderfully symbolic number, came into the world that was Egypt to be greeted by their savior.

In the world of Egypt, "the children of Israel were fruitful, and increased abundantly, and multiplied, and waxed exceeding mighty," so that "the land was filled with them" (Exodus 1:7). It is also part of the Plan of Salvation that we begin to acquire posterity here in a literal and symbolic preparation for posterity without number in the celestial kingdom; that is, we have been commanded to multiply and fill the earth and to begin to become "a great nation" here and now. While none of us ever realizes fully this part of the Abrahamic promise in this life, the concern for the fulfillment illustrates one of the reasons that families are so important. It is also one of the reasons that a different "king over Egypt" who "knew not Joseph" (Exodus 1:8), in a remarkable prefiguring of the tenth plague, tried to destroy the families of God's chosen people by ordering the destruction of the male babies born to the Hebrews. (King Herod would try again in the New Testament with a striking postfiguring of the tenth plague.)

As is always the case in mortality, Egypt began to subvert the children of God and to co-opt them for its own selfish purposes. Thus it was, after several hundred years of living in the world called Egypt, that the children of Israel had no doubt lost the living memory of the Promised Land and had forgotten that Egypt was never intended to be their final inheritance, just as this earth was never intended to be the sum of our existence. And like us, they could not escape on their own the condition in which they found themselves. Such a situation called for an unusual means of rescue, a prophet extraordinaire. Out of their midst, Moses was called, and in remarkable symbolism of our own existence, he was born a Hebrew but raised an Egyptian. He was in the world but not of the world.

With good reason, many people see in Moses a Christ figure. For example, like Christ, Moses did for the Israelites what they could not have done on their own, namely, release them from slavery. In our case, Christ has freed us from spiritual bondage. However, without rejecting Moses as a messianic figure, it is also possible to see Moses as the archetypal prophet. First of all, he was called from his "own nation and tongue" (Alma 29:8), as God usually calls prophets. In spite of being brought up in the household of the king of Egypt, he knew that he was not one of them, but rather one of the Hebrews. But as long as he was in the household of the king of the world that was Egypt, he could not be called as the prophet, because no one of this world can become a prophet. Neither can the world bestow the legitimate priesthood through a descendant of one who "would fain claim it from Noah, through Ham" (Abraham 1:27). Through a series of events, Moses was led to stand on hallowed ground, outside the purview of Egypt. There he received his Melchizedek Priesthood ordination (see D&C 84:6) and his assignment to lead God's people back to the Promised Land (see Exodus 3), that is, back to God's presence.

Moses knew that at least some, if not many, of God's people would be reluctant to leave the world of Egypt. After all, they had a good life there with plenty to eat and, most importantly, time to create large families.

No matter that they were enslaved and that they had complained to God about their situation. Perhaps they had naively asked, "O God, can't you do something about my overbearing overseer? But don't ask me to stop making adobes and to start wandering out into the desert." Therefore, Moses' first task was to convince the Hebrews of the need to return to the Promised Land. It is no easy task, as any missionary can attest, to convince people who are comfortable of the need for a paradigm shift. In addition, while trying to convince the people of God to leave the world of Egypt, he also had to convince the Egyptians to allow God's people to leave—no simple task by any measure.

In the beginning, Moses made only a modest request, namely, that Pharaoh should let the people of God go "three days' journey into the desert, and sacrifice unto the Lord [their] God" (Exodus 5:3), that is, to temporarily leave the employ of Egypt in order to serve God. But even this modest request was denied because the self-proclaimed king of this world does not want his subjects serving the true God or truly serving their fellow beings, even if for only a short time. The king of this world wants us to believe that there is no time for extraneous activities that divert attention away from his manufactured distractions. He even warns us about leaving his employ. He would rather keep people busy constructing the adobe bricks of his kingdom and engaged in other mundane activities that distract the children of God from what should be their primary concern, making the journey back to God. Making a living, getting an education, going to social events, tending a garden, shopping for clothing, fixing up old cars, hunting, seeking political office, serving on various committees, writing academic papers and presenting them—while these activities are often necessary in and of themselves, they can become the equivalent of making adobes if they distract us from serving our God or detain us in Egypt when we should be journeying to the Promised Land.

Even though each of the various plagues that afflicted the Egyptians has its symbolism, I will only touch upon the tenth plague. This last plague was designed to demonstrate "how that the Lord doth put a difference between the Egyptians and Israel" (Exodus 11:7), that is, the children of God, though living in the world, are not supposed to be of the world. They are supposed to be peculiar, not in the sense that they are weird and strange, but in the sense that they belong to God and not to the world.

The plague itself was the death of the firstborn of those who did not avail themselves of the Passover. In the ancient world, the firstborn often had rights and obligations above and beyond the other children. Primarily, the firstborn was to preside over the family estate upon the death of the parents. In other words, the firstborn was to perpetuate the heritage of the family. Therefore, the death of the firstborn symbolized, among other things, the symbolic end of that family's heritage. Or, as Malachi stated, "all that do wickedly" shall be consumed by the Lord and left with "neither root nor branch" (Malachi 4:1).

The Passover is a powerful metaphor or symbol that most Latter-day Saints—indeed, most Christians who read Exodus—understand in its more salient features clearly. The "lamb . . . without blemish, a male of the first year" (Exodus 12:5) stands for Christ, the Messiah, who "came . . . to give his life a ransom for many" (Mark 10:45). It is the blood of the paschal lamb that spares the children of God from the death of their firstborn, just as it is Christ who "washed us from our [mortal] sins in his own blood" (Revelation 1:5).

The less salient details of the Passover are just as telling. In Old Testament times, the door of one's tent, or the gate of the city (if one lived in the city), was the place where official business was conducted. By synecdoche, the door or the gate stood for the whole of the dwelling or city. Thus, applying the blood of the sacrifice to the jambs and lintel of the door symbolized the application of the Atonement of Christ to all of one's household, that is, to every aspect of one's life, but particularly to the family's heritage here on earth and throughout the eternities.

Applying the blood of the sacrifice and eating the roasted lamb occurred in family units. The symbolism is obvious, namely, that salvation comes through family organization, that is, through God's family organization. The fact that the whole lamb was to be roasted and totally consumed before morning probably indicates that we are not allowed to pick and choose what parts of the gospel we will enjoy; we are to consume all of the gospel completely, leaving nothing undone in this life.

In other places in scripture, the Holy Ghost is described as a fire or His influence as a burning. It may be that the roasting of the lamb, rather than being "sodden [boiled] at all with water" or eaten raw (Exodus 12:9), was intended to indicate that all gospel content must be consumed in and through the medium of the Holy Ghost.

As part of the preparation for celebrating the Passover and for the departure out of Egypt, the Israelites were to completely rid their dwellings of leaven, eating only unleavened bread for a week (see Exodus 12:19). When they left Egypt they were not to take any Egyptian leaven with them on their journey to the Promised Land (see Exodus 12:34). Christ defined the symbolism of leaven in the New Testament when He warned His disciples about the leaven of the Pharisees, meaning their doctrine (see Matthew 16:11–12). Of all the ingredients in bread, of whatever kind, yeast or leaven is unique because it is the only ingredient that is alive. Yeast makes the whole loaf come alive and grow. The Pharisees could never produce a spiritually satisfying loaf of bread in all its goodness because their doctrine would never leaven the loaf in the way the Lord wanted. Like the ancient Israelites, we are to eschew the doctrines of the world. We are to cleanse our house of worldly doctrines. And, on our trip back to the celestial kingdom, we are not to take with us any doctrines of the world.

Yet in leaving Egypt, the Israelites were told to take with them all the best that Egypt had to offer, that is, to spoil Egypt of its wealth (see Exodus 3:22). So we too are commanded to "seek . . . out of the best books words of wisdom, seek learning even by study and also by faith" (D&C 109:7), but we are not to leaven our loaf with the doctrines of the world. We can study them, use them, or even scorn them, but we should not allow them to give life to our loaf and thereby change the nature of our gospel bread.

After the Israelites left their Egyptian homes behind them, the first striking occurrence must have been the appearance of the "pillar of a cloud" to lead them by day and a "pillar of fire" to give them light by night. The cloud and the fire were one and the same; in broad daylight only the smoke of the fire was visible, whereas by night only the fire could be seen.[13] Passages such as "And the Lord descended in the cloud, and stood with him there, and proclaimed the name of the Lord" (Exodus 34:5) suggest that the cloud and the fire symbolize the Lord. To be more precise, they symbolize the presence of the Lord. Therefore, perhaps the cloud and the fire also symbolize the Holy Ghost, who is present when God makes an appearance. As already mentioned, the Holy Ghost is associated with fire (see 2 Nephi 31:14), with leading the way (see 1 Nephi 4:6), and with showing us everything we need to do (see D&C 39:6). Thus it is that the children of God were led, from the time they left Egypt until they entered the Promised Land, by the visible symbol of the Holy Ghost, which in turn made the invisible presence of the Lord possible. Our journey from the beginnings of our conversion in this life until we reach the ultimate goal, the celestial king-dom, also must be guided by the Lord and mediated by the Holy Spirit, who communicates to us "all things" that we "should do" (2 Nephi 32:5).

The Exodus teaches also that while following the Plan of Salvation we cannot turn our back on the world and expect to be left alone. If, like the children of Israel, we have managed to leave the world and set out on our quest to reach the celestial kingdom, the world, like Pharaoh and his hosts, will come after us to bring us back into bondage. No matter what it is that we have repented of, the ruler of this world will pursue us and try to convince us to come back and make adobes. It is only the presence of a member of the Godhead that protects our blind side from an unwar-ranted and unwanted attack and at the same time points the way forward.

The departure from Egypt was marked by passing through the Red Sea. Our departure from the world is also symbolized by passing through the waters of baptism. The Apostle Paul understood this metaphor when he stated, speaking of the ancient Israelites, "All our fathers were un-der the cloud [a reference to the pillar of fire], and all passed through the sea; and were all baptized unto Moses in the cloud and in the sea" (1 Corinthians 10:1–2). That is, they were baptized by water and by the Holy Ghost. Even today, it is the Holy Ghost that will guide God's chil-dren to the waters of baptism, if they will let Him. Prior to baptism, the forces of this world will be marshaled to prevent individuals from enter-ing the water. Only the Holy Ghost, if we allow Him to, will provide pro-tection. Once having passed through the water, the world will continue to call after us and entice us with its bright lights, but it cannot follow after us. However, we can turn again on our own toward the world, long for it, sigh for it, delay our journey, or even return back to it, but only as an act of willful rebellion against the directions of the Holy Ghost.

Between passing through the Red Sea and crossing the Jordan River—that is, between baptism and entering the Promised Land of the celestial kingdom—the Exodus story maps out certain consequential and instructive events concerning the Plan of Salvation. The most obvious of these is the manna from heaven. From the New Testament we know that the manna of the Exodus, the bread from heaven, symbolized Christ, "the true bread from heaven" (John 6:32). "Jesus said unto them, I am the bread of life: he that cometh to me shall never hunger" (John 6:35). Christ is capable of supplying all of our day-to-day spiritual food. In fact, He knows exactly how much spiritual nourishment to provide each day, and any attempt to appropriate more than He has allotted usually produces at best nothing more than a rearrangement of ignorance.

Besides needing bread for our journey back to Heavenly Father's presence, we also need water to sustain life; we need the Water of Life. During the Exodus, when the people thirsted for water and complained to Moses, he struck a rock, and life-sustaining water poured out to quench the immediate thirst of the Israelites (see Exodus 17:6). The symbolism of the rock throughout the Old Testament is clear; it represents the God of Israel, Jehovah, the Messiah. "The Lord [Jehovah] is my rock" (Psalm 18:2). From Christ, the Rock of our Salvation, comes the water that was promised the Samaritan woman at the well: "Whosoever drinketh of the water that I shall give him shall never thirst" (John 4:14).

One of the teachings the Exodus story sets forth through its presentation of the Plan of Salvation is that all those who could remember Egypt, with two exceptions, were not allowed to enter the Promised Land (see Numbers 14:30). The two exceptions, Joshua and Caleb, were allowed to enter the Promised Land, probably because they were ready to enter the Promised Land the first time they had the chance. The other representatives of the twelve tribes refused to enter the Promised Land the first time they were given that chance (see Numbers 14:22–24). Instead, they and all the rest of the Israelites were consigned to wander in the wilderness until all of that early generation had died off, a forty-year odyssey (see Numbers 14:33–34; Joshua 5:6). The number forty symbolizes the period of human gestation.[14] The meaning for us should be obvious: before entering the celestial kingdom, we must pass through the Sinais of mortality in order to become new creatures, untainted by the world, tried in the harness, proven worthy by having jettisoned all iniquity and other mortal trappings, and by having become as a little child.

On our journey between our conversion and entering the celestial kingdom, we are also symbolically and ceremonially introduced into the presence of God. The Israelites, similar to Latter-day Saints, were supposed to become "a kingdom of priests, and an holy nation" (Exodus 19:6) unto God. However, the Israelites rejected God's invitation to ascend the mountain (see Deuteronomy 9:23), saying to Moses, "Speak thou with us, and we will hear: but let not God speak with us, lest we die" (Exodus 20:19), ironically missing the opportunity to become alive in the fullest sense. It was not supposed to be that way, and it should not be that way for Latter-day Saints on our journey. Latter-day Saints are to embrace, and by and large have embraced, the Melchizedek Priesthood, and, if faithful, shall become kings and queens, priests and priestesses (see Revelation 5:10), calling upon God without the use of an intermediary, and accepting the obligations that come with being symbolically and ritually introduced into the celestial kingdom in the Temple.

During the trek, the children of Israel were organized along strict lines, with specific instructions about who was to lead out in their travels (the priests) and where each tribe was to encamp in relation to the Tabernacle, the transportable House of God, which formed the center of each encampment. We too should expect a hierarchical organization to help shepherd us on our individual journeys to the celestial kingdom, the Temple playing a central role in our sojourn.

In addition, detailed instructions are given concerning how to deal with iniquity while trying to follow the Plan of Salvation. For example, if a person had a skin disease (a disease of the skin is symbolic of superficial and therefore curable sin), that person must show the disease (i.e., sin) to the priest (i.e., bishop), who will determine if it is serious or not. If it is serious, the person must leave the camp of Israel (i.e., be excommunicated) and remain outside the camp until the disease is overcome. When the person believes that the disease has abated, the person must again show the diseased skin to the priest, who will determine if the person has been truly cured. If the disease has been overcome, the person then must wait a set amount of time and be examined again. If the cure has taken, the person then has to be ritually cleansed by the shedding of the blood of a sacrifice and must put on new, clean, pure clothing. The old clothing, the old trappings of sin, must be washed and cleansed also (see Leviticus 13–14).

The Plan of Salvation does not promise a free ride to anyone. The journey to the Promised Land can be and is fraught with perils if we are not careful. On one occasion some Israelites longed for the pleasures of Egypt, for "the fish, which we did eat in Egypt freely; the cucumbers, and the melons, and the leeks, and the onions, and the garlick" (Numbers 11:5). As tasty as these things might have been to an inhabitant of Egypt, how tawdry this list must seem when compared with the banquet set for the marriage feast of the Lamb, "A feast of fat things, of wine on the lees well refined; . . . yea, a supper of the house of the Lord, well prepared" (D&C 58:8–9). In other words, for those of us on our way to the Promised Land, rather than longing for the things of the world, we should be satiated at the banquet the Lord has set with the Bread of Heaven and the Water of Life.

Temptations may also come in the form of worshipping other gods, as some Israelites did at Baal-Peor (see Numbers 25:1–5). But those who do will be destroyed from among the children of God (see Deuteronomy 4:3). The First Presidency message for June 1976, written by President Spencer W. Kimball, warned the present-day members of the Church about "the false gods we worship." "Whatever thing a man sets his heart and his trust in most is his god; and if his god doesn't also happen to be the true and living God of Israel, that man is laboring in idolatry." He went on to say that it was his "firm belief that when we read [the Old Testament] . . . we will see many parallels between the ancient worship of graven images and behavioral patterns in our very own experience" today. Becoming more specific, President Kimball continued:

> We are a warlike people, easily distracted from our assignment of preparing for the coming of the Lord. When enemies rise up, we commit vast resources to the fabrication of gods of stone and steel—ships, planes, missiles, fortifications—and depend on them for protection and deliverance. When threatened, we become antienemy instead of pro-kingdom of God; we train a man in the art of war and call him a patriot, thus, in the manner of Satan's counterfeit of true patriotism, perverting the Savior's teaching:
>
> "Love your enemies, bless them that curse you, do good to them that hate you, and pray for them which despitefully use you, and persecute you;

"That ye may be the children of your Father which is in heaven." (Matt. 5:44–45.)

We forget that if we are righteous the Lord will either not suffer our enemies to come upon us (see 2 Nephi 1:7) . . . or he will fight our battles for us.[15]

It is also significant that at the end of the forty years, the crossing of the Jordan into the Promised Land happened as the priests, who represent us and who were carrying the ark, waded into the river (see Joshua 3:14–16). But that is a lesson for another time.

Suffice it to say that God has made all basic gospel teachings available to those who seek and knock. He has promised us, "For by my Spirit will I enlighten them, and by my power will I make known unto them the secrets of my will—yea, even those things which [the mortal] eye has not seen, nor [mortal] ear heard, nor yet entered into the heart of [the natural] man" (D&C 76:10).

In summary, like Jacob and his sons, we too had to leave the Promised Land before we could inherit it permanently. We had to enter mortality where an elder brother had prepared a place for us. But we must also be willing to give up that life of the world when God's prophet comes to lead us back to the Promised Land. The journey begins with the sacrifice that represents the Atonement and continues with the reception of the Holy Ghost and baptism. If we are true and faithful, we will be led symbolically and ceremonially back into God's presence on the Mountain of the Lord. We will eat the Bread of Heaven and drink the Water of Life and be satisfied. After jettisoning all our sins, even our favorite ones, the time will come when we will cross the Jordan River into the Promised Land, never to leave again.

And thus, God in his mercy has given to all the world an outline and many of the details of the great Plan of Salvation for those who have eyes to see, ears to hear, and hearts to understand the plain and precious parts in His scriptures.

NOTES

1. Besides the Genesis account, there are the two accounts of the Creation in the Pearl of Great Price, both from Old Testament times.

2. The books of Abraham and Moses in the Pearl of Great Price are examples of additional texts or revelations containing plain and precious parts of the gospel.

3. Alexander Roberts and James Donaldson, eds., *Ante-Nicene Fathers*, vol. 8, *Fathers of the Third and Fourth Centuries*, American edition, rev. A. Cleveland Coxe (Peabody, MA: Hendrickson, 1995), 83a. For a discussion of the date, see the introduction on page 74. I thank my colleague Matthew Roper for this reference.

4. Seeing history as teaching about the Savior has led to the theological school called Heilsgeschichte.

5. See any Christian printing of the Old Testament wherein the passages that speak of the Messiah are printed in red. For example, The Holy Bible, Red Letter Edition (Oxford: Oxford, n.d.), states on the title page, "The Old Testament prophecies concerning the Lord Jesus Christ, His Messianic dignity and redeeming work, printed in red letters."

6. James E. Talmage, *Jesus the Christ* (Salt Lake City: Deseret News, 1915), 297.

7. Interwoven with the Plan of Salvation in these books are other gospel teachings. But I confine myself here to the more salient parts of the Plan of Salvation. Admittedly, I have chosen convenient but somewhat arbitrary beginning and ending points for my explanation.

8. For illustrations of questionable conclusions that might result from careless eisegesis, see Alonzo Gaskill's chapter on the church fathers in this volume. For an entire novel about bad eisegesis, see Umberto Eco's *Foucault's Pendulum*.

9. In addition to the types and shadows of the Plan of Salvation in the Hexateuch, there are also many allusions to Temple material. I do not discuss these allusions in this paper.

10. See, for example, 2 Nephi 2:10; 9:22, 38; Alma 11:41, 44; 42:23; Helaman 14:15–17; and Mormon 9:12–13. I thank my colleague D. Kelly Ogden for these references.

11. For a discussion of early eastern Christian interpretations of Joseph as a type of Christ, see the excellent article by Kristian S. Heal, "Joseph as a Type of Christ in Syriac Literature," *BYU Studies* 41, no. 1 (2002): 29–49, with much detail and copious footnotes. For a Latter-day Saint viewpoint on ways in which Joseph symbolizes Christ, see also Andrew C. Skinner, *Prophets, Priests, and Kings: Old Testament Figures Who Symbolize Christ* (Salt Lake City: Deseret Book, 2005), 45–53.

12. Just because a number has symbolic meanings does not mean that it cannot also be literal.

13. See passages such as "They have heard that thou Lord art among this people, that thou Lord art seen face to face, and that thy cloud standeth over them, and that thou goest before them, by day time in a pillar of a cloud, and in a pillar of fire by night" (Numbers 14:14).

14. The commonly expressed period of human gestation is nine months. But my friend Joseph Cannon mentioned to me one day in the fall of 2007 that the more precise length of human gestation is actually closer to forty weeks than it is to nine months.

15. Spencer W. Kimball, "The False Gods We Worship," *Ensign*, June 1976, 4, 6.

5

THE WHOLE MEANING OF THE LAW: CHRIST'S VICARIOUS SACRIFICE

Jennifer C. Lane

In "The Living Christ," modern-day prophets and apostles testify that Christ gave "His life to atone for the sins of all mankind" and that this was "a great vicarious gift in behalf of all who would ever live upon the earth."[1] As Latter-day Saints, we often take this doctrine of vicarious sacrifice for granted as a basic Christian belief, but in the modern world the idea of substitutionary suffering can be difficult for many to believe, even within a Christian framework. Since the Enlightenment, many forms of Christian theology have moved away from this belief as different interpretations of the meaning of Christ's suffering and death developed that reject the need for a vicarious or substitutionary sacrifice to atone for human sin.[2] These lines of thinking emphasize the love and mercy of God and argue that God did not need Christ's suffering on our behalf in order to be able to forgive us, but that Christ's suffering was merely a way to show God's love, thereby moving us to repentance and remorse to accept the forgiveness that he was already prepared to give us. In this model, the idea of God's wrath seems foreign, and it begins to seem unnecessary to have an intermediary.

Jennifer C. Lane is an associate professor of religion at Brigham Young University–Hawaii.

In this alternate vision of the Atonement, the seriousness of sin and the consequences of our sinfulness are subtly downplayed as God's mercy is emphasized. If there were no price that needed to be paid or no consequences of eternal death or banishment from God's presence, then it would not make sense to talk about Christ as a substitute, giving "His life to atone for the sins of all mankind." If God were in a position to forgive our uncleanness and debt merely by mercifully declaring the debt waived and our impurity irrelevant, then we would not need Christ's suffering and death as "a great vicarious gift in behalf of all who would ever live upon the earth." The affirmation of the doctrine of the vicarious Atonement of Christ is central to the message of the restored gospel. This paper argues that the truths about the Atonement affirmed in the Restoration correspond to those taught in the Old Testament, particularly those found in the law of Moses in Exodus and Leviticus and also in Isaiah's teachings about the suffering Messiah in Isaiah 53. I will show that the substitutionary sacrifice that we see under the law of Moses is explained by Isaiah as pointing to the vicarious sacrifice of the Messiah. Together these practices and prophetic teachings can strengthen our faith in the Atonement of Christ.

THE ISSUE OF VICARIOUS ATONEMENT

This question of the meaning of Christ's Atonement becomes central to the question of how to read the Bible.[3] While the issue of the Atonement is debated by many, it is essential to note that there are other Christians, particularly many evangelical Christians, that also defend the teachings of the Bible and the doctrine of vicarious Atonement. As Latter-day Saints, we can stand with our evangelical friends in defense of a belief in vicarious Atonement, but we have even more to bring to this defense since we are blessed to have additional scriptures providing further witness of both this doctrine of substitutionary Atonement and its role in the Bible.[4]

The Restoration also brings an additional witness to the Bible as the word of God. Given the Restoration's affirmation of the vicarious aspect of Christ's Atonement and what the Bible teaches about it, I hope to show how we can closely study the Bible and take seriously the descriptions about the nature of God and our relationship to him that are found therein. Taking the message of the Bible seriously allows us to appreciate the spiritual truths taught in the law of Moses about the reality of the wrath of God, our uncleanness before God, and the mercy extended through a suffering Messiah that came as an intercessor to bear our sins and iniquities.

The Book of Mormon and New Testament testify of the role of the law of Moses to provide us with a model of our relationship to God and our need for a vicarious sacrifice to cleanse us and pay the price for our being reconciled with God. We know from the Book of Mormon that the vicarious sacrifices of the law of Moses were given with the intent to persuade "them to look forward unto the Messiah, and believe in him to come as though he already was" (Jarom 1:11). This clarification works together with the New Testament witness that Jesus Christ is the Lamb of God, "the Lamb slain from the foundation of the world" (Revelation 13:8) and that we have been redeemed not "with corruptible things . . . but with the precious blood of Christ, as of a lamb without blemish and without spot" (1 Peter 1:18–19).

While the New Testament, Book of Mormon, Doctrine and Covenants, and Pearl of Great Price give additional witness to the vicarious nature of Christ's Atonement, the Old Testament stands as the first witness of this foundational doctrine. In this paper I seek to summarize some of what the Old Testament has to teach us about the Savior's "great vicarious gift" for all mankind. One of the key witnesses of this doctrine of vicarious, substitutionary sacrifice can be found in the law of Moses. Here we see the strict demands of God's holiness and come to appreciate how death and separation from God are consequences for sin. In the requirements of this sacrificial law, we also learn how provisions have been made to reconcile God and humans through the offering of a sacrifice. These sacrifices serve both to cleanse and to ransom the sinner who has offended God and his holiness. As taught in the rituals of the Day of Atonement, through these sacrifices it becomes possible to enter the presence of God. It is the aspect of the law of Moses that deals with substitutionary sacrifice that will be the focus of this paper.

In addition to the example of reconciliation through the substitutionary sacrifice of animals found in Exodus and Leviticus, we also find in Isaiah 53 prophetic interpretation of how the vicarious sacrifice prescribed in the law of Moses points to Christ. Isaiah 53 is a unique text in the Old Testament, and it is essential in showing how the law, particularly the element of vicarious or substitutionary sacrifice, pointed towards a messianic Suffering Servant. We often read Isaiah 53 as simply looking forward to the life of Jesus Christ, but close reading reveals how it specifically points to how the Suffering Servant would suffer vicariously as did the animals sacrificed under the law of Moses. Isaiah's interpretation allows us to see the law with an eye focused on the idea of vicarious or substitutionary sacrifice providing reconciliation. Better understanding of the law of Moses will "serve to strengthen [our] faith in Christ" (Alma 25:16).

THE MEANING OF THE LAW

Few of us spend much time thinking about the law of Moses, and when we do look at it, the specifics of sacrifice can feel overwhelming and mystifying. Many of our own feelings of puzzlement in reading the provisions of the law of Moses are expressed by Gordon J. Wenham in his discussion of how to explain Old Testament sacrifice. "How should sacrificial ritual be interpreted? . . . With the sacrifices, the rites of ordination, and even the day of atonement ceremonies the problems of interpretation are often baffling. The rites are usually carefully described, but we are left with few clues as to what was said during them or why they should be performed in a particular way."[5]

As Christians and Latter-day Saints, we are blessed to see how the meaning of the Mosaic sacrificial rituals receives ample discussion in both the New Testament and the Book of Mormon. In these additional scriptures we clearly learn that these rituals point to Christ and his great and last sacrifice on our behalf. In saying that, however, we often then stop looking closely at the sacrificial rituals. We know the "meaning" of the reference point and so we stop looking at the referent altogether. If, however, we wish our understanding of Christ's Atonement to be deepened and informed by the law of Moses, we must seek out the significance that these rituals held for the Israelites, which would have been clear even when they did not understand that these rituals were pointing them toward a suffering Messiah.

Speaking of the lack of explanation given of the ritual requirements and sacrifices in the Old Testament, Wenham argues that "the reason for this obscurity is not far to seek. Evidently the meaning of these rites was so obvious that it was unnecessary to spell it out in words."⁶ He then goes on to list some things that seem clear from within the ritual itself:

> Opposition between life and death is fundamental to the whole ritual law. God is the source of life, so that everything brought near to God whether sacrificial animal or priest must be physically unblemished. Death is the great evil, and everything suggesting it, from corpses to bloody discharge to skin disease, makes people unclean and therefore unfit to worship God. Another theme is the election of Israel: that the Lord has made an exclusive covenant with Israel explains the choice of animals for sacrifice and why some animals are unclean and therefore not to be eaten by Israelites. Thirdly, in sacrifice it appears that the worshipper identifies himself with the animal he offers. What he does to the animal, he does symbolically to himself. The death of the animal portrays the death of himself. In the animal's immolation on the altar his own surrender to God is portrayed.⁷

When we see the type and shadow of spiritual truths in the law's physical requirements, we realize how they echo the basic doctrines of the gospel. The law points to Christ by setting up a framework within which we can understand the role of the suffering and death of Jesus. As Amulek taught, "This is the whole meaning of the law, every whit pointing to that great and last sacrifice; and that great and last sacrifice will be the Son of God, yea, infinite and eternal" (Alma 34:14). The law of Moses was a strict law designed to teach about the price and consequences of sin and also the possibility of ransom and purification (see Mosiah 13:29–30). We are familiar with the expression of this concept from the New Testament: "The wages of sin is death" (Romans 6:23). The same principle was foundational to understanding the law of Moses and the role of sacrifices within that law. Without the sacrifices to reconcile Israel and God, they would be unclean and unfit to have God's presence in their midst.

The high standard of holiness required of the people in order to have the Lord dwell among them is easy for us to miss. We might take for granted the Lord's presence in their midst in his holy house, but the law of Moses was designed to constantly reinforce the need to purify the people, and even the Temple itself, of the people's sinfulness, which would make them unworthy. The Lord, however, after establishing the requirements of the law and its provisions for making atonement for uncleanness, re-emphasized the need to be worthy to have his presence. In Leviticus 26, he summarizes the blessings that would come "if ye walk in my statutes, and keep my commandments, and do them" (v. 3), promising that only if this is the case, "I will set my tabernacle among you: and my soul shall not abhor you" (v. 11). The consequences for not keeping the commandments and for becoming unclean are equally stark—the covenant people will be cast out of the promised land: "And I will scatter you among the heathen, and will draw out a sword after you: and your land shall be desolate, and your cities waste" (v. 33). In this way the spiritual principle that "no unclean thing can enter into his kingdom" (3 Nephi 27:19) was taught in terms of obedience to the law and worthiness to dwell in the land and have the presence of the Lord in their midst.

As we shall see, one of the central roles of the element of sacrifice under the law of Moses will be to "make atonement" for those that are unclean—to cleanse and to ransom. This redeeming and cleansing process was essential if the Lord's presence was to remain in their midst. The Lord declared death as the consequence of uncleanness but also provided a means through which the consequence of death could fall upon a vicarious substitute. Even before the giving of the law of Moses, the role of sacrifice as a vicarious substitute is clearly pointed to in the stories of the Old Testament. We can, for example, see this function of the animal as a vicarious substitute in the account of the sacrifice of Isaac. "And Abraham lifted up his eyes, and looked, and behold behind him a ram caught in a thicket by his horns: and Abraham went and took the ram, and offered him up for a burnt offering in the stead of his son" (Genesis 22:13). Here the phrase "in the stead of his son" can be understood as a substitution—the animal's death took the place of Isaac's death.[8]

Another example of an animal's death substituting for a human's can be found in the account of Passover in Exodus chapter 11.[9] The Israelites were spared the death of their firstborn sons when the destroying angel came because of the blood of the lamb which they had been told to put on their doorposts and lintels. The death of the lambs and the application of their blood kept the Israelite sons from dying. Just as with the ram that was sacrificed, the lamb here took the place of a human death. Both of these forms of substitutionary death clearly point to the gospel message of Christ's role as our substitute, dying in our place and thereby shielding us from death. The importance of this symbolism in pointing to Christ is clearly underlined in the institution of the Feast of Passover as an annual commemoration in the law of Moses and in its eventual transformation into the institution of the sacrament at the Last Supper.

This idea of substitution also plays out in the non-sacrificial part of the law in Exodus. In Exodus 21 we see an example of how a ransom could be seen as substitution for the life that might otherwise be required to balance the life that was taken. In this situation, if a man's ox kills someone's family member, the negligent owner is to forfeit his own life: "But if the ox were wont to push with his horn in time past, and it hath been testified to his owner, and he hath not kept him in, but that he hath killed a man or a woman; the ox shall be stoned, and his owner also shall be put to death" (v. 29). But if the family agrees to accept the ransom or redemption (*koper*) as a settlement, then "he [the ox's owner] shall give for the ransom of his life whatsoever is laid upon him" (v. 30). This ransom functions as a substitution. The legal term *koper* shares the same root as the term "to make atonement for." In its noun form, "it denotes the material gift that establishes an amicable settlement between an injured party and the offending party."[10] Rather than requiring justice or compensation—a vendetta as seen in the concept of "an eye for an eye"—this ransom functions as a substitute that allows the injured party to extend mercy and be reconciled.

Within the provisions in the law of Moses, the death of a sacrificial animal can likewise be understood as a substitution for the death of the sinner. Wenham notes significantly that "all the animal sacrifices have a common procedural core, i.e. gestures that occur in every sacrifice, laying on of the hand, killing the animal, catching the blood and using it, burning at least part of the flesh on the altar. It therefore seems likely that every sacrifice has a common core of symbolic meaning. . . . The animal is a substitute for the worshipper. Its death makes atonement for the worshipper."[11] This principle of substitution of the animal's suffering and death for human suffering and death seems to be suggested in Leviticus 17:11: "For the life of the flesh is in the blood: and I have given it to you upon the altar to make an atonement for your souls: for it is the blood that maketh an atonement for the soul." In reading this passage as a ransom, the blood (the life) of the animal makes an atonement for (ransoms) the soul of the sinner. In commenting on this reading of the passage, Wenham argues that "it is this interpretation that seems to fit the burnt offering best. God in his mercy allowed sinful man to offer a ransom payment for sins, so that he escaped the death penalty that his iniquities merit."[12]

The means by which the animal's death "makes atonement" can be seen as the very heart of the system of sacrifice. Lang argues that "the fundamental structure of atonement in Priestly practice finds full expression in [Leviticus] 19:22: 'With this ram the priest shall make atonement before Yahweh for the sin which he has committed.'"[13] Just as the *koper* or ransom brought reconciliation and saved the owner of the ox from death, so the priest's offerings on behalf of himself and others can save them from spiritual death. "The priest acts as a mediator, removing the tension through a sacrifice, provided by the guilty party and sacrificed by the priest. Frequently the text mentions where the act of atonement takes place: 'before Yahweh,' i.e., in the temple. It is the priest who performs the act of atonement—generally on behalf of others, but also on behalf of himself and his family (Leviticus 16:6, 11; etc.)."[14]

This principle of substitution is clearly illustrated in certain kinds of sacrifices which require a laying on of one (or both) hand(s) upon the sacrificial animal. This pattern can be seen in Leviticus 1:4: "And he [the person bringing the sacrifice] shall put his hand upon the head of the burnt offering; and it shall be accepted for him to make atonement for him." The animal takes the place of the person in the sacrifice. In addition to its role in the burnt offering, the laying on of hands as symbolizing substitution is even clearer in the Day of Atonement ritual with the scapegoat.[15] We read in Leviticus 16:21 that "Aaron shall lay both his hands upon the head of the live goat, and confess over him all the iniquities of the children of Israel, and all their transgressions in all their sins, putting them upon the head of the goat, and shall send him away by the hand of a fit man into the wilderness." Here the idea of substitution and vicarious sacrifice is spelled out explicitly. It is particularly significant that in this ritual on the Day of Atonement, it is directly stated that the animal will "bear on itself" all their iniquities (see Leviticus 16:22).[16] The sacrifices of the law of Moses functioned as a way for individuals to have their transgressions transferred and thereby become clean before the Lord. In this "system" the gospel message is clear—God provides a Lamb. We are unclean and in danger of being cut off and dying, but in his mercy God provides means by which a substitute can take our place and make us clean.

While the many specifics of the sacrifice prescribed under the law of Moses can be daunting to grasp, this concept of vicarious sacrifice to reconcile God and humans brings unity to the system and helps point to the message of the gospel of Jesus Christ. Wenham suggests a helpful way to see the various forms of sacrifice under the law of Moses:

> The sacrificial system therefore presents different models or analogies to describe the effects of sin and the way of remedying them. The burnt offering uses a personal picture: of man the guilty sinner who deserves to die for his sin and of the animal dying in his place. God accepts the animal as ransom for man. The sin offering uses a medical model: sin makes the world so dirty that God can no longer dwell there. The blood of the animal disinfects the sanctuary in order that God may continue to be present with his people. The reparation offering presents a commercial picture of sin. Sin is a debt which man incurs against God. The debt is paid through the offered animal.[17]

All of these models can then be further connected with the role of Christ's sacrifice. He dies in our place as in the burnt offering. His blood cleanses us to allow us to dwell in the presence of God as in the sin offering. His suffering and death pays the debt that we owe to God through our sin as in the reparation offering.[18] It is significant that the Hebrew root translated "to make atonement" (*kipper*) can be seen as having a root meaning of to ransom, to purify, and, possibly, to cover.[19] Many scholars will suggest that while the exact etymology of the term may be uncertain, the different senses of this term can be found in Old Testament usage. Each of these concepts points to the role of the atoning sacrifice of Jesus Christ.

ISAIAH 53 AND THE LAW OF MOSES

With this background we can better understand the role of animals as a vicarious sacrifice in the sinner's place as they "make atonement" with their suffering and death—they both ransom or redeem and purify. This understanding prepares us to better appreciate the startling role of the Suffering Servant in Isaiah 53. The sacrifices under the law of Moses give us a framework to understand how his suffering and giving his life can function as a vicarious sacrifice.

Isaiah's message is that the mission of the messianic Suffering Servant is to be a vicarious and substitutionary sacrifice. The general idea of Christ's suffering replacing our suffering is very clear in the text. We can first see this in the contrast set up between the suffering that might initially be regarded as divine punishment: "He is despised and rejected of men; a man of sorrows, and acquainted with grief: and we hid as it were our faces from him; he was despised, and we esteemed him not" (Isaiah 53:3). Isaiah specifically states that those looking at him from the outside might think that he was "smitten of God" (v. 4). But then it is revealed that while the Servant is suffering, it is not for his own sins or transgressions. Isaiah emphasizes that "*he* hath borne *our* griefs," "[*he*] carried *our* sorrows" (v. 4; emphasis added), that "*he* was wounded for *our* transgressions, *he* was bruised for *our* iniquities: the chastisement of *our* peace was upon *him*; and with *his* stripes *we* are healed" (v. 5; emphasis added), and finally that "the Lord hath laid on *him* the iniquity of *us all*" (v. 6; emphasis added). The text builds upon the contrast between the expectation that suffering is a consequence for sin and the surprise that this suffering is vicarious or substitutionary. The Suffering Servant has taken our place and endured the consequences of our sins and iniquities.

In addition to these statements, the message of the Suffering Servant giving his life as a vicarious sacrifice is strengthened by specific references to the sacrifices prescribed under the law of Moses. These connections to the sacrifices of the law serve as a very important addition to the general sense of Christ's vicarious suffering gathered in this chapter. These references specifically link the Suffering Servant to the sacrifices offered in the Temple to reconcile God and Israel. Not only is Isaiah prophesying about the future suffering and death of the coming Messiah, but he is linking it to the suffering and sacrificial death of the animals that ritually redeemed and cleansed the children of Israel under the law of Moses.

The most explicit connection to the law of Moses is Isaiah 53:10: "Thou shalt make his soul an offering for sin." The Hebrew text behind the translation "an offering for sin" is *asham*, the name of a sacrifice under the law of Moses discussed in Leviticus 5–7, what the King James Version refers to as the "guilt offering."[20] This sacrifice is also referred to as a trespass offering or sacrifice of reparation.[21] This passage in Isaiah 53:10 is saying that "the Messianic servant offers himself as an [asham] in compensation for the sins of the people, interposing for them as their substitute."[22] The phrasing in Isaiah 53 is unusual in that with the reparation offering, people are normally described as "bringing it," but here the phrase is "laying down," which follows Abraham laying Isaac down on the altar (see Genesis 22:9).[23] On the significance of the Servant's death being described as an *asham*, Hartley comments: "The choice of [asham] to describe his sacrificial death may be twofold. First, it communicates that the servant's death compensates God fully for the damages he has incurred by mankind's sinning. Second, the servant's sacrifice provides expiation for every kind of sin, inadvertent and intentional. That is, the servant's sacrifice provides expiation for any person who appropriates its merits to himself, no matter how grave his sin."[24]

Another striking phrase in Isaiah 53 identifies Christ's death as that of a lamb.[25] The statement that "he is brought as a lamb to the slaughter" (v. 7) takes on new significance in this context of ritual language. Christ is like the lambs that were used in sacrificial offerings. This would have been central to Passover (see Exodus 12), of course, and also many other sacrifices under the law of Moses. Because of the New Testament testimony of John the Baptist, "Behold the Lamb of God, which taketh away the sin of the world" (John 1:29), we take this identification of the Messiah as the Lamb of God for granted. As a consequence, this imagery can seem so familiar as to lose its meaning. In other words, we assume that the Messiah came to suffer and die. But for the Jews at the time of Jesus the idea of a suffering Messiah was actually not prevalent; rather, they assumed that the Messiah was coming as a political deliverer.[26] It seems very likely, then, that this idea of a suffering Messiah may have easily slipped away at other times when the Israelites were in states of apostasy.[27] To appreciate how fresh and powerful Isaiah's vision of a suffering Messiah would have seemed to those personally familiar with the sacrifices of the law of Moses, consider how consistently the coming Messiah was revealed to Nephi as the Lamb of God (see 1 Nephi 11–14). This would seem to fit with Nephi's confidence in Isaiah's words' power to "more fully persuade . . . to believe in the Lord their Redeemer" (1 Nephi 19:23).

From the perspective of the sacrifices under the law of Moses, another phrase in Isaiah 53 takes on additional meaning. We read that Christ was "cut off out of the land of the living" (Isaiah 53:8), language that evokes the scapegoat ritual of Leviticus 16. On Yom Kippur, the Day of Atonement, when all of Israel was cleansed, two goats were selected. One was sacrificed and its blood sprinkled on the mercy seat in the Holy of Holies to cleanse the Temple and the people (see Leviticus 16:15–20). The other had hands laid upon its head to transfer to "him all the iniquities of the children of Israel, and all their transgressions in all their sins, putting them upon the head of the goat" (Leviticus 16:21). Then that goat was "cut off out of the land of the living," sent "into a solitary, literally, 'cut-off land' . . . , recalling the Servant's being cut off from the land of the living."[28] Leviticus 16:22 specifically says that "the goat shall bear upon him all their iniquities unto a land not inhabited." This clear statement is unique in regards to sacrificial animals and finds a parallel in Isaiah 53:12, where the Servant "bare the sin of many," again a unique usage in the Bible for a human being.[29]

When we can see this dimension of vicarious sacrifice embedded in Isaiah's message we gain a tremendous depth of understanding of the role of redemption and sacrifice. We better appreciate how Isaiah both looked forward to Christ and also backwards to the law of Moses (or, rather, sideways since the sacrifices would have been ongoing in his day). We can better understand the requirement of payment and cleansing to allow us to be in the presence of God and become as he is and how through vicarious sacrifice our ransom and cleansing is brought about. The role of Christ's sacrifice becomes clearer with an examination of this dimension of vicarious suffering under the law.

THE WHOLE MEANING OF THE LAW

The sacrifices of the law of Moses lay out for us a vivid picture of how we are reconciled to God. We are unclean and the consequence of our sin and uncleanness is spiritual death, to be forever cut off from the presence of God. Rather than separating himself from us and leaving us to the condition that we merit, God in his mercy provides a means by which we

THE WHOLE MEANING OF THE LAW 79

can be reconciled. The giving of the life of the sacrificial offering vicariously takes the place of our lives, and by applying this blood we are made clean. Mercy is extended, but justice and the demands of the righteousness of God are not ignored. No unclean thing can dwell in the presence of God, and we cannot cleanse ourselves on our own.

This doctrine of vicarious suffering is taught in the law of Moses. Then in Isaiah 53 we find a prophetic interpretation of how God's forgiveness comes. It is not in the death of the animals that we truly find cleansing and redemption, but in the suffering and death of the messianic Suffering Servant who suffers and dies in our place. Isaiah's connection of the role of the Messiah and the sacrifices under the law of Moses finds ample additional witness by Book of Mormon prophets. In fact, the messianic reading of the law seen in Isaiah 53 finds a fascinating parallel in the words of Abinadi. Understanding the dimension of vicarious sacrifice in Isaiah 53 and its connection to the law of Moses helps to explain why Abinadi quoted this passage to the priests of King Noah in its entirety. They thought they could be saved by obedience to the law alone (see Mosiah 12:32). By sharing Isaiah 53, he was showing them how they should understand the law of Moses. With Abinadi's prophetic interpretation of Isaiah 53, it is clear that the Suffering Servant "brought as a lamb to the slaughter" (Isaiah 53:7) is Christ, who "shall be led, crucified, and slain, the flesh becoming subject even unto death" (Mosiah 15:7).

To a people who believed that with their own actions in following the law's provisions they were saving themselves, Abinadi emphasized that the law pointed to the true source of redemption: "For were it not for the redemption which he hath made for his people, which was prepared from the foundation of the world, I say unto you, were it not for this, all mankind must have perished" (Mosiah 15:19). As we have seen in the provisions of the law of Moses, the priests "made atonement" (cleansed, ransomed) for their sins and the sins of the people through the sacrifices. Under the law, provisions were made for human sin and transgression, and people could be made right with God again. The danger with this ritual system is that it can seem closed and under our control. If we do all the right things, participate in the required ordinances, then we might feel as though we have saved ourselves.

The deep irony of this perspective is that the rituals that people participated in were specifically designed to point to our profound uncleanness and spiritual death, being cut off from the presence of God without divine intervention. Abinadi ended his commentary on the question whether we could be saved by the law of Moses by answering: "And now, ought ye not to tremble and repent of your sins, and remember that only in and through Christ ye can be saved? Therefore, if ye teach the law of Moses, also teach that it is a shadow of those things which are to come—teach them that redemption cometh through Christ the Lord, who is the very Eternal Father" (Mosiah 16:13–15).

Like the people living under the law of Moses, in our day we can also overlook the underlying message of the ordinances provided to cleanse us and bring us into the presence of God. We might be tempted to feel that it is our obedience to these ordinances that saves us. Understanding the message of vicarious and substitutionary sacrifice at the heart of the law of Moses can also help us look and see Christ's vicarious and substitutionary sacrifice manifest in the ordinances of our day. As we recognize our own condition of uncleanness and spiritual death, separated from the presence of God, we are better able to appreciate how God reaches out to cleanse and ransom us from our unclean state.

Isaiah begins chapter 53 by asking, "Who hath believed our report? and to whom is the arm of the Lord revealed?" (v. 1). He then proceeds to explain how the arm of the Lord is revealed—in the suffering and death of the Messiah as a vicarious sacrifice on our behalf. As Christ spoke to the shattered and chastened Nephites in 3 Nephi 9, he specifically referred to this arm of mercy that he has extended to us: "Yea, verily I say unto you, if ye will come unto me ye shall have eternal life. Behold, mine arm of mercy is extended towards you, and whosoever will come, him will I receive" (v. 14). Isaiah shows us the price that was paid for that arm of mercy to be extended toward us. He also reminds us how much we need mercy and that our obedience alone cannot save us. "All we like sheep have gone astray; we have turned every one to his own way; and the Lord hath laid on him the iniquity of us all" (Isaiah 53:6).

Learning to better understand the law of Moses and its symbolic teaching about the Atonement helps provide us with a framework to appreciate the fulness of the gospel. These elemental images of life and death, cleanness and impurity, and of substitutionary sacrifice help us learn to see the symbols that point to our relationship to God as we receive the blessings of the ordinances in our day. Recognizing that "all we like sheep have gone astray" brings us down into humility when we recognize that our ability to enter into the presence of the Lord comes only through his arm of mercy. Like the scapegoat whose death cleansed the people and allowed the Lord's presence to remain in their midst, even so with Christ—"The Lord hath laid on him the iniquity of us all." As Amulek testified, "This is the whole meaning of the law, every whit pointing to that great and last sacrifice; and that great and last sacrifice will be the Son of God, yea, infinite and eternal" (Alma 34:14).

While the idea that mercy is available simply out of the loving goodness of our Father may sound like an attractive doctrine, the Old Testament bears witness to the true source of mercy. The provisions of the law of Moses teach that the consequence of our uncleanness, our sins and transgressions, is to be banished from the presence of God and to die. The provisions of the law of Moses also teach that mercy is possible through the suffering and death of a substitute. In Alma's words, "mercy cometh because of the atonement" (Alma 42:23). Isaiah testifies that "he hath poured out his soul unto death: and he was numbered with the transgressors; and he bare the sin of many, and made intercession for the transgressors" (Isaiah 53:12). The Lord speaks to us today, pleading that we accept the mercy that he has made available to us through the Restoration. "Listen to the voice of Jesus Christ, your Redeemer, the Great I Am, whose arm of mercy hath atoned for your sins" (D&C 29:1). His arm of mercy has been revealed in our day and he invites us to accept his invitation to leave behind spiritual death and uncleanness. He invites us into his presence.

NOTES

1. "The Living Christ: The Testimony of the Apostles," *Ensign*, April 2000, 2.

2. An overview of these different views addressing the question of Jesus' death can be found in James Beilby and Paul R. Eddy, eds., *The Nature of the Atonement: Four Views* (Downers Grove, IL: InterVarsity Press, 2006) and Derek Tidball, David Hilborn, and Justin Thacker, eds., *The Atonement Debate: Papers from the London Symposium on the Theology of Atonement* (Grand Rapids, MI: Zondervan, 2008). A brief history of the changing views on the meaning of Christ's life can be found

in works such as John McIntyre's *The Shape of Christology: Studies in the Doctrine of the Person of Christ*, 2nd ed. rev. (Edinburgh: T&T Clark, 1998) and John Macquarrie, *Jesus Christ in Modern Thought* (London: SCM Press; Philadelphia: Trinity Press International, 1990).

3. An example of how the assumptions of the Enlightenment frame how to interpret the Bible can be seen in John Goldingay's rejection of seeing vicarious suffering in Isaiah 53. He sees this nonvicarious reading as preferable because "it thus does not fall foul of Immanuel Kant's argument that in connection with guilt and punishment one person cannot stand in the place of another person. By its nature guilt is not transferable. A court does have the power to decide not to punish a person for their guilt, and also to pardon them so that they cease to be guilty" (John Goldingay, *The Message of Isaiah 40–55: A Literary-Theological Commentary* [London: T&T Clark, 2005], 484). He will, however, argue for a kind of vicariousness to the Servant's suffering in that "the speakers' first new realization about the servant's suffering would then be that it came about not because of his own wrongdoing but because he was sharing their fate as wrongdoers. Like the suffering of someone such as Jeremiah, the servant's suffering issues from his identification with the lot of the people as a whole" (Goldingay, *Message of Isaiah 40–55*, 501). For an argument for reading Isaiah 53 as vicarious suffering, see J. Allan Groves, "Atonement in Isaiah 53," in *The Glory of the Atonement: Biblical, Theological & Practical Perspectives*, ed. Charles E. Hill and Frank A. James (Downers Grove, IL: InterVarsity Press, 2004), 61–89.

4. For summaries and overviews of other Christians' defense of substitutionary sacrifice see such discussions as Simon Gathercole, "The Cross and Substitutionary Atonement," *Scottish Bulletin of Evangelical Theology* 21 (2003): 152–65; Steve Jeffery, Michael Ovey, and Andrew Sach, *Pierced for Our Transgressions: Rediscovering the Glory of Penal Substitution* (Wheaton, IL: Crossway Books, 2007); Thomas R. Schreiner, "The Penal Substitution View," in *The Nature of the Atonement: Four Views*, ed. James Beilby and Paul R. Eddy (Downers Grove, IL: InterVarsity Press, 2006), 67–116; Sylvain Romerowski, "Old Testament Sacrifices and Reconciliation," *European Journal of Theology* 16, no. 1 (2006): 13–24.

5. Gordon J. Wenham, "The Theology of Old Testament Sacrifice," in *Sacrifice in the Bible*, ed. Roger T. Beckwith and Martin J. Selman (Carlisle, UK: Paternoster Press; Grand Rapids, MI: Baker Book House, 1995), 76–77. An older but classic study of the theology of sacrifice in the Old Testament and its connection to Christ is Andrew Jukes's *The Law of the Offerings: The Five Tabernacle Offerings and Their Spiritual Significance* (Grand Rapids, MI: Kregel Classics, 2004). It was originally published in the mid-nineteenth century, and this reprint is of the seventeenth edition. A classic twentieth-century text that also continues to be appreciated by those looking to the law of Moses as a type of Christ is Leon Morris's *The Apostolic Preaching of the Cross* (Grand Rapids, MI: Eerdmans, 1960). While both of these works have helpful insights and continue to be important resources for the Christian perspective on the sacrifices of the law of Moses, I will be drawing primarily on the more recent scholarship of Gordon J. Wenham. Other contemporary discussions of these issues are listed in note 3.

6. Wenham, "Theology," 77.

7. Wenham, "Theology," 77.

8. Speaking of how to interpret the imposition of hands on the sacrificial victim, Wenham argues that "the most probable explanation of the imposition of the hand in sacrifice is that thereby the victim is identified with the offerer. This has been identified by Edmund Leach who states, 'the plain implication is that, in some metaphysical sense, the victim is a vicarious substitution for the donor himself.'" He continues, "This interpretation is strengthened by the comment in some Hittite texts that the animal is a substitute for the worshipper. It is further confirmed by [Genesis] 22:13 which states that Abraham offered up the lamb 'as a burnt offering *instead of his son*'. Now while this could be taken simply as a statement of fact, it seems more probable that Genesis 22, like many stories in Genesis, is also paradigmatic and elucidates the OT understanding of sacrifice in general. It shows an animal suffering vicariously in a man's place" (Wenham, "Theology," 79–80).

9. See the discussion in David Peterson, "Atonement in the Old Testament," in *Where Wrath and Mercy Meet: Proclaiming the Atonement Today*, ed. David Peterson (Carlisle, UK: Paternoster, 2001), 4.

10. B. Lang, "Kipper," *Theological Dictionary of the Old Testament*, ed. G. Johannes Botterweck, Helmer Ringgren, and Heinz-Josef Fahry (Grand Rapids, MI: Eerdmans, 1995), 7:301.

11. He continues, "Its immolation on the altar quietens God's anger at human sin. But to say that every animal sacrifice has a common core of ritual meaning is not to say that in other respects the sacrifices are not very different and have a diversity of symbolic meaning" (Wenham, "Theology," 82).

12. Gordon J. Wenham, *The Book of Leviticus*, New International Commentary on the Old Testament (Grand Rapids, MI: Eerdmans, 1979), 61. It is important to note that this passage is heavily debated and those who hold different views on how to read it will have correspondingly different views on the role of substitutionary sacrifice in the law of Moses.

13. Lang, "Kipper," 292.

14. Lang, "Kipper," 292.

15. Wenham observes: "The laying on of hands may indicate that the animal is taking the place of the worshipper. The worshipper is offering himself to God through the sacrificial victim. 'The plain implication is that, in some metaphysical sense, the victim is a vicarious substitution for the donor himself.' Or alternatively the laying on of hands transfers the worshipper's sins symbolically to the animal. Both of these meanings seem to be attested in Scripture." He continues, "It does not seem necessary to decide between these explanations. Both fit in well with sacrifices making atonement, i.e., the animal serving as a ransom for the life of man. One may regard the animal either as dying in the worshipper's place as his substitute, or as receiving the death penalty because of the sin transferred to it by the laying on of hands" (Wenham, *Leviticus*, 62).

While noting that this is a debated question, Wenham argues against those who simply see laying on of hands as indicating ownership, arguing that the meaning of pressing (*samak*) is stronger and that "the very action of pressing down on the animal's head suggests an attempt to establish an identity between worshipper and victim." He continues, "Another possibility is that the imposition of hands conveys the worshipper's sins to the animal, which then dies in the worshipper's place. This is certainly the most probable interpretation of [Leviticus] 16:21, where in the day of atonement ceremony the high priest lays *both* his hands on the scapegoat's head, confesses 'over him all the iniquities of the people of Israel . . . all their sins; and he shall put them upon the head of the goat, and send him away into the wilderness'" (Wenham, "Theology," 79; emphasis in original).

16. See Peterson, "Atonement in the Old Testament," 15.

17. Wenham, *Leviticus*, 111.

18. Wenham suggests that "it may not be necessary, however, to choose between the idea of substitutionary atonement, of the ram dying in the sinner's place, and of reparation, of the ram somehow compensating God for the loss he has suffered as the result of sin. In some degree substitution seems to form part of the theology of all the sacrifices: reparation may be the specific component of the reparation offering, just as purification is the distinctive aim of the purification offering" (*Leviticus*, 111).

19. The debate over how to interpret *kipper* is wide-ranging. Part of it is connected to various possible cognates in other Semitic languages. Part of it is connected to theological issues of interpretation, related to the question of whether this should be understood as expiation or propitiation. For a summary of several of these points see B. Lang, "Kipper," in *Theological Dictionary* and Richard E. Averbeck, "Kipper," in *The New International Dictionary of Old Testament Theology and Exegesis*, ed. Willem A. Van Gemeren (Grand Rapids, MI: Zondervan, 1997), 2:689–710. Both review the scholarship and give summaries of several influential interpretations. Simply put, the etymological issues stem from possible roots with the Hebrew term *koper*, "ransom," and the Akkadian "to purify" or "to cover," and from the Arabic cognate, which both Lang and Averbeck suggest has generally been seen as having difficulties (see Lang, 290; Averbeck, 692). Several suggest that both purification and substitution should be seen as the meaning of *kipper*; see, for example, Émile Nicole, "Atonement in the Pentateuch," in *The Glory of the Atonement*, ed. Ch.E. Hill (Downers Grove, IL: InterVarsity Press, 2004), 47–49.

20. For a discussion of the translation of *asham*, how the *asham* was offered, and a debate over *asham* as sacrifice, see J. E. Harley, *Leviticus*, Word Biblical Commentary (Dallas: Word, 1992), 76–79. Kellerman illustrates the debate over interpreting this term, noting that as some see it as "restitution for trespasses," or "to atone for a sacrilege," others see it limited to "unintentional, inadvertent transgressions," but another sees it as "atonement for intentional sins," while some see it as a "fine" or "restitution" (D. Kellerman, "Asham," *Theological Dictionary of the Old Testament*, ed. G. Johannes Botterweck and Helmer Ringgren, trans. John T. Willis, rev. [Grand Rapids, MI: Eerdmans, 1974], 1:432).

21. Francis Brown, S. R. Driver, and Charles A. Briggs, *A Hebrew and English Lexicon of the Old Testament: With an Appendix Containing the Biblical Aramaic* (Oxford: Clarendon Press, 1997), 79–80 on trespass offering; Joseph Blenkinsopp, *Isaiah 40–55: A New Translation with Introduction and Commentary*, The Anchor Bible (New York: Doubleday, 2002), 354 on sacrifice of reparation. Blenkinsopp notes: "This type of sacrifice was

the indispensable means for the removal of guilt and liability for punishment in especially serious cases of encroachment on holy objects and places. It also served to make reparation for a range of transgressions (probably not listed exhaustively in the relevant ritual text, [Leviticus] 5:14–26 [5:14–6:7]), such as theft, fraud, and the swearing of false oaths" (p. 254).

22. Brown, Driver, and Briggs, *A Hebrew and English Lexicon*, 80.

23. John Goldingay and David Payne, *A Critical and Exegetical Commentary on Isaiah 40–55* (London: T&T Clark, 2006), 2:320.

24. John E. Hartley, *Leviticus*, Word Biblical Commentary (Nashville, TN: Thomas Nelson Publishers, 1992), 80.

25. The term can also be understood more generally and could also be translated "goat" (Wenham, *Leviticus*, 110).

26. This can be seen even in the case of the Apostles. Consider, for example, Matthew 16:21–23.

27. On the question of the influence of this text see Blenkinsopp, *Isaiah 40–55*, 81–92. He has a discussion of the impact of Isaiah 53 in biblical times and comments: "One would think that the depth and originality with which the religious idea of prophetic instrumentality is worked out in [Isaiah] 40–55, most remarkably in the form of substitutionary suffering in 52:13–53:12, could hardly fail to leave its mark on religious thinking in the later Second Temple period. It has nevertheless proved difficult to pin down clear and substantial indications of its influence in the extant literature prior to the common era (see most recently the survey by Martin Hengel 1996, 49–91). The situation provides another occasion for regret at the scarcity of source material for the period and the uncooperative nature of the few sources that we do possess" (84).

Another insight on the difficulty of knowing the impact of Isaiah 53's vision of a suffering Messiah can be seen in this comment by Martin Hengel: "We cannot claim that Isa. 53 had no kind of messianic interpretation in pre-Christian Judaism. It is simply the case that too few texts have come down to us from the pre-rabbinic period." He continues, "So far, then, we have no clear text from pre-Christian Judaism which speaks of the vicarious suffering of the Messiah in connection with Isa. 53. Of course, this does not rule out the possibility of such a tradition, and there are some indications in favour of it, but the basis provided by our sources is too restricted. At all events, a suffering Messiah did not belong to the widespread popular Messianic hope in the time of Jesus and a crucified Messiah was a real blasphemy" (*The Atonement: The Origins of the Doctrine in the New Testament*, trans. John Bowden [Philadelphia: Fortress, 1981], 59).

28. Blenkinsopp, *Isaiah 40–55*, 351. Also, Wenham says "'cutting off' could refer to the fact that the place to which the goat was led was 'cut off' from the camp, perhaps by a deep valley, so that the animal had no chance of returning to Israel and bringing back the guilt of their sins. Alternatively, it could refer to the fact that it was taken to a place where its life was 'cut off'" (*Leviticus*, 233).

29. Peterson, "Atonement in the Old Testament," 15.

6

THE SANCTIFYING POWER
OF TRUE RITUAL WORSHIP

Carol Frogley Ellertson

Religious ritual is central to all past great civilizations. The ancient Greeks, Romans, and Egyptians—as well as most Near and Far Eastern ancient societies—depended on ceremonial manifestations of God, "the gods," or "the divine" to give structure and orientation to the world. Because the rites were communal in nature, they served as a fundamental mechanism that held a society together. The rituals generated common emotions linked to symbols that formed the basis for belief, morality, and culture.[1] This ritual foundation established a sacred order in the lives of the people. The order usually centered around a temple where kings were crowned, religious law went forth, and sacred ceremonies were performed. Some of these communal rituals included religious festivals, processions, choruses, dramas, and games.[2]

In contrast, the modern secular world emphasizes a different value structure to govern the social order of our lives. The secularization of society means that religious ideas, practice, and organizations have lost much of their influence in the face of scientific and other knowledge.[3]

Carol Frogley Ellertson is a doctoral candidate at Brigham Young University.

Western culture in general values individual autonomy and emphasizes pleasure seeking and material satisfaction.[4] Ritual performances that build religious communities do not have the prominence they had anciently. At times they can even connote negative stereotypes as religious discourse and worship is increasingly pushed out of the public sphere.

Though we live in an "enlightened" secular culture, members of The Church of Jesus Christ of Latter-day Saints are involved in sacred religious rituals from a young age. These rituals, called ordinances, include baptism, the sacrament, the laying on of hands for blessing and healing, and other rites involved in consecrating, dedicating, and covenant making. Sometimes, however, we experience tension between the secular and the sacred. This tension may be felt more acutely when we enter the Temple for the first time. Our secular world is the "water in which we swim." Ancient, sacred rituals are generally not part of our cultural mindset in the same way they were to Saints in earlier dispensations. That is not to say that Saints of old did not feel pulled between the sacred and the profane, but secularism is the cultural view of our modern world.

We can receive insight into the great and sacred nature of ritual performance involved in covenant making by studying God's dealings with his people in the ancient world. The purpose of this essay is to define what ritual is and then to show how sacred ritual worship is particularly illustrated in the Old Testament. It will focus on three aspects of true ritual: (1) its immediate enlivening power, (2) its increased power through renewal and remembrance, and (3) its long-term sanctifying power to bring us to Christ. After this I will focus on specific Old Testament rituals and ritual objects that illustrate these aspects and then compare ancient and modern qualifications to enter Temples. Some ancient rituals are similar to those in the latter-day Church. They illustrate commonalities between ancient and modern-day practice. This is one way in which we see that God is the same yesterday, today, and forever (see 2 Nephi 27:23). There is great wisdom in the Old Testament for those who have eyes to see and ears to hear.

In my own experience, I have struggled in the past to understand why the Lord uses symbols and rituals in some of the most important covenants that we make. When I adopted an in-depth study regimen of the Old Testament over a long period, the Temple came alive for me in ways

I had not anticipated. I received unexpected understanding of the importance of ritual symbolism and the great eternal nature of God's dealings
with his children. As one writer expressed, "What a critical blessing it is
. . . to be able to see Church practices . . . from our Heavenly Father's perspective. That perspective . . . protects us from disenchantment, offense,
or misunderstanding that can fester in our souls and take us out of the
Church."⁵ By learning about ritual ordinances in the Old Testament, I
feel I have an increased perspective on mortality and eternity.

WHAT IS RITUAL?

A ritual or rite is a carefully prescribed procedure. A performance
is an act or deed. Though similar, a ritual may be more repetitive and
structured than a performance. Both call for set action. In a gospel sense,
a sacred ritual revealed by God is a ceremonial procedure that is a physical
demonstration of an eternal truth. Put another way, it is the expression
of truth through prescribed symbolic action. The concept of sacred ritual
has been described by some scholars as one element in a kind of universal temple typology. Initiation rites have been part of sacred worship in
the temples of many ancient cultures.⁶ In this context, the primordial
purpose of these rites was to open up communication to higher states or
realms.⁷ This definition is certainly part of a gospel understanding.

However, Latter-day Saints view sacred ritual in a more narrow sense.
It is the symbolic act that is also known as an ordinance. *Ordinance* means
"precept, given by one in authority." Over time, ordinance has come to
mean a ritual act because God's precepts or laws were often given through
ritual. Ordinance can also mean the act of conferring or receiving something that is holy. The biblical Hebrew "ordinance" (*huqqah*) usually
means "law," "statute," or occasionally "rite." Thus Leviticus 18:4, "Keep
mine ordinances, to walk therein," means "obey my laws and follow my
decrees." *Ordinance* is derived ultimately from the Latin *ordinare*, which
means to set in order or to arrange in ranks to prepare for battle.⁸ Taken
altogether, these definitions imply that holy rituals prepare us for battle.
Because God is a God of order (see 1 Corinthians 14:33), he requires specific physical acts to prepare us for the battles of this life. Many of these
ritual acts are given in the "house of order," the Temple (D&C 109:8).

How does the physicality of these ordinances prepare us for the battles of life and to be worthy to see the face of God?

The Prophet Joseph Smith said that the power of godliness must be manifested to "men in the flesh": It is "in the ordinances . . . [that] the power of godliness is manifest. And without the ordinances thereof, and the authority of the priesthood, the power of godliness is not manifest unto men in the flesh; for without this no man can see the face of God, even the Father, and live" (D&C 84:20–22). In other words, it is through ordinances that God's power is manifest, not just spiritually but physically. God's ordinances must involve the physical body for his power to be manifested.

The rituals involved in gospel ordinances are the physical indications of what is happening inwardly. The whole person is involved in the act, whatever it may be, in order to show God that we are participating with our whole souls, our complete beings. In this way both our bodies and spirits are changed and given the power of godliness promised. In the Old Testament, the Hebrew *nefesh* refers to the whole living person. For example, when Jacob sought the birthright blessing from Isaac, he said, "Arise, I pray thee, sit and eat of my venison, that thy soul [*nefesh*] may bless me" (meaning a physical laying on of hands) (Genesis 27:19). *Nefesh* was translated into the Greek Bible as *psyche*. Greek thought, which considered the body evil and corrupt,[9] influenced the meaning of the term *soul* until it came to connote the unembodied moral essence of a person. The notion that the soul includes both body and spirit (see D&C 88:15–16) was eventually lost. Today, it is mostly unique to Latter-day Saint thought.

The ancient Hebrew sense of ordinances was nonmetaphysical. They existed only as they were expressed in a person. In other words, spiritual truths remained unfounded until they were experienced. The Lord said, "Yea, behold, I will tell you in your mind and in your heart, by the Holy Ghost, which shall come upon you and which shall dwell in your heart" (D&C 8:2). How does the Holy Ghost "dwell in your heart"? It is received and experienced. Joseph Smith observed, "Reading the experience of others, or the revelation given to *them*, can never give *us* a comprehensive view of our condition and true relation to God. Knowledge of these things can only be obtained by experience through the ordinances of God set forth for that purpose. . . . I assure the Saints that truth, in reference to these matters, can and may be known through the revelations of God in the way of his ordinances."[10] In other words, eternal truths are not completely learned until they are experienced. They are experienced in the mind and the heart, in the body, and in the soul.[11] When Christ appeared to the Nephites at their temple site in Bountiful, they fell down before him in awe or fear. He invited them to see and feel his wounds. It was after experiencing the wounds of Christ one by one that they then felt an adoring reverence for him and shouted "Hosanna," meaning "Save us now." This physical witnessing of the wounds of Christ revealed to them their true condition in mortality (see 3 Nephi 11:12–17).

Truths reside and are expressed within people. "Activity in a physical body is the most fundamental category of Hebrew thought. . . . The way something is defines what it is. . . . How something is and what it is are inseparable."[12] This Hebrew sense is conveyed when Jesus Christ said, "I am the way, the truth, and the life" (John 14:6). To embody truth is to live and act like Christ. It follows, then, that expressions in sacred ritual ordinances are expressions of truth. The physicality of ritual reflects the importance that God places upon the body and its eventual glorification for those who do his works.

THE ENLIVENING POWER OF RITUAL

As we attempt to grasp the function and meaning of ritual worship as individuals, we may react similarly to Adam of old when the angel asked why he offered sacrifices. He replied, "I know not, save the Lord commanded me" (Moses 5:6). The angel then taught Adam that his sacrifice had within it a symbol and a pattern that brought great meaning to his life. It was in similitude of the great sacrifice of Christ who was to come (see Moses 5:7–8). In fact, the physical performances of ritual ordinances, if done in faith, help to make us *alive* in Christ.

The Old Testament prophet Ezekiel referred to this "aliveness" when he prophesied of a new spirit and a new heart for believers in the latter days. The Lord spoke through Ezekiel concerning the power that observing ordinances have to renew us: "And I will give them one heart, and I will put a new spirit within you; and I will take the stony heart out of their flesh, and will give them an heart of flesh: that they may walk in my statutes, and keep mine ordinances, and do them: and they shall be my people, and I will be their God" (Ezekiel 11:19–20). Also, the Lord states in Jeremiah 31:33, "But this shall be the covenant that I will make with the house of Israel; After those days, saith the Lord, I will put my law in their inward parts, and write it in their hearts; and will be their God, and they shall be my people." How does the Lord write his law in our hearts and in our inward parts? How does he give us hearts of flesh? Though these passages do not mention specific rituals, the implication is there in the phrase "I will put my law in their inward parts." He gives us his law and statutes in an interactive covenant process with the Spirit of the living God to be put in the fleshy tables of our hearts (see 2 Corinthians 3:3). Rather than stone, or something lifeless, he gives us hearts of flesh, meaning we come alive and are reborn through a covenant process (see Hebrews 8:10–11; Mosiah 13:11).

The enlivening power of true ritual is attended by efficacy, virtue, and force (see D&C 132:7). After Joseph Smith and Oliver Cowdery baptized one another, they immediately experienced "great and glorious blessings from our Heavenly Father" and began to prophesy and rejoice. They received discernment in interpreting scripture (Joseph Smith—History 1:73–74). Their baptism was enlightening to the mind and enlivening to the whole soul. Similarly, Adam was immediately "quickened in the inner man" after he was baptized (Moses 6:65). These passages demonstrate that sacred ritual quickens and invigorates our bodies and increases powers of discernment and revelation. This supports Joseph Smith's claim that "being born again, comes by the Spirit of God through ordinances."[13]

The enlivening power of a symbolic act is illustrated when Moses invited the children of Israel to look upon the brazen serpent to be healed from the bites of fiery serpents. Most did not understand this symbolic act. The serpent represented Christ raised up on the cross (see Numbers 21:6–9; Helaman 8:14–15). The performance was simple, to come and cast their eyes upon a symbol that could "enliven" them physically and spiritually. However, we learn from Alma in the Book of Mormon that some of the children of Israel "would not look, therefore they perished" (Alma 33:20). Others who did "look and live" did not understand the meaning of the symbol (Alma 33:19–20).

In the first group, "the reason they would not look is because they did not believe that it would heal them" because of the hardness of their hearts (Alma 33:20). They lacked faith, and thus they perished. But the second group who did "look and live" must have had enough faith to be healed. Alma described them *also* as having a hardness of heart. He noted that even though *many* did look and live, *"few* understood the meaning of those things [the symbol of the brazen serpent], and this because of the hardness of their hearts" (Alma 33:20; emphasis added). Perhaps this group's hardness of heart was a lack of sensitivity or open-mindedness toward *practices* with which they were not familiar. Here was a symbol alluding to Christ and his saving power. Was it because they were un-familiar with such a symbol or that it did not fit their cultural paradigm for healing that they were not willing to try to understand it? With our twenty-twenty hindsight, it is easy to judge their actions as ignorant and foolish. On the other hand, should we not ask ourselves about our own attitudes when we do not understand or have respect for the symbols and rituals the Lord has given to save us?

POWER OF RITUAL INCREASED THROUGH
RENEWAL AND REMEMBRANCE

One way to gain understanding and respect for symbolic rituals is to repeat them often. When replicated, the power of ritual increases. This is done in two ways. First, the ritual becomes a memorial of the original act or covenant. Second, the ritual is renewed and strengthens the cov-enantal relationship.

A memorial serves as a remembrance of a person or an event. The Lord refers to the fact that some of the ordinances done today are a memorial for those done anciently. He told the Saints of this dispensa-tion, "I commanded Moses that he should build a tabernacle . . . that those ordinances might be revealed which had been hid from before the world was. Therefore, verily I say unto you, that . . . your *memorials for your sacrifices by the sons of Levi* . . . are ordained by the ordinance of my holy house" (D&C 124:38–39; emphasis added). This notion of memorial, or commemorating an earlier event through a later ordinance, was evident when the feast of the Passover was instituted. The Lord said, "This day shall be unto you for a memorial; and ye shall keep it a feast to the Lord throughout your generations; ye shall keep it a feast by an ordinance for ever" (Exodus 12:14). "Ye shall blow with the trumpets over your burnt offerings, and over the sacrifices of your peace offerings; that they may be to you for a *memorial* before your God" (Numbers 10:10; emphasis added).

Baptism and the sacrament are rituals that memorialize Christ's death, Resurrection, and atoning sacrifice. Along with serving as a memorial, the sacrament renews the original covenant relationship the person has made with God. The person receives forgiveness of sins and strength through the Holy Ghost. This covenant includes a willingness to bear others' burdens, which strengthens communal bonds. It also includes a promise to take upon ourselves Christ's name, which implies renewing all other priesthood and Temple covenants we have made.[14] Those who return to the Temple for proxy work find spiritual refuge, renewal, hope, and revelation. By remembering and commemorating the recent or ancient past, these ordinances instill a genuine optimism about the future.[15]

Is the concept of renewal, of sealing the ritual into our souls through repetition, merely figurative, or is there a literal manifestation of this repetition in our bodies? Perhaps this is one way in which we receive his image "engraven" upon our countenances (see Alma 5:14, 19). Apart from our minds, do our physical bodies have memory? Some social scientists assert that memory resides not just in our mind or brain but in all parts of our body.[16] Such questions have implications for what our bodies will be like in the Resurrection. There "our works will condemn us" (Alma 12:14) if they have not been "holy works" (Alma 12:30).

Others believe memory can also reside within a culture or community.[17] Communal rituals or performances such as Temple dedications, solemn assemblies, ward and Churchwide fasts, weekly sacramental ritual, and even regular conferences where God's people gather to hear the law go forth from the prophet all invoke communal memory that strengthens God's people.

Ritual objects and actions are given to us by God through priesthood channels. In other words, the physical symbols (such as those in the sacrament) remind us of the Lord's sacrifice, but they are also tied to God because he gave them to us. One writer expounds on the importance of "memory" in ritual objects. He muses on the meaning of his wedding ring as a ritual object of his marriage. As a symbol it is connected to memory because when he wears it, it always reminds him of the day he got married. But it is more than just a reminder. Because his wife gave it to him, it has a physical relation to her and is a memorial of their relationship. It demands an attitude of fidelity when it is worn. It gives order to his world.[18] Likewise, sacred rituals and objects (such as sacred clothing or sacramental emblems) give order to our world and demand a certain attitude and behavior. God gave them to us, and they tie us to him. They were instituted from before the foundation of the world, and they sanctify, honor, and glorify the performer when the rites to which they are connected are done with faith in Jesus Christ (see D&C 124:34, 39). In this sense, ritual covenant making becomes the foundation of eternal relationships with God and with beloved family members.

Long-Term Sanctifying Power

Sacred ritual has power to sanctify, which means "to make holy or to set apart for sacred use." Additional meanings from the Hebrew for sanctify, *qadōš*, are "to consecrate, hallow, dedicate, prepare, appoint, and purify." The Lord sanctifies us to enter his presence as well as to use us for his purposes on the earth. The Lord commanded Moses to bring Aaron to the tabernacle and "sanctify him" to minister in the priest's office (see Exodus 40:13–15). Aaron and his sons were set apart and made holy in order to "*sanctify* the most holy things, he and his sons for ever, to burn incense before the Lord, to minister unto him, and to bless in his name for ever" (1 Chronicles 23:13; emphasis added). The law of Moses commanded that "all the firstling males that come of thy herd and of thy flock thou shalt sanctify unto the Lord thy God" (Deuteronomy 15:19). Likewise, the Lord set apart the house of Israel: "When the most High divided to the nations their inheritance, when he separated the sons of Adam, he set the bounds of the people according to the number of the children of Israel" (Deuteronomy 32:8). The Lord sanctified one day for Israel. "I gave them my sabbaths, to be a sign between me and them, that they might know that I am the Lord that sanctify them" (Ezekiel 20:12). To sanctify a people and a day is more than to just separate them, but to make them holy.

God's people often spurned their identity as a sanctified people. The Lord said to Abraham, "My people have gone astray from my precepts, and have not kept mine ordinances, which I gave unto their fathers; and they have not observed mine anointing, and the burial, or baptism wherewith I commanded them" (Joseph Smith Translation, Genesis 17:4–5). Centuries later, Hezekiah reigned over the wayward Southern Kingdom of Judah during the time that the Northern Kingdom was carried away by the Assyrians. The people of the Southern Kingdom had corrupted sacred rituals and had lost the sanctifying power of covenantal ordinances. Hezekiah is known for bringing about religious reforms, especially concerning how and where sacrifice was performed. "He removed the high places, and brake the images, and cut down the groves, and brake in pieces the brasen serpent that Moses had made" (2 Kings 18:4) because the children of Israel were burning incense to it. He admonished the priests, "Hear me, ye Levites, sanctify now yourselves, and sanctify the house of the Lord God of your fathers, and carry forth the filthiness out of the holy place" (2 Chronicles 29:5). This passage implies that the priests were to once again consecrate and make hallow the Temple and themselves through a ritual process. Hezekiah was reinstituting the sanctifying process in Israel. Rituals sanctify by carrying away filthiness that may reside in us and in our holy places. We have this sanctifying process often close at hand in chapels and Temples. If we yield ourselves to the Lord, we can be consecrated and set apart for his purposes. The sanctifying process builds on itself throughout our lives as we prove our fidelity to God by keeping the rites and ordinances of his Church.

PATTERNS OF SACRED RITUAL IN THE OLD TESTAMENT

God has established rituals as essential elements of his plan on earth. Ancient practices of ritual worship are evident during Adam's day, the patriarchal period, and the time when the law of Moses was instituted. They include the use of altars, ritual prayers, washings and anointings, and the donning of sacred vestments, to name a few. Additionally, the law of sacrifice had many iterations during Adam's day, as well as the patriarchal and Mosaic periods. Similar patterns of these rituals and performances are practiced today in the restored Church. By focusing on certain ancient rituals, we can discern significance and meaning in these practices from the scriptural text. We gain insight to the eternal importance of ritual to save us.

The use of altars. Adam learned the meaning of sacrifice at an altar (see Moses 5:5–8). Noah built an altar on the first land that emerged from the Flood, which is seen as a renewal of the original creation ritual (see Genesis 8:20). Abraham had important spiritual experiences at several places where he built altars unto the Lord and called upon his name. When the Lord appeared to him and promised, "Unto thy seed will I give this land," he built an altar at that place (Genesis 12:7). God appeared to Jacob "when he fled from the face of his brother," Esau. The spot became sacred space, so he built an altar there and called the place El-beth-el (The God of the House of God) (Genesis 35:7). During the Mosaic period, Moses, Joshua, David, Elijah, and other prophets also built altars that became sacred space because God was manifest there.[19]

These and other ancient prophets built altars of stone according to the prescribed command given in Exodus 20:24–25: "An altar of earth thou shalt make unto me, and shalt sacrifice thereon thy burnt offerings. . . . If thou wilt make me an altar of stone, thou shalt not build it of hewn stone." In other words, the stones were to be of the earth, not cut or made by man. One writer observed that this passage in Exodus suggests that an altar's construction (to be made of earth) "is associated with the creation of the earth and God's covenants with humankind. As the waters of creation receded, dry land appeared and was known as the primordial mound (first hill). Here, according to legend, the gods stood in order to complete the Creation. Because of divine presence, this spot became sacred or holy ground, a point of contact between this world and the heavenly world."[20] Another ritual that connects the holy altar to creation is the pouring ritual of the Second Temple period. Blood was a symbol of mortal life. Leviticus 17:11 says: "For the life of the flesh is in the blood: and I have given it to you upon the altar to make an atonement for your souls: for it is the blood that maketh an atonement for the soul." By pouring blood upon the altars of the Temple, the process of creation was ritualized.[21]

Thus a holy altar is considered sacred space because it represents this point of contact with heaven. Indeed, some ancient Near Eastern temples were in actuality seen by their people as giant altars.[22] The word translated as "altar" in Ezekiel 43:15 is the Hebrew *Har'el*, which means "mountain of God." Altars thus symbolize the Creation and the presence of God.

In general, altars in the Tabernacle and the Temple were also made of dirt or unhewn stone but were usually boxed in with wood and overlaid with finery. Altars had horns raised from each corner upon which the priests would smear the blood of the sacrifice in order to bring the atonement nearer to heaven. The ancients built altars not only to make offerings but to lift up prayers and devotion unto the Lord. Today altars are found in Church meetinghouses (as sacrament tables) and Temples throughout the world. Their function is similar in that they serve as specific sacred sites to bring us nearer to heaven, often through the acts of sacrifice and prayer.

Ritual prayer. The Temple is known as a "house of prayer" (Isaiah 56:7). Of the four altars within the Jerusalem Temple complex,[23] the altar of incense was directly in front of the veil of the Temple. This was an altar of prayer. John describes the smoke ascending from this altar as a symbol of the prayers of all the Saints ascending to heaven (see Revelation 5:8; 8:3–4). David's psalm indicates this connection as well: "Lord, I cry unto thee: make haste unto me; give ear unto my voice, when I cry unto thee. Let my prayer be set forth before thee as incense" (Psalm 141:1–2). The Holy of Holies was a place of ritual prayer once a year when the high priest supplicated the Lord on Israel's behalf. Many remarkable prayers were given by ancient prophets and Saints.

The ritual nature of these prayers is indicated in the prescribed position of those praying. Solomon "stood before the altar of the Lord in the presence of all the congregation of Israel, and spread forth his hands toward heaven: and he said, Lord God of Israel, there is no God like thee, in heaven above, or on earth beneath, who keepest covenant and mercy with thy servants that walk before thee with all their heart" (1 Kings 8:22–23; see also D&C 109:1). Joseph Smith used similar language to Solomon's in the dedicatory prayer for the Kirtland Temple. Both Temple prayers beseech the Lord in Israel's behalf.

Prayers were offered standing or kneeling with hands spread toward heaven (see 1 Kings 8:22; Ezra 9:5; Isaiah 1:15). They were offered in the Sanctuary (see 1 Samuel 1:9–12; Psalm 42:2, 4; 1 Kings 8) or looking toward the Sanctuary (see 1 Kings 8:44, 48; Daniel 6:10; Psalm 5:7).[24] Hezekiah sought deliverance from the Assyrians by going "up into the house of the Lord" to beseech his help (2 Kings 19:14). At the evening sacrifice, Ezra prayed with hands "spread out" and confessed the sins of his people (Ezra 9:5); Nehemiah recorded that the Levites "stood up in their place" and blessed the Lord God for ever and ever in prayer

(Nehemiah 9). Daniel, in exile without a Temple, nevertheless prayed for all scattered Israel (see Daniel 9:7). Likewise today, ritual prayers of supplication for both gathered and scattered Israel are lifted up unto the Lord continuously from early morning until night from altars in Temples throughout the world.

Sacrifice—an ordinance of atonement. In addition to prayer, one of the chief functions of an altar in the Old Testament was to offer sacrifices of various kinds. Adam offered sacrifices as a symbol of the Atonement of Christ (see Moses 5:6–7). Sacrifices included the firstlings of the flock and, later, first fruits of the field (see Exodus 22:29; 23:19). Sacrifices were considered so important that God commanded the observance of this ritual ordinance directly following Adam and Eve's expulsion from the garden. Abraham sacrificed at altars in Jershon, the plains of Moreh, between Bethel and Hai, and in the plain of Mamre (see Genesis 12; 13:18, Abraham 2). Abraham's wrenching encounter in offering up his son Isaac underscores the extreme gravity given to the law of sacrifice by the ancients. The Lord gives this law whenever there are true believers on the earth, and it is administered by priesthood authority. Sacrifices are accompanied by prayer, devotions, and thanksgiving for life and blessings.

A paramount concern in Pharoah's freeing of the Hebrews surrounded the urgency with which Moses and his people yearned to fulfill this law of regular sacrifice. With each plague that came upon the Egyptians, Moses pressed Pharoah to let Israel go in order that they could travel "three days' journey into the desert, and sacrifice unto the Lord our God; lest he fall upon us with pestilence" (Exodus 5:3). Consider a hypothetical modern parallel. Imagine that members of the Church today were forbidden to partake of the sacrament—a vital key to renewing our covenants and feeling invigorated and rededicated to the Lord. How lost and unanchored we might become! Without this regular ritual renewal, it might be more difficult to repent or resist the temptation to stray. This was a key reason that Moses kept importuning Pharoah, "Let us go, we pray thee, three days' journey into the desert, and sacrifice unto the Lord our God" (Exodus 5:3).

The law of sacrifice was observed in various forms throughout the Old Testament down through the ages in both true and corrupted forms (see Exodus 22:20; Deuteronomy 32:17; 2 Kings 18:22). One early account of the corruption of a ritual offering is that of Cain just before "he listened not any more to the voice of the Lord" (Moses 5:26). When Cain brought his offering of the fruit of the ground, "the Lord had respect unto Abel and his offering: but unto Cain and to his offering he had not respect. And Cain was very wroth, and his countenance fell" (Genesis 4:4–5). Why did the Lord not respect Cain's offering? Was it because he had an evil disposition (see 1 John 3:12)? Was it because the offering was motivated by greed? One of the reasons behind this rejection is explained by Joseph Smith. He indicated that Cain "could have no faith, or could not exercise faith contrary to the plan of heaven. It must be shedding the blood of the Only Begotten to atone for man; for this was the plan of redemption . . . to offer a sacrifice contrary to that, no faith could be exercised, . . . consequently Cain could have no faith; and whatsoever is not of faith is sin."[25] Apparently, offerings of the fruit of the ground were acceptable at other times, especially under Mosaic law; however, for this particular offering, the Lord required the shedding of blood.

Cain's offering was also not accepted because Satan commanded it (see Moses 5:18); it was the wrong offering, and it was performed without faith in the Lord (see Hebrews 11:4). In other words, Cain had already cultivated hardness in his heart. The Lord knew his heart, and Cain's performance of this ritual became a mockery, "for without faith no man pleaseth God" (D&C 63:11). Perhaps his participation brought even more "damnation to his soul" for performing it unworthily (see 3 Nephi 18:29), though the Lord indicates he still was in a position to repent. The Lord warned that Cain would rule over Satan if he did not repent (see Moses 5:23).

This event indicates that rejecting the covenants made before the Lord at sacred altars allows Satan to gain power in our lives. It is an illustration of the seriousness of covenant making in the eyes of God. The Lord said to Jeremiah, "And I will give the men that have transgressed my covenant, which have not performed the words of the covenant which they had made before me, . . . I will even give them into the hand of their enemies, and into the hand of them that seek their life" (Jeremiah 34:18, 20).

What was the nature of these sacrifices? Within the law of Moses, the ritual acts were very specific and intricate. Full explanations of these ordinances are given elsewhere.[26] However, the following are some main points of the law of sacrifice: One of the purposes of the peace offering (also known as the vow or thank offering) was a recommitment to covenants the children of Israel had made. It had similar value then as the sacramental ordinance has for us today.[27]

Also reminiscent of our sacramental ordinances were the sin offering and the trespass offering. The sin offering had to do with repenting of inward sins—sins of omission or sins in one's heart and thoughts that were not usually outwardly manifest. In contrast, the trespass offering was performed when repenting of outward transgressions.[28] These ordinances pointed to the Savior's redemptive power and were done on a regular basis. The Prophet Joseph Smith said, "Whenever the Lord revealed himself to men in ancient days, and commanded them to offer sacrifice to him, . . . it was done that they might look forward in faith to the time of his coming, and rely upon the power of that atonement for a remission of their sins."[29]

In the Jerusalem Temple complex, the sacrifices performed on the altar directly outside the Temple proper were done more publicly than the others and can be compared to the altar of our sacrament table.[30] However, today we do not bring animal sacrifices as in days of old. The emblems of the bread and water represent Christ's body and blood. In turn, the Saints both anciently and in latter days "offer [their] whole souls as an offering unto him" (Omni 1:26) with a "broken heart and contrite spirit" (3 Nephi 9:20). The ritual emblems of bread and water tie us to the performance of his "great and last sacrifice" (Alma 34:10).

Washings and anointings. One kind of washing done anciently was immersion, or baptism.[31] We know that Adam, Enoch, and Noah all practiced baptism (see Moses 6:59; 7:11; 8:24). According to Jewish legend, it was a ritual of conversion to Judaism.[32] The Lord explains in Doctrine and Covenants 84:25–27 that when the holy priesthood was taken out of the midst of the children of Israel in the wilderness, "the lesser priesthood continued, which priesthood holdeth the key of the . . . preparatory gospel; which gospel is the gospel of repentance and of *baptism*, and the remission of sins" (emphasis added). In Joseph Smith Translation, Genesis 17:4–7, the Lord said, "My people have gone astray from my precepts, . . . and they have not observed mine anointing, and the burial, or baptism wherewith I commanded them."

Another form of washing done anciently was the initiation rite of cleansing at the door of the Temple. Priests in ancient Israel were required to be washed and anointed with oil and then clothed in a ceremonial fashion before they could enter the Tabernacle or Temple complex: "And thou shalt bring Aaron and his sons unto the door of the tabernacle of the congregation, and wash them with water. And thou shalt put upon Aaron the holy garments, and anoint him, and sanctify him; that he may minister unto me in the priest's office, . . . for their anointing shall surely be an everlasting priesthood throughout their generations" (Exodus 40:12–15). Notice the Lord indicates the purpose of washing, anointing, and clothing. It is for Aaron to be sanctified, or made holy. He is to be set apart and purified in order to participate in other ordinances.

Again, here we have an outward representation of an inward change. The physical washing was an emblem of spiritual cleansing. It signified the cleansing from pollutions for the Lord's people.[33] Aaron and his sons were to be purified in order to enter the house of the Lord. Similarly, we must be clean in order to dwell in the presence of the Lord. This requires a cleansing—new birth into the kingdom of God on earth and then an ongoing renewal of this cleansing. The constant renewal is a personal journey that sanctifies us for his presence.

Anointings were to be done with scented olive oil. Oil was generally considered to be a symbol of the Holy Spirit (see D&C 45:56–57) and was used in the calling of prophets and kings anciently.[34] It symbolized an outpouring of the Spirit upon the person anointed. Isaiah wrote, "The Spirit of the Lord God is upon me; because the Lord hath anointed me" (Isaiah 61:1). When Samuel anointed Saul to be king of Israel, he "took a vial of oil, and poured it upon his head" and said to him, "the Spirit of the Lord will come upon thee, and thou shalt prophesy with them, and shalt be turned into another man" (1 Samuel 10:1, 6). Again, the ordinance emphasizes the newness and quickening into "another [or new] man," a man of discernment.

Washings and anointings are an outward representation of inward purification and consecration. These particular ordinances of the biblical period have a parallel today. Baptism was formally introduced when the Church was formed in April of 1830, and washings and anointings were introduced in the Kirtland Temple in 1836. The Lord told Joseph Smith to gather the Saints and "to prepare them for the ordinances and endowments, washings and anointing."[35]

Sacred clothing. Following the ritual washing and anointing in ancient times, the initiate was clothed in sacred vestments, but the Lord has commanded the donning of sacred clothing from the beginning. He clothed Adam and Eve in sacred garments just before their expulsion from the garden. "Unto Adam also and to his wife did the Lord God make coats of skins, and clothed them" (Genesis 3:21). In the sacrifice of the animals killed for their skins is a symbol that points to the great atoning sacrifice of the Savior. These skins covered Adam and Eve's nakedness. One root word translated as "nakedness" is the Hebrew, *erwah*, or uncleanness and shame.[36] Additionally, the Hebrew word for "atonement" is *kaphar.* The exact meaning of *kaphar* is not known though it is often interpreted as "covering."[37] The Day of Atonement in Judaism is the high, holy day of Yom Kippur, which could mean "day of covering." The sacrifice done in Adam and Eve's behalf effectually covered their actual nakedness while figuratively covering their transgression and shame. They received a garment that reminded them of the sacrifice of the Lord who covers sins (nakedness). The actual Day of Atonement performed by Jesus Christ could be called a day when he covered our sins, guilt, and shame as well as our infirmities and sicknesses (see Alma 7:11–14)—everything that Adam's Fall has brought into our mortal lives. The garment of the holy priesthood is a rich symbol with many levels of meaning, including the covering of atonement we can have here in mortality.

Following this pattern, we assume that all the prophets down through the ages have been clothed with skins or garments to remind them of the sacrifice of the Lord and of the covenants they have made. This clothing ritual is usually associated with a Temple setting, such as the Garden of Eden, a mountain, or a sacred place. Enoch "went up on the mount" and was "clothed upon with glory," a metaphor for a type of sacred clothing (Moses 7:3). Moses was commanded to make special clothing for those who would enter the Tabernacle (see Exodus 28:1–3). Hugh Nibley identified the garment taken by Shem and Japheth and put upon Noah as a robe of the priesthood, or perhaps even the original skin given to Adam that was passed down to subsequent prophets (see Genesis 9:23).[38] Isaiah rejoiced when he said, "God . . . hath clothed me with the garments of salvation, he hath covered me with the robe of righteousness" (Isaiah 61:10). Here, Isaiah's word "clothed" is written in the Greek as *enduo*, which is the root for our English "endow." This passage seems to explicitly refer to the endowment.

We know that Joseph was given the birthright by Jacob along with a "coat of many colours" (Genesis 37:3, 23, 32). Here, the Hebrew word for "coat," *kuttonet*, also means "robe or garment of linen." There is discussion among scholars as to the exact meaning of the Hebrew word for "colors" (*passim*). One interpretation is that it may actually refer to the length of the garment, which reached to the palms and feet. Thus, "coat of many colors" could mean "a garment of linen reaching to the palms and feet."[39] Some believe that Joseph was given this garment to represent the priestly birthright in order to lead his family in the patriarchal system of the time.[40]

These ancient patterns of ritual clothing are similar to the patterns for the Saints today. Memory is associated with the ritual object of the garment. Elder Carlos Asay said, "I like to think of the garment as the Lord's way of letting us take part of the temple with us when we leave. It is true that we carry from the Lord's house inspired teachings and sacred covenants written in our minds and hearts. However, the one tangible *remembrance* we carry with us back into the world is the garment. And though we cannot always be in the temple, a part of it can always be with us to bless our lives."[41]

Elder Asay also commented on allusions to the garment in the scriptures. "Don't forget that the word *garment* is used symbolically in the scriptures and gives expanded meaning to other words such as *white, clean, pure, righteous, modesty, covering, ceremonial, holy, priesthood, beautiful, perfection, salvation, undefiled, worthy, white raiment, shield, protection, spotless, blameless, armor, covenants, promises, blessings, respect, eternal life,* and so forth. All of these words occupy special places in the vocabularies of people sincerely [striving] to become Saints."[42]

QUALIFICATIONS FOR ENTERING HOLY TEMPLES

We turn our discussion now to those in ancient Israel who were qualified to enter the Temple. Psalm 24 is presumably a hymn referring to the Sanctuary on the Holy Mount. David asks, "Who shall ascend into the hill of the Lord? or who shall stand in his holy place?" Then the answer to these questions is presented: "He that hath clean hands, and a pure heart; who hath not lifted up his soul unto vanity, nor sworn deceitfully." David then recounts the blessings for those who qualify in this manner, "He shall receive the blessing from the Lord, and righteousness from the God of his salvation. This is the generation of them that seek him, that seek thy face" (Psalm 24:3–6). Some commentators have identified these verses as sort of a set of ancient Temple recommend questions.[43] Donald Parry cites some biblical scholars who suggest that a priest might have actually posed these questions to Temple visitors at the Temple gate, or written them on the doorposts of the Temple, or that these qualifications were even sung by worshippers or priests in the Temple courtyard.[44] In any case, they seem to indicate standards for Temple entrance in ancient Israel, and they also reflect some similarities to Temple entrance standards today.

If Psalm 24 indicates that temple entrants were required to have "clean hands, and a pure heart," what does that mean? With a careful reading, it is apparent that clean hands and pure hearts represent two different things, possibly even two categories of things. The first, clean hands, is indicative of outward preparatory qualifications, some of them ritual oriented and some performance oriented. These qualifications may be compared to modern ritual preparations for the Temple such as baptism, receipt of the Holy Ghost, and priesthood ordination (formal rituals). Other less-formal acts are paying tithing, keeping the Word of Wisdom, attending Church meetings, sustaining Church leaders, meeting financial obligations and family responsibilities, wearing the garment correctly, and acting honestly. These are "the clean hands," or outward performances. It is interesting to note that we can fulfill all of these outward performances without having proper motives.

However, the second kind of qualification in Psalm 24, pure hearts, *does* represent untainted motives for ancient Israel. Likewise, similar requirements of pure motives are part of Temple entrance qualifications today: having faith in the Godhead, having a testimony of the Atonement of Christ, having a testimony of the current prophet, desiring to keep our covenants, feeling worthy to attend the Temple, and so forth. These requirements cannot be met without proper motives or "pure hearts." In a conference address, Elder David A. Bednar touched upon the meaning of "clean hands and pure hearts." He declared, "It is possible for us to have clean hands but not have a pure heart. Please notice that both clean hands and a pure heart are required to ascend into the hill of the Lord and to stand in His holy place."[45] He observed that prophets throughout the ages have emphasized the dual requirements of (1) acting good and (2) being good. But Elder Bednar takes this teaching even further in recognizing that our clean hands and pure hearts are not what ultimately save us here and now or in the eternities. Our outward actions can sanctify us only if they are done with pure motives and faith in Jesus Christ. In other words, having a heart made pure through Jesus Christ is what makes clean hands efficacious. Elder Bednar continues, "Prophets throughout the ages have emphasized the dual requirements of (1) avoiding and overcoming bad and (2) doing good and becoming better. . . . All of our worthy desires and good works, as necessary as they are, can never produce clean hands and a pure heart. It is the Atonement of Jesus Christ that provides both a *cleansing and redeeming power* that helps us to overcome sin and a *sanctifying and strengthening power* that helps us to become better than we ever could by relying only upon our own strength."[46]

SUMMARY

The sanctifying power of ritual ordinances is illustrated in the Old Testament. This power can change us into new people whose hands are clean and hearts are pure. The power of these sanctifying actions should not be underestimated. The resulting blessings were described by Isaiah as he foretold of faithful Saints who would enter the Lord's house to receive an everlasting name: "Even unto them will I give in mine house and within my walls a place [sometimes translated as *hand*] and a name better than of sons and of daughters: I will give them an everlasting name, that shall not be cut off. . . . Every one that keepeth the sabbath from polluting it, and taketh hold of my covenant; even them will I bring to my holy mountain, and make them joyful in my house of prayer: their burnt offerings and their sacrifices shall be accepted upon mine altar; for mine house shall be called an house of prayer for all people" (Isaiah 56:5–7). The beauty and effectiveness of sacred rites and ordinances illustrated in the Old Testament are similar to patterns that exist for Latter-day Saints, often leading to revelation and great blessings for the participants.

NOTES

1. Erika Summers-Effler, "Ritual Theory," in *The Handbook of the Sociology of Emotions*, ed. Jan E. Stets and Jonathan H. Turner (New York: Springer, 2006), 135.

2. Hugh Nibley, *The Ancient State* (Salt Lake City: Deseret Book; Provo, UT: FARMS, 1991), 99–147; see discussions about the "sacred and profane," and the term "hierophany," which signifies a manifestation of the sacred, in Mircea Eliade, *Patterns in Comparative Religion* (Lincoln: University of Nebraska Press, 1996), 1–37; Walter Burkert, *Greek Religion* (Boston: Harvard University Press, 1987); see also Ramsay MacMullen, *Paganism in the Roman Empire* (New Haven: Yale University Press, 1981).

3. See Kenneth McLeish, *Key Ideas in Human Thought* (New York: Prima Publishing, 1995).

4. See the discussion of modernity in Charles Taylor, *Sources of the Self: The Making of the Modern Identity* (Cambridge, MA: Harvard University Press, 1989), 285–91.

5. Andrew C. Skinner, *Temple Worship* (Salt Lake City, Deseret Book, 2007), 131–32.

6. See John M. Lundquist, "What Is a Temple? A Preliminary Typology," in *Temples of the Ancient World*, ed. Donald W. Parry (Salt Lake City: Deseret Book; Provo, UT: FARMS, 1994), 83–117; John M. Lundquist, "Fundamentals of Temple Ideology from Eastern Traditions," in *Revelation, Reason, and Faith: Essays in Honor of Truman G. Madsen*, ed. Donald W. Parry, Daniel C. Peterson, and Stephen D. Ricks (Salt Lake City: Deseret Book; Provo, UT: FARMS, 2002), 651–702.

7. See Lundquist, "Temple Ideology," 678.

8. *Webster's New Universal Unabridged Dictionary*, 1st ed., s.v. "ordinance"; Douglas Harper, *Online Etymology Dictionary*, http://www.etymonline.com/index.php?term=ordinance.

9. John M. Dillon, "Platonism," in *Anchor Bible Dictionary*, ed. David Noel Freedman (New York: Doubleday, 1992), 5:378–81.

10. Joseph Smith, *Teachings of the Prophet Joseph Smith*, comp. Joseph Fielding Smith (Salt Lake City: Deseret Book, 1976), 324–25.

11. See James E. Faulconer, *Scripture Study* (Provo, UT: FARMS, 1999), 135–53; Thorleif Boman, *Hebrew Thought Compared with Greek* (New York: Norton, 1970).

12. Faulconer, *Scripture Study*, 139–41.

13. Smith, *Teachings*, 162.

14. Dallin H. Oaks, "Taking Upon Us the Name of Jesus Christ," *Ensign*, May 1985, 81.

15. See Skinner, *Temple Worship*, 21.

16. Though this is a new and somewhat controversial field in medicine and the social sciences (see Madhulika A. Gupta, "Somatization Disorders in Dermatology," *International Review of Psychiatry* 18, no. 1 [February 2006]: 41–47), it has been addressed by phenomenological philosophers for some time (see Thomas Fuchs, "The Tacit Dimension," *Philosophy, Psychiatry, & Psychology* 8, no. 4 [December 2001]: 323–26; see also Thomas Fuchs, University of Heidelberg, paper entitled "The Memory of the Body," http://www.klinikum.uni-heidelberg.de/fileadmin/zpm/psychatrie/ppp2004/manuskript/fuchs.pdf; see also Babette Rothschild, *The Body*

Remembers: The Psychophysiology of Trauma and Trauma Treatment [New York: Norton, 2000]).

17. Charles Golden, "Where Does Memory Reside, and Why Isn't It History?" *American Anthropologist* 107, no. 2 (2005): 270–74.

18. James E. Faulconer, "Remembrance," in *FARMS Review* 19, no. 2 (2007): 71–87.

19. Terrence L. Szink, "Altar of Stones," in *Book of Mormon Reference Companion*, ed. Dennis L. Largey (Salt Lake City: Deseret Book, 2003), 44.

20. Bruce H. Porter, "Altar," in *Encyclopedia of Mormonism*, ed. Daniel H. Ludlow (New York: Macmillan, 1992), 36–37.

21. Margaret Barker, *The Great High Priest: The Temple Roots of Christian Liturgy* (London: Continuum International, 2003), 287–88.

22. Geoffrey W. Bromley, ed., *International Standard Bible Encyclopedia* (Grand Rapids, MI: Eerdmans, 1988), s.v. "Religions: Assyria and Babylonia."

23. (1) The altar of sacrifice or burnt offering in the court of Israel; (2) the altar of incense in the holy place; (3) the table of shewbread which held twelve loaves of bread, frankincense, and a drink offering; and (4) the ark of the covenant in the Holy of Holies where the high priest represented all Israel in covenant prayer once a year on the Day of Atonement (see Porter, "Altar," *Encyclopedia of Mormonism*, 36–37).

24. Bible Dictionary, "Prayer," 752.

25. Smith, *Teachings*, 58.

26. See Bible Dictionary, "sacrifices," 765–67; see also Gary A. Anderson, "Sacrifice and Sacrificial Offerings," in *Anchor Bible Dictionary*, 5:870.

27. For a full discussion of Mosaic sacrifices and their comparison to the gospel of Jesus Christ, see Edward J. Brandt, "The Law of Moses and the Law of Christ," in *Sperry Symposium Classics*, ed. Paul Y. Hoskisson (Salt Lake City: Deseret Book; Provo, UT: Religious Studies Center, Brigham Young University 2005), 133–53.

28. Brandt, "The Law of Moses and the Law of Christ," 137.

29. Smith, *Teachings*, 60–61.

30. Porter, "Altar," *Encyclopedia of Mormonism*, 36–37.

31. See Moses 6:65; Robert J. Woodford, "How Much Do We Know about Baptism before Christ's Time?" *Ensign*, July 1991, 74.

32. See Louis Ginzburg, *The Legends of the Jews* (Philadelphia: The Jewish Publication Society of America, 1939), 3:88.

33. Donald W. Parry, "Washings and Anointings," in *Encyclopedia of Mormonism*, 1551.

34. Matthew B. Brown, *The Gate of Heaven* (American Fork, UT: Covenant, 1999), 127; Joseph Fielding McConkie, *Gospel Symbolism* (Salt Lake City: Bookcraft, 1986), 114–15; Immo Luschin, "Ordinances," in *Encyclopedia of Mormonism*, 3:1032–33.

35. Smith, *Teachings*, 308.

36. Francis Brown, S. R. Driver, and Charles A. Briggs, *A Hebrew and English Lexicon of the Old Testament* (Oxford: Oxford University Press, 1968), 788.

37. Brown, Driver, and Briggs, *Hebrew and English Lexicon*, 497.

38. Hugh Nibley, "On the Sacred and the Symbolic," in *Temples of the Ancient World*, ed. Donald W. Parry (Salt Lake City: Deseret Book; Provo, UT: FARMS, 1994), 579.

39. Brown, Driver, and Briggs, *Hebrew and English Lexicon*, 509.

40. William Wilson, *Old Testament Word Studies* (Grand Rapids, MI: Kregel, 1978), s.v. "colour."

41. Carlos E. Asay, "The Temple Garment: An Outward Expression of an Inward Commitment," *Ensign*, August 1997, 19; emphasis added.

42. Asay, "Temple Garment," 21.

43. Both Psalm 15:1, "Lord, who shall dwell in thy tabernacle? who shall dwell in thy holy hill?" and Isaiah 33:14, "Who among us shall dwell with the devouring fire? who among us shall dwell with everlasting burnings?" are also presumed to be Temple entrance hymns. According to Joseph Smith, "everlasting burnings" refers to where God is enthroned with glory (see *Teachings*, 347).

44. Donald W. Parry, "Temple Entrance Hymns," in *Revelation, Reason, and Faith*, 734–39; Brown, *Gate of Heaven*, 62.

45. David A. Bednar, "Clean Hands and a Pure Heart," *Ensign*, November 2007, 80–83.

46. Bednar, "Clean Hands," 82–83.

7

CUTTING COVENANTS

Jared T. Parker

Covenants have always been a critical part of the gospel, meaning both the fulness of the gospel and the preparatory gospel that was part of the law of Moses (see D&C 84:26–27). The Bible Dictionary teaches, "The gospel is so arranged that principles and ordinances are received by covenant, placing the recipient under strong obligation and responsibility to honor the commitment."[1] The importance of covenants is emphasized by the fact that some form of the word *covenant* is found 555 times in the standard works, almost as often as *faith* (627 occurrences) or *repent* (628 occurrences).[2] Indeed, the Lord has called the fulness of the gospel "the covenant" (D&C 39:11) and the "everlasting covenant" (D&C 66:2).

A covenant is an agreement between at least two parties. The English word *covenant* comes from the Latin *convenire*, meaning "to come together, agree."[3] Such an agreement can be between parties of equal standing, like many voluntary contracts in Western society today, or between parties of widely different standing, like God and man, where one party dictates the terms of the agreement and the other accepts them. In the scriptures,

Jared T. Parker is a product specialist coordinator in the medical division of W. L. Gore & Associates in Flagstaff, Arizona.

the term *covenant* sometimes refers to agreements between people, but more often denotes an agreement between God and his children. Latter-day Saints can better understand the Lord's expectations of his people by studying how covenants were made anciently. We can benefit from knowing about ancient covenant making in at least three ways: (1) improved understanding of the scriptures, (2) increased appreciation of modern covenants, and (3) deepened personal commitment.

Hebrew Wording

In the Old Testament, the English phrase "make a covenant" is most often a translation of the Hebrew *kārat berît*, which literally means "cut a covenant."[4] The verb *kārat* means "cut off, cut down,"[5] and the noun *berît* means "covenant,"[6] similar in meaning to the words *pact, compact, treaty, alliance,* and *league*. While other Hebrew verbs are sometimes used with *berît*, such as *qûm* ("establish" or "confirm") and *nātan* ("give"),[7] *kārat* occurs ninety times in the Hebrew Bible in reference to making covenants.[8] In a few of these instances, only *kārat* is found in the Hebrew text; the King James translators added "covenant" so the English text would make sense.[9]

Why does biblical Hebrew regularly speak of "cutting" covenants? Certainly this idiomatic wording is used metaphorically in some cases, but more importantly it seems to reflect ancient covenant-making practices. In our day, a contract often becomes legally binding when the parties sign a document detailing the terms of the agreement. In a similar way, ancient covenants often became binding by killing and cutting an animal. This may sound foreign to us in modern society, but the phrases "cut a deal" and "strike a bargain" appear to have come into English from the wording of ancient covenant-making practices involving animal slaughter.[10]

Two Old Testament examples give some detail about how a covenant was literally "cut." The first involves Jehovah and Abram (about 1900 BC), and the second involves Zedekiah and the people of Judah (about 590 BC). In both of these accounts, we read that at least one animal was killed, cut into two pieces, and that someone (or something) passed between the divided pieces (see Genesis 15:7–21; Jeremiah 34:8–22). Unfortunately for modern readers, these passages do not explain why the events occurred as they did or what they meant. Nevertheless, extrabiblical sources offer information to help us better understand these scriptural accounts. Therefore, to provide a context for analyzing the biblical passages, we will first briefly review extrabiblical covenant-making practices that involved killing and cutting animals.

ANIMAL SLAUGHTER IN EXTRABIBLICAL COVENANTS

Over the last 150 years, many ancient extrabiblical texts have been discovered that help students of the Bible better understand its historical context and content.[11] From these sources it is clear that covenant-making rituals were a common practice for hundreds of years among different cultures and societies who spoke many languages.[12] To provide an overview of animal slaughter in these rites, selected examples will be grouped according to two time periods—the second and first millennia BC.[13] These periods are approximately equivalent to the time from the birth of Abram to King David's reign and from King David's reign to the birth of Christ.[14]

Second millennium BC covenants. Two of the earliest extrabiblical texts describing the slaughter of an animal to make a covenant are from the eighteenth century BC. In a letter found in the ancient city of Mari in modern Syria, Ibal-Il reported to King Zimri-Lim: "I went to Aslakka to 'kill an ass' between the Hanu and Idamaras. . . . I caused the foal of an ass to be slaughtered. I established peace between the Hanu and Idamaras."[15] The expression "kill an ass" apparently "means simply 'make a treaty,' which was solemnized by the sacrifice of a young ass."[16] In another text found in the ancient city of Alalakh in modern Turkey, we read that Abban "placed himself under oath" to give Alalakh to Iarimlim "and had cut the neck of a sheep," saying, "If I take back that which I gave thee!"[17] The implication is that Abban's life would be cut off if he took the city back from Iarimlim.

Most of the other currently known examples of covenants made in the second millennium are Hittite treaties from the fourteenth to twelfth centuries BC, the majority of which are between a king and a vassal.[18] Regarding the ratification ceremony of these treaties, apparently much variety existed, but it was "frequently associated with the sacrifice of an animal," and it is generally assumed that after "the animal was killed, the vassal could expect the same fate if he violated his oath."[19] Because the texts of the treaties from this period "do not contain a verbal oath formula," the animal sacrifice is thought to be "the *enactment* of the oath" such that "a verbal formula is unnecessary in the *text* of the treaty itself."[20]

First millennium BC covenants. Several extrabiblical texts describe covenants from the first millennium BC in which the cutting or killing of an animal represents what would happen to a vassal who violated his agreement with the king. This is evidenced by simile curses in the treaties where the offending vassal is graphically identified as becoming "like" or "as" a slaughtered animal. From the eighth century BC Sefire inscription, we have a treaty between King Barga'yah and Matti'el that includes this statement: "[As] this calf is cut up, thus Matti'el and his nobles shall be cut up."[21] Note the slaughter of a calf as part of making the covenant and the curse—Matti'el and his associates will become as the cut-up calf if they break the agreement.

Also from the eighth century BC is a treaty between King Ashurnirari V of Assyria and Mati'ilu (possibly the same as Matti'el above). A part of this treaty reads:

This spring lamb has been brought from its fold not for sacrifice, not for a banquet, not for a purchase; . . . it has been brought to sanction the treaty between Ashurnirari and Mati'ilu. If Mati'ilu sins against (this) treaty made under oath by the gods, then, just as this spring lamb, brought from its fold, will not return to its fold. . . . Mati'ilu, together with his sons, daughters, officials, and the people of his land . . . will not return to his country, and not behold his country again. This head is not the head of a lamb, it is the head of Mati'ilu, it is the head of his sons, his officials, and the people of his land. If Mati'ilu sins against this treaty, so may, just as the head of this spring lamb is torn off, . . . the head of Mati'ilu be torn off.[2]

From the seventh century BC we have another Assyrian example in which King Esarhaddon sought to secure the throne for his sons through a treaty with his vassals. This treaty was made under oath and contains numerous simile curses, including the following: "Just as this ewe is cut open and the flesh of its young placed in its mouth, so may he . . . make you eat in your hunger the flesh of your brothers, your sons, and your daughters. Just as (these) yearlings and spring lambs, male and female, are cut open and their entrails are rolled around their feet, so may the entrails of your sons and daughters be rolled around your feet."[23] Again we see that animal slaughter represented the curse for violating a covenant during this period.[24]

Evolution in covenant rituals. In analyzing extrabiblical second and first millennia BC covenants, scholars have identified differences that suggest evolution in the rituals. For example, it is thought that the slaughtered animal was both a ratifying sacrifice and symbolic of the curse for violating the covenant in the earlier texts, although only the latter is found in the later texts.[25] Moreover, the second millennium texts "include not only curses (a litany of disasters and misfortunes to befall a disobedient vassal) but also blessings (a litany of benefits to befall a faithful vassal)."[26] In contrast, the first millennium texts "contain only curses."[27] It appears there was evolution in the practices over time, and this should be considered as we now turn our attention to examine scriptural accounts of covenant cutting.

JEHOVAH AND ABRAM

The first Old Testament example of cutting covenants comes from the middle part of Abram's life (about 1900 BC). Jehovah had promised to give Abram and his seed certain lands forever, make his posterity innumerable, and cause the priesthood and the gospel to continue in his family in order to bless all nations (see Abraham 2:6, 9–11, 19; Genesis 12:7; 13:14–17). However, Abram had no children and was concerned that his steward would become his heir. When he expressed this, the Lord reaffirmed that he would give Abram a land forever and innumerable posterity (see Genesis 15:3–7). Abram "believed in the Lord; and he counted it to him for righteousness" (Genesis 15:6).

Even though Abram trusted the Lord completely, he wanted some sort of confirmation of Jehovah's promise to him about the land. "And he said, Lord God, whereby shall I know that I shall inherit it?" (Genesis 15:8). Jehovah responded, "Take me an heifer of three years old, and a she goat of three years old, and a ram of three years old, and a turtledove, and a young pigeon" (Genesis 15:9). Abram brought the various kinds of animals and slaughtered them. Next he "divided them in the midst [in half], and laid each piece one against another: but the birds divided he not" (Genesis 15:10). Then Abram waited on the Lord, protecting the two rows of carcasses from scavenging birds of prey, and subsequently fell into "a deep sleep"[28] during which he experienced "an horror of great darkness" (Genesis 15:12). After this, Jehovah revealed to Abram his posterity's future, including their bondage in Egypt, eventual deliverance, and return to Canaan (see Genesis 15:13–16). Finally, the experience culminated with God giving Abram a dramatic sign: "And it came to pass, that, when the sun went down, and it was dark, behold *a smoking furnace, and a burning lamp that passed between those pieces.* In that same day the Lord made [or 'cut' in Hebrew] a covenant with Abram, saying, Unto thy seed have I given this land, from the river of Egypt unto the great river, the river Euphrates" (Genesis 15:17–18; emphasis added).[29]

Various aspects of Abram's experience have prompted much discussion among commentators.[30] For example, why did the Lord instruct Abram to use three different animals, each three years old, and two birds? Were the slaughtered animals actually sacrificed or just cut in two? What did the divided animals symbolize? Were the two birds killed or left alive? Did the Lord actually swear an oath and take upon himself a curse? Did Abram swear an oath as part of the experience? Though the scriptural account does not provide answers to all these questions, an understanding of ancient covenant-making practices, coupled with modern revelation, can help us gain additional insight into Abram's experience.

From what we know of second millennium BC covenant rituals, it seems clear that Jehovah condescended to cut a covenant with Abram. Instead of a parity treaty or loyalty oath on Abram's part, God instructed Abram to slaughter three animals and divide them so he could demonstrate the absolute surety of his promises. Evidently, the smoking furnace and burning lamp represented God's presence, analogous to the cloud and pillar of fire that accompanied Israel later (see Exodus 13:21–22). Thus the implication is that the Lord passed between the divided animals and, in effect, swore an oath that he would lose his own life if he did not give Abram and his seed the land for an inheritance.[31] This idea is supported by Jehovah's later revelation wherein he confirmed the same promise of land to Isaac, saying, "Unto thee, and unto thy seed, I will give all these countries, and I will perform the oath which I sware unto Abraham thy father" (Genesis 26:3). Since God cannot swear by anything greater than his own life (see Hebrews 6:13), Jehovah's promise could not have been more sure. Certainly this was an extremely powerful message to Abram, a man who lived in various places in the ancient Near East and who must have been very familiar with covenant-cutting practices.

Given the prevalence of oath taking in the second millennium BC, we might wonder if Abram passed between the animal pieces and took an oath. However, there is nothing to suggest this in the text. We know the Lord gave Abram covenants that he promised to keep, but this does not necessarily mean Abram passed between the animals and swore an oath in Genesis 15. Rather, it is probably best to think of the account as a gracious act by God to confirm his promises, prompted by Abram's great faith. In support of this, the Apostle Paul cited Genesis 15:6 as evidence that Abram was justified by faith rather than works (see Romans 4:1–3).

Various proposals have been made relative to the animals Abram used and what they symbolized. Many have observed that the five different kinds of animals comprise all those that were later acceptable as sacrifices under the law of Moses.[32] Some have thought that the animals were actually sacrificed (blood poured out, carcasses burned on an altar) as part of the covenant-making ritual in addition to being slaughtered and divided. Though later extrabiblical retellings of Abram's experience suggest the animals were sacrificed,[33] there is no indication of this in the scriptural account and the normal sacrificial elements are notably absent. Lastly, most think the two birds were killed, though the text is not explicit.[34]

One explanation of the symbolism in Genesis 15 is based on the Lord's revelation that Abram's posterity would become slaves in Egypt and later return to Canaan (see vv. 13–16). In other words, Abram's experience can be seen as a type of his posterity's future. In this approach, the smoking furnace and burning lamp represent God's presence, foreshadowing the cloud and pillar of fire during the Exodus (see Exodus 13:21–22). The five different animals, comprising all the clean animals for sacrifice under the law of Moses, are seen as the whole house of Israel. Since birds of prey are seen as unclean in the law of Moses (see Leviticus 11:13–19), they represent oppressive foreign nations. Thus the "rite pictures Abram's descendants, in the form of sacrificial animals, protected by the Abrahamic promises from attacks by foreigners, the birds of prey. After Abram's death, his 'falling asleep,' the Lord (the smoking pot and torch of fire) will walk among them."[35] This seems to be a useful approach based on the existing biblical text.

Latter-day Saints have the benefit of modern revelation which can expand our understanding of Abram's covenant-cutting experience. The Joseph Smith Translation adds to the biblical account that the Lord revealed he would give Abram the land for an everlasting inheritance after his death by virtue of Christ's Resurrection. "And the Lord said, Though thou wast dead, yet am I not able to give it thee? And if thou shalt die, yet thou shalt possess it, for the day cometh, that the Son of Man shall live; but how can he live if he be not dead? he must first be quickened. And it came to pass, that Abram looked forth and saw the days of the Son of Man, and was glad, and his soul found rest" (Joseph Smith Translation, Genesis 15:10–12).[36] In other words, the promise of land to Abram was not limited to Israel inheriting Canaan after the Exodus, but was also an individual promise to Abram that would be fulfilled in eternity. Furthermore, modern revelation teaches that the promise of an everlasting inheritance of land is a key part of the fulness of the gospel because it refers to inheriting the earth when it becomes a celestial kingdom (see D&C 38:17–20; 88:17–20).[37] Thus it seems clear that Jehovah actually cut a gospel covenant with Abram.

Another way modern revelation can help us gain additional insight into Genesis 15 is to consider it a Temple text and compare it to our latter-day understanding of the plan of salvation.[38] This can be seen by identifying parallels with Jacob's later experience at Bethel and ancient Israel's Tabernacle-Temple. First, at Bethel we understand that Jacob had a dream wherein he saw a ladder reaching to heaven, with angels ascending and descending on it, and that he received from Jehovah the same promises Abram did in Genesis 15 (see Genesis 28:12–14). The Prophet Joseph Smith taught that Jacob's ladder had "three principle rounds" representing "the telestial, the terrestrial, and the celestial glories or kingdoms,"[39] and Latter-day Saints understand modern Temples to be "all what Bethel was to Jacob."[40] Clearly Jacob's experience at Bethel, which means "house of God" in Hebrew (see Genesis 28:19, footnote a), was a Temple experience. Second, we recognize that the ancient Tabernacle-Temple exhibited three gradations of holiness, like Jacob's ladder, which Latter-day Saints understand to represent the telestial, terrestrial, and celestial levels.[41] Now, if we apply the Temple connotations associated with Bethel and the ancient Tabernacle-Temple to Abram's experience, we could think of the three different animals in Genesis 15, each three years old, as representing three gradations of holiness, and thereby signifying the three degrees of glory. The two birds with their ability to fly can be seen as representing angels, like those Jacob saw at Bethel (see Genesis 28:12) and the cherubim on the mercy seat in the Holy of Holies of the ancient Tabernacle-Temple (see Exodus 25:18, 22). God's passing between the animal pieces can be thought of as foreshadowing the high priest in ancient Israel and Christ, the great High Priest, who passed through the telestial, terrestrial, and celestial divisions of the ancient Tabernacle-Temple (see Hebrews 9). Putting all these ideas together, Genesis 15 could signify that by cutting covenants, God would bring Abram through the telestial, terrestrial, and celestial levels, back into his presence. Of course this approach to Genesis 15 goes well beyond the existing account, but it is consistent with what modern revelation tells us about Abram and should not seem too unusual when we remember that all things God has given to man typify Christ in some way (see 2 Nephi 11:4). In short, latter-day revelation helps us see how the covenant cutting in Genesis 15 can be viewed as a Temple text.

ZEDEKIAH AND THE PEOPLE OF JUDAH

The second Old Testament example of covenant cutting we will consider concerns Zedekiah, king of Judah, and his people during the ministry of the prophet Jeremiah (about 590 BC). The time frame is shortly after Lehi's group left Jerusalem (see 1 Nephi 1:4) and the city was besieged by the king of Babylon. Zedekiah wanted the Lord's help, so he caused his people to cut a covenant in which they would fulfill the law of Moses requirement to liberate their Hebrew slaves in the seventh year (see Exodus 21:2). Through Jeremiah, the Lord explained that he was pleased with the covenant they had cut in the Temple: "And ye were now turned, and had done right in my sight, in proclaiming liberty every man to his neighbour; and ye had made [cut] a covenant before me in the house which is called by my name" (Jeremiah 34:15). After the threat of Babylon appeared to pass, the people profaned the Lord's name and violated the covenant they had made by reenslaving their servants (see Jeremiah 34:16). In consequence, those who broke the covenant were cursed: "Therefore thus saith the Lord; Ye have not hearkened unto me, in proclaiming liberty, every one to his brother, and every man to his neighbour: behold, I proclaim a liberty for you, saith the Lord, to the sword, to the pestilence, and to the famine; and I will make you to be removed into all the kingdoms of the earth" (Jeremiah 34:17). The next part of the curse is especially revealing as it relates to the covenant the people had cut. "And the men who transgressed my covenant and did not keep the terms of the covenant which they made [cut] before me, *I will make like the calf which they cut in two and passed between its parts*—the princes of Judah, the princes of Jerusalem, the eunuchs, the priests, and all the people of the land *who passed between the parts of the calf*" (Revised Standard Version, Jeremiah 34:18–19; emphasis added).[42] Those who broke the covenant were to become as the cut-up calf, and animals would feed on their carcasses. "I will even give them into the hand of their enemies, and into the hand of them that seek their life: and their dead bodies shall be for meat unto the fowls of the heaven, and to the beasts of the earth" (Jeremiah 34:20). The Lord explained that this severe punishment would occur because he would bring Babylon back to destroy Jerusalem. "Behold, I will command, saith the Lord, and cause them [the Babylonians] to return to this city; and they shall fight against it, and take it, and burn it with fire: and I will make the cities of Judah a desolation without an inhabitant" (Jeremiah 34:22). Sadly, not long after this prophecy was given, Babylon did destroy Judah, and these curses were fulfilled because of the people's disobedience.

The account of Zedekiah and his people is an example of a covenant cut under the law of Moses that is consistent with extrabiblical covenants from the first millennium BC. An animal was slaughtered, cut into two, and the people passed between the divided pieces to ratify the covenant. The severe punishment Jehovah pronounced makes it clear that those who entered the covenant had taken upon themselves a self-curse. The text does not tell us if this was only implied by passing between the divided calf or if it was associated with a verbal oath. Considering extrabiblical covenant rituals from this period, it seems likely that an oath was verbalized as part of the ratification ceremony. Assuming this was the case, we can postulate how it might have happened. First, the person taking the covenant oath most likely raised his hand as part of the ritual. This is reflected in biblical Hebrew because the "raising of the hand accompanies the taking of an oath and therefore 'to raise the hand' means 'to take an oath.'"[43] Second, the individual probably repeated a phrase similar to self-curses in which a person said, "God do so to me, and more also," signifying that the individual expected to be cursed if they did not live up to their oath. This type of curse formula is attested from the eleventh to the eighth centuries BC among Israelites (Eli, Saul, Jonathan, Abner, David, Solomon) and non-Israelites (Ruth, Jezebel, Ben-hadad)[44] and seems to be linked to covenant-cutting oaths where the imagery of the divided animal was invoked as the consequence for violating the agreement. Thus it is not unreasonable to think that Zedekiah and others of his people passed between the slaughtered calf, raised their hands, and said something like, "God do so to us and more also if we keep not the terms of this covenant."[45] Regrettably, the people were not true to the covenant they had made and ended up suffering greatly. This graphically demonstrates how seriously the Lord views covenants his people make and the devastating consequences of violating those covenants.

ECHOES OF COVENANT CUTTING

Now that we have analyzed the two most prominent instances of covenant cutting in the Old Testament, we are in a position to consider various echoes of the practice.[46] Here we will focus on a few examples related to gospel covenants in the Old Testament.

Circumcision. Some years after the events recorded in Genesis 15, Jehovah appeared to Abram, reaffirmed his promises to the patriarch, and changed his name to Abraham (see Genesis 17:1–8). "And God said to Abraham, Thou shalt keep my covenant therefore, thou, and thy seed after thee in their generations. This is my covenant, which ye shall keep, between me and you and thy seed after thee; Every man child among you shall be circumcised, . . . and it shall be a token of the covenant betwixt me and you" (Genesis 17:9–11). Circumcision became the "token of the Abrahamic covenant" during Old Testament times and those who were circumcised "enjoyed the privileges and undertook the responsibilities of the covenant."[47] In other words, circumcision was a gospel covenant given to Abraham that continued as a requirement of the law of Moses until it was fulfilled. It has been suggested that the institution of circumcision with Abraham was "a ratification of the covenant" in Genesis 15 and that the "symbolic signification of circumcision is the same as that of the divided victims."[48] This association is supported by the fact that not being circumcised meant breaking the covenant and resulted in a severe "cutting" penalty. The Lord said, "And the uncircumcised man child . . . shall be cut off from his people; he hath broken my covenant" (Genesis 17:14). Here the Hebrew verb for "cut off" is *kārat*, the same as for cutting a covenant, and reminds us of the self-curse for violating one's promise. While circumcision is related to other things in the gospel,[49] it seems to echo the practice of cutting covenants and the promise of seed to Abraham. It appears that circumcision regularly reminded males of the covenant God had cut with Abraham and the consequences of failing to keep that covenant.

The Sinai covenant. Many times in the Hebrew Bible we read that the Lord cut a covenant with Israel at Sinai.[50] Significantly, echoes suggesting this was a literal covenant cutting are recorded in Exodus 24, before the Lord revoked the fulness of the gospel from Israel (compare Joseph Smith Translation, Exodus 34:1–2), thereby giving us another example of gospel covenant cutting. We read that Moses wrote down the Lord's commandments, built an altar, and instructed that oxen be slaughtered for burnt and peace offerings (see Exodus 24:4–5). Then he took "*half of the blood, and put it in basons; and half of the blood he sprinkled on the altar.* And he took the book of the covenant, and read in the audience of the people: and they said, All that the Lord hath said will we do, and be obedient. *And Moses took the blood, and sprinkled it on the people*, and said, Behold the blood of the covenant, which the Lord hath made [cut] with you concerning all these words" (Exodus 24:6–8; emphasis added).

Since an intensive form of the Hebrew root *kpr* means "cover over"[51] and is often translated "make an atonement,"[52] the sprinkling of the people with the sacrificial blood seems to indicate they were "covered" with the blood of Christ and protected by his Atonement. In addition, the sprinkling of half of the blood on the altar and the other half on the people reminds us of the animals divided in half in Genesis 15.[53] It appears this was "a symbolic action in which the people were identified with the sacrificed animal, so that the fate of the latter is presented as the fate to be expected by the people if they violated their sacred promise (i.e., it is a form of self-curse)."[54] Therefore, the sacrificed animal can be seen as typifying Christ, who blesses the obedient by vicariously taking the curses of disobedience upon himself (that is, he becomes the sacrificed animal), and also typifying the disobedient, who will suffer the curses themselves (that is, they become the sacrificed animal). Thus the symbolism of the covenant ritual appears to have been twofold—blessings for obedience and curses for disobedience. This idea is consistent with the many blessings and curses of the covenant recorded later (see especially Deuteronomy 28). Not surprisingly, one of these curses echoes the slaughtered animals: "And thy carcase shall be meat unto all fowls of the air, and unto the beasts of the earth" (Deuteronomy 28:26).[55]

It is noteworthy that the covenant curse came upon the generation of Israelites who were led out of Egypt. After these people had provoked the Lord numerous times (see Numbers 14:11, 22–23), Jehovah finally enforced the curses of the covenant by causing them to wander forty years in the wilderness so they would die there and not inherit the land he promised to Abram. The Lord said, "*Your carcases shall fall in this wilderness* . . . Doubtless ye shall not come into the land, concerning which I sware to make you dwell therein. . . . And your children shall wander in the wilderness forty years, and bear your whoredoms, *until your carcases be wasted in the wilderness* . . . and ye shall know my breach of promise. . . . I will surely do it unto all this evil congregation, that are gathered together against me: in this wilderness they shall be consumed, and there they shall die" (Numbers 14:29–30, 33–35; emphasis added).

The failure of the first generation of Israelites to keep their covenant with Jehovah may be related to an apparent renewal of the Sinai covenant when Israel finally entered Canaan. Shortly after entering the promised land, Joshua fulfilled an earlier commandment of Moses's (see Deuteronomy 11:26–29; 27:12–13) that echoes elements of the covenant at Sinai and the covenant with Abram. Joshua built an altar, slaughtered animals for burnt and peace offerings, and wrote upon stones a copy of the law of Moses (see Joshua 8:30–32), reminding us of Moses's actions at Sinai (see Exodus 24:4–8). Then Joshua divided Israel in half and placed the ark of the covenant in the valley between Mount Gerizim and Mount Ebal. Next, half of the priests declared the blessings of the law from Gerizim, and the other half of the priests declared the curses of the law from Ebal: "And all Israel, and their elders, and officers, and their judges, stood on this side the ark and on that side before the priests the Levites, . . . *half of them over against mount Gerizim, and half of them over against mount Ebal.*

. . . And afterward *he read all the words of the law, the blessings and cursings*, according to all that is written in the book of the law" (Joshua 8:33–34; emphasis added). Animal sacrifices, division of the people into halves on opposing mountains, and the reading of the blessings and curses of the law all echo the covenant cutting that occurred at Sinai. The division of the people into halves also reminds us of the animals divided in half in Genesis 15 and reinforces the idea that the people were identified with the sacrificed animals if they violated the covenant. Thus, it appears the Lord wanted the Israelites who would actually inherit the promised land to effectively reenact what occurred at Sinai and renew their covenant with him.

A new covenant. The last echo of covenant cutting we will consider is the Lord's promise through the prophet Jeremiah that he would cut a new covenant with his people. "Behold, the days come, saith the Lord, that I will make [cut] a new covenant with the house of Israel, and with the house of Judah: Not according to the covenant that I made [cut] with their fathers in the day that I took them by the hand to bring them out of the land of Egypt" (Jeremiah 31:31–32). Certainly Jesus sought to establish a new covenant with his people during his mortal ministry (see Matthew 26:28; Hebrews 12:24), but in reference to Jeremiah's prophecy, the Prophet Joseph Smith taught: "This covenant has never been established with the house of Israel, nor with the house of Judah, for it requires two parties to make a covenant, and those two parties must be agreed, or no covenant can be made. Christ, in the days of His flesh, proposed to make a covenant with them, but they rejected Him and His proposals, and in consequence thereof, they were broken off, and no covenant was made with them at that time."[56] From modern revelation and other teachings of the Prophet Joseph, we understand that the fulfillment of Jeremiah's prophecy pertains to our dispensation.[57] In other words, Jeremiah was prophesying of a time in the last days when the Lord would cut a new gospel covenant with Israel and Judah.

Since we know Jeremiah was familiar with literal covenant cutting (he was the prophet when Zedekiah and his people cut a covenant), we might wonder if his prophecy should be interpreted literally or figuratively. Even if Jeremiah's prophecy is only figurative, it may be useful to compare it to the dramatic event when the Jews will recognize Jesus Christ as their Messiah. The prophet Zechariah portrays this experience in an interesting way as part of the destruction of Jerusalem in the last days (see Zechariah 14:1–2). "And his [the Lord's] feet shall stand in that day upon the mount of Olives, which is before Jerusalem on the east, and the mount of Olives shall cleave in the midst thereof toward the east and toward the west, and there shall be a very great valley; and *half of the mountain shall remove toward the north, and half of it toward the south*. And ye shall flee to the valley, . . . and the Lord my God shall come" (Zechariah 14:4–5; emphasis added). "And then shall the Jews look upon me and say: What are these wounds in thine hands and in thy feet? Then shall they know that I am the Lord; for I will say unto them: These wounds are the wounds with which I was wounded in the house of my friends. I am he who was lifted up. I am Jesus that was crucified. I am the Son of God. And then shall they weep because of their iniquities; then shall they lament because they persecuted their king" (D&C 45:51–53). The coming of the Lord to the Mount of Olives and its division into halves could be seen as echoing the divided animals with Abram, the division of the sacrificial blood into halves at Sinai, the division of the Israelites into halves with Joshua, and the calf divided into halves with Zedekiah. The Savior's showing of the marks of his atoning sacrifice to the Jews may be thought of as an echo of the sacrificed animals of covenant cutting and the imagery of Jehovah between the divided halves of the mountain might remind the Jews of when Jehovah passed between the animals Abram divided. Whether or not all these parallels are intended, it appears that through this experience the Jews will finally accept Jesus Christ as their Messiah and their God, suggesting it may be one part of the fulfillment of Jehovah's promise to cut a new covenant with his people.

APPLICATION TODAY

The principles of covenant cutting shed light on many other scriptural passages. In addition to those already discussed, some scriptures to consider in light of covenant cutting include Jesus's parable about eagles gathering to a carcass (see Matthew 24:28; Luke 17:37); the righteous covenants made by King Benjamin's people (see Mosiah 2–6), the Anti-Nephi-Lehies (see Alma 24:17–19; Alma 53:11–17), and those associated with Moroni's title of liberty (see Alma 46:19–22); the wicked covenants of secret combinations (see Alma 37:27–29; Helaman 6:21, 25–30;

Ether 8:13–16; Moses 5:29–30, 49–50; 6:29); and the oath and covenant of the priesthood (see D&C 84:33–41; Joseph Smith Translation,
Genesis 14:25–31). If we are attuned to covenant-cutting ideas, we can
improve our understanding of these and other scriptures.

Thinking of modern covenants in light of ancient covenants can
help us better appreciate their significance. Though certain elements of
covenant cutting are not practiced today, such as animal sacrifice (see
3 Nephi 9:19), the principles are still relevant. For instance, in modern Temples we enter into covenants that will bring us back into God's
presence (the endowment) and receive the promises made to Abraham
(Temple marriage). The Prophet Joseph Smith taught that modern
Temple ordinances are the restoration of "the ancient order of things,"[58]
suggesting these covenants may be better understood in light of ancient
practices. If we are knowledgeable of ancient covenant making, we will
not be confused by things that are ancient in nature and less familiar
to us in modern society. As we see parallels between ancient and modern covenants, we will better appreciate the covenants that have been
restored in our day.

Finally, perhaps the most important benefit of studying covenant cutting concerns our individual commitment. God does not change and expects the same complete commitment from his people today as he did anciently. Do we view gospel covenants today as seriously as we should? Do
we need to deepen our commitment to keep our covenants? Just as was
dramatized by ancient covenant cutting, we as Latter-day Saints should
view keeping our covenants as more important than losing our own lives.
"I have decreed in my heart, saith the Lord, that I will prove you in all
things, whether you will abide in my covenant, even unto death, that you
may be found worthy. For if ye will not abide in my covenant ye are not
worthy of me" (D&C 98:14–15). If we keep our covenants with complete
faithfulness, we will be found worthy to receive the great blessings the
Lord has promised us. If we do not, we will eventually find ourselves cut
off from the blessings and protection of the covenant.

SUMMARY

Covenants are a key aspect of the gospel of Jesus Christ in the Old
Testament. The phrase "cut a covenant" reflects ancient practices where

animals were slaughtered and cut up to ratify an agreement, graphically illustrating the curse for violating the covenant. Numerous examples or echoes of covenant cutting can be found in the scriptures, many of which are associated with the fulness of the gospel. We, as Latter-day Saints, can benefit from studying ancient covenant-cutting practices through improved scriptural understanding, increased appreciation of modern covenants, and deepened personal commitment to keep our covenants today as if our own lives depended on it.

NOTES

1. Bible Dictionary, s.v. "covenant."

2. According to a search of the English text of the scriptures in The Church of Jesus Christ of Latter-day Saints, *The Scriptures: CD-ROM Resource Edition 1.0* (Salt Lake City: Intellectual Reserve, 2002).

3. *Random House Webster's College Dictionary*, 2nd ed. (New York: Random House, 1998), s.v. "covenant."

4. Jacob Weingreen, *A Practical Grammar for Classical Hebrew*, 2nd ed. (Oxford: Oxford University Press, 1959), 304.

5. Francis Brown, S. R. Driver, and Charles A. Briggs, *The Brown-Driver-Briggs Hebrew and English Lexicon: With an Appendix Containing the Biblical Aramaic* (Peabody, MA: Hendrickson Publishers, 2000), 503.

6. Brown, Driver, and Briggs, *Hebrew and English Lexicon*, 136.

7. Warren Baker and Eugene Carpenter, *The Complete Word Study Dictionary: Old Testament* (Chattanooga, TN: AMG Publishers, 2003), 166.

8. According to a search of the text of the Hebrew Bible in *The Scriptures: CD-ROM Resource Edition 1.0.*

9. See how "covenant" is italicized (added by translators) in 1 Samuel 11:2; 20:16; 1 Kings 8:9; 2 Chronicles 5:10; Nehemiah 9:38; and Isaiah 57:8.

10. See Bruce William Jones, "Cutting Deals and Striking Bargains," *English Today* 12, no. 2 (1996): 35–40.

11. See James B. Pritchard, ed., *Ancient Near Eastern Texts Relating to the Old Testament*, 3rd ed. with supplement (Princeton, NJ: Princeton, 1969), xix. Pritchard has conveniently compiled English translations of many extrabiblical texts related to the Old Testament into one volume. This source will be cited whenever possible since it is more accessible for most readers.

12. See David Noel Friedman, ed., *The Anchor Bible Dictionary* (New York: Doubleday, 1992), s.v. "covenant."

13. This approach is based on David Noel Friedman, ed., *Eerdmans Dictionary of the Bible* (Grand Rapids, MI: Eerdmans, 2000), s.v. "covenant." In compiling this section, and in other areas of this paper, I have been aided by the references in Jones,

"Cutting Deals and Striking Bargains" and David L. Peterson, "Covenant Ritual: A Traditio-Historical Perspective," *Biblical Research* 22 (1977): 7–18.

14. According to the dates in David R. Seely, "Chronology, Bible," in *Book of Mormon Reference Companion*, ed. Dennis L. Largey (Salt Lake City: Deseret Book, 2003), 192–95. Note that this paper is not intended to evaluate biblical chronology or the accuracy of textual dates but to use estimated dates to provide a framework for understanding the topic.

15. Pritchard, *Ancient Near Eastern Texts*, 482.

16. Pritchard, *Ancient Near Eastern Texts*, 482.

17. Donald J. Wiseman, "Abban and Alalaḫ," *Journal of Cuneiform Studies* 12, no. 4 (1958), 129; see also J. D. Douglas and N. Hillyer, eds., *The Illustrated Bible Dictionary* 1 (Leicester, UK: InterVarsity Press, 1980), s.v. "Alalah."

18. See Friedman, *Anchor Bible Dictionary*, s.v. "covenant."

19. Friedman, *Anchor Bible Dictionary*, s.v. "covenant."

20. Friedman, *Anchor Bible Dictionary*, s.v. "covenant"; emphasis in original.

21. Pritchard, *Ancient Near Eastern Texts*, 660, brackets in original.

22. Pritchard, *Ancient Near Eastern Texts*, 532.

23. Pritchard, *Ancient Near Eastern Texts*, 539.

24. For a brief discussion of Persian and Greek examples from the first millennium BC, see Jones, "Cutting Deals and Striking Bargains," 37–38.

25. See Moshe Weinfield, "The Covenant of Grant in the Old Testament and in the Ancient Near East," *Journal of the American Oriental Society* 90, no. 2 (1970), 184–203. Another view is that the development was sequential, from a ratifying sacrifice to a dramatized curse (see Peterson, "Covenant Ritual: A Traditio-Historical Perspective," 7–18).

26. Friedman, *Eerdmans Dictionary of the Bible*, 291.

27. Friedman, *Eerdmans Dictionary of the Bible*, 291.

28. It appears this was divinely induced to prepare Abram for revelation, as suggested by the use of the Hebrew word *tardēmāh*, which is also used for when the Lord caused "a deep sleep" to come upon Adam so he could create Eve (Genesis 2:21; see also Baker and Carpenter, *The Complete Word Study Dictionary: Old Testament*, 1246).

29. While God's promises to Abram are found in prior revelations, this is the first time the King James Version says Jehovah "made a covenant" with Abram, which corresponds to the first occurrence of *kārat berît* in the Hebrew Bible. Earlier in the Joseph Smith Translation, we read that God "made" a covenant with Enoch, Noah, and Abram (see Joseph Smith Translation Genesis 14:27; 9:11; 13:14), but since there is no indication these covenants were actually "cut," Genesis 15 may be considered the first scriptural example of its kind.

30. For example, see the bibliography and discussion in Gordon J. Wenham, *Genesis 1–15*, Word Biblical Commentary (Waco, TX: Word Books, 1987), 322–35.

31. See Weinfield, "The Covenant of Grant in the Old Testament and in the Ancient Near East," 196. Some have argued that God would not have taken upon himself a curse since this was done by the inferior party in king-vassal loyalty oaths. However, this need not be problematic since Jehovah stipulated what should happen,

and his willingness to condescend is found in many scriptures (see Isaiah 53:3–10; 1 Nephi 11:26–33; 19:8–10; Mosiah 3:5–7).

32. For example, see Wenham, *Genesis 1–15*, 331.

33. *Apocalypse of Abraham* (see chapter 15), Flavius Josephus's *Antiquities of the Jews*, Book 1, *The Pseudepigraphic Book of Jubilees* (see chapter 14), all add sacrificial elements in their retelling of Genesis 15 (see Christopher T. Begg, "Rereadings of the 'Animal Rite' of Genesis 15 in Early Jewish Narratives," *Catholic Bible Quarterly* 50 [1988]: 36–46).

34. The *Apocalypse of Abraham* suggests the birds were left alive to carry Abram to heaven (see James H. Charlesworth, ed., *The Old Testament Pseudepigrapha* [New York: Doubleday, 1983], 1:696).

35. Wenham, *Genesis 1–15*, 335.

36. The wording here suggests Jesus referred to Abram's experience in Genesis 15 when he said to the Jews, "Your father Abraham rejoiced to see my day: and he saw it, and was glad" (John 8:56).

37. See also Church Educational System, *Old Testament Student Manual: Genesis–2 Samuel*, 2nd ed. (Salt Lake City: The Church of Jesus Christ of Latter-day Saints, 1981), 71.

38. I appreciate Robert J. Norman of the Church Educational System, who has taught about cutting covenants for many years, for introducing me to the idea of Genesis 15 as a Temple text and several aspects of the scriptural echoes discussed later.

39. Joseph Smith, *Teachings of the Prophet Joseph Smith*, comp. Joseph Fielding Smith (Salt Lake City: Deseret Book, 1976), 305.

40. Marion G. Romney, "Temples—The Gates to Heaven," *Ensign*, March 1971, 16.

41. See *Old Testament Student Manual: Genesis–2 Samuel*, 155–56.

42. The Revised Standard Version is used here rather than the King James Version because it follows the proposed emendation of the Hebrew text noted in *Biblia Hebraica Stuttgartensia* (the Masoretic version of the Hebrew Bible often used by scholars). This emendation only changes a single Hebrew letter, but then reads that the covenant breakers will become *like* the cut-up calf.

43. Weingreen, *Practical Grammar for Classical Hebrew*, 182. For a scriptural example, see Genesis 14:22–23. This practice continues today with the swearing in of government officials and witnesses who testify in court.

44. See Ruth 1:17; 1 Samuel 3:17; 14:44; 20:13; 25:22; 2 Samuel 3:35; 19:13; 1 Kings 2:23; 19:2; 20:10; 2 Kings 6:31.

45. Matthew Black and H. H. Rowley, eds., *Peake's Commentary on the Bible* (London: Thomas Nelson and Sons, 1962), 557; see also George Arthur Buttrick, ed., *The Interpreter's Bible* 1 (Nashville: Abingdon Press, 1956), 5:1058.

46. The idea of "echoes" is drawn from Donald W. Parry, Daniel C. Peterson, and John W. Welch, eds., *Echoes and Evidences of the Book of Mormon* (Provo, UT: FARMS, 2002).

47. Bible Dictionary, s.v. "circumcision."

48. Black, *Peake's Commentary on the Bible*, 191.

49. For example, Joseph Smith Translation Genesis 17:11 explains that circumcision was given to Abraham as a constant reminder that children are not accountable until they are eight years old.

50. These instances include while Israel was at Mount Sinai (see Exodus 24:8; 34:10, 27), when Israel was about to enter Canaan (see Deuteronomy 4:23; 5:2–3; 31:16), during the time of the kings (see 1 Kings 8:21; 2 Kings 17:15, 35, 38), and during the time of Jeremiah (see Jeremiah 11:10; 31:32; 34:13).

51. Brown, Driver, and Briggs, *Hebrew and English Lexicon*, 497.

52. There are many examples of this, especially in Leviticus, such as chapters 4 (vv. 20, 26, 31, 35); 5 (vv. 6, 10, 13, 16, 18); 14 (vv. 18–21, 29, 31, 53); and 16 (vv. 6, 10–11, 16–18, 24, 30, 32–34).

53. This connection was first suggested to me by Peterson (see "Covenant Ritual: A Traditio-Historical Perspective," 11).

54. Friedman, *Anchor Bible Dictionary*, s.v. "covenant."

55. The awful nature of this curse seems in part related to the importance of having a proper burial (see Douglas, *Illustrated Bible Dictionary*, s.v. "Burial and Mourning").

56. Smith, *Teachings*, 14–15.

57. Compare Jeremiah 31:31–34 with D&C 84:57, 98 and Smith, *Teachings*, 149.

58. Smith, *Teachings*, 237.

8

CHRIST, COVENANTS, AND THE *CAPH*

Shon Hopkin

For some modern Christian religions, there is a fundamental discon-
nect between the gospel of Jesus Christ and the need for priesthood
covenants and ordinances. Covenants and ordinances are seen as connected to an antiquated system of worship not directly connected to the
personal grace found in Jesus Christ. This interpretation comes primarily
from an overemphasis on certain statements in the epistles of Paul, and
forces an interpretation of Old and New Testament passages given directly by Christ, which separates the grace of Christ offered to members
of his Church from sacred ordinances. This viewpoint de-emphasizes the
responsibility of Christians to make and keep sacred covenants by participating in priesthood ordinances such as baptism, the sacrament, and
the bestowal of the gift of the Holy Ghost.

An example of the impact that this noncovenant, nonordinance interpretation has on these religions' views of Christ's gospel is evidenced
by a statement in Spiros Zodhiates' *Complete Word Study Dictionary of the
New Testament*. Zodhiates refers to Christ's well-known statement about

---

*Shon Hopkin is a seminaries and institutes coordinator and a PhD candidate in Hebrew studies at
the University of Texas, Austin.*

the importance of baptism and the gift of the Holy Ghost, found in John 3:5, which states, "Except a man be born of water and of the Spirit, he cannot enter into the kingdom of God." Zodhiates states, "Water is mentioned in the discourse of the Lord Jesus to Nicodemus in John 3:5, the mention of which has given some the idea that the Lord Jesus was speaking of baptism. Such a presumption, however, is unjustified."[1] This statement is followed by some lengthy linguistic reasoning about why this verse cannot refer to baptism. Only partway through the passage does the author mention the thought that shapes his reasoning, a heavily tilted view of a statement by the Apostle Paul: "Paul very clearly states in 1 Cor. 15:50 'that flesh and blood cannot inherit the kingdom of God.' This means that there is no physical means whereby man can enter this spiritual kingdom of God. . . . Jesus Christ does not become the King of our hearts and live in us through water baptism. Nowhere in the Scriptures is anything of the kind stated. . . . If the Lord meant to convey the idea of water baptism here, He would have said so. He does not in any shape or form refer to baptism."[2]

It is not surprising to find that this author's argument is colored by his own previous conception of the scriptures.[3] However, it is bothersome that the author does not clearly state the viewpoints that guide his thinking before he offers his interpretation. Instead, the thread of his logic is interwoven within his explanation, making it difficult to tell how fundamentally important the assumption is to his argument.

In contrast, the fundamental position of this study should be understood clearly from the outset. The assumptions are these: (1) The fulness of the gospel of Jesus Christ has been restored to the earth through the teachings of The Church of Jesus Christ of Latter-day Saints; and (2) sacred covenants through true priesthood ordinances exist in the Church, and these covenants and ordinances are an essential part of the gospel. Or, as the third article of faith declares, "We believe that through the Atonement of Christ, all mankind may be saved, by *obedience to the laws and ordinances* of the Gospel" (emphasis added). This gospel pattern has existed since the beginning of the world, in each dispensation of the gospel. The Prophet Joseph Smith has clearly stated:

> We all admit that the Gospel has ordinances, and if so, had it not always ordinances, and were not its ordinances always the same?

... It will be noticed that, according to Paul, (see Gal. iii:8) the Gospel was preached to Abraham. We would like to be informed in what name the Gospel was then preached, whether it was in the name of Christ or some other name. If in any other name, was it the Gospel? And if it was the Gospel, and that preached in the name of Christ, had it any ordinances? If not, was it the Gospel? And if it had ordinances what were they? ... Now taking it for granted that the scriptures say what they mean, and mean what they say, we have sufficient grounds to go on and prove from the Bible that the gospel has always been the same; the ordinances to fulfil its requirements, the same; and the officers to officiate, the same; and the signs and fruits resulting from the promises, the same: therefore, as Noah was a preacher of righteousness he must have been baptised and ordained to the priesthood by the laying on of the hands, &c.[4]

In light of the foregoing statement, we should not be surprised to find evidence of the connection between Christ, covenants, and priesthood ordinances in either the New or Old Testament, or in any of the scriptures of the restored gospel. The following analysis of the scriptures seeks to answer these questions: (1) Can evidence be found in the Old Testament for the Latter-day Saint view that there is a fundamental connection between covenants, priesthood ordinances, and personal salvation through the grace of Christ? (2) Did the prophets of the Old Testament teach that covenants and priesthood ordinances lead and connect to Christ and his blessings, or are these blessings to be gained without the power of covenants and priesthood ordinances, as some teach today? This study will rely primarily on Old Testament texts to demonstrate the central role of covenants and ordinances from the earliest ages of the earth and that these covenants and ordinances centered in Jesus Christ in antiquity, just as they center in him today.

COVENANTS AND CURSE REVERSAL IN THE OLD TESTAMENT

To recognize the importance and spiritual ramifications of covenants in the Old Testament, it is essential to understand the pattern of cause and effect that the Lord sets up early in the scriptural account. God establishes a relationship with his people in which he sets the conditions or commandments. He grants the blessings when his people choose to obey the commandments and be a part of the covenant relationship, and he designates the consequences when his people transgress against that covenant relationship. Thus, in Genesis 1, the Lord offers to Adam and Eve the blessing of all his creations and the blessing and commandment to exercise dominion over them. He offers the blessing of a companion to Adam with the blessing and commandment to be fruitful and multiply. However, when the Lord's commandments are disobeyed or transgressed, he also designates the consequences of this disobedience. These promises to Adam and Eve, dependent on their faithfulness, bring them into a "partnership" or covenant relationship with the Lord. After they had transgressed the law to not partake of the fruit of the tree of knowledge of good and evil, Adam and Eve are told, "Because thou hast . . . eaten of the tree, of which I commanded thee, saying, Thou shalt not eat of it: *cursed* is the ground for thy sake; in sorrow shalt thou eat of it all the days of thy life; thorns also and thistles shall it bring forth to thee; and thou shalt eat the herb of the field; in the sweat of thy face shalt thou eat bread, till thou return unto the ground" (Genesis 3:17–19; emphasis added).

In these verses, the cursing, or consequence of eating the fruit, reverses some of the earlier blessings promised to Adam by the Lord. He had been promised dominion over an earth that would provide for him plentifully, but now he will live in an earth with which he has to struggle for dominion. Adam and Eve are also told, "I will greatly multiply thy sorrow and thy conception; in sorrow thou shalt bring forth children" (Genesis 3:16). They had been promised the ability to multiply and replenish the earth, but now those blessings would come with significant hardship.

The Book of Mormon clarifies the purpose of the cursing or consequences of the Fall when Lehi teaches his son that "Adam fell that men might be; and men are, that they might have joy" (2 Nephi 2:25). While the Fall obviously made the world a more difficult place in which to live, with pain, sickness, hardship, and death, it also provided immense opportunities designed by a loving Father for our benefit. These difficulties are connected to the many joys that also spring from the Fall, including the ability to have and raise children, the joy of overcoming difficult challenges, the opportunity to become more like our Heavenly Father, and the joy of a saving reliance upon the Lord developed in consequence of our need for him in a fallen world. The consequences of the Fall draw the hearts and minds of God's children constantly back to the Lord, help them overcome their weaknesses, and fill them with a desire to enter into covenant relationships with him. Thus the word *curse* should be understood in the light of Nephi's teachings that "[God] doeth not anything save it be for the benefit of the world; for he loveth the world, even that he layeth down his own life that he may draw all men unto him. Wherefore, he commandeth none that they shall not partake of his salvation" (2 Nephi 26:24).

While the descendants of Adam and Eve are not accountable for our first parents' transgression (see Articles of Faith 1:2), we do live in a world affected by their choices. In addition, we also transgress and sin in our own lives. When any child of God willfully moves away from him, this behavior also leads to consequences. The Old Testament offers a reminder of this pattern in the chapter of Genesis right after the Fall. After Cain's transgression of the law in the murder of his brother Abel, he is told, "And now art thou *cursed* from the earth, which hath opened her mouth to receive thy brother's blood from thy hand; when thou tillest the ground, it shall not henceforth yield unto thee her strength; a fugitive and a vagabond shalt thou be in the earth" (Genesis 4:11–12; emphasis added). It should again be noted that while these consequences were difficult for Cain, they were designed by a loving Father, who desired to draw Cain's heart toward goodness to help him overcome the weaknesses that motivated him to "murder and get gain" (see Moses 5:31), and to create the need for him to rely upon the Lord in his difficulties.

The consequences that followed the transgression in the Garden of Eden affected future covenants that the Lord would offer his people. In effect, through the making and keeping of sacred covenants, the Lord would offer to *reverse* the effects of the consequences of the Fall under which his people operate. He would also offer to redeem them from the consequences of their own sins. Therefore, when the Lord later covenanted with Abraham, he stated: "I am the Almighty God; walk before me, and be thou perfect. And I will make my *covenant* between me and thee, and will multiply thee exceedingly. . . . And I will make thee exceeding fruitful, and I will make nations of thee, and kings shall come out of thee. . . . And I will give unto thee, and to thy seed after thee, the land wherein thou art a stranger, all the land of Canaan, for an everlasting possession; and I will be their God" (Genesis 17:1–2, 6, 8; emphasis added).

God offered Abraham again the same thing he had offered to Adam and Eve, namely, dominion over a land and greatness in posterity. The reversal through the Abrahamic covenant of the curse on the land, dependent on Abraham's obedience, becomes even clearer in God's description of the promised land to Abraham's descendant, Moses. "I am come down to deliver [the Israelites] out of the hand of the Egyptians, and to bring them up out of that land unto a good land and a large, unto a land flowing with milk and honey" (Exodus 3:8). This description is a vivid reminder of the paradise that existed in the garden of Eden.

Nowhere is the triumphant power of covenants to reverse the consequences of sin more evident than in the writings of the Old Testament prophets, and most particularly the writings of Isaiah. Again and again, Isaiah uses language which is biblically connected to covenant breaking and to covenant making in order to teach that the consequences of sin are real, but that these consequences can be reversed for God's people if they will return to a correct covenantal relationship with him. Most frequently the blessings of the covenant are promised in the form of a cursed land returning to its precurse, Edenic state, as man returns to a right relationship with God: "Let the wicked forsake his way, and the unrighteous man his thoughts: and let him return unto the Lord, and he will have mercy upon him; and to our God, for he will abundantly pardon. . . . *Instead of the thorn* shall come up the fir tree, and *instead of the brier* shall come up the myrtle tree: and it shall be to the Lord for a name, for an *everlasting sign* that shall not be cut off" (Isaiah 55:7, 13; emphasis added). Blessings that follow after the covenant, such as those mentioned in this verse from Isaiah, act as physical *signs* of the reality of the Lord's covenant promises.

The reversal of the consequences of sin is often described in terms of water coming to a land that has been cursed with drought:

> For I the Lord thy God will hold thy *right hand*, saying unto thee, Fear not; I will help thee. . . .
> When the poor and needy seek water, and there is none, and their tongue faileth for thirst, I the Lord will hear them, I the God of Israel will not forsake them.

I will open rivers in high places, and fountains in the midst of the valleys:

I will make the wilderness a pool of water, and the dry land springs of water.

I will plant in the wilderness the cedar, the shittah tree, and the myrtle, and the oil tree; I will set in the desert the fir tree, and the pine, and the box tree together: That they may see, and know, and consider, and understand together, that the hand of the Lord hath done this, and the Holy One of Israel hath created it. (Isaiah 41:13, 17–20; emphasis added)

The effects of the Fall are also overcome in Isaiah 55, where the ability to obtain food and water without having to purchase them (by the sweat of one's brow), again hearkens to the Edenic state: "Ho, every one that thirsteth, come ye to the waters, and he that hath no money; come ye, buy, and eat; yea, come, buy wine and milk without money and without price. Wherefore do ye spend money for that which is not bread? and your labour for that which satisfieth not? hearken diligently unto me, and eat ye that which is good, and let your soul delight itself in fatness. Incline your ear, and come unto me: hear, and your soul shall live; and *I will make an everlasting covenant with you*, even the sure mercies of David" (Isaiah 55:1–3; emphasis added).

We can also clearly see a reversal of the effects of the Fall as it relates to a greater abundance of descendants, which appear to spring up almost without any effort, in these verses by the prophet Isaiah: "Thus saith the Lord.... Fear not, O Jacob, my servant.... For I will pour water upon him that is thirsty, and floods upon the dry ground: I will pour my spirit upon thy seed, and my blessing upon thine offspring: And they shall spring up as among the grass, as willows by the water courses. One shall say, *I am the Lord's*; and another shall call himself by the name of Jacob; and another shall subscribe with his hand unto the Lord, and *surname himself by the name of Israel*" (Isaiah 44:2–5; emphasis added).

The offspring are given the same name—Israel—that the Lord gave to Jacob when making a covenant with him (see Genesis 32:28), and they become the Lord's. It is interesting to note that this process is followed precisely in the covenant-making process of new members of The Church of Jesus Christ of Latter-day Saints. Through baptism they become the

Lord's. As they receive their patriarchal blessing, they learn that they are descendants of Israel and can be called by his name.[5]

Of course, the curses and the blessings mentioned in Isaiah are to a great degree symbolic of more important spiritual changes that will come upon the individual. Where the individual spirit has been dry and unproductive, providing only weeds and thistles, the Lord will send water to bring forth an abundance of knowledge, peace, and joy.[6] Where the spiritual womb has been barren, not bringing any blessings to others or joy to the individual, it will spring forth with life to bless all those around and bring joy to the bearer. These spiritual blessings, more important than the physical, reverse the consequences that separate people from the Lord because of their wickedness. A reminder of these spiritual consequences of sin, followed by a promise of their reversal, when the covenant is renewed and obeyed, is beautifully described by the prophet Isaiah:

> Hear the word of the Lord, ye rulers of Sodom; give ear unto the law of our God, ye people of Gomorrah. . . .
>
> When ye spread forth your hands, I will hide mine eyes from you: yea, when ye make many prayers, I will not hear: your hands are full of blood.
>
> Wash you, make you clean; put away the evil of your doings from before mine eyes; cease to do evil. . . .
>
> Come now, and let us reason together, saith the Lord: though your sins be as scarlet, they shall be as white as snow; though they be red like crimson, they shall be as wool.
>
> If ye be willing and obedient, ye shall eat the good of the land:
>
> But if ye refuse and rebel, ye shall be devoured with the sword: for the mouth of the Lord hath spoken it. (Isaiah 1:10, 15–16, 18–20)

The theme of the glorious power of covenants in the reversal of the consequences of sin develops throughout the scriptures and in an overview of the entire plan of salvation from the Garden of Eden through the Millennium. The foregoing examples serve as ample witness that God does make covenants with his people and that his people are required to obey the stipulations of that covenant. When they do not obey, they receive the consequences that flow from their actions. These consequences come from a loving Father who desires to strengthen his people and to call them back to him. When the Lord's people do obey, God reverses the consequences of sin and blesses them. However, while the power of the Lord is always most important in the covenant relationship, the Old Testament clearly supports the teachings of the restored gospel of Jesus Christ that disciples of Christ have an important role to play and are required to be obedient to these covenants to the best of their ability. There is abundant evidence that "through the Atonement [grace, mercy] of Christ, all mankind may be saved, *by obedience to the laws and ordinances of the gospel*" (Articles of Faith 1:3; emphasis added).

PRIESTHOOD ORDINANCES IN THE OLD TESTAMENT

Thus far, this study has analyzed the vital role covenants have played in God's interaction with his children from the beginning. However, what of the importance of priesthood ordinances as emphasized by the Prophet Joseph Smith? Covenants are an essential part of God's dealings with his people, but is there evidence in the Old Testament that these covenants are solemnized, entered into, and made valid through priesthood ordinances? Is it sufficient to feel that God has spiritually called one into a covenant relationship, or is a priesthood ordinance an important part of the pattern?

In order to determine whether ordinances are important in covenant making, first it is important to understand what is meant by the word *ordinance*. The *Encyclopedia of Mormonism* states:

The word "ordinance" is derived from the Latin *ordinare*, which means to put in order or sequence; or to act by authorization or command. Members of The Church of Jesus Christ of Latter-day Saints regard religious ordinances not as arbitrarily established but as purposefully instituted by God and eternal in scope.

The power to perform ordinances whose validity is recognized by God is inseparably connected with the divine authority conferred on mortal man, that is, the priesthood of God. . . .

Ordinances in the Church contain instructions and rich symbolism. Anointing with consecrated oil (e.g., as in the temple) is reminiscent of the use of sacred oil in the coronation of kings and the calling of prophets in ancient days. *Laying hands* on the head of the sick symbolically suggests the invocation and transmission of power from on high.[7]

So, according to Latter-day Saint usage, priesthood ordinances are sacred rituals, designed to teach eternal truths, with the important purpose (along with other purposes) of solemnizing and validating covenants between God and man.

The Hebrew word for "ordinance" is *huqqah*. This word comes directly from the Hebrew verb *haqah* or *haqaq* ("to engrave").[8] Ordinances engrave, cement, or seal upon the individual the reality of the covenant.[9] One who is marked by the physical reality of an ordinance cannot with impunity pretend that the covenant never took place or that the commandment was never taught. The individual is completely accountable for the covenant and for the consequences of obeying or disobeying the laws of that covenant.

The connection between covenant and ordinance becomes clearer when we notice the Lord regularly requiring a physical demonstration (or, according to Latter-day Saint usage, an ordinance) of his covenants with man. Thus in Genesis 17, the proclaiming of the covenant from God is followed by a physical demonstration of the reality of that covenant, in the nature of circumcision: "And God said unto Abraham, Thou shalt keep my covenant therefore, thou, and thy seed after thee in their generations. This is my covenant, which ye shall keep, between me and you and thy seed after thee; Every man child among you shall be circumcised. And ye shall circumcise the flesh of your foreskin; and it shall be a *token of the covenant* betwixt me and you" (Genesis 17:9–11).

Of course, this ordinance would be much more than the symbolic "engraving" of the covenant through a physical act. It would literally engrave the reality of the covenant upon the flesh of the Israelite males.

Again, when God renewed his covenant with the children of Israel before their departure from Egypt, he solemnized that renewal with the ordinance of the Passover sacrifice and feast: "And this day shall be unto you for a memorial; and ye shall keep it a feast to the Lord" (Exodus 12:14). This ordinance was perpetuated by Christ in his New Testament Church when he instituted the sacrament as a continuation of the ancient ordinance of the Passover lamb, remembered by the Passover feast (see Luke 22:15, 19–20).

The sacrifice of the Passover feast, along with previous Old Testament sacrifices, points forward to ordinances that the Lord would later initiate in the Tabernacle/Temple setting with the children of Israel. These ordinances, including animal sacrifices, would serve as constant, physical reminders to them of the covenants they had made with the Lord. The Temple was the place where the majority of covenant-ratifying ordinances were completed. Isaiah frequently reminds the reader of the importance of a Temple setting and covenants: "And it shall come to pass in the last days, that the mountain of the Lord's house [i.e., the Temple] shall be established in the top of the mountains, and shall be exalted above the hills; and all nations shall flow unto it. And many people shall go and say, Come ye, and let us go up to the mountain of the Lord, to the house of the God of Jacob; and he will teach us of his ways, and we will walk in his paths: for out of Zion shall go forth the law, and the word of the Lord from Jerusalem" (Isaiah 2:2–3). It is important to note that Isaiah is referring to the Temple, with which the Old Testament Israelites would have been familiar, but prophesies of its importance "in the last days," indicating that the importance of the Temple and Temple ordinances was not just for Old Testament times.

Isaiah offers a powerful example of how the ordinances of the Temple would reverse the consequences of sin. When the tribes of Israel were at Mount Sinai, they had lost the full blessings of the higher law of the gospel through transgression and were given a lesser law in which the lower priesthood was only held by the Levites. However, Isaiah prophesied that in the last days, members of the covenant would bring true Israel from among the Gentile nations to the Temple, and there, connected to priesthood offerings and ordinances, God will make all of these true Israelites a part of his holy priesthood:

> And I will set a *sign* among them, and I will send . . . them unto the nations . . . that have not heard my fame, neither have seen my glory; and they shall declare my glory among the Gentiles.
>
> And they shall bring all your brethren for an offering unto the Lord out of all nations upon horses, and in chariots, and in litters, and upon mules, and upon swift beasts, to my holy mountain [i.e., the Temple] Jerusalem, saith the Lord, as the children of Israel bring an *offering* in a clean vessel into the house of the Lord.

And I will also take of them for priests and for Levites, saith the Lord.
(Isaiah 66:19–21; emphasis added)

Thus the consequences of Israel's transgression at Mount Sinai would be reversed, and they would again become a "kingdom of priests, and an holy nation" (Exodus 19:6).

Christ in the New Testament demonstrates that covenants, with their spiritual blessings and manifestations, must be connected with the outward manifestations of priesthood ordinances. In his well-known discussion with Nicodemus in John 3, mentioned above, Christ is most intent on teaching about the importance and spiritual benefits of being born of the Spirit and focuses on the Spirit throughout his discussion. However, he does not leave out the importance of a physical manifestation of the ordinance. "Except a man be born *of water* and of the Spirit, he cannot enter into the kingdom of God" (John 3:5). Both are necessary. Being born of the Spirit engraves the disciples' spirit with the image and power of Christ. However, since we are both physical and spiritual beings, it is necessary for the physical "engraving" to take place as well. The necessity of this outward ordinance is restated by Christ in the Gospel of Mark: "He that believeth and is baptized shall be saved" (Mark 16:16).

Not surprisingly, it is the Book of Mormon that makes an important connection with the Old Testament. The prophet Alma teaches that through being born again, the disciple can receive Christ's image in his countenance. "And now behold, I ask of you, my brethren of the church, have ye spiritually been born of God? Have ye received his image in your countenances? Have ye experienced this mighty change in your hearts?" (Alma 5:14). Shortly thereafter, Alma connects receiving Christ's image with the engraving process: "I say unto you, can ye look up to God at that day with a pure heart and clean hands? I say unto you, can you look up, having the image of God *engraven* upon your countenances?" (Alma 5:19; emphasis added). As we would expect, Alma finishes his powerful discourse with priesthood ordinations and with the ordinance (or engraving) of baptism (see Alma 6:1–2). In such a way, through priesthood ordinances, the image of Christ can begin to be engraven, stamped, or sealed upon the countenances of the disciples of Christ. The Old Testament, the New Testament, and the Book of Mormon have provided clear illustration of the teaching of the Prophet Joseph Smith, that "being born again, comes by the Spirit of God *through ordinances.*"¹⁰ Or, as the Doctrine and Covenants states it, "In the ordinances [of the priesthood], the power of godliness is manifest. And without the ordinances thereof, and the authority of the priesthood, the power of godliness is not manifest unto men in the flesh" (D&C 84:20–21).

Priesthood Ordinances and the *Caph*

The passage quoted above from the *Encyclopedia of Mormonism* mentions the laying on of hands as an example of a priesthood ordinance. There are many instances in the restored gospel in which the laying on of hands is essential as an important part of priesthood ordinances, such as ordaining to the priesthood, setting apart for a calling, conferring the gift of the Holy Ghost, giving priesthood blessings of health, and even naming and blessing babies. Other ordinances, such as baptism, with the raised right arm of the priesthood holder as the baptismal prayer is offered, also demonstrate the importance of the hand in the making of sacred covenants.

There are various words for hand in Hebrew: *yad* refers to the hand as a whole, *ha-yamin* refers to the right hand, and *caph* refers to the palm of the hand. Scholars of other faiths have discussed the significance of the hand in the Hebrew language, as summarized below. For the ancient Israelites, the hand symbolized divine might, power, and authority. Human hands could be used in ways that indicated their possession of some of God's power and authority. Thus hands could be stretched out to offer a priesthood blessing. When laid upon the head, they could confer blessings from God, as when Jacob blessed Ephraim and Mannaseh (see Genesis 48:13–19). This example, when Joseph verbally shows preference for the father's right hand of blessing, offers evidence of the symbolic importance of the right hand. The right hand was used to make important marks or place seals of authority on communications. The grasping of right hands signified the entering into of a relationship, whether through treaty, obligation, or formal friendship. The right hand could be raised into the air as a formal gesture that the statement or oath being made was of special importance and weight, or it could be raised in the offering of a blessing.¹¹ The importance of the right hand in the context of covenants in the Latter-day Saint Church is obvious to those who have watched a baby blessing or who have witnessed a baptism.

As discussed by James Hastings in his *Encyclopedia of Religion and Ethics*, the biblical phrase that is used to signify formal consecration or appointment to priesthood office through priesthood ordinance literally means "to fill the hand (*yad*)," most likely symbolizing the priestly hand being filled with that which it needed to fulfill its work (such as incense in the hand of a priest) or with a symbol of authority (such as a scepter in the hand of a king).[12] The *caph* is the name of the Hebrew letter כ. For ancient Jewish/Israelite readers, the shape of the letter *caph* represented the curved shape of the palm of the hand and would have described the part of the hand that could be "filled" with priesthood authority and blessings. *Caph* was also one of the names given to spoons, cups, incense holders, and bowls in the Hebrew Bible, which, of course, are designed to be filled.[13] According to Hastings, the "filling of the hand" would have occurred at the time when the ancient Levitical priest was consecrated in his office to serve at the Temple or sanctuary, with the implicit receipt of blessings, power, and authority from heaven. This "filling of the hand" could also symbolize the receipt of those items or blessings that would have allowed the priest to serve the Lord (and to serve the house of Israel). This action might then imply a subsequent passing of the received blessings on to others through the laying on of hands, through priesthood service, or through a worthy offering made to the Lord after the priest's hand had been filled with the appropriate item of sacrifice.

For the Latter-day Saint, our hands become filled when we receive direction, authority, and blessings from the Lord to fulfill the duty to which we have been called or ordained. With regard to the Atonement, Christ accepted his divinely appointed mission when he drank from the "bitter cup" (D&C 19:18), which had been filled with the sins and suffering of all people. His plea to the Father to "let this cup pass from me: nevertheless not as I will, but as thou wilt" (Matthew 26:39) was an acknowledgment of the Father's directive power in the mission that had been placed in Christ's hands. Significantly, Christ's mention of the "cup" comes only twelve verses after Christ's institution of the sacrament, fulfilled in part by filling a cup with wine, a symbol of his atoning blood, and passing it to his apostles' waiting hands. In the modern-day symbolism of the sacrament ordinance, Latter-day Saints also accept the emblems of Christ's sacrifice into their hands with the divinely appointed responsibility to "always remember" Christ with the attendant blessing that they may be filled with the Spirit (D&C 20:77, 79).

These priesthood and gospel connections with the palm of the hand (*caph*), the hand (*yad*), and the right hand (*yamin*) become important in scriptural examples.[14] The importance of the hand in Isaiah 41:13 was already mentioned: "I the Lord thy God will hold thy right hand" (i.e., according to scholars of Jewish symbolism, this action brings the Lord and Israel into a formal, close relationship).[15] Three verses earlier is a mention of the protective power of God's right hand: "I will uphold thee with the right hand of my righteousness" (Isaiah 41:10). In the context of the covenant nature of these verses, this phrase might appropriately be interpreted, "I will uphold you through the power of my covenants." Later, the Lord utilizes the importance of the right hand in making oaths or promises when he states, "The Lord hath sworn by his right hand, and by the arm of his strength" (Isaiah 62:8). Each instance witnesses of the importance of an outwardly visible ordinance or sign in the making of covenants.[16]

THE *CAPH* AND THE CHRIST

Having established the importance of hands as associated with priesthood power, we are prepared to answer a final question: Does the Old Testament provide evidence that these covenants and ordinances are connected to Christ? And are these covenants and ordinances necessary in order to receive a full measure of Christ's saving grace? In part, of course, the question has already been answered. It has been clear that God uses covenants, ratified through ordinances, to offer blessings to his people and reverse the effects of sin. But does the Old Testament specifically connect this important process with Christ?

While there are many prophecies of the Messiah throughout the Old Testament, three specific examples are useful as they describe Christ's priesthood power and authority and point specifically to his role in reversing the effects of sin, employing "hand" symbolism to make his priesthood authority clear. One of these is found in Isaiah 22:20–25. These messianic verses need to be analyzed closely: "And it shall come to pass in that day, that I will call my servant Eliakim the son of Hilkiah: and I will clothe him with thy robe, and strengthen him with thy girdle, and I will commit thy government into his hand [*yad*]: and he shall be a father to the inhabitants of Jerusalem, and to the house of Judah. And the key of the house of David will I lay upon his shoulder; so he shall open, and none shall shut; and he shall shut, and none shall open" (Isaiah 22:20–22).

Eliakim, meaning "God shall cause to arise," was to serve at the king's right hand, just as Joseph did with Pharaoh and just as Christ does with the Father. As part of this symbolically Christ-centered position, Eliakim carried out all of the king's wishes, held the authority of the king to act in his stead, and held the power to grant a petitioner audience with the king or to deny that access, i.e., to open or to shut.

The clothing of Eliakim/Christ with a robe and girdle points the Old Testament reader immediately to the first act of clothing which occurred in the beginning of the world, as God began through covenant to reverse the effects of Adam and Eve's Fall by providing them with a "coat of skins" (Genesis 3:21).[17] Just as the garment of Adam and Eve surrounded and protected them from the elements of a fallen world, even so the children of God, which have been stripped of premortal glory by sin and by the effects of the Fall, can again become surrounded and protected by the power of God through the restoring effects of covenants. In addition, the vestments of robe and girdle in these verses, and the "filling of the hand" with the authority of government committed "into his [Eliakim's/Christ's] hand" (Isaiah 22:21), also clearly point to the priestly consecrations that occurred in Old Testament ordinations to the Levitical priesthood, in which the priest was clothed with a robe and girdle and consecrated (see Leviticus 8:7 for the robe and girdle; also see Leviticus 8:33 for "consecration" or the "filling of the hand"). Eliakim/Christ is clothed in an outward sign or evidence of the inward reality of his priesthood authority. Blessings connected to offspring are restored as Eliakim/Christ is made the "father" of all of the house of Judah (see Isaiah 22:21). Eliakim's/Christ's authority to act in the king's name is made complete by the key which is laid upon his shoulder (see Isaiah 22:22). This Davidic key of authority (see Revelation 3:7), connected with power to "open and none shall shut" and to "shut and none shall open" (Isaiah 22:22) points forward to Christ's offering of keys of authority to Peter. Peter is promised that what he binds on earth will be bound in heaven and what he looses on earth will be loosed in heaven (see Matthew 16:15–19).

This symbolic bestowal of authority points most specifically to Christ as evidenced by the permanent nature of the reversal of the effects of the Fall: "And I will fasten him as a nail in a sure place; and he shall be for a glorious throne to his father's house. And they shall hang upon him [Christ] all the glory of his father's house, the offspring and the issue" (Isaiah 22:23–24).

Eliakim/Christ is to be fastened as a "nail in a sure place" in "his father's house" (v. 23). Thus Christ (unlike other humans, for whom the blessings of the covenant are dependent upon continued obedience) is never to be removed from his position in his Father's house, which is located at God's throne in heaven or in the Tabernacle/Temple at his symbolic throne on earth. He is fastened there for all eternity, having overcome for himself forever the spiritual curse which separates man from God.

In addition, these verses state that not only is Eliakim/Christ to be "fasten[ed] as a nail" in his Father's house, he is also to serve as a "glorious throne" in that house, upon which all the blessings, glory, and *"offspring"* (since he is now the father of Judah) "hang" (Isaiah 22:24). All of the future blessings of Judah, the possibilities of overcoming the effects of the Fall and the possibility of their position on a throne (signifying authority) in the house of God "hang" on, or hinge on Christ. Paul brings the symbolism of nailing full circle, centered in Christ's Atonement: "And you, being dead in your sins and the uncircumcision of your flesh, hath he quickened together with him, having forgiven you all trespasses; blotting out the handwriting of ordinances that was against us [i.e., the record of the transgression of laws/ordinances, which transgression causes a loss of blessings], which was contrary to us, and took it out of the way, *nailing* it to his cross" (Colossians 2:13–14).

The supreme act of sacrificial Atonement for mankind's trespasses that caused Christ to be nailed to the cross ensured that he would be secured or "nail[ed] in a sure place" in his Father's house forever. However, as Paul states, this same glorious act also caused Christ to become "sin for us" (2 Corinthians 5:21). The Atonement of Christ laid upon his shoulders the trespasses of all mankind, "nailing [them] to his cross" (Colossians 2:14), and with those trespasses hung all of mankind's potential glory and blessings. Isaiah finished his Christ-centered message in this way: "In that day, saith the Lord of hosts, shall the nail that is fastened in the sure place be removed, and be cut down, and fall; and the burden that was upon it shall be cut off: for the Lord hath spoken it" (Isaiah 22:25). When the nail that held Christ to the cross was removed, his great act of atoning sacrifice was completed. The burden was finished, removed, and cut off from God's sight, so that Christ could be fastened permanently into his Father's house as the throne or foundation of all our hopes in heaven, judging when to open and when to shut or when to reverse the effects of sin and when to leave them intact.

A second example of the Old Testament connection between Christ and restoration of lost blessings through covenants is found in the famous messianic prophecy of Isaiah 53 and makes reference to the burden laid upon Christ's shoulders, as in the previous example. This passage is full of the evidence of the Fall and of the loss of blessings occasioned by apostasy. The effects of a rejected covenant are exemplified in Christ, who will suffer those effects vicariously for all of mankind and restore the covenant relationship between God and all those who are willing to accept his atoning sacrifice. Christ is to grow up out of "dry ground" (v. 2), wherein all the blessings of life and growth have been removed. Notwithstanding the effects of the apostasy and sin around him, he will have life and vitality as a "tender plant" in the midst of a benighted land (v. 2). However, by all external appearances, Christ appears to carry the effects of transgression himself. He has no beauty of form nor comeliness (see v. 2), in contrast to his glorious appearance in the premortal and postmortal life. He appears to be stricken and smitten of God (see v. 4). He is bruised by God, oppressed, full of grief, and cut off from the land of the living (see vv. 3, 7, 10). God has laid transgressions upon his shoulders (see v. 6). He suffers with the same type of "travail" (v. 11) that came to Adam and Eve as a result of their transgression. The very act that causes him to appear smitten and stricken of God is the same act that will ensure the salvation of others. This act causes him to become a father to all the house of Israel as he provides the possibility of the reversal of the effects of the Fall for all mankind. "With his stripes we are healed. . . . When thou shalt make his soul an offering for sin, he shall see his seed, he shall prolong his days, and the pleasure of the Lord shall prosper in his hand" (vv. 5, 10). As in the symbolism of Eliakim, Christ's offering will allow him to serve at the throne (or mercy seat) in his Father's house: "[He] made intercession for the transgressors" (v. 12).

One final example from the prophet Isaiah will further illustrate the connection between Christ, covenants, and priesthood ordinances, as symbolized by the hand, which in this example is the Hebrew word *caph*: "Sing, O heavens; and be joyful, O earth; and break forth into singing, O mountains: for the Lord hath comforted his people, and will have mercy upon his afflicted. But Zion said, The Lord hath forsaken me, and my Lord hath forgotten me" (Isaiah 49:13–14). The curse of affliction is being reversed, but Zion/Israel is still not confident that the Lord will remember her. The memory of her affliction is too fresh and vivid. So, the Lord seeks to convince her of the reality of his love: "Can a woman forget her sucking child, that she should not have compassion on the son of her womb? yea, they may forget, yet will I not forget thee. Behold, I have *graven* thee upon the palms of my hands" (Isaiah 49:15–16; emphasis added). How does the Lord prove to his people that he remembers them and will bless them with joy? He points to a physical reminder or ordinance of the covenant he has made with them. He points to the palms of his hands (*caphím*), upon which he has engraven (*haqqah*) them. The physical engraving of the wounds that remain upon Christ's hands is a physical ordinance (*huqqah*) reminding his people of the reality of his covenant with them. As his physical, resurrected body is a reminder of his spiritual power, so are the wounds in his hands a physical reminder of his love. This engraving/ordinance has been carried out in the palm of his hand (*caph*), symbolizing the power and authority of Christ's consecrated sacrifice, acceptable before Heavenly Father. Heavenly Father "filled Christ's hand" or consecrated and authorized his performance of the Atonement, as symbolized by the wounds in his hands, for the good of all mankind.

This is one of the primary reasons why when Christ appears to the Apostles in Jerusalem and later to the Nephites in the Americas, he first reminds them of the bitter cup from which he has drunk (see 3 Nephi 11:11) and then invites them to touch the wounds in his hands (see 3 Nephi 11:14–15). Those wounds in his resurrected body serve as a palpable, physical reminder to his disciples that Christ remembers his spiritual covenant with them and that God the Father has accepted Christ's sacrifice in their behalf.

CONCLUSION

That Christ has physically engraven us upon his hands reminds us that we must have Christ's image engraven upon our countenances through physical ordinances (see Alma 5:19), which ratify our covenants with the Lord. Therefore, Christ invites us to engage in physical ordinances such as baptism and the sacrament, which remind us of the reality of Christ's atoning sacrifice. These ordinances mark us and who we are as Christ's sacrifice marked him and who he is. They provide outward evidence to all who would come and see of the inner covenant that has been made with Christ. They are also outward symbols ratifying the reversal of the spiritual loss and separation that has come into our lives through sin. We can become connected to Christ through covenants, cemented and made real through ratifying ordinances. And through the Atonement of Christ, we can be forgiven of our sins, be healed of our destitute and barren spiritual condition, be born again, have the Spirit of God with us always, be reunited with Christ, and overcome the distance separating us from God. Again, as the Prophet Joseph Smith said, "Being born again, comes by the Spirit of God *through ordinances*."[18]

The Old Testament testifies eloquently of the necessity of covenants to restore us from our separated state and bring us back into God's presence. Mankind cannot receive the full blessings of God's mercy without making and keeping sacred covenants. Those covenants must be ratified and made efficacious through priesthood ordinances. And those covenants and priesthood ordinances point to and are centered in the example, power, and Atonement of Jesus Christ. It is the power of the Atonement of Christ that allows a full return of blessings lost, that allows ordinances to have real effect in the lives of his disciples, and that will give his disciples power to eventually enter back into the presence of their Heavenly Father.

NOTES

1. Spiros Zodhiates, *The Complete Word Study New Testament* (Chattanooga, TN: AMG Publishers, 1992), 907.

2. Zodhiates, *Complete Word Study New Testament*, 908.

3. Indeed, all writers and scholars have biases and preconceived notions which shape their view of the scriptures. An important key for students of the scriptures is to be aware of their preformed assumptions and to ensure to the best of their

abilities that these viewpoints conform with God's viewpoints. An important step in scripture scholarship is for scholars to be open and forthcoming about their assumptions so that the reader knows what lens is guiding the scholarship.

4. Larry Dahl, ed., *Encyclopedia of Joseph Smith's Teachings* (Salt Lake City: Bookcraft, 1997), "Gospel."

5. For this use of the name Israel when referring to Latter-day Saints, see D&C 103:17. For popular usage and understanding of this concept, see the Latter-day Saint hymn "Israel, Israel, God Is Calling," no. 7; "Hope of Israel," no. 259, and others (*Hymns* [Salt Lake City: The Church of Jesus Christ of Latter-day Saints, 1985]).

6. Famine is clearly used by the prophet Amos to symbolize separation from God. Amos 8:11 declares, "Behold, the days come, saith the Lord God, that I will send a famine in the land, not a famine of bread, nor a thirst for water, but of hearing the words of the Lord." Water is often used as a symbol for spiritual knowledge or revelation in the Old Testament. Habakkuk 2:14 provides an excellent example: "For the earth shall be filled with the knowledge of the glory of the Lord, as the waters cover the sea."

7. Immo Luschin, "Ordinances," in *Encyclopedia of Mormonism*, ed. Daniel H. Ludlow (New York: Macmillan, 1992), 3:1032.

8. *The Brown-Driver-Briggs Hebrew and English Lexicon* (New York: Houghton Mifflin, 1906), 349. It is important to clarify that there are many shades of meaning of the word *ordinance* in English. It can refer to (1) a command or order, (2) a custom or practice established by long usage, (3) a Christian rite, or (4) a statute or regulation. These variations are connected to the Latin meaning of the word, "to set in order." In the King James Version of the Bible, ordinance was translated from the Hebrew word *huqqah*, which indicates something that is engraved. Another Hebrew word, *mishpat*, which is sometimes translated "ordinance" in the King James Version, refers more to the shade of meaning of a statute or regulation. Latter-day Saint usage of the word *ordinance* focuses specifically on the physical act which declares or demonstrates (or physically engraves and sets in order) a priesthood covenant.

9. An excellent example of a spiritual covenant being cemented and made real by a physical act of engraving occurred when the Lord's finger engraved the Ten Commandments upon the stone tablets (see Exodus 31:18).

10. Joseph Smith, *Teachings of the Prophet Joseph Smith*, comp. Joseph Fielding Smith (Salt Lake City: Deseret Book, 1976), 162.

11. Ellen Frankel, *The Encyclopedia of Jewish Symbols* (New Jersey: Jason Aronson, 1992), 70; see also Maurice Farbridge, in *Studies in Biblical and Semitic Symbolism* (E. P. Dutton & Co., 1923), 274–75.

12. James Hastings, *Encyclopedia of Religion and Ethics* (Edinburgh: T&T Clark, 1914), 12:494; see Exodus 28:41, 29:9, 29:33, 32:29; Leviticus 8:33, 16:32, 21:10; Numbers 3:3; Judges 17:5, 17:12; 1 Kings 13:33; 1 Chronicles 29:5, 29:31; Jeremiah 44:25; Ezekiel 43:26. This concept is also supported by E.W. Bulliger, in *Number in Scripture*: "[This] means to *fill the hand*, especially with that which is the sign and symbol of office, *i.e. to fill the hand with a scepter* was to consecrate to the office of king. To fill the hand with certain parts of sacrifices was to set apart for the office of priest, and to

confirm their right to offer both gifts and sacrifices to God. (Ex. 29:22–25, 28:41; 29:9; 32:29; see also Heb. 5:1, 8:3–4.) A ram of 'consecration' (or of filling) was a ram with parts of which the hands of the priests were filled when they were set apart to their office. Whenever the word refers to official appointment, or separation to a work or dignity, it is the sovereign act of God, and the accompanying symbolic act was the filling of the hand of the person so appointed with the sign which marked his office" (Whitefish, MT: Kessinger Publishing, 2003), 145.

13. See Exodus 25:29; Exodus 37:16; Numbers 5:7; Numbers 7:14; 1 Kings 7:50; 2 Chronicles 4:22; 2 Kings 25:14; Jeremiah 52:18–19; 2 Chronicles 24:14.

14. As stated above, there are various words for "hand" in the Hebrew language. The *caph* (palm of the hand) is a part of the *yad* (hand), which in turn may be distinguished as the *yamin* (right hand), each of these having connection with covenants and ordinances. In the scriptures which will be quoted regarding the hand, ordinances, and Christ, only the last, Isaiah 49:15–16, which is the most important reference, utilizes the Hebrew word *caph*. However, all refer to the hand, which, of course, contains the *caph*.

15. Frankel, *Encyclopedia of Jewish Symbols*, 70.

16. While the examples cited here are metaphorical actions, they would only be significant to the Israelites as they represented physically understood realities. Thus the image of God swearing by his right hand would be significant only if the Israelites understood the physical use of the right hand to confirm statements. Examples are found in Genesis 14:22 and Exodus 6:8. Similarly, God holding Israel by the right hand would only be significant if the right hand held special meaning for the Israelites. Examples are found in 2 Kings 10:15, Jeremiah 1:15, and Ezekiel 17:18.

17. In Genesis 3, the symbolism of the coat of skins shows God's willingness to protect Adam and Eve (as the coat would do in the newly fallen world) and provide for them (as he did when he gave them the coat). An understanding of the importance of covenants and ordinances reveals the Lord's tender offering of the coat of skins as a renewal of the covenant and a partial reversal of the curse upon them. The act of clothing Adam and Eve would partially reverse the effects of the Fall, when they "knew that they were naked." Also, the providing of a coat of skins by the Lord after the Fall would certainly have entailed a memorable physical act (or ordinance), cementing and teaching the relationship of God as the protector of Adam and Eve. The physical act would have been even more memorable in a setting where death with all its difficulties and dangers had newly been introduced into the world, along with the need for a protective covering and the ability for the first time to obtain that covering from a slain (possibly sacrificed) animal. Of course, the physical reversal of the curse with a physical covering more importantly represents a symbolic reversal of Adam's and Eve's loss of Edenic glory, reversed symbolically with God's "covering." The spiritual symbolism of the "covering" becomes even more clear when we understand that the word for "atonement" in Hebrew is *kippur*, or "covering." Christ provided for Adam and Eve's Fall, and for our sins, with the "covering" of the Atonement, represented by the coat or "covering" of skins, which clothed and protected Adam and Eve with God's redemptive glory.

18. Smith, *Teachings*, 162.

9

THE PATH OF ANGELS: A BIBLICAL PATTERN FOR THE ROLE OF ANGELS IN PHYSICAL SALVATION

Taylor Halverson

Among the characters that populate the biblical landscape, angels play a particularly noteworthy, though not always fully understood, role. Because of their pervasive presence in the Restoration, we as Latter-day Saints may feel especially familiar with angels and what we see as their work: bearing testimony of Jesus Christ and his gospel. Yet I believe we can expand our understanding of the role of angels through an investigation of select Old Testament passages. What I hope to portray is a pattern of how angels are involved in the physical salvation[1]—or destruction—of individuals and groups so that God's promises can be fulfilled and his purposes can roll forth.

Angels' involvement in physically saving people in order to lead them to God's blessings typically follows the pattern presented below:[2]

1. Someone petitions God (usually in distress).
2. God responds (perhaps God convenes the heavenly council).
3. An authorized messenger is sent (an angel or a prophet).

Taylor Halverson is a faculty consultant for Brigham Young University's Center for Teaching and Learning.

4. The messenger speaks as God's representative (sometimes speaking as God).[3]
5. The messenger commands the petitioner to do something.
6. The messenger conveys God's promises.
7. The petitioner responds to the commands.
8. The messenger saves the petitioner from physical death.
9. The petitioner receives or realizes blessings from God.

This chapter will first briefly review common Latter-day Saint beliefs about the roles of angels. Then I will share the underlying meanings of the scriptural Greek and Hebrew words for *angel*. Second, I will place angels in the context of the ancient Israelite culture, in which they belong to God's heavenly council and serve as his authorized messengers. Fourth, I will review several significant passages in the biblical record that follow, fully or in part, the pattern expressed above, depicting angels delivering messages that save people from death. Finally, I will explain how the Old Testament depiction of angelic roles can add to our understanding of angels' work from the history of the Restoration and the pages of restoration scripture.

RESTORATION PERSPECTIVES ON ANGELS

The modern-day Restoration has acculturated us to certain views and perspectives about angels. Indeed, the Restoration was in many regards constructed revelation-by-revelation through angelic mediation. The angel Moroni instructed Joseph Smith at length on numerous occasions about the plan of God in the latter days (see D&C 2).[4] The sacred location of the Book of Mormon would have remained quietly concealed without Moroni's revelatory disclosure.[5] Other angels heralded the restoration of priesthood keys. Peter, James, and John restored the Melchizedek Priesthood (see D&C 128:20), and John the Baptist the Aaronic Priesthood (see D&C 13).[6] Other angels, including Moses, Elijah, and Elias, appeared to Joseph Smith over time, each to deliver keys and knowledge necessary for the building of God's kingdom (see D&C 110).

The Book of Mormon narrative influences us to feel especially familiar with the role and purpose of angels.[7] We hear of angels visiting both Jacob (see 2 Nephi 9:3) and King Benjamin (see Mosiah 3:1–3) with heavenly testimony of the gospel and Jesus Christ. Or we might think of the angel who visited Alma the Younger at various stages in his life. As a rebellious youth, Alma was struck dumb by the thunderous voice of an angel (see Mosiah 27:11–12). Yet in later righteous years, that same angelic voice penetrated Alma's heart with words of blessing (see Alma 8:14–17). These few episodes from the Book of Mormon underscore our perspective that angels convey the word of God to mankind. In this regard, the passage that "angels speak by the power of the Holy Ghost; wherefore, they speak the words of Christ" (2 Nephi 32:3) dominates the Latter-day Saint perspective on the function of angels.

Thus Restoration scripture has given us the understanding that angels testify of the gospel and of Jesus Christ, share priesthood keys and powers to further the work of God, and deliver God's promises to the faithful. This study proposes, through an investigation of select Old Testament texts, to expand our perspective of the role of angels to allow us to see that angels were also authorized by God to physically save or destroy individuals or groups so that God's promises and purposes could be realized.

"Angels"—Definitions from Two Languages

The English word *angel* derives from the Greek *aggelos*, which means "messenger."[8] *Aggelos* is based on the root verb *aggello*, which means "to tell, to inform."[9] These definitions suggest that the basic role of an *aggelos* is to deliver a message.

As helpful as these Greek definitions are (especially since we can readily see the linguistic connection between the English *angel* and the Greek *aggelos*), the Old Testament was not written in Greek, but rather in Hebrew.[10] So what is the underlying Hebrew word for our English translation of angel? *Mal'ach*.[11] The basic definition of the agent noun *mal'ach* is "one who is sent forth," usually with a message.[12] As we saw with the Greek definition of *aggelos*, the term *mal'ach* is sufficiently straightforward to declare the primary function of an angel—one who goes forth with a message.

We should highlight that the Greek *aggelos* and the Hebrew *mal'ach* make no distinction between heavenly or earthly messengers. The Old Testament refers to God's authorized messengers as *mal'achim* whether they are of heavenly origin (which in our day we consider to be angels) or of earthly origin (some Old Testament prophets fill the role).[13] It wasn't until Jerome's late fourth century AD Latin translation of the Bible (the Vulgate) that an attempt was made to distinguish between heavenly messengers (Latin *angelus*) and earthly messengers (Latin *nuntius*).[14]

In this study, I confine my investigation to deal only with passages where a *mal'ach* is part of the story. Hence, I do not consider cherubim, seraphim, sons of God, or holy ones as angels, because, from a linguistic standpoint, none of them is a *mal'ach*, or messenger. With this rather pedestrian understanding of the meaning of the word *angel*—a messenger—what message do these messengers convey? Who sends them on their errand? And for what purpose?

ANGELS IN GOD'S HEAVENLY COUNCIL

Ancient Israelites believed that God resided in heaven, surrounded by his heavenly council.[15] Just as a royal court consists of different members with different roles and purposes (e.g., counselor, messenger, jester, warrior, or bodyguard), so too God's heavenly court was composed of a variety of heavenly beings. According to the Old Testament, God's heavenly council consisted of beings such as the sons of God (see Psalm 89:7; Job 38:7), gods (see Psalms 58:1[16]; 82:1[17]; 97:7; 138.1), the stars (see Job 38:7), members of the council of God (see Job 15:8), members of the assembly of holy ones (see Psalm 89:5–6[18]; Job 5:1[19]), ministers (see Psalm 103:21), prophets (see Amos 3:7), and angels.[20]

Angels participated in the heavenly council as plenipotentiary messengers. Their role included serving as mediators, guardians, servants to beings of higher rank in the council (called "gods" in Psalms),[21] and spokespersons for the council. Angels depicted in the Old Testament primarily served the great Master of the court, Jehovah; they acted in his name, conveyed his messages, and did his will to bring either physical salvation or physical destruction to people, being commissioned in the council to do so.

According to some ancient texts,[22] God's heavenly council functioned in the following way: God assembled the members of his council whenever there was an issue to discuss and a decision to be made. Next, God carefully listened to the various proposals and then rendered a decision. It was at this point that an angel (or a prophet)[23] who had participated in the heavenly council was commissioned to go forth from the heavenly council in God's name and share on earth whatever had been decreed in heaven, whether unto physical salvation or death.[24]

A rare but valuable scriptural description of God's heavenly council is found in 1 Kings 22 (see especially verses 19–23). In this chapter, wicked king Ahab contemplates going to war against his enemies. Ahab gathers together his hundreds of prophets, who all predict success. However, these prophets are afflicted with a lying spirit—they say whatever the king wants to hear. Another prophet, Micaiah, who has been commissioned of the Lord, comes to the royal court and describes that he has participated in God's heavenly council. Micaiah risks his life by sharing the message decreed in God's heavenly council of Ahab's physical destruction: Ahab would die in battle. Sure enough, Ahab dismisses Micaiah's warning, goes forth to battle (in disguise), and is killed by an errant arrow (see 1 Kings 22:34–38).

Angels as Agents of Physical Salvation or Destruction in the Old Testament

With these angelic perspectives and definitions, we will now examine seven Old Testament stories that display or at least play on the pattern presented above, highlighting the crucial role angels perform to physically protect someone so that God's promises might be fulfilled or, on the other hand, to destroy people who threaten God's purposes.

The angel of the Lord saves Hagar (see Genesis 16).

Then Sarai dealt harshly with [Hagar], and she ran away from her.

The angel of the Lord found her by a spring of water in the wilderness. . . .

And he said, "Hagar, slave-girl of Sarai, where have you come from and where are you going?"

She said, "I am running away from my mistress Sarai."

The angel of the Lord said to her, "Return to your mistress, and submit to her."

The angel of the Lord also said to her, "I will so greatly multiply your offspring that they cannot be counted for multitude."

And the angel of the Lord said to her, "Now you have conceived and shall bear a son; you shall call him Ishmael, for the Lord has given heed to your affliction. . . .

So she named the Lord who spoke to her, "You are El-roi"; for she said, "Have I really seen God and remained alive after seeing him?" (New Revised Standard Version, Genesis 16:6–11, 13)

This passage represents the first biblical appearance of an angel. In studying how well it stacks up against the proposed pattern of angelic intervention, we find that it contains, implicitly or explicitly, all nine features of the pattern. First, Hagar is in distress, though no explicit petition to the Lord is cited. Nevertheless, God responds to her grievance by sending forth a messenger who speaks authoritatively for him. Following a short interrogation as to why Hagar fled, the angel commands her to return and submit to Sarah. Then the angel pronounces the stunning promise, "I will so greatly multiply your offspring that they cannot be counted for multitude" (v. 10).

The angel's appearance and blessing evoke two surprises, one for us and one for Hagar. Most of us are familiar with the language of blessing as it pertains to the Abrahamic promise, but we may be surprised to hear that Hagar receives the same promise of a multitude of offspring as Abraham. Upon further reflection, we see this connection as entirely logical and necessary—those who bear Abraham's seed have the same promises extended to them of countless multitudes of descendants. Without Sarah,[25] Hagar, and Keturah, the promises so often associated with Abraham can never be realized. As if to underscore the future reality of Hagar's multitudinous offspring, the angel announces that Hagar is pregnant with a child who shall be named Ishmael ("God hears"), a name fitting to memorialize God's hearing her in her afflictions.

The other surprise is for Hagar. So thoroughly does this angel represent the Lord, that Hagar mistakenly believes she has seen God.[26] After the angel leaves, Hagar questions, "Have I really seen God and remained alive after seeing him?" (v. 13). Notice that Hagar is surprised that she is still alive. The common conception in Old Testament times was that no one could see the face of God and live; at the very least, anyone who did come into the presence of God would have felt the vast difference between the overwhelming holiness of the Lord and his or her own thorough uncleanliness (compare Isaiah in his theophany recorded in Isaiah 6:1–6). What we are to conclude from her statement is that so fully does the angel authoritatively represent the Lord that Hagar believes that she has encountered the Lord himself.

The conclusion of this episode is that the angel saves the life of Hagar and, by extension, the lives of all members of Abraham's posterity descended through her. Had Hagar not obeyed the command to return to the tent of Abraham and submit to the hand of Sarah, she likely would have famished in the wilderness. The angel's message and Hagar's adherence to that message are the means of Hagar's personal, physical preservation. Her obedience helps realize God's mighty promises. Had she failed to heed the angel's admonition to be humble, she never would have realized (in the fullest sense) the promised blessings.

Angels save Lot from Sodom's destruction (see Genesis 18–19). The next instance of angelic intervention occurs in Genesis 18–19. Three men visit Abraham in Genesis 18 to reiterate the promise that he will inherit a large posterity.[27] Due to ambiguities in the text, it seems that the three men are the Lord and two angels. As the narrative progresses, the Lord stops to counsel with Abraham concerning the impending destruction of Sodom and Gomorrah (see vv. 17–33). Meanwhile, the men who have come to visit Abraham continue their journey (see v. 22) to Sodom and Gomorrah as messengers of physical salvation and destruction for the inhabitants of the cities. Those who heed the messengers' warning (Lot and his family) are temporally saved, while those who reject the messengers are duly destroyed. Similar to Hagar's story, the evidence is clear that angels play a significant part in the physical salvation of God's chosen people.

This episode fulfills all nine elements of angelic intervention. In Genesis 18 there is an outcry to God because of the wickedness at Sodom and Gomorrah (see v. 20). God responds by sending angels[28] to Sodom (see vv. 20–22), who say that the Lord has sent them to destroy the city (see Genesis 19:13).[29] However, in Genesis 19 when the angels command Lot to take his family and get out of town (see v. 15), Lot lingers.[30] When the angels see Lot lingering, they physically drag him and his family out of the city. This is the second time in as many days that the angels have to touch Lot to literally save him (they had dragged him into his house the night before to save him from the angry mob; see vv. 9–11).

In most instances, someone is saved not because an angel reaches out and touches them but rather because they respond in faith to the commands of God. And by so responding to God, they remove themselves from harm's way or return to an environment of protection. The analogy here is that God calls us to "come unto him" (Alma 5:34–36) but will not force us into his arms (see Mormon 6:17). However, in Lot's circumstance, the situation is apparently sufficiently dire and his response sufficiently tardy that the angels pull him out of danger. This is physical salvation at its best.

The pattern of angelic involvement continues. The angels command Lot to escape to Zoar and not look back (see vv. 15, 17, 22), promising him safety there (see v. 21). Finally, Lot heeds the message, flees to Zoar, and secures the blessing of life (see vv. 21, 29).

In summary, what we learn from Lot's story is that God will send forth his angels to warn. Those who heed the warnings achieve physical safety and see the blessings of God realized in their lives, even if it is the most basic (and yet the most precious) of all God's blessings—life itself. On the other hand, those who do not heed the message of God's messengers are wiped out, such as Lot's sons-in-law, the wicked inhabitants of Sodom, and even Lot's wife, who at first heeds the angelic message but then turns and rejects it to her own salty demise.

The angel of God saves Hagar and Ishmael (see Genesis 21). Some years after Hagar's first encounter with an angel, she once again faces death in a trackless wilderness because of conflict with Sarah. Sarah does not want Hagar's son Ishmael to receive the family inheritance (see v. 10), so she requires Abraham to thrust Hagar out to secure Isaac's position as the child of the promise (see v. 10). Abraham reluctantly sends Hagar on her way only after the Lord tells Abraham to hearken to the voice of his wife (see v. 12).

After wandering for some time in the desert until her food and water are spent, Hagar casts Ishmael under a bush (see v. 15) while she sits a ways off not wanting to see him die. In this dire situation, God hears the boy crying. He sends an angel to call out to Hagar from heaven to reclaim the boy, reminding her of his original promise that Ishmael would be a great nation (see vv. 17–18). God opens her eyes and she sees a well of water that quenches their thirst and saves them from death (v. 19).

This episode fulfills all the elements of the pattern; the angel speaks for God (see v. 17), renews God's promises to Hagar, and delivers a message that requires action on her part to secure physical salvation for herself and her son (see v. 18). When her eyes are opened to see the well of water, she goes forth to drink and shares with her son to stave off his death in the desert (see v. 19). The reward for responding faithfully to God's angel-delivered message was immediate salvation from physical death (see v. 19) and the eventual fulfillment of Ishmael's portion of the Hagar-Abrahamic promises: "And God was with the lad" (v. 20). Just as we see in the first passage of angelic intervention in Hagar's life, had she not listened and responded to the angel, she would have died in the desert with Ishmael and thus forfeited the grand promises as coheir with Abraham.

The angel of the Lord saves Isaac (see Genesis 22). The *Akedah* story, also known as "the Binding of Isaac" or "the Sacrifice of Isaac," is one of the most memorable stories in scripture. It provides both a foundation for discussing the principles of faith, obedience, and sacrifice and a foreshadowing of the sacrifice of Jesus Christ. With remarkable reticence, the nearly tragic story is told with minimal detail and in a vacuum of emotion. These narrative features heighten the intensity of the near-death drama when Abraham's hand is raised to strike his son with the fatal blow of sacrificial slaughter (see v. 10). Just when the unimaginable is about to happen, and in what appears to be a last-second voice of salvation, an angel of the Lord calls out from heaven to Abraham, "Lay not thine hand upon the lad" (v. 12). Abraham hearkens to the voice of God's messenger, the crisis is averted, and the victory of faith is assured (see v. 13).

Because of Abraham's unswerving righteousness in an enormously difficult spiritual test replete with the traumatic horrors of memories past,[31] the angel of the Lord calls out to Abraham a second time with promises as great as the stars of heaven: "By myself have I sworn, saith the Lord, for because thou hast done this thing, and hast not withheld thy son, thine only son: That in blessing I will bless thee, and in multiplying I will multiply thy seed as the stars of the heaven, and as the sand which is upon the sea shore; and thy seed shall possess the gate of his enemies; And in thy seed shall all the nations of the earth be blessed; because thou hast obeyed my voice" (Genesis 22:16–18).

In this episode, God sends forth an angel, who gives a command speaking *as* God; Abraham dutifully obeys; and Isaac's physical salvation is secured (see vv. 11–13). God's promises to Abraham are renewed (see vv. 16–18) and can now be fulfilled because Isaac has survived.[32]

The notable observation that this pattern points out to us is that the angel of the Lord is the agent who physically saves the righteous, so long as they hearken to his message. Those who heed God's voice will receive the magnanimous blessings promised by the messenger. We also see that God tests the faithful to the very limits of physical existence. He then reaches out to save them through his commissioned angels. Finally, he grants blessings of an eternal nature to those who accept physical salvation.

The angel of God saves the Israelites from the Egyptians (see Exodus 14). The biblical episodes reviewed so far have centered on the physical salvation of a specific individual (Hagar, Ishmael, Isaac) or a small group (Lot and his family) and the blessings promised to, or secured for, them for faithfully hearkening to the voice of an angel. In this next passage, a version of the pattern appears, but this time the beneficiary is the entire host of Israel, while Moses and the angel of the Lord share the responsibility of being the Lord's messenger.

In Exodus 14, the Israelites are fleeing the Egyptian army. Finding themselves hemmed in between the sea and Pharaoh's deadly fighting force, the Israelites cry out to the Lord in complaint against Moses, believing that he has led them into a death trap (see vv. 10–11). However, instead of death, the Israelites find physical salvation through the mediation of the angel of the Lord: "And the angel of God, which went before the camp of Israel, removed and went behind them; and the pillar of the cloud went from before their face, and stood behind them: And it came between the camp of the Egyptians and the camp of Israel; and it was a cloud and darkness to them, but it gave light by night to these: so that the one came not near the other all the night" (Exodus 14:19–20).

The angel of the Lord stands between the Egyptian armies and the Israelites, casting darkness upon the former and bringing light to the latter. The Israelites are protected throughout the night from the onslaught of the Egyptian army. The next day, Moses stretches his hand out over the sea, and the Israelites pass through unmolested, while the pursuing Egyptians, to the very last, are sunk in the depths of the sea (see

Exodus 14:21–31). So concludes what is likely the foundational moment of Israelite identity. God's promises to Abraham of posterity and property[33] would have been entirely overthrown had the angel not physically protected the Lord's people from the advancing Egyptians.

What is slightly different in this angelic episode from the others we have reviewed is that the Israelites are physically tested to the limits and then asked to hearken to the words of Moses and not a *mal'ach*, or angel (see v. 16). God commands Moses to tell the people to move forward (see vv. 15–16), which provides the opportunity for the people to demonstrate faith in God's word and claim physical salvation and, by extension, the promises to Abraham's posterity. Although Moses is not explicitly called a *mal'ach* in this story, he plays the role of a *mal'ach*, an angel, a divinely authorized messenger who comes in a time of crisis, bearing a message from God that, if acted upon, will lead to physical salvation.

The angel of the Lord saves Jerusalem (see Isaiah 37). The next example we will consider comes from the time of the prophet Isaiah and the righteous king Hezekiah of Judah (circa 701 BC). The narrative is repeated in both Isaiah 37 and 2 Kings 19.[34] The historical context is that the mighty Assyrian army has advanced against Jerusalem with more than 185,000 troops to subject Hezekiah's kingdom to paying tribute. The point is forcefully clear: Jerusalem faces imminent destruction. Up against this fearsome army and with surrender appearing to be the only option for physical deliverance, Hezekiah bows in fervent prayer (see vv. 15–20). He pleads that God might save his people and use that victory so that "all the kingdoms of the earth may know that thou art the Lord" (v. 20).

In response to Hezekiah's prayer, the prophet Isaiah delivers a message as the mouth of God, playing the role of an angel as God's emissary, much like Moses had done during the Exodus: "Then Isaiah the son of Amoz sent unto Hezekiah, saying, Thus saith the Lord God of Israel, Whereas thou hast prayed to me against Sennacherib king of Assyria . . . , He shall not come into this city, nor shoot an arrow there, nor come before it with shields, nor cast a bank against it. By the way that he came, by the same shall he return, and shall not come into this city, saith the Lord. For I will defend this city to save it for mine own sake, and for my servant David's sake" (Isaiah 37:21, 33–35). True to his promises, God sends an angel that very night to destroy the Assyrian army: "Then the angel of the

Lord went forth, and smote in the camp of the Assyrians a hundred and fourscore and five thousand: and when they arose early in the morning, behold, they were all dead corpses" (Isaiah 37:36).

This episode has some interesting connections to and variants from the pattern we have seen so far. Similar to some of the other angelic stories, God's faithful people call out to him in their distress (see vv. 15–20). He responds to them verbally through his appointed messenger (see vv. 21–35). As in the Exodus story, a prophet plays the role of the appointed messenger conveying God's message. Still, it is the angel of the Lord (or God himself in the Exodus story) that brings the physical ruin of the enemy army (see v. 36). Promises from God are declared (see vv. 33–35), and the people are physically saved (see v. 36). What is significantly different in this passage is that neither Hezekiah nor the people are required to act on any of God's words to partake of physical salvation. In previous examples, an individual (Hagar, Lot) or a group (the children of Israel) have had to act and follow through with a command from God's messenger in order to realize the physical salvation made possible by the words and deeds of the angel. But in this case, God declares that he will defend Jerusalem for his *own* sake and for the sake of promises to *one individual*, King David. As the scripture records, God does defend Jerusalem. Physical salvation comes at the hands of the angel of the Lord who goes through the camp of the Assyrians destroying everyone but the Assyrian king and a few others who escape to tell the tale.

Malachi (my messenger) comes again to save God's people (see Malachi 4). This study concludes with one final example that demonstrates how important angels are in physically saving God's people. Significantly, this example also links us as readers to the pattern of angels' role in physical salvation demonstrated in other biblical passages. The prophetic book of Malachi (especially chapter 4)[35] holds prominence in Latter-day Saint thought and theology because Christ quoted it to the Nephites (see 3 Nephi 25), the angel Moroni employed it as a textbook to train Joseph Smith on the Restoration, and we understand the latter days in part through the lens of these passages.

Significant to the overall discussion presented in this study is the fact that the name *Malachi* may not even be the real name of the prophet, but rather his title. As can readily be seen, the name *Malachi* is directly related to the Hebrew word *mal'ach* (messenger, angel). *Malachi* means "my messenger" or "my angel." What more appropriate title could there be for a prophetic book that speaks of God calling out to his people in the last days to heed his messengers and be saved (first physically and then spiritually)?

Let us take a moment to see how well Malachi 4 matches the pattern of angelic intervention that has guided us so far:

> For, behold, the day cometh, that shall burn as an oven; and all the proud, yea, and all that do wickedly, shall be stubble: and the day that cometh shall burn them up, saith the Lord of hosts, that it shall leave them neither root nor branch.
>
> But unto you that fear my name shall the Sun of righteousness arise with healing in his wings; and ye shall go forth, and grow up as calves of the stall.
>
> And ye shall tread down the wicked; for they shall be ashes under the soles of your feet in the day that I shall do this, saith the Lord of hosts.
>
> Remember ye the law of Moses my servant, which I commanded unto him in Horeb for all Israel, with the statutes and judgments.
>
> Behold, I will send you Elijah the prophet before the coming of the great and dreadful day of the Lord:
>
> And he shall turn the heart of the fathers to the children, and the heart of the children to their fathers, lest I come and smite the earth with a curse. (Malachi 4:1–6)

Although there is no explicit petition to God of distress, it may be implicit in verse 2. God's response may be contained in the sending of two authorized messengers: Moses in verse 4 and Elijah in verses 5–6. Both of these messengers of God are important to the salvation of God's people in the final days. Those who heed God's command to remember the law of Moses (see v. 3) will be prepared to accept the message of Elijah (see vv. 5–6), thus avoiding physical death at the burning destruction awaiting the wicked who reject God (see vv. 1, 5–6).

What makes this example so important is that *we* in the present day are brought into the Old Testament narrative and into the pattern of angelic intervention. Significantly, two elements in the pattern ("the

Episode	Passage	1. Someone petitions God	2. God responds	3. Authorized messenger is sent
The angel of the Lord saves Hagar	Genesis 16:6–15	Implicit in Gen. 16:6	Implicit in Gen. 16:7	Gen 16:7
Angels save Lot from Sodom's destruction	Genesis 18–19	Gen. 18:20	Gen. 18:20	Gen. 18:21–22
The angel of God saves Hagar and Ishmael	Genesis 21:14–20	Gen. 21:16–17	Implicit in Gen. 21:17	Gen. 21:17
The angel of the Lord saves Isaac	Genesis 22:1–19	(Perhaps implicit in Genesis 22:9–10)	Implicit in Gen. 21:11	Gen. 22:11
The angel of God saves the Israelites from the Egyptians	Exodus 14:10–28	Ex. 14:10	Ex. 14:15–18	Ex. 14:19–20
The angel of the Lord saves Jerusalem	Isaiah 37	Isaiah 37:15–20	Implicit in Isaiah 37:21	Isaiah 37:21–35
Malachi ("my messenger") comes to save God's people in the latter days	Malachi 4	(Perhaps implicit in Mal. 4:2)	Implicit in Mal. 4:2	Mal. 4:5–6

petitioner responds to the commands" and "the messenger saves the petitioner from physical death") are not found directly in the scripture; they are awaiting fulfillment from us. It is now time for the people of the latter days to respond to God's heavenly council and realize the blessings he has in store for the faithful. Just as the faithful in the Old Testament realize physical salvation if they heed the words of angels, so too do people in the latter days find physical deliverance from the burning oven on the "great and dreadful day of the Lord" if they respond faithfully to God's messengers (see v. 3).

CONCLUDING THOUGHTS ON THE ROLE OF ANGELS IN THE OLD TESTAMENT

Although a thorough investigation of every Old Testament passage referencing angels is not possible here, a definite pattern emerges from the passages presented. Angels are the Lord's divinely commissioned messengers, authorized to speak the will of the Lord in response to human crisis. They provide people an opportunity to faithfully respond to

4. Messenger speaks as God's representative	5. Command to act	6. Promises made	7. Petitioner responds	8. Salvation from death	9. Blessings realized
Gen. 16:10, 13	Gen. 16:9, 11	Gen. 16:10	Implicit in Gen. 16:15	Implicit in Gen. 16:15	Gen. 16:15
Gen. 19:13	Gen. 19:15, 17, 22	Gen. 19:17, 21	Gen. 19:16, 20, 23	Gen. 19:10, 16, 25, 28–29	Gen. 19:20–21, 29
Gen. 21:17	Gen. 21:17–18	Gen. 21:18	Gen. 21:19	Gen. 21:20	Gen. 21:20
Gen. 22:12, 16	Gen. 22:12	Gen. 22:17–19	Gen. 22:13	Gen. 22:13	Gen. 22:19
NO	Ex. 14:16	Ex. 14:14	Ex. 14:22	Ex. 14:29–31	Ex. 14:27–28
Isaiah 37:33–35	NO	Isaiah 37:33–35	NO; God acts for his sake and David's sake.	Isaiah 37:36	Implicit in Isaiah 37:36
Perhaps Mal. 4:3	Mal. 4:3–4	Mal. 4:1, 5–6	Yet to be written. It's our day. We have to respond.	Mal 4:1, 6	Implicit in Mal. 4:6

God's message and thereby be saved from some physical calamity. The passages we have reviewed are stories of God's chosen people, encountering moments of crisis where life is threatened. Their faithful response to God's urgent angelic messengers has meant the difference between life and death. Their faithful response has also meant the difference between their claiming or forfeiting, for themselves and their descendants, God's Abrahamic promises; for who can claim the promises of property and posterity if death closes in before either is achieved?

Finally, it is important to connect the work of angels in the Old Testament to angelic work throughout the scriptures. Though the pattern of angelic intervention in the Old Testament appears to focus heavily on saving people from physical calamity, compared to Restoration scriptures where angels openly preach the gospel and testify of Jesus Christ, the evidence presented here has also strongly demonstrated that physical salvation is first and foremost necessary for claiming spiritual salvation. Alma clearly and succinctly teaches this truth: "And we see that death comes upon mankind, yea, the death which has been spoken of by Amulek, which is the temporal death; nevertheless there was a space granted unto man in which he might repent; therefore this life became a probationary state; a time to prepare to meet God; a time to prepare for that endless state which has been spoken of by us, which is after the resurrection of the dead" (Alma 12:24).

Those moments of crisis in the Old Testament provide God's people an opportunity to be tested, to choose life or death (in quite a literal sense). Those who physically survive these crises because they faithfully respond to God's authorized messengers can then lay claim to far greater spiritual promises from God.

NOTES

1. Please note that my use of "physical salvation" in this paper can also be understood as "temporal salvation." Furthermore, my use of the terms "physical salvation" and "physical destruction" do not necessarily connote bodily contact between angels and humans.

2. See above the matrix display of this pattern set against the seven Old Testament passages discussed in this study.

3. The doctrine of divine investiture of authority can help us to understand how and why angels or prophets speak as God. The doctrine of divine investiture of authority, in its simplest expression, means that God's representative (whether Jesus Christ, an angel, or a prophet) speaks as though God himself were present. So fully do they represent God that it is not always possible to ascertain whether God or his representative is present (James E. Talmage, *Articles of Faith* [Salt Lake City: Deseret Book, 1981], 424).

4. Joseph Smith, *History of the Church of Jesus Christ of Latter-day Saints*, ed. B. H. Roberts, 2nd ed. rev. (Salt Lake City: Deseret Book, 1980), 1:9–16.

5. Smith, *History of the Church*, 1:11–13.

6. Smith, *History of the Church*, 1:39–41.

7. For an accessible and thoughtful summary of the role of angels in the Book of Mormon, see Mary Jane Woodger, "The Restoration of the Doctrine of Angels as Found in the Book of Mormon," in *The Book of Mormon: The Foundation of Our Faith*, ed. Joseph F. McConkie and others (Salt Lake City: Deseret Book, 1999), 257–70.

8. J. P. Louw and E. A. Nida, eds., *Louw-Nida Greek-English Lexicon of the New Testament Based on Semantic Domains*, 2nd ed. (New York: United Bible Societies, 1988), s.v. "aggelos."

9. Louw and Nida, *Greek-English Lexicon*, s.v. "aggello."

10. More precisely, the Old Testament was written in Hebrew, with a few sections written in Aramaic: Genesis 31:47 (just two words); Ezra 4:8–68 and 7:12–26; Jeremiah 10:11; and Daniel 2:4–7:28.

11. Francis Brown, S. R. Driver, and Charles Briggs, eds., *Hebrew-Aramaic and English Lexicon of the Old Testament* (Peabody, MA: Hendrickson Publishers, 1996), s.v. "mal'ach." Please note that *mal'ach* is not related to the Hebrew *malak/melek*. The former refers to a messenger, the latter to a king or ruler. Though English transliterations of these two words appear to be related, they are based on entirely different Semitic root words: *l'k* ("to send") versus *mlk* ("to rule, govern").

12. Though the Hebrew root word *l'k* ("to send") does not appear in the Old Testament, it does exist in other Semitic languages related to Hebrew (such as Ugaritic). We can feel fairly confident that the root word either existed in ancient Hebrew or that the ancient Israelites borrowed the word from their surrounding Semitic environment.

13. In Greek translations of the Old Testament, such as the Septuagint, the Hebrew *mal'ach* is often translated as the Greek *aggelos*.

14. David Noel Freedman, ed., *The Anchor Bible Dictionary* (New York: Doubleday, 1992), s.v. "Angels (Old Testament)."

15. For a lengthy description of the divine council in Ugaritic and Hebrew literature, see E. Theodore Mullen Jr., *The Divine Council in Canaanite and Early Hebrew Literature* (Chico, CA: Scholars Press, 1980).

16. The Hebrew word *'elim* (gods) is translated in the King James Version (KJV) as "congregation."

17. The Hebrew word *'el* (God) is translated in the KJV as "mighty," hence this passage could also read "congregation of God."

18. The Hebrew word *k'doshim* (holy ones) is translated in the KJV as "saints" in this passage.

19. The Hebrew word for "holy ones" is translated in the KJV as "saints" in this passage as well.

20. Over the centuries, the concept of angel was erroneously applied to all beings who resided in God's heavenly court, even though, from a technical standpoint, these other beings were not angels. That being the case, the Old Testament passages analyzed in this study do not include passages that refer to "sons of God," "holy ones," or "ministers," because these heavenly beings are not technically angels.

21. Sang Youl Cho, *Lesser Deities in the Ugaritic Texts and the Hebrew Bible: A Comparative Study of Their Nature and Roles* (Piscataway, NJ: Gorgias Press, 2007), 137.

22. Examples of ancient texts that portray the heavenly council are the Old Babylonian *Enuma Elish*, the Ugaritic *Kirta* epic, and Psalm 89:6–9. For a concise summary of the heavenly council in ancient thought, see Freedman, *Anchor Bible Dictionary*, s.v. "Divine Assembly."

23. The heavenly council is sometimes called in Hebrew *sod* ("council, assembly, secret counsel"). Therefore, the well-known passage in Amos 3:7, "Surely the Lord God will do nothing, but he revealeth his secret unto his servants the prophets," envisions a scenario where a prophet participates in the heavenly council (Hebrew *sod*) and then is commissioned to share (or reveal) the council's decision.

24. See especially the discussion in the section "The Messenger of the Council and the Prophet" in Mullen, *The Divine Council in Canaanite and Early Hebrew Literature*, 209–26, where Mullen provides substantial evidence that God's messengers,

whether angels or prophets, stand in the heavenly council, hear God's pronounce-
ments, and then are sent forth with authority to share the divine pronouncement
in the name of God.

25. In addition to blessing Hagar and Abraham, God also blessed Sarah in a revelation to Abraham: "I will bless her, and she shall be a mother of nations; kings of
people shall be of her" (Genesis 17:16).

26. Admittedly, the biblical text is a bit ambiguous about who exactly Hagar is communicating with (we see a similar vagueness in Genesis 18 and 19). The text indicates
that the angel of the Lord communicated with Hagar (see Genesis 16:9–11), and yet
the angel of the Lord speaks as though the Lord himself is speaking: "I will multiply
thy seed exceedingly" (Genesis 16:10). We see a similar situation of textual ambiguity
in 2 Kings 18:17–37 in the story of the Assyrian Rabshakeh who is sent to convince
Hezekiah through parley to submit to the Assyrian emperor. Rabshakeh (literally
"cup-bearer") was the plenipotentiary representative of the Assyrian emperor. As he
attempts to convince Hezekiah to submit to Assyria, Rabshakeh slips in and out of
speaking in the first person on behalf of his master and speaking in the first person
on behalf of himself. When we read this story, it is clear that the Assyrian emperor is
not personally present, even though his representative is speaking as though he were.
So too in the stories of the angel of the Lord, the Lord himself is not personally present, but is fully, authentically, and authoritatively represented by his divinely chosen
messenger.

27. In interesting contrast with Hagar's reception of God's promises through angelic intermediation, God communicated promises to Abraham directly, without
the medium of an intermediary—by direct verbal encounter (see Genesis 12 and 13),
through a lucid vision (see Genesis 15), and by a personal visitation (see Genesis 17).
Not until Genesis 18 does God involve other heavenly beings to convey his promises
to Abraham.

28. According to Joseph Smith Translation, Genesis 19:1, *three* angels arrive in
Sodom. We cannot be entirely certain who the three angels are, though it is reasonable to suppose that they are the three men who visited Abraham in Genesis 18.
Elder Bruce R. McConkie taught that these three angels were the First Presidency
of that day (*Doctrinal New Testament Commentary* [Salt Lake City: Bookcraft, 1965–73],
3:235).

29. Though both cities were marked for destruction, the angels visited only
Sodom because only in that city were there any righteous to be saved (Lot and his
family).

30. As an instructive comparison, think of how the Book of Mormon story might
have been different, or nonexistent, had Lehi lingered in Jerusalem!

31. As a young man, Abraham himself had been bound to an altar of sacrifice
because of his father (Terah). It was only by a last-minute intervention of divine
proportions that Abraham was delivered from a gruesome death on the altar of
priestcraft. Just as in the story of Isaac's deliverance from the altar, it was an angel of
the Lord who saved Abraham from physical death and then made promises to him
of greatness, priesthood, and posterity (see Abraham 1:1–20).

32. It may be that Isaac, Abraham, and Sarah were all silently pleading to God that Isaac would be saved.

33. In the Old Testament, God's promises to Abraham of property and posterity are primarily found in Genesis 12, 13, 15, 17, and 22.

34. For the sake of simplicity, I will work just with the Isaiah 37 text and not address the authorial and text-critical issues of comparing these two accounts.

35. In our KJV Bibles, Malachi is the final book of the Old Testament. However, in the Hebrew Bible, the final book of the Old Testament is Chronicles.

10

"HOW EXCELLENT IS THY LOVINGKINDNESS": THE GOSPEL PRINCIPLE OF *HESED*

Dan Belnap

The concept of *hesed* (pronounced *khesed*)[1] is unfamiliar to most Bible readers. This is partly due to the fact that it is a Hebrew word; thus we will never come across the word *hesed* anywhere in our King James English Version (KJV); moreover, the term is difficult to translate, the KJV providing no less than fifteen different terms to signify the presence of *hesed* in the text, the most common being "mercy," "kindness," and "loving-kindness."[2] Yet the principle of *hesed* may be one of the most important doctrinal concepts in the Old Testament, as it appears 245 times in the Hebrew Bible and embodies both the manner in which Israel was expected to act and the true nature of God. Thus, by studying the *hesed* references within their contexts and discerning the pattern in which this gospel principle is revealed, we can recognize its importance, particularly through its emphasis on acts of deliverance in the Old Testament narratives and its insight on what it means to be like God in our own personal journeys toward salvation.[3]

Dan Belnap is an assistant professor of ancient scripture at Brigham Young University.

Before we get into the references, we need to note some basics. To begin, *hesed* is a noun. Moreover, *hesed* is often the object of the sentence, not the subject; thus the verb that precedes *hesed* is an important indicator as to what *hesed* is. While not every *hesed* reference is found in a verb-object relationship, of those that are, the vast majority follow the verb *asah*, translated in the KJV as "shew(-eth, -ed, etc.)." This term, however, is the common Hebrew verb meaning "to do, to make, to perform"; thus when translating *asah* with *hesed* as the object, it is more correct to say that one "does" *hesed*.[4] Also important is the predominance of God as the one who does *hesed*. Of the 245 references, two-thirds of them either describe God as one who does *hesed* or are praises to God because he does *hesed*. Of the remaining third, about half of those also mention *hesed* in connection with God. Thus *hesed* is clearly associated with the divine and may even be used to define godly experience. Yet, though it is a predominantly divine action, *hesed* can be done by mortals, and this suggests that *hesed* is a characteristic common to both natures. Of course, these details still have not told us exactly what *hesed* is. Thus we need to look at some of the references.

MAN AS DOER OF *HESED*

The first reference to *hesed* in the Hebrew Bible is in the words of Lot to the angels who had come to warn him of the impending destruction of Sodom and Gomorrah. After they told him to leave and travel some distance, Lot responded by asking if he could travel to a nearby town: "Behold now, thy servant hath found grace in thy sight, and thou hast performed great *hesed* (magnified thy mercy), which thou hast done (shewed) unto me in saving my life. . . . Behold, now, this city is near to flee unto" (Genesis 19:19–20; this and subsequent passages are author's translation, with original KJV in parentheses).[5] As this passage shows, Lot began his request by recognizing that God, or God's messenger in this case, had already done *hesed* by warning Lot of the impending destruction. Thus Lot was asking for another act of *hesed*, as implied by virtue of his mentioning that God had already performed *hesed* on his behalf.

Like his nephew, Abraham was acquainted with *hesed*, both as a giver and a receiver. In Genesis 20, Abraham asked Sarah to show him *hesed* by saying that she was his sister when they met potentially life-threatening individuals: "I said unto her, This is thy *hesed* (kindness) which thou shalt do for me (shew unto me); at every place whither we shall come, say of me, He is my brother" (Genesis 20:13). Later, in Genesis 21, Abimelech, one of Abraham's neighbors and rivals, wishing to avoid future confrontations, entered into a covenant relationship with Abraham that included the following oath: "Now therefore swear unto me here by God that thou wilt not deal falsely with me, nor with my son, nor with my son's son: but according to the *hesed* (kindness) that I have done unto thee, thou shalt do unto me, and to the land wherein thou hast sojourned" (v. 23).

A few chapters later, in Genesis 24, Abraham's servant recognized the role of *hesed* in the eventual success of his journey to find Isaac a wife. In verse 12 the servant prayed that God would "do *hesed* (shew kindness) unto my master Abraham" by granting him quick success. In verse 14 he specified the sign by which he would know that *hesed* had been enacted: if the woman at the well would offer both him and his camels water, "thereby shall I know that thou hast done *hesed* (shewed kindness) unto my master." Rebekah did this, whereupon the servant then declared, "Blessed be the Lord God of my master Abraham, who hath not left destitute my master of his *hesed* (mercy) and his truth" (v. 27).

Abraham's great-grandson Joseph is also associated with *hesed*. In Genesis 39:21, following Joseph's confrontation with Potiphar's wife, which ended with his imprisonment, the narrator tells us that "the Lord was with Joseph, and performed for him *hesed* (shewed him mercy), and gave him favour in the sight of the keeper of the prison," thus ensuring that his prison stay was a relatively pleasant one. In the next chapter, Joseph was ultimately released from prison by an act of *hesed*. After explaining to the pharaoh's chief butler the meaning of his dream, Joseph asked, "Think on me when it shall be well with thee, and do *hesed* (shew kindness), I pray thee, unto me" (Genesis 40:14). Unfortunately, the cupbearer forgot Joseph upon his release, but when the pharaoh had his dream of the seven fat cattle and the seven lean cattle, his servant remembered Joseph, and Joseph was released. Finally, near the end of his life, Joseph's father, Jacob, called Joseph to his side and asked his son for an act of *hesed*: "If now I have found grace in thy sight, put, I pray thee, thy hand under my thigh, and perform *hesed* (deal kindly) and truly with me; bury me not, I pray thee, in Egypt" (Genesis 47:29). Thus, in the narratives of all four patriarchs, *hesed* played fundamental roles in their ability to fulfill their divine purposes.

In the case of Abraham and Abimelech, the principle of *hesed* was one of the primary means by which Israel interacted with their neighbors upon entering the promised land. Similarly, early in the book of Joshua, the subject of the exchange between Rahab, the woman of Jericho, and the spies of Israel was one of *hesed*: "Swear unto me by the Lord, since I have done you *hesed* (shewed you kindness), that ye will also do *hesed* (shew kindness) unto my father's house" (Joshua 2:12–14). The specific act she requested is that they deliver her and her family from the destruction of Jericho. The spies responded, "Our life for yours. . . . And it shall be, when the Lord hath given us the land, that we will deal *hesed* and truth (kindly and truly) with thee" (v. 14). In this scene her promise to help them was recognized as an act of *hesed*, and their agreeing to help her was their act of *hesed*. This same reciprocal scenario was played out later in Judges 1 when the tribe of Joseph took over Bethel. In Judges 1:24 the spies of the tribe saw a man leave the city and approached him: "Shew us, we pray thee, the entrance into the city and we will perform thee *hesed* (shew thee mercy)." Like Rahab and her family, the act of *hesed* done for the man was his survival: "And when he shewed them the entrance into the city, they smote the city with the edge of the sword; but they let go the man and all his family" (v. 25).

Following the establishment of Israel in the promised land, the enacting of *hesed* was recognized as a kingly trait. Saul did *hesed* early in his reign when before destroying the Amalekites he allowed the Kenites to flee: "Go, depart, get you down from among the Amalekites, lest I destroy you with them: for ye performed *hesed* (shewed kindness) to all the children of Israel, when they came up out of Egypt" (1 Samuel 15:6). In chapter 20, Saul's son, Jonathan, who was a close friend of David's, was approached by David to ask for an act of *hesed* on his behalf—to cover for David's absence from the new moon feast: "Therefore thou shalt perform *hesed* (deal kindly) with thy servant" (v. 8). Jonathan agreed, but asked in return for a future act of *hesed* from David, that when David became king, he would not destroy Jonathan's line: "And thou shalt not only while yet I live do me *hesed* (shew me the kindness)of the Lord, that I die not: But also thou shalt not cut off thy *hesed* (kindness) from my house for ever" (vv. 14–15).

These promises of complementary acts of *hesed* were fulfilled later. After David had established his throne, 2 Samuel 9:1, 7 mention David's desire to remember his promise of *hesed*: "Is there yet any that is left of the house of Saul, that I may enact *hesed* (shew him kindness) for Jonathan's sake?" (v. 1). This act was realized as he took Mephibosheth, Jonathan's son, and brought him to his palace with this declaration: "Fear not: for I will surely do thee *hesed* (shew thee kindness) for Jonathan thy father's sake, and will restore thee all the land of Saul thy father; and thou shalt eat bread at my table continually" (v. 7).

Like Saul, David also used *hesed* in his political relationships. In 2 Samuel 2:5–6, while establishing his throne, David praised the men of Jabesh-gilead, supporters of Saul, for their act of *hesed*: "Blessed be ye of the Lord, that ye have performed this *hesed* (shewed this kindness) unto your lord, even unto Saul, and have buried him. And now the Lord acts in *hesed* and truth (shew kindness and truth) unto you . . . because ye have done this thing." In 2 Samuel 10:2, David, upon hearing of the death of Nahash, his Ammonite contemporary, wished to offer condolences and congratulations to Hanun, Nahash's son: "I will perform *hesed* (shew kindness) unto Hanun the son of Nahash, as his father performed *hesed* (shewed kindness) unto me. And David sent to comfort him by the hand of his servants for his father." Finally, David also left instructions to his son concerning acts of *hesed* after his death. In 1 Kings 2:7 David instructed Solomon to "do *hesed* (shew kindness) unto the sons of Barzillai the Gileadite, and let them be of those that eat at thy table: for so they came to me when I fled because of Absalom thy brother."

At least three other kings of Israel are associated with *hesed*: "Now the rest of the acts of Hezekiah, and his *hesed* (goodness), behold they are written in the vision of Isaiah the prophet, the son of Amoz, and in the book of the kings of Judah and Israel" (2 Chronicles 32:32); "Now the rest of the acts of Josiah, and his *hesed* (goodness), according to that which was written in the law of the Lord, and his deeds, first and last, behold, they are written in the book of the kings of Israel and Judah" (2 Chronicles 35:26–27); the third kingly reference is associated with Ahab and will be discussed in detail later.

No discussion of *hesed* would be complete without mentioning its role in the interactions of Naomi, her Moabite daughter-in-law Ruth, and the redeemer Boaz.[6] Mentioned three times in the book of Ruth, the term is used to describe the acts of Ruth and God explicitly and the works of

Boaz implicitly. The first reference is in chapter 1, verse 8, as Naomi gives the following blessing upon both of her daughters-in-law in response to their desire to return her safely to her homeland: "Go, return each to her mother's house: the Lord deal *hesed* (kindly) with you, as ye have dealt with the dead, and with me." This blessing was given in response to their accompanying Naomi home to protect her on the journey.[7]

Later, Naomi noted God's *hesed*, this time referring to the manner in which Boaz had provided sustenance for both Naomi and Ruth: "Blessed be he of the Lord, who hath not left off his *hesed* (kindness) to the living and to the dead" (Ruth 2:20). In this case, while Boaz may have performed the act of *hesed*, the honor of it was given to God, as it was he who was truly aware of Naomi's condition. Finally, when Ruth helped Boaz to accept his role as redeemer in the family, he responded with a blessing upon her: "Blessed be thou of the Lord, my daughter: for thou hast done more *hesed* (shewed more kindness) in the latter end than at the beginning, inasmuch as thou followedst not young men, whether poor or rich" (Ruth 3:10). In other words, her final act of *hesed* led to her choosing Boaz as the family's redeemer, demonstrating her awareness of his true worth, based not on appearances or simple physical attractiveness, which is temporary, but on more firm principles of leadership and authority. These acts of *hesed* only underscore the importance of the book of Ruth, for the acts of *hesed* ultimately lead to the birth of David, the chosen of God, which was likely the act of *hesed* requested by Naomi in Ruth 1.[8]

Already we can begin to see a pattern of the nature of *hesed*. So far, all of these acts of *hesed* have been associated with deliverance from either an actual or perceived loss of life, which includes threats against the family's futurity. Thus Abimelech and Abraham's servant, while not necessarily threatened physically, recognized that *hesed* was necessary for the continuation of the family lineage. Similarly, Jonathan requested an act of *hesed* to preserve his line, and David asked for an act of *hesed* to save his life. The book of Ruth is all about the continuation of Naomi's family.

In most, if not in all of these cases, a mutuality in enacting *hesed* is assumed in the relationship. Abimelech expected *hesed* because he himself had done *hesed*. David wished *hesed* on the men of Jabesh-gilead because they did *hesed* earlier. The same goes for Rahab, the man of Bethel, and the Kenites; in each case they were granted *hesed* because they themselves had done *hesed*. Importantly, all the acts of *hesed*, while requested, were not required or forced. They were freely offered or provided; thus *hesed* is an act of agency. But the obligatory nature of *hesed* reveals one more element—that it is an act that comes from an awareness of another. One cannot unconsciously do *hesed*. As we shall see, every one of these elements is reflected in those passages concerned with the primary performer of *hesed*—God.

GOD AS DOER OF *HESED*

It was mentioned that two-thirds of all the references to *hesed* speak of *hesed* that God has done, the general recognition that God continues to do *hesed*, or the hope that God will perform *hesed* in the future. We have already seen God's *hesed* in the above references. The words of Lot and Abraham's servant both recognize the *hesed* of God in the events in which they were involved. Naomi requested that God do *hesed* on Ruth's behalf, and David asked that God provide *hesed* to his friends and associates. Other references specify different acts of *hesed* that God has performed. Not surprisingly, these other references also note the act of God's *hesed* as one of deliverance from harm, the most famous being God's deliverance of Israel from Egypt.

As early as the Song of Moses, recorded in Exodus 15:13, we find God's *hesed* described as an act of redemption: "Thou in thy *hesed* (mercy) hast led forth the people which thou hast redeemed: thou hast guided them in thy strength unto thy holy habitation." Later, while in the wilderness, Moses relied on God's *hesed* to save the people from themselves after they had provoked the Lord, eliciting his declaration that he would destroy them and raise another, more righteous Israel. Responding to this, Moses intervened by relying on God's history of *hesed* acts: "Pardon, I beseech thee, the iniquity of this people according to the greatness of thy *hesed* (mercy), and as thou hast forgiven this people, from Egypt even until now" (Numbers 14:19). In Psalm 106:7 we are told that Israel did not remember God's acts of *hesed* in Egypt, nor in the wilderness, again demonstrating that ancient Israel understood that their deliverance from Egypt was the quintessential act of *hesed*.

God's *hesed* as an act of deliverance is also attested to in a more general manner. In Psalm 143:12, the Psalmist prayed, "By thy *hesed* (Of thy

mercy) cut off mine enemies, and destroy all them that afflict my soul."
In one of the communal lament psalms, the Psalmist cried out: "Arise for
our help, and redeem us for the sake of thy *hesed* (for thy mercies' sake)"
(Psalm 44:26). In 31:7–8 the Psalmist declared, "I will be glad and rejoice in thy *hesed* (mercy): for thou hast considered my trouble . . . and hast
not shut me up into the hand of the enemy." Psalm 85:7 reads, "Perform
for us thy *hesed* (Shew us thy mercy), O Lord, and grant us thy salvation."
Similarly, Psalm 109:26 includes the plea "Help me, O Lord my God: O
save me according to thy *hesed* (mercy)." Finally, at least one psalm rejoices
in the protecting power of God's *hesed* that he has already performed:
"But I will sing of thy power; yea, I will sing aloud of thy *hesed* (mercy) in
the morning: for thou hast been my defence and refuge in the day of my
trouble" (Psalm 59:16).[9]

The Old Testament also describes God's spiritual deliverance of the
individual as an act of *hesed*. We have already seen in Numbers 14 that
Moses recognized God's *hesed* as the means by which he forgave Israel.
Similarly, in Psalm 86:13 we read, "For great is thy *hesed* (mercy) toward me:
and thou hast delivered my soul from the lowest hell." Though the term
hell brings up certain images, the Hebrew term is *sheol*, the most common
Hebrew term for the abode of the dead. Thus the Psalmist recognizes his
deliverance from the spirit world as an act of God's *hesed*. Elsewhere God's
hesed is recognized in forgiving sin. In Psalm 51:1 we read, "Have mercy
upon me, O God, according to thy *hesed* (lovingkindness): according unto
the multitude of thy tender mercies blot out my transgressions," and in
Proverbs 16:6 the connection between forgiveness and divine *hesed* are
explicitly tied together: "By *hesed* (mercy) and truth iniquity is purged." In
light of these references, divine *hesed* is always an act of deliverance, but
is of greater magnitude when it delivers man from death and hell, and as
such, reflects the understanding of the Atonement as described in latter-
day scripture and revelation.

Divine *hesed* also incorporates the reciprocation found in the mortal experiences of *hesed*. Yet, although mortal to mortal *hesed* acts lead to
the deliverance of one mortal to another, one cannot respond in kind to
God's acts of *hesed*; in other words, man cannot deliver God. Instead, the
expected mutuality arising from divine *hesed* is manifested in one's obedience to God's word. In the Decalogue, we are told to "not bow down

[before idols], . . . for I the Lord thy God . . . enacting *hesed* (shewing mercy) unto thousands of them that love me, and keep my commandments"[10] (Exodus 20:5–6). In Deuteronomy 7:12–13, Moses promised Israel, "If ye hearken to these judgments, and keep, and do them, that the Lord thy God shall keep unto thee the covenant and the *hesed* (mercy) which he sware unto thy fathers: And he will love thee, and bless thee, and multiply thee."

The same relationship between obedience and *hesed* exists in texts outside the Pentateuch. In Psalm 103:11 we are told, "Great is his *hesed* (mercy) toward them that fear him." Psalm 25:10 tells us, "All the paths of the Lord are *hesed* (mercy) and truth unto such as keep his covenant." Psalm 36:10 records, "O continue thy *hesed* (lovingkindness) unto them that know thee." The same principle is taught in Proverbs 14:22: "*Hesed* (mercy) and truth shall be to them that devise good."

At least two references suggest that this obedience is ultimately demonstrated by performing *hesed* on others. In Micah 6:8 we read his rhetorical question: "He hath shewed thee, O man, what is good; and what doth the Lord require of thee, but to do justly, and to love *hesed* (mercy), and to walk humbly with thy God?" Similarly, in Zechariah the righteous are exhorted, "Execute true judgment, and perform *hesed* (shew mercy), and compassions every man to his brother" (Zechariah 7:9). Moreover, as we obey the Lord, not only can we expect an act of divine *hesed* in return, but more importantly, we will comprehend the nature of *hesed*: "Whoso is wise, and will observe these things, even they shall understand the *hesed* (lovingkindness) of the Lord" (Psalm 107:43).[11] Finally, *hesed* includes the intent and not just rote action, as Hosea explains, "For I desired *hesed* (mercy), and not sacrifice; and the knowledge of God more than burnt offerings" (6:6).[12] This last reference is especially significant in that it suggests that the intent, the mental state one is in, is as much a characteristic of *hesed* as the act itself.

HESED, TRUTH, AND REMEMBERING

This last observation can be understood best by recognizing the relationship between the concept of *hesed* and the concept of truth. In Exodus 34:6 we are told that God is "abundant in *hesed* (goodness) and truth."[13] In Psalm 61:7 the plea is that God "prepare *hesed* (mercy) and truth," and Psalm 85:10 rejoices that in God "*hesed* (mercy) and truth are met together." Though we often use the word *truth* to describe the validity or the veracity of a concept or the words of another ("That principle is true," "What he said is true," and so forth), the word originally referred to the concepts of trust, fidelity, constancy, and steadfastness.[14] In other words, truth is concerned with the reliability of an object or person. It is this reliability, or constancy, that gives concepts validity.[15] The reliability of a given thing allows for the exercise of power, since knowing of its truthfulness allows us to act upon it. Thus the reception of truth gives us power to act in ways previously thought impossible.

When tied with *hesed*, truth highlights the eternal nature of and describes an aspect of God's *hesed*, which is that he also gives us the power to change ourselves as well as delivering us out of situations that we cannot control. For instance, in Psalm 57:3, following a plea that God save the individual, it reads, "God shall send forth his *hesed* (mercy) and his truth," suggesting that the manner in which the individual will be delivered is through not only the reception of revelatory truths, giving one power to act, but also a specific act of deliverance by God.

In light of the association of truth with *hesed*, it is not surprising to find other references acknowledging the relationship of trust to *hesed*. Psalm 13:5 declares, "I have trusted in thy *hesed* (mercy)," and Psalm 52:8 makes the same claim, "I trust in the *hesed* (mercy) of God for ever and ever," while Psalm 32:10 suggests that "he that trusteth in the Lord, *hesed* (mercy) shall compass him [about]." Psalm 36:7 relates, "How excellent is thy *hesed* (lovingkindness), O God! therefore the children of men put their trust under the shadow of thy wings." Finally, in Psalm 89:14, the phrase "*hesed* (mercy) and truth shall go before thy face" tells us that these two concepts defined the work of God for ancient Israel.[16]

The association of *hesed* with truth suggests that *hesed* is more than merely an act; it includes the mental activity that governs such acts. In 2 Chronicles 6:42, Solomon ends his temple dedicatory prayer by requesting that God "remember the *hesed* (mercies) of David thy servant." Elsewhere, in Nehemiah 13:22, Nehemiah asks that God "remember me . . . and spare me according to the greatness of thy *hesed* (mercy)." In Psalm 25, verses 6 and 7 ask God to remember his *hesed* and thereby his relationship to Israel: "Remember, O Lord, thy tender mercies and thy *hesed* acts (lovingkindnesses), . . . Remember not the sins of my youth, nor my transgressions: according to thy *hesed* (mercy) remember thou me for thy goodness' sake." This last line is especially intriguing because it suggests that God may actually be performing *hesed* by "remembering" or remaining aware of the individual.

Psalm 98:3 suggests that God's care of Israel throughout the ages is because "he hath remembered his *hesed* (mercy) and his truth toward the house of Israel: all the ends of the earth have seen the salvation of our God." Finally, at least one reference suggests that God remembering his *hesed* may happen because Israel has performed earlier *hesed* acts toward others: "Remember me, O my God . . . and wipe not out my good *hesed* acts (deeds) that I have done for the house of my God" (Nehemiah 13:14). In other words, if God's remembering is an act of *hesed*, it is done in recognition of the *hesed* acts performed by the righteous.

The relationship between remembering and *hesed* may explain why *hesed* is so often associated with an answer to prayer. For instance, in Psalm 66:20 the answer to prayer is equated to an act of *hesed*: "Blessed be God, which hath not turned away my prayer, nor his *hesed* (mercy) from me." Similarly, in Psalm 17:6–7 the Psalmist cries: "incline thine ear unto me, and hear my speech. Perform (shew) thy marvelous *hesed* (lovingkindness), O thou that savest by thy right hand them which put their trust in thee." Psalm 69:13 says, "My prayer is unto thee, O Lord, in an acceptable time: O God, in thy abundant *hesed* (the multitude of thy mercy) hear me." In Psalm 86:5 the same theme is present: "For thou, Lord, art good . . . and plenteous in *hesed* (mercy) unto all them that call upon thee," and in Psalm 143:8 the individual prays for the means to receive God's *hesed*: "Cause me to hear thy *hesed* (lovingkindness) in the morning."[17]

Yet just as God is asked to remember his *hesed* acts on Israel's behalf, so Israel is expected to remember them as well to receive continued *hesed*: "I have not concealed thy *hesed* (lovingkindness) and thy truth from the great congregation. Withhold not thou thy tender mercies from me, O Lord; let thy *hesed* (lovingkindness) and thy truth continually preserve me. For innumerable evils have compassed me about" (Psalm 40:10–12). Moreover, there are references which detail what happened to Israel when one did not do *hesed*. In Judges 8, the horrible spiritual state of Israel is summed up in the last two verses of the chapter: "And the children of Israel remembered not the Lord their God, who had delivered them out of the hands of all their enemies, . . . neither did they return *hesed* acts (shewed they kindness) to the house of Jerubbaal . . . in return for [according to] all the goodness which he had done (shewed) unto Israel" (Judges 8:34–35). The result was internal fighting among the sons of Gideon and the eventual defeat of Israel by the Shechemites. Psalm 106:7 suggests that Israel's continued provoking of the Lord during the exodus and their subsequent sinful state came about because "they remembered not the abundant *hesed* of God (multitude of thy mercies)."[18] Here, the mutuality of *hesed* also meant that a lack of doing *hesed* acts resulted in a lack of receiving *hesed* acts. Psalm 109 describes just such a state: "Let there be none to extend *hesed* (mercy) to him. . . . Let his posterity be cut off . . . because that he remembered not to perform *hesed* (show mercy) . . . but persecuted the poor and needy" (vv. 12, 13, 16).[19] In other words, because the individual did not remember to do *hesed*, *hesed* should not be extended to him.

Finally, according to 1 Kings 20:31–43, not remembering God's word can negate what would potentially be an act of *hesed*. In the text, Ahab, king of Israel, defeated the Syrian king Ben-Hadad, whereupon Ben-Hadad's servants suggested that he plead for mercy from Ahab because "we have heard the kings of the house of Israel are kings of *hesed* (merciful kings): let us, I pray thee . . . go out to the king of Israel: peradventure he will save thy life" (v. 31). Ben-Hadad did so, and Ahab promptly proclaimed him as a brother entering into a covenant relationship with him. At this point, it would appear that Ahab did *hesed* by delivering the Syrian king from death, similar to other *hesed* accounts studied so far. But verse 42 suggests this is not the case: "Because thou hast let go out of thy hand a man whom I appointed to utter destruction, therefore thy life shall go for his life, and thy people for his people." Indeed, before the battle Ahab had been told explicitly that God would deliver the opposing army into his hands and that in so doing, Ahab would "know" God (vv. 13, 28). Thus, Ahab's later actions went contrary to God's will as he "forgot" God instead of "knowing" him.

"Because He Delighteth in *Hesed*"

The above has provided us with an understanding of *hesed* as an act of deliverance, either physical or spiritual. When performed by a mortal on behalf of another, a reciprocal act is expected, but not required, at some later point. When the *hesed* act is performed by God, he expects obedience, ultimately exemplified in *hesed* acts performed on behalf of others, since we cannot truly reciprocate in kind to God. *Hesed* is associated with the concept of truth and is thus a reliable, "real" concept that we can trust. God's reliability is proven by his acts of *hesed*, which in turn demonstrate his continued, conscious awareness of the individual who receives the act of *hesed*. In some cases, the very knowledge that he has "remembered" his people is the act of *hesed* that delivers them in their time of need.

As significant as these insights are, they do not answer one important question: why is *hesed* performed? Many have noted that a relationship exists between performing *hesed* and participation in a covenant relationship.[20] Certainly this has been borne out in the *hesed* references listed above. In at least four relationships, *hesed* is expected of one who enters, or who has already been engaged in, a covenant. Abraham and Abimelech established a covenant between themselves and their offspring, promising *hesed* from both, and established because one did *hesed* earlier. Similarly, Jonathan and David entered into a covenant promising to do *hesed* for one another and their descendants. Though the covenant relationship between Abraham and Sarah is not explicit, it is their marriage that Abraham relied on for *hesed* on his behalf. Even the example of Ahab and the Syrian king, though not a true *hesed* act, demonstrates that covenants were associated with the performance of *hesed*. Psalm 25:10 tells us, "All the paths of the Lord are *hesed* (mercy) and truth unto such as keep his covenant," and in Isaiah 55:3 God promises to enact *hesed* by actually entering into a covenant as he did with David: "Incline your ear, and come unto me: hear, and your soul shall live; and I will make an everlasting covenant with you, even the sure *hesed* acts (mercies) of David." In other words, the eternal covenant God makes with us is characterized by the same true, reliable *hesed* acts he did for David.[21]

Yet not all of the relationships are covenantally bound. Saul's *hesed* act with the Kenites is not described in covenantal terms, neither are those acts between the spies of Israel and Rahab and the spies of Ephraim and the man of Bethel. Ruth may or may not be covenantally bound to Naomi, but she is certainly not yet covenantally bound to Boaz when she performs her act of *hesed* for him. Psalm 107:8 suggests that all mankind, whether or not in a covenantal relationship like Israel, should "praise the Lord for his *hesed* (goodness), and for his wonderful works to the children of men!" Thus it is not just a covenant that brings about *hesed* and therefore cannot be the only factor in which *hesed* is done. So what else is there? Two verses in the Old Testament provide one other reason for God's *hesed* acts. In Jeremiah 9:24 the Lord reveals, "I am the Lord which exercise *hesed* (lovingkindness), judgment and righteousness, in the earth: for in these things I delight." Micah points out that he retaineth not his anger forever because he "delighteth in *hesed* (mercy)" (Micah 7:18). In other words, God performs *hesed* because he likes to do it. It is more than simply his responsibility to do so because of his covenant relationship; it is his desire to continue doing this work.

This may have been what Moses meant when he declared that delivering man was not just God's work, but also his glory (see Moses 1:39). He loves what he does and does what he loves. It is his very nature to do such acts, and in recognizing this, we can begin to discern our true nature, for as was stated above, God's expectation is that we too perform acts of *hesed*. As we do so, we find ourselves doing the same things God does, engaging in the work of deliverance, and learning to think like he does, perceiving the world around us in a divine manner. Thus, we become aware of our true nature as heirs of our Father in Heaven: beings whose very desire is to serve and deliver others.

NOTES

1. The first letter of this Hebrew word is what is known as a guttural and represents a sound that is not common in the English language. As awkward as this consonantal cluster may be, it is the best approximation of an English translation.

2. Gordon R. Clark, "חסד—A Study of a Lexical Field," in *Abr-Nahrain* 30 (1992), 34: "It is widely acknowledged that חסד [*hesed*] . . . is extremely difficult to translate into English—and, for that matter, into many other languages. . . . The King James Version used mercy words 155 times, kindness words 43 times, lovingkindness 30 times, goodness words 14 times, but love words are never used. In the Revised Standard Version, love words occur 182 times, kindness words 29 times, loyalty words 21 times, but mercy words only twice." For a more comprehensive study on *hesed*, see Gordon R. Clark, *The Word Hesed in the Hebrew Bible*, Journal for the Study of the Old Testament Supplement Series 157 (Sheffield, England: JSOT Press, 1993).

Beyond Clark's study mentioned above, two excellent studies are Katherine Doob Sakenfeld, *The Meaning of* Hesed *in the Hebrew Bible*, Harvard Semitic Monographs 17 (Missoula, Montana: Scholars Press, 1978) and "hesed" in *Theological Dictionary of the Old Testament* V, ed. G. Johannes Botterweck and Helmer Ringgren (Grand Rapids, MI: Eerdmans, 1977), 44–64.

3. Not all 245 references need to be reviewed, since many of them are found in formulaic expressions that are repeated again and again. Where the formulas or textual narrative provide insight into the meaning of *hesed*, these references are discussed.

4. The verb *shew* is the Early Modern English spelling of the modern *show*. The translation of the verb as "shew" may be to emphasize the visible, manifesting nature of acts of *hesed*, yet this translation implies a passivity that is not necessarily found in the original Hebrew.

5. In order to emphasize *asah* ("doing") and *hesed*, I have provided my own translations of the Bible passages cited in this paper. For purposes of comparison, I have also included the original KJV text in parentheses.

6. According to some Jewish sources, the very purpose of the book of Ruth is to teach about *hesed*. See Susan Schept, "Hesed: Feminist Ethics in Jewish Tradition," *Conservative Judaism* 57 (2004), 21–29.

7. This blessing reflects an interesting use of *hesed* in farewell benedictions. In 2 Samuel 15:20, David tells his friend Ittai the Gittite goodbye in the following manner: "Return thou, and take back thy brethren: *hesed* (mercy) and truth be with thee."

8. Following her request for *hesed* on Ruth's behalf, Naomi continues to ask specifically that God would "give" (the Hebrew verb *natan*) Ruth security and place in the house of a husband. In Ruth 4:13, after Ruth marries Boaz, we are told that God "gave" (*natan*) Ruth conception of a male child, securing her place and security in the house of her husband and thereby fulfilling the blessing. "At long last Ruth had the . . . place of settled security, which Naomi at first wished her (Ruth 1:9) and later schemed for her (3:1). Thus her case illustrates the biblical truth that God does reward *hesed*" (Robert L. Hubbard Jr., *The Book of Ruth*, New International Commentary on the Old Testament [Grand Rapids, MI: Eerdmans, 1988], 267–68).

9. The act of singing in the morning about God's *hesed* may have been a recognized Temple procedure. In 2 Chronicles 5:13, part of the ritual associated with the dedication of Solomon's Temple included the following: "It came even to pass, as the trumpeters and singers were as one, to make one sound to be heard in praising and thanking the Lord, and when they lifted up their voice with the trumpets and cymbals and instruments of musick, and praised the Lord saying, For he is good; for his *hesed* (mercy) endureth for ever." This refrain was also sung at the introduction of the ark to Jerusalem as described in 1 Chronicles 16. Hundreds of years later, as Ezra was laying the foundation for the new Temple, the refrain was again sung to commemorate the event. The Psalms suggest that *hesed* was to be sung about: "Enter into his gates with thanksgiving, and into his courts with praise. . . . For the Lord is good; his mercy is everlasting; and his truth endureth to all generations"

(Psalm 100:4–5). Certainly contemplating God's *hesed* was a worthy Temple experience: "We have thought of thy *hesed* (lovingkindness), O God, in the midst of thy temple" (Psalm 48:9; see also Psalms 5:7; 23:6).

10. This phrase was carried down through the generations. It was still part of the priestly recital, which was recorded almost a thousand years later (Nehemiah 9:32).

11. This verse ends Psalm 107, a psalm that begins with an exhortation to thank God for the eternal nature of his *hesed* and then goes on to recount the great acts God has done on Israel's behalf, interspersed throughout with the refrain: "Oh that men would praise the Lord for his *hesed* (goodness), and for his wonderful works to the children of men."

12. In his study "On the Use and Meaning of Hosea vi. 6 in Matthew's Gospel," *New Testament Studies* 24 (1977), 107–19, David Hill suggests that the concept of *eleos*/*hesed* is a common theme in the arrangement of Matthew's Gospel.

13. Interestingly, a number of New Testament scholars suggest that this reference is alluded to in John 1:14 and that the phrase "grace and truth" found in the New Testament reference is the equivalent of "*hesed* and truth" as found here. See Anthony Hanson, "John i. 14–18 and Exodus," *New Testament Studies* 23 (1976), 90–101. If this is true, then we may have greater insight into the role of *hesed* as part of God's work since the clause "grace and truth" is found throughout restoration scripture.

14. *Oxford English Dictionary*, online version, s.v. "truth." Similarly, the Hebrew terms translated as "truth," *amunah* and *emet*, both include the same connotation of reliability, steadfastness, and unchangeability.

15. In latter-day scripture, truth is defined as knowledge "of things as they really are" (Jacob 4:13; D&C 93:24). This definition coincides with the above statements, as the "realness" of a thing testifies to its reliability. Since truth does not change, it can be relied on to provide a foundation upon which to build. The contrast between the way things are and the way things appear is, at its core, one that distinguishes between that which can be relied on and that which cannot.

16. Interestingly, in Moses 7:31, Enoch uses a similar phrase to describe the work of God: "And thou hast taken Zion to thine own bosom, from all thy creations . . . and mercy shall go before thy face and have no end."

17. At least three psalms appear to be prayers or songs of thanksgiving emphasizing God's *hesed* acts: Psalms 107 and 118 begin with the refrain, "O give thanks unto the Lord, for he is good: for his *hesed* (mercy) endureth for ever." Psalm 118 also ends with this phrase.

18. The sin of forgetting is mentioned throughout this Psalm. Verse 13 relates that Israel "soon forgat his works," and in verse 21 "they forgat God their saviour." According to these verses, Israel forgot God by making the golden calf and worshipping it. This latter reference reveals an important difference between biblical forgetting and our contemporary meaning. The English word *forget* means literally "to miss or lose one's hold"; this suggests that one may wish to retain, or hold on to, but cannot. Forgetting, then, is not necessarily a conscious decision, but something that may happen by accident. The biblical term, on the other hand, has the nuance of "to ignore" or "to take lightly." Thus forgetting God is not the same in meaning

as forgetting to pick up the milk. While one may completely forget that instruction, when Israel made the golden calf, they didn't forget that God existed; they ignored or trivialized his role.

19. This psalm actually references *hesed* four times: the first two listed here, as well as verses 21 and 26 (mentioned in an earlier section of this study). Walter Brueggemann, in his study "Psalm 109: Three Times 'Steadfast Love,'" *Word & World* 5, no. 2 (1985): 144–54, suggests that *hesed* is the theme of the entire psalm: "I propose that the main flow of the argument of the poem can be traced through the uses of this word" (149).

20. This is the theme of Nelson Glueck's seminal study, *Hesed in the Bible*, trans. Alfred Gottschalk (Cincinnati: The Hebrew Union College Press, 1967).

21. The relationship between *hesed* and God's covenant with David is one recognized elsewhere in the Old Testament. Psalm 89, in particular, emphasizes the two. According to verse 28, God does *hesed* for David eternally: "My *hesed* (mercy) will I keep for him for evermore, and my covenant shall stand fast with him." In this reference, the two stand in parallel: God's *hesed* is also his covenant. This may provide an answer as to what exactly the sure *hesed* acts of David are. It is also possible that this sure *hesed* is associated with the key of David mentioned in Revelation 3:7, which appears to be the priesthood keys of kingship. David's line is promised kingship culminating in the kingship of Jesus Christ, but the Isaiah reference suggests that anyone who comes unto God can have the same covenant with the attendant *hesed* acts. Ann N. Madsen discusses the role of *hesed* and covenant briefly in her study, "'His Hand Is Stretched Out Still': The Lord's Eternal Covenant of Mercy," in *Revelation, Reason, and Faith: Essays in Honor of Truman G. Madsen*, ed. Donald W. Parry, Daniel C. Peterson, and Stephen D. Ricks (Provo: Brigham Young University, 2002), 704–21.

11

RUTH, REDEMPTION, COVENANT, AND CHRIST

Kerry Muhlestein

The book of Ruth is one of the most loved stories of the Old Testament. Yet sometimes it remains just that: a story from which some readers gain little in the way of doctrine or application. We identify with the story because the principal actors are neither kings nor prophets but the average people of a typical village. There are neither mighty warriors nor great conflicts, but there are intense struggles for surviving life's difficulties and genuine battles with grief. We love the story because it is so well told, because it has characters we can identify with, because it weaves a plot we can relate to that has a wonderful resolution. Yet we often do not recognize a deeper symbolism in the text.

The book of Ruth carries within its pages some of the most fundamental and powerful doctrines of the kingdom. It speaks of and symbolically demonstrates God's redeeming power; it teaches us of how we can access that power and exemplifies how we should emulate our Redeemer. Numerous elements of the story serve as types of Christ. It is about hope in Israel. I believe that some of the reason we love the story so much is

———————

Kerry Muhlestein is an associate professor of ancient scripture at Brigham Young University.

because, whether we realize it or not, our souls intuitively resonate with the redemption of Ruth; we long for what happened to her on a mortal level to happen to us in both a mortal *and* eternal way. Ruth satisfies some of our soul's yearning for deliverance. It highlights our reasons for hope. We often sense this message without picking up on its full development.

These powerful messages are conveyed by one of the Bible's most able writers. While we do not know who the author of Ruth is nor when he wrote the book, we can recognize in this writer an extraordinary talent. Realizing this does not take away from the potency of the message, nor from the reality of Ruth's, Naomi's, and Boaz's lives. On the contrary, we can see in this biblical author attributes similar to Isaiah's or Neal A. Maxwell's in the employment of a God-given gift so that the message of salvation he carries can be delivered all the more meaningfully.

The biblical author's message is conveyed so smoothly and stylishly, yet its vehicle is a myriad of details. No other book of scripture gives us so many insights into daily life in ancient Israel in so few pages. For the author's contemporaries, these details were easily understood; they were a part of their everyday world. For us, they must be decoded. They are aspects of a culture strange and foreign. As we delve into such minutia, we run the risk of becoming detained in the details or distracted from the message that flows through the story. Thus we will first dive into the details and then return to many of the same items in a more comprehensive way, having acquired the knowledge that the writer of Ruth assumed his audience had. This will enable the story's symbols to distill upon us the way the author spoke to our Israelite ancestors.

Cultural Caring, Covenant, and Redemption

We must first understand some important cultural and legal aspects of ancient Israel. The ancient Near East in general—and Israel in particular—incorporated into their culture many ways of providing for those who could not care for themselves. The law of Moses is filled with stipulations regarding how such caring should take place and to whom it was applied. Typically the widow, the orphan, the poor, and the resident alien were among the groups most in need. Prophets continually reminded Israel of their duty to provide for these groups. The law made particular allowances for them.[1] Ruth takes advantage of these allowances in her efforts to sustain herself and her mother-in-law.

One of the ways the Mosaic law provided for the poor was through the practice of gleaning. "And when ye reap the harvest of your land, thou shalt not wholly reap the corners of thy field, neither shalt thou gather the gleanings of thy harvest. And thou shalt not glean thy vineyard, neither shalt thou gather every grape of thy vineyard; thou shalt leave them for the poor and stranger: I am the Lord your God" (Leviticus 19:9–10). When reaping with a scythe, the swinging-arm movement naturally created a circular motion which would leave the square corners of fields untouched without an extra step. The Lord commanded the Israelites not to take this extra step and to leave those corners for the poverty-stricken. Additionally, anything that fell was left for the destitute. Also, some grapes were to be intentionally left for the needy in each vineyard. Through these practices, Israel furnished a way for the impoverished to provide for themselves as long as they were willing and able to engage in some arduous labor. Similarly, in Deuteronomy 24:19 the Lord instructs Israel, "When thou cuttest down thine harvest in thy field, and hast forgot a sheaf in the field, thou shalt not go again to fetch it: it shall be for the stranger, for the fatherless, and for the widow: that the Lord thy God may bless thee in all the work of thine hands." These laws were given of God to help Israel aid those most in need of help: the poor, the stranger (or foreigner), the widow, and the orphan. Ruth, a poor, foreign widow, would look to these laws in her efforts to provide for herself and Naomi.

Many more elements of Israelite culture and law were aimed at helping those in need. One such needy group was the elderly. Israel had no pension plans, no social security, no assisted living. The responsibility to care for the elderly fell upon their families. It was first the responsibility of children to provide for the aged and the widow; this is one reason why the loss of children was such a staggering blow. David was even willing to waive capital punishment for a murderer in order to forestall a woman being bereft of any children to sustain her (see 2 Samuel 14:4–11).

Ancient Near Eastern societies valued having children both because of the need to care for the elderly and because of the importance of carrying on family lines.[2] Hence, most Near Eastern cultures, including Israel, followed some form of the levirate law of marriage.[3] We understand little of how Israelite levirate marriages worked, but we know enough to decipher the basic principles. If a married man died without children, his brothers were responsible to care for his wife. Part of this care was for one brother to marry and impregnate the new widow; therewith the firstborn child bore the dead brother's name and served as his heir. This process is spoken of in Deuteronomy: "Her husband's brother shall go in unto her, and take her to him to wife, and perform the duty of an husband's brother unto her. And it shall be, that the firstborn which she beareth shall succeed in the name of his brother which is dead, that his name be not put out of Israel" (Deuteronomy 25:5–6).[4]

This duty was so important that it includes the only stipulated example of public humiliation[5] in the law of Moses for those who were unwilling to take upon themselves the levirate duty:

> And if the man like not to take his brother's wife, then let his brother's wife go up to the gate unto the elders, and say, My husband's brother refuseth to raise up unto his brother a name in Israel, he will not perform the duty of my husband's brother.
>
> Then the elders of his city shall call him, and speak unto him: and if he stand to it, and say, I like not to take her;
>
> Then shall his brother's wife come unto him in the presence of the elders, and loose his shoe from off his foot, and spit in his face, and shall answer and say, So shall it be done unto that man that will not build up his brother's house.
>
> And his name shall be called in Israel, The house of him that hath his shoe loosed. (Deuteronomy 25:7–10)

Clearly, failure to provide for a widow under levirate customs was viewed as a shameful thing. But how does this relate to the symbolism of taking off the shoe? While many have wrangled over the meaning, I have a suggestion. When shoes are used symbolically in the Old Testament, wearing them denotes a readiness, a preparation to do what needs to be done (see Exodus 12:11; 1 Kings 2:5; and Isaiah 5:27).[6] Given the context of the Deuteronomy passage just cited, it seems that removing someone's shoe shows their unwillingness to do what needs to be done. If having a shoe on indicates preparation for doing one's duty, having the sandal taken off signifies a *refusal* to perform that same duty. The shame of those who are unwilling to serve as levirate husbands is that they will be known as someone who fails to fulfill his obligations. Since some of the reasoning behind a man refusing levirate duty likely had to do with the thought that raising up a child to another man would take inheritance away from his own family, the entire family was to share in the stigma of shame if the father did not fulfill his duty. Such a reprisal would have the effect of making a man who was thinking of his own children and their inheritance reconsider the ramifications that avoiding his responsibility would have on his children.

As noted above, the levirate husband was responsible to care for his brother's widow and her new child. As the mother and her new husband grew old, that child would assume responsibility for himself and his mother using his dead father's inheritance. Thus the levirate law both provided for the widow, partially by keeping family land within the family, and prevented family lines from dying out.[7]

Apparently, levirate duty could apply to relatives beyond immediate brothers. It was the responsibility of the entire family to sustain a widow, both in the short term by providing for her needs and in the long term by furnishing her with a child that would provide care in her old age. Societies who continue this practice today speak of protection of the widow as the primary consideration.[8] In ancient Israel, if this system were properly carried out, no widow would find herself without support; she would always be visited in her affliction, brought under the wing of a protective family.

In Israel, the family had another responsibility in looking after its members who had come under hardship. Israel and her ancient Near Eastern neighbors required that all possible means be taken in order to meet a debt. If an individual had difficulty in paying his debt, family land and even family members, including the debtor, were required to be sold as an attempt to meet the obligation. No allowances were made in justice, which demanded debt repayment. Yet the law of Moses also provided a way for mercy to be extended through family members. The closest family member had a right and an obligation to redeem, or buy back, family land or family members who had been sold.[9] "After that he is sold he may be redeemed again; one of his brethren may redeem him: either his uncle, or his uncle's son, may redeem him, or any that is nigh of kin unto him of his family may redeem him; or if he be able, he may redeem himself" (Leviticus 25:48–49). The man who bought his family land or kinsman back was known as the redeemer, or in Hebrew, the *gō'el*. This was not free deliverance; this was deliverance at a price, and the *gō'el* paid that price.[10] He met the debt owed by his relative which that kinsman could not pay on his own.

Symbolically, it is important that not just anyone could serve as a redeemer, that only close family members had that right, beginning with the closest relative.[11] This law reminded Israel that they had once been bond servants in Egypt and that the Lord had served as their redeemer. Their covenant with him, beginning with Abraham, had made them eligible for redemption. "But because the Lord loved you, and because he would keep the oath which he had sworn unto your fathers, hath the Lord brought you out with a mighty hand, and redeemed you out of the house of bondmen, from the hand of Pharaoh king of Egypt" (Deuteronomy 7:8).[12]

The Lord had created a custom among his chosen people in such a way that for those in darkest need a hope was provided;[13] for all such Israelites, the concept of a redeemer must have served as a strand of hope in the midst of despair. The existence of a kinsman redeemer, the *gō'el*, was the hope of Israel. This divinely mandated role stood as a bright shining comfort for those in most desperate need.

It is from the book of Ruth that we learn that levirate marriage and the right of redemption were connected.[14] Apparently in some places and times in Israel, the closest kinsman had the duty and obligation to serve as both the levirate husband and the *gō'el*.[15] The family was to rally in support of those in need and to do for them that which they could not do for themselves, whatever that need may be.

The Mosaic law's abundant mercy and concern for all—especially those most in need—also included a provision for those who were destitute of both material means *and* family. If no family ties existed, they could be established by covenants (formed in a variety of ways), which created family ties between people.[16] It is this "creation of an 'adoptive relationship' by covenant that is the basis for the Lord's acts of redemption."[17]

One group necessitating extra care was the foreigners who had chosen to live among Israel.[18] The Lord extended special aid to these resident aliens in the Mosaic law, often counting them among the widows and orphans as people in particular need.[19] These foreigners did not naturally possess a land inheritance as an Israelite did and thus were at an inherent disadvantage. Besides the laws designed to protect them, the Lord often reminded Israel of their obligation to care for the foreigner—or stranger—who sojourned among them. "Thou shalt neither vex a stranger, nor oppress him: for ye were strangers in the land of Egypt" (Exodus 22:21).

While the law does not address the process by which a foreigner became an Israelite, it is clear that it was possible. Before leaving Israel, Moses renewed God's covenant with them *and* with the foreigners who dwelt among them (see Deuteronomy 29:10–13). Resident aliens were among the group with whom Joshua reestablished that covenant at Mount Ebal (see Joshua 8:30–35). Shortly thereafter he made a covenant with the Gibeonites that incorporated them into the house of Israel (see Joshua 9). Likewise, the Passover indicates that foreigners could join Israel. "And when a stranger shall sojourn with thee, and will keep the passover to the Lord, let all his males be circumcised, and then let him come near and keep it; and he shall be as one that is born in the land: for no uncircumcised person shall eat thereof. One law shall be to him that is homeborn, and unto the stranger that sojourneth among you" (Exodus 12:48–49). Since circumcision was the mark of Israel's covenant with Jehovah, its application to a foreigner along with his inclusion in the Passover ritual indicates that the foreigner could, through covenant, become part of Israel.[20] While we do not know the exact mechanism for the covenant which changed a foreigner into an Israelite, clearly such a mechanism and covenant existed.[21] Having become Israelites, these people would have full access to the protections and blessings available through the Mosaic law and God's covenant with his chosen people.[22] These principles were important for Ruth, who was a native Moabite.

This covenant segues to one last point which must be addressed in order to more fully understand the book of Ruth. There was a special kind of love, mercy, and kindness available only within the context of a covenant. The Hebrew word for this was *hesed*, an extra measure of kindness and love available to those within a covenant relationship.[23] The greatest acts of *hesed* were those performed by God on behalf of his people. In many ways, all of the provisions God made for those who were in need and could not care for themselves were provisions of *hesed*.

With a basic understanding of these cultural elements, we can more fully examine the narrative, finding ourselves more able to draw forth meaning from this powerful book.

RUTH, NAOMI, AND BOAZ WITHIN THE COVENANT

The story takes place during the period of the judges, before Israel has come together under a king. The book of Ruth begins with a familiar theme. A famine has come into the land of Canaan, and some choose to escape this famine by journeying to a foreign land. In this case it is Elimelech, his wife Naomi, and two sons. These sons soon take Moabite women as wives, but do not have children by these wives (despite spending ten years in Moab). In time, tragedy strikes the family as first the father and then the sons die. Besides the grief which would naturally attend the loss of her children, Naomi is now faced with the prospect that she will have no one to care for her in her old age. Confronted with these hardships and having learned that the famine in Judah has ceased, Naomi decides to return to her native home.

Initially, both of her daughters-in-law accompany Naomi on this journey, intent on remaining with her. Somewhere along the way, Naomi must have given much thought to the plight of the two women who were at her side. Being young, they still had the opportunity for remarriage and thus for a family life that could bring them joy and security. Acting on these thoughts, Naomi entreats her loyal daughters-in-law to return home and make a life for themselves. Both Ruth and Orpah maintain that they wish to remain with Naomi, but when Naomi insists, Orpah eventually gives in to her wishes.

Three things are worth noting in this situation. Naomi is very aware that the women who were accompanying her, who were her family by covenant, were volunteering to undergo extreme hardship for the rest of their lives in order to help Naomi. Thus she says to them, "Go, each of you return to your mother's house; may the Lord perform *hesed* for you as you have done for the dead and for me" (see Ruth 1:8; author's translation). Naomi recognizes the covenantal kindness, or *hesed*, that these women are carrying out. Being aware that she was incapable of performing *hesed* for them, she asks the Lord to do so. At least in the case of Ruth, the Lord will eventually show *hesed*, but he will do this through the acts of a mortal: Boaz. Ruth's intense love and loyalty, manifestations of *hesed*, are particularly inspiring to us. We cannot read of her devotion without hoping that we will always have a Ruth in our lives, and simultaneously aspiring to be a Ruth for others. Whether we understand the term or not, Ruth motivates us to perform similar acts of *hesed*; the devotion in her soul-felt expression feels its way into our souls.

Second, the narrative is not written in a way that portrays Orpah in a bad light. Indeed, this worthy daughter has been fulfilling all that could be expected of her in a stalwart way. It is not a shortcoming on the part of Orpah that is highlighted here, but instead Orpah's goodness is contrasted with Ruth's greatness. In a theme that will recur during the narrative, Ruth shows that she is willing to go beyond what is expected of her; she will be extraordinary in her service.[24]

Finally, in insisting that she will accompany Naomi throughout her life, Ruth has altered who will pay the greatest price. Naomi is faced with finishing her life alone, having no one to care for her and see her through the hardships of life. Ruth is willing to forestall that fate for Naomi. However, in staying with Naomi, which seems to dictate that Ruth will not remarry nor have children, Ruth ensures that it is she who will face old age all alone. Ruth is fully willing to take Naomi's potential suffering upon herself, providing relief for a loved one by experiencing that fate instead. This emulation of the Savior is not an accidental message of the story—it is one of its main themes.

When Ruth declares she will stay with Naomi, we learn of Ruth's conversion. The bold statement "Thy people shall be my people, and thy God my God" (Ruth 1:16) confirms that Ruth has become an Israelite in her heart. While we are unaware of what covenant and rite must have accompanied the formalization of these thoughts, we are left in no doubt as to the actuality of Ruth's conversion.[25]

The great tragedies that have struck Naomi, seemingly undeservedly, raise the age-old question of the justice of God in allowing the innocent to suffer. The author of Ruth artfully raises this theme when Naomi replies to her long-lost friends: "The Almighty hath dealt very bitterly with me. I went out full, and the Lord hath brought me home again empty: why then call ye me Naomi, seeing the Lord hath testified against me, and the Almighty hath afflicted me?" (Ruth 1:20–21). While Naomi's lament does not accuse God directly, it certainly complains of the unjust-ness of her situation and implies that God is unjust. Her complaint is not addressed at this point in the story but will receive a resounding answer as the narrative moves on and will be fully resolved when Naomi praises God in the middle of the story, as well as when her friends praise him at the end of the story.

The next scene in our narrative begins by making the reader privy to knowledge which Ruth does not possess (see Ruth 2:1). It is crucial to the plot for us to know that Boaz is a man of great worth—a double meaning implied, for he is a man of means and character—*and* that he is a kinsman of Naomi. We benefit from understanding this while reading of the in-teractions between Ruth and Boaz, but Ruth has no idea. The actions of these two characters are not influenced by any thought of a possible *gōʾel* relationship; instead we see them acting out of true intent.

Plainly, when the writer says of Ruth that "her hap" was to come to Boaz's field (Ruth 2:3), he does not intend for us to understand that it was pure luck. The story is full of happenstances which bring about the Lord's purposes, underscoring that all of these events are directed by God and that the happy conclusion of the story is orchestrated by him as he pours out his *hesed* on this family.

Our introduction to Boaz wastes no time in establishing him as a man of character and compassion. He goes to great lengths to help Ruth in her efforts. He instructs her to stay in his fields and to work with his maidens under the watchful eye of his men (see Ruth 2:8–9), a measure of invita-tion and protection that must have served as immeasurable comfort to a foreigner who was earnestly engaged in her first day of labor. He also tells her to partake of the water drawn for his workers, an important commod-ity in an arid land during heavy work (see Ruth 2:9). He further invited her to partake of the meal he provided for his workers, a great boon to Ruth because it not only provides her with food (see Ruth 2:14) but does so when she is not in a position to have aught with which to prepare any meal for herself. The parched corn she partakes of is more important than we typically realize. Israel and her neighbors followed a custom with grain harvesting that many Middle Eastern societies continue today. Some of the grain is harvested just before it is ripe. It is then roasted, producing a caramelized food that is both tasty and serves as a high-energy food source for its consumers. While the preharvest production and preparation of this meal is expensive for the owner of a field, today workers are often given this food at midday because it enables them to continue their work with vigor throughout the hot afternoon.[26] When Ruth received such a meal, it must have served as a great physical and emotional boost.

Moreover, Boaz secretly charged his workers to leave extra grain for Ruth (see Ruth 2:16). Thus, without her knowledge, her workload was made lighter and her production ability increased. As with Ruth, we see in Boaz someone not only willing to do what the law required but also zealous in keeping the spirit of the law. As a man who far exceeded that which was expected or asked of him, Boaz possessed a greatness of generosity and love to match Ruth's.

All of Boaz's efforts proved extremely beneficial for Ruth. When we calculate how much she gathered in one day against known ration amounts and extrapolate that rate to the entire harvest season, it appears that she would have been able to gather enough food for nearly a year while spending time in Boaz's fields.[27] Such a rate must have been gratifying to her and Naomi.

To me the most impressive thing about Boaz is the reason he did all of this for Ruth. He tells her plainly, "It hath fully been shewed me, all that thou hast done unto thy mother in law since the death of thine husband: and how thou hast left thy father and thy mother, and the land of thy nativity, and art come unto a people which thou knewest not heretofore" (Ruth 2:11). Boaz's wish is that "the Lord recompense thy work, and a full reward be given thee of the Lord God of Israel, under whose wings thou art come to trust" (Ruth 2:12). We find not only that Boaz is part of fulfilling this wish but that the picture of coming under God's wing is both a moving image and an important phrase that will come to play later in the story.

Ruth's success as a gleaner led to difficulty in her journey back to the city, for she had to carry all that she gleaned for the entire distance. The burden of the harvest she gleaned made it obvious to Naomi that someone has shown her kindness. When Ruth reveals that Boaz is the kind man, Naomi immediately sees a possible redemption, and further, she sees the hand of God in the fortuitous turn of events: "May he be blessed by the Lord, who hath not abandoned his *hesed* to the living and to the dead. And Naomi said to her, the man is near of kin to us, he is one of our redeemers" (see Ruth 2:20; author's translation). Once she has realized how kindly disposed Boaz is toward Ruth, Naomi sees that the wish she made in Moab for the Lord to show *hesed* to Ruth is being fulfilled. The opportunity for redemption and levirate marriage under the Mosiac law is obvious to Naomi. The possibility of a levirate marriage leading to the continuation of her husband's and son's seed is the reason she states that the Lord is showing *hesed* to the dead. Furthermore, Naomi's lament in the first chapter wherein she wondered why the Lord was allowing tragedy to happen to her seems to be fully satisfied in her mind. Her words affirm that she sees the Lord is in control of things and is bringing about a merciful plan for her.

What a wonderful turn of events in the lives of these poor women! The day must have been one of hope and suspense—their first try at providing for themselves. Gleaning was a difficult and uncertain job, relying on it for their sustenance must have been a daunting and foreboding prospect, full of anxiety. Yet in that day of darkness, a potential redeemer must have been a source of great hope. Just as Israel's hope during their darkest hour while in Egypt was answered by a deliverer, Ruth and Naomi found hope in a righteous Israelite who could serve as a redeemer. They had a hope in Israel.

The fact that Naomi recognized that Boaz was "*one* of our redeemers" (emphasis added) denotes that she realized there were others; she was probably even aware that there was a kinsman closer to her than Boaz. Yet because of Boaz's kindness, her hopes were pinned on this magnanimous man. Her hopes were well placed. It seems that Naomi's plan for Ruth was already hatching. She merely waited for the perfect time to put it into effect.

Such a time came during the threshing. Threshing was a joyful and meaningful event for Israelite farmers, as it represented a successful conclusion to a long series of labors.[28] It simultaneously represented an excellent opportunity for thieves, so husbandmen often stayed on the threshing floor after the threshing. This time of rejoicing and import, along with its assurance that Ruth could find a private audience with Boaz, seemed to be the perfect opportunity for Naomi's plan to be put into motion. She explained very carefully to Ruth what she should do, had Ruth prepare herself by washing and dressing (presumably in the best clothes she had), and then let events unfold.

Our writer cloaks the beginning of this scene in darkness and with shrouds of seclusion.[29] Boaz has been merry, has drunk, and has fallen into a heavy sleep on the threshing floor. Ruth has carefully marked where he will lie, and waits for the full cover of darkness to approach her potential redeemer. Here the tension of the story reaches its apex, heightened by the combination of Ruth's quest and the uncertainty of the outcome that is magnified by images of secrecy and darkness. In this episode of the story, we encounter only the principal actors; no one else knows of their meeting or their plans. Phrases such as "the man" and "a woman" (Ruth 3:8, 16, 18) used in place of their names are further devices of the shroud of secrecy contrived by the writer. Boaz's insistence that no one know that "a woman" had been there (Ruth 3:14), coupled with his and Naomi's initial inabilities to recognize Ruth (see Ruth 3:9, 16), and Ruth's departure before people could recognize each other (see Ruth 3:14) serve to convey this same mood. In contrast to the public lights of the following day, this climactic scene is set in seclusion and dramatic suspense.

These elements of isolation may serve to heighten another dramatic element in the story. The Hebrew words employed by the writer for *lying down*, *uncovering*, and *feet* are words often used as sexual euphemisms in the Hebrew Bible and were sexually charged words. It is possible that these words and this mood was chosen to raise in the mind of the reader the possibility of an intimate encounter. If this is the case, it seems most likely that our writer only did so in order that he might crush the idea, using the potential of impropriety to contrast the reality that nothing of the kind happened.[30] When Boaz invites her to stay until morning, the writer does not use the word for *lying down* (see Ruth 3:13) but rather for *lodging*—a word that never carries sexual connotations in the Hebrew Bible. Most likely the trip home would have been too dangerous a journey for Ruth to undertake in the full dark of night, and hence Boaz instructs her to lodge until the grey hours of the morning. It is possible that suspense about this issue was intentionally raised in order to highlight Boaz's action. Both before and after this episode, Boaz proves himself to be a man who does things exactly the way they should be done or even better. That characteristic is also exemplified on the threshing floor, where the carefully chosen words demonstrate that Boaz does not do anything out of its proper order. Time and again our story presents Ruth or Boaz with choices, and each time they choose valiantly. This quality is strongly highlighted by creating a situation suggestive of sin and using it as a contrast to what actually happened.

Perhaps the most meaningful lines of the story take place there, in the middle of the night, on the threshing floor. There Ruth makes her plea to Boaz, and Boaz affirms his willingness to comply with that request. Most Bible translations—including the King James Version—leave out a few crucial clues that heighten the import of this conversation.

In the King James Version, when Boaz asks who is at his feet, Ruth replies, "I am Ruth thine handmaid: spread therefore thy skirt over thine handmaid; for thou art a near kinsman" (Ruth 3:9).[31] We can reach deeper levels of understanding by providing a more literal translation: "I am Ruth thy handmaid. Spread thy wing over thy handmaid, for thou art a redeemer." To understand the implications of this phrase we must remember Boaz's statement to Ruth during their first meeting, when he said, "The Lord recompense thy work, and a full reward be given thee of the Lord God of Israel, under whose wings thou art come to trust" (Ruth 2:12). On the threshing floor, Ruth uses similar language. By asking Boaz to spread his wing over her, Ruth draws upon Boaz's own imagery, implying that he is the fulfillment of Ruth's coming under the Lord's wings. Boaz's power to redeem her gives him the ability to fulfill this blessing. Boaz's redemption of Ruth would justify her trust in the Lord. That act by Boaz would simultaneously spread his and the Lord's wings over the plaintive Moabite. One of the major motifs of the book of Ruth is that people are often the Lord's means for pouring forth his blessings, or *hesed*. Here Ruth asks Boaz to be the Lord's wings.

This idea is furthered by Boaz's reply to Ruth: "Blessed be thou of the Lord, my daughter, for thou has shown more *hesed* in the end than in the beginning; for thou didst not follow after young men, either rich or poor" (see Ruth 3:10; author's translation). Boaz is also referring to their first conversation, wherein he noted Ruth's kindness to Naomi. Here Boaz expresses his belief that while Ruth had shown *hesed* to Naomi (something Naomi has already expressed), she has also shown *hesed* to Boaz for asking him to be her redeemer and levirate husband. This implies that

Boaz was older and probably even unmarried and childless, though we cannot be sure of the latter suppositions. In any case, he feels that Ruth's covenantal kindness to Naomi leads her to seek a covenantal action from Boaz, which results in a covenantal kindness being shown to him as well.

What heightens this circle of covenant and *hesed* is the fact that Naomi had viewed the arrival of Boaz (a potentially willing redeemer) as an act of *hesed* from the Lord, or as the fulfillment of her desire for the Lord to show *hesed* to Ruth. Thus we have Naomi, Ruth, and Boaz all performing acts of kindness to each other within the context of the covenant, which in turn makes them all recipients of acts of godly kindness. This is heightened by each person realizing that *they* are all expressions of God's covenantal kindness *to each other*. The circle of covenant and reciprocity involving God and these three exemplifies what a covenant community is designed to achieve. These acts and attributes create a small Zion.

Such reciprocity being noted, we must also remain aware that Ruth is the driving force behind all of this. Ruth is the one who accompanies Naomi. Ruth is the one who gleans and thus initiates contact with Boaz. While Naomi conceives the plan, Ruth is the one who puts it into action. While Boaz is generous and willing, Ruth is the one who approaches him and who asks for redemption. In the story we have three magnanimous actors, but the resolution of everyone's plights hinges on Ruth. Her virtue, courage, and action are the engine of the events. That being said, it is symbolically significant that with all of her character, charisma, and drive, Ruth must depend upon another to find full resolution. She is in need of redemption herself.

As mentioned above, Boaz is a man who does things the way they should be done. It is this attribute that leads him to inform Ruth that there is a kinsman who is a closer relation and who thus has the first right to be a redeemer. Boaz is unwilling to attempt to circumvent the proper fulfillment of the laws, so he tells Ruth that he will take care of the matter in the morning, but that it will be done in accord with proper practices (see Ruth 3:12–13). He then sends her home with a measure of food for herself and Naomi.

Perhaps one of the greatest compliments that can be paid to Boaz is found in Naomi's response to how Ruth carried out her plan. When she learns of Boaz's intent, she tells Ruth, "Sit still, my daughter, until thou know how the matter will fall: for the man will not be in rest, until he have finished the thing this day" (Ruth 3:18). In Naomi's mind there is no doubt that once Boaz has set his mind to doing this thing, it will be accomplished in short order.

Naomi's faith is well placed. It also seems clear that the Lord is involved in the matter, for when Boaz goes to the gate in the morning in hopes of resolving this matter with the closer kinsman, "behold, the redeemer of whom Boaz spoke came by" (see Ruth 4:1; author's translation). Our writer did not intend for us to think of this fortuitous meeting between Boaz and Naomi's nearest relative as coincidence. Instead, as Boaz set about his task in the early hours, the Lord assisted him by bringing the right person to the right place at that same early time.

The right place to which they went was the city gate. This is where the official business of ancient cities took place. There Boaz gathers ten elders of the city and asks them to sit as witnesses and judges. Boaz informs Naomi's kinsman of the right to redeem Naomi's land. Boaz also expresses his own willingness to act as redeemer if the right is refused. The kinsman agrees to redeem the land, and then Boaz makes his move. It is only after the kinsman has agreed to buy land that Boaz informs him that with the land comes the care of both Naomi and Ruth. It is obvious that a levirate marriage would be part of the redemption. This would not be as intimidating if the redemption involved only Naomi. But including Ruth in the matter not only added another woman, it added the care of a child he must sire who would eventually take Naomi's land inheritance away from his family. Such a redemption would require the kinsman to use his own means to purchase the field, and these means would not go to the children he already had. They would instead go to Ruth's child, who would be considered of the family of Elimelech. Not wanting to siphon these means away from his own children's inheritance, the kinsman refuses his right of redemption. He formally does this by his words and by removing his sandal and presenting it to Boaz, demonstrating his unwillingness to perform the duty of the redeemer (see Ruth 4:8). Boaz then claims his right to redemption, being willing to sacrifice his estate in order to support Ruth, Naomi, and their heritage.[32]

Boaz does all of these acts in the most legal and public way possible. The elders who are present recognize the greatness of both Boaz and

Ruth and wish for them blessings similar to Rachel, Leah, and Tamar. The Lord immediately blesses Ruth with conception, and all that Naomi or Ruth had ever hoped for is realized. The wording here is significant. In the first chapter, when Naomi had entreated Orpah and Ruth to leave them and return home to look for new husbands, she said, "May the Lord give you that you may find rest, each of you, in the house of her husband" (see Ruth 1:9; author's translation). The resolution of this verse is phrased thus: "the Lord gave conception to her" (Ruth 4:13; author's translation). The verb that Naomi uses when she wishes that her daughters-in-law will be given rest is the same verb used when the Lord gives Ruth conception. This is the only time in the Hebrew Bible when that verb is used to describe conception.[33] This parallel verb usage cannot be coincidental. Instead the author is highlighting that Naomi's wish has been fulfilled. By the grace of God, Ruth has found rest in the house of her new husband. That rest culminates in the conception of a son who will ensure that Ruth will continue to find rest and care throughout her life. Again the shadows of the Messiah are striking.

At this point in the story, Naomi's friends praise the Lord, almost as a bracket to Naomi's lament in the first chapter. "Blessed be the Lord, who hath not left thee this day without a redeemer" (see Ruth 4:14; author's translation). Clearly it is the Lord who has brought about this wonderful resolution. They also recognize how the Lord had worked through Ruth, because they sing of how Ruth's child "will be unto thee a restorer of life, and a nourisher of thine old age; for thy daughter-in-law, who loveth thee, who is better to thee than seven sons, hath borne him" (see Ruth 4:15; author's translation). These women aptly point out that the Lord had honored his covenantal *hesed* and had done so by the *hesed* of others, most especially Ruth. It was through the attempt of many to keep *their* covenants that God had kept *his* covenant. Each actor became an expression of God's efforts to bless his children.

This is most true of Ruth. Part of the resolution of the story is the reward Ruth receives for her efforts, especially for her willingness to care for Naomi despite the eventual price she would have to pay for this generosity. Ruth had lost her own husband, but in the midst of her own pain she was willing the bear the burden of another. In this way she serves as a poignant symbol of the Savior. While Ruth was willing to take Naomi's suffering upon herself, eventually she did not need to because of the mercy of a redeemer. There would be no such escape for the Savior.

The redemption of Ruth was accomplished because of a number of factors. First, she chose to enter a covenant, both with Naomi and with the Lord. These covenants gave her access to blessings from the Lord and a right to a redeemer. Without this covenant, Ruth was not eligible for redemption. Having made the covenant, Boaz was obligated to redeem her. Second, the Lord built into his plan for Israel a way to deliver those who could not deliver themselves. He provided for a redeemer in order to save those who were put in a position of bondage and destitution. Third, the Lord put in place a righteous man who was both able and willing to serve as Ruth's redeemer. Thus because of her covenants, God's plan, and the righteousness of a redeemer, Ruth received redemption for herself and her loved ones. The offspring of this redemption eventually led to Israel's greatest political king, David, and to Israel's greatest spiritual deliverer, king, and redeemer, Christ. She who was willing to save, and was in turn saved by another, was ancestress to *the* Savior. It is not coincidence that our Redeemer descended from a line of redemption. I believe it is fully intentional that the Savior is progeny of a woman who was willing to take upon herself the suffering of another, and a man who was willing to redeem.

The fulfillment of hope for those who were most in need of help speaks of the Hope of Israel. These events happened and are told "in a manner that thereby the people might know in what manner to look forward to [God's] Son for redemption" (Alma 13:2). In a manner of speaking, Ruth's redemption is our own. From Ruth we can better understand the Savior, his covenants with us, the rest God has in store for us, and Christ's glorious redeeming power.

NOTES

1. Paula S. Hiebert, "'Whence Shall Help Come to Me?': The Biblical Widow," in *Gender and Difference in Ancient Israel*, ed. Peggy L. Day (Minneapolis: Augsburg Fortress, 1989), 134–37.
2. Victor P. Hamilton, "Marriage," in *The Anchor Bible Dictionary*, ed. David Noel Freedman (New York: Doubleday, 1992), 4:559–69; Michael C. Kirwen, *African Widows: An Empirical Study of the Problems of Adapting Western Christian Teachings on Marriage*

to the Levíratic Custom for the Care of Widows in Four Rural African Societies (Maryknoll, NY: Orbis Books, 1979), 12.

3. Millar Burrows, "Levirate Marriage in Israel," *Journal of Biblical Literature* 59, no. 1 (March 1940): 23–33.

4. G. Johannes Botterweck and Helmer Ringgren, eds., *Theological Dictionary of the Old Testament*, trans. David Green (Grand Rapids, MI: Eerdmans, 1986), s.v. "*ybm; yābām; yᵉbāmâ.*"

5. Hamilton, "Marriage," 4:559–69.

6. In light of the Deuteronomy passage only, this may seem as if it were related to hospitality customs of the ancient Near East, namely that the woman removes the shoe, but instead of washing the feet, she spat on the face. But in light of what happens in Ruth, where the person himself removes his shoe and no spitting happens, we must conclude that there is something else afoot here.

7. Philip J. King and Lawrence E. Stager, *Life in Biblical Israel* (Louisville, KY: Westminster John Knox, 2001), 56–57; Hamilton, "Marriage," 561; Millar Burrows, "The Ancient Oriental Background of Hebrew Levirate Marriage," *Bulletin of the American School of Oriental Research*, no. 77 (February 1940): 2–3; and Burrows, "Levirate Marriage," 31–32.

8. Kirwen, *African Widows*, 232, table 39; and Hamilton, "Marriage," 4:559–69.

9. Jennifer Clark Lane, "The Lord Will Redeem His People: 'Adoptive' Covenant and Redemption in the Old Testament," in *Thy People Shall Be My People and Thy God My God: The 22nd Annual Sidney B. Sperry Symposium* (Salt Lake City: Deseret Book, 1994), 50–51, 57.

10. Lane, "The Lord Will Redeem," 53; and Jennifer Clark Lane, "The Redemption of Abraham," in *Astronomy, Papyrus, and Covenant*, ed. John Gee and Brian M. Hauglid (Provo, UT: FARMS, 2005), 169.

11. Jennifer Clark Lane, "Not Bondage but Adoption: Adoptive Redemption in the Writings of Paul" (master's thesis, Brigham Young University, 1994), 35; and Robbert Hubbard Jr., "The Go'el in Ancient Israel: Theological Reflections on an Israelite Institution," *Bulletin for Biblical Research* 1 (1991): 3.

12. See also Lane, "Abraham," 171–72.

13. Michael S. Moore, "Haggo'el: The Cultural Gyroscope of Ancient Hebrew Society," *Restoration Quarterly* 23 (1980): 31.

14. Raymond Westbrook, *Property and the Family in Biblical Law* (New York: Sheffield Academic, 1991), 68–89; Raymond Westbrook, "The Law of the Biblical Levirate," *Revue internationale des droits de l'antiquite* 24 (1997). Hector Avalos, "Legal and Social Institutions in Canaan and Ancient Israel," in *Civilizations of the Ancient Near East*, ed. Jack Sasson (New York: Scribner and Sons, 1995), 1:616, advises that the combination of the two customs here may be a literary contrivance, though he does not espouse this position. Neither do I. See also Millar Burrows, "The Marriage of Boaz and Ruth," *Journal of Biblical Literature* 59, no. 4 (December 1940).

15. Eryl W. Davies, "Ruth IV 5 and the Duties of the gō'el," *Vetus Testamentum* 33 (April 1983).

16. William Most, "A Biblical Theology of Covenant in a Covenant Framework," *Catholic Biblical Quarterly* 29 (January 1967): 1–19; Stanislas Lyonnet and Leopold

Sabourin, *Sin, Redemption, and Sacrifice: A Biblical and Patristic Study* (Rome: Biblical Institute Press, 1970), 121; Lane, "The Lord Will Redeem," 54; and Lane, "Abraham," 169.

17. Lane, "The Lord Will Redeem," 54.

18. Orlo J. Price, "The Biblical Teaching Concerning the Hireling and the Pauper," *Biblical World* 29, no. 4 (April 1907): 269–83.

19. Christoph Auffarth, "Protecting Strangers: Establishing a Fundamental Value in the Religions of the Ancient Near East and Ancient Greece," *Numen* 39 (December 1992): 206.

20. Christiana van Houten, *The Alien in Israelite Law* (Sheffield, England: JSOT Press, 1991), 133–38.

21. Van Houten, *The Alien*, 155; and Julian L. Greifer, "Attitudes to the Stranger: A Study of the Attitudes of Primitive Society and Early Hebrew," *American Sociological Review* 10, no. 6 (December 1945): 739–45.

22. Van Houten, *The Alien*, 16.

23. For further discussion on the term *hesed*, see Daniel Belnap's article on the subject in this volume.

24. Edward F. Campbell Jr., *The Anchor Bible: Ruth* (New York: Doubleday, 1975), 78, 82.

25. For an independently reached but similar conclusion, see Campbell, *Ruth*, 80–82. See also Regina Schwartz, *The Curse of Cain: The Violent Legacy of Monotheism* (Chicago: University of Chicago, 1991), 90–91.

26. Amr Al-Azm, "The Importance and Antiquity of Frikkeh: A Simple Snack or a Socioeconomic Indicator of Decline and Prosperity in the Ancient Near East," in *Ethnobotanist of Distant Pasts: Papers in Honour of Gordon Hillman*, ed. A. S. Fairbairn and E. Weiss (Oxford: Oxbow Press, forthcoming).

27. K. Lawson Younger Jr., "Two Comparative Notes on the Book of Ruth," *Journal of the Ancient Near Eastern Society* 26 (1999): 124–25.

28. For the importance of the event and its applicability to Ruth, see Brian Britt, "Death, Social Conflict, and the Barley Harvest in the Hebrew Bible," *Journal of Hebrew Scriptures* 5 (2004–5): 15–16.

29. See Campbell, *Ruth*, 130.

30. Campbell, *Ruth*, 131, independently reaches the same conclusion.

31. For more on this term, see Younger, "Two Comparative Notes," 127–28; and Daniel L. Belnap, "Handmaids of God and Mothers of Kings: A Study of the Terms 'Gebirah' and 'Amah' as Used in the Hebrew Bible" (Provo, UT: master's thesis, Brigham Young University, 1999).

32. On the sacrifice of Boaz as opposed to that of Onan (or his lack thereof) in Genesis 38, see R. G. Abrahams, "Marriage and Affinal Roles: Some Aspects of the Levirate," in *The Character of Kinship*, ed. Jack Goody (Cambridge: Cambridge University Press, 1973), 167.

33. I am grateful to Dr. Daniel Belnap for pointing this out.

12

ISAIAH'S "OTHER" SERVANT SONGS

Terry B. Ball

The latter chapters of Isaiah contain a series of beautiful poetic prophecies about a servant who would bless the world through his life, labors, and suffering. Collectively these prophecies are known as the "Servant Songs" or the "Servant Psalms." Though an issue of some debate, a typical list of the Servant Songs includes Isaiah 42:1–6; 49:1–6; 50:4–9; 52:13–15; 53:1–12.[1]

Through the centuries, scholars, saints, and students have debated the identity of the servant. Some speculate the servant is Isaiah himself. Others suggest that perhaps the servant is Cyrus, the great and magnanimous king who united the Medes and Persians, conquered Babylon, and allowed the Jews to return to Judah. One of the songs, Isaiah 49:1–7, specifically identifies Israel as the servant. Still others see Moses, Jeremiah, and Abraham as fulfillments of the prophecies.[2] Indeed, a case can be made for each of these individuals or entities, and others, to be a fulfillment of some of the Servant Song prophecies, but Latter-day Saints and other Christians typically identify "the Servant"

Terry B. Ball is a professor of ancient scripture at Brigham Young University.

as Jesus Christ, for it can be shown that he fulfills all the prophecies of the Servant Songs and some only he can fulfill. Thus while other individuals or entities such as Isaiah, Cyrus, or Israel appear to fulfill certain portions of the Servant Songs' prophecies, in that capacity they can appropriately be viewed as a type or a symbol for Jesus Christ—the Servant who fulfills them all.

While a study of what the Servant Songs may have meant in their ancient context in regards to these other entities who have been identified as the servant is a fascinating and worthwhile endeavor, this study will focus primarily on how, from a Latter-day Saint perspective, the Servant Songs can be applied to Christ and what important truths they can reveal about our Savior. Arguably, the best known of the Servant Songs is Isaiah 53. This beloved chapter can be understood to foretell the mortal Messiah's humble beginnings and appearance, as well as his sorrows, suffering, and ultimate atoning sacrifice. This study will not review Isaiah 53 in any detail, but rather, focus on the other, lesser-known Servant Songs that likewise can be interpreted to tell us much about the mortal Messiah's ministry and mission.

Song 1

Behold my servant, whom I uphold; mine elect, in whom my soul delighteth; I have put my spirit upon him: he shall bring forth judgment to the Gentiles.

He shall not cry, nor lift up, nor cause his voice to be heard in the street.

A bruised reed shall he not break, and the smoking flax shall he not quench: he shall bring forth judgment unto truth.

He shall not fail nor be discouraged, till he have set judgment in the earth: and the isles shall wait for his law.

Thus saith God the Lord, he that created the heavens, and stretched them out; he that spread forth the earth, and that which cometh out of it; he that giveth breath unto the people upon it, and spirit to them that walk therein:

I the Lord have called thee in righteousness, and will hold thine hand, and will keep thee, and give thee for a covenant of the people, for a light of the Gentiles;

To open the blind eyes, to bring out the prisoners from the prison, and them that sit in darkness out of the prison house. (Isaiah 42:1–7)

The voice in this first Servant Song is Jehovah, speaking in the first person on behalf of the Father. The opening verse of the song (see Isaiah 42:1) tells us much about the sacred relationship between our Heavenly Father and the Servant, his Son, Jesus Christ. We learn from the passage that Christ serves the Father and that the Father upholds and supports the Son. We are taught that God elected or chose the Son for the work and delights in him. We are further taught that Christ has the Spirit of God upon him as he serves. The verse helps us understand that the relationship between the Father and the Son is one of unity, love, trust, and support.

This first verse of the song closes with the assurance that the Servant's labors will bring "judgment" or justice to the Gentiles.[3] The Hebrew term *mishpat*, translated here as "judgment," can refer to either a favorable or unfavorable verdict or sentence.[4] Likely those in Isaiah's day who had suffered at the hands of some of the Gentile nations preferred to understand this promised "judgment" to be a punishment to be poured down upon those who had oppressed them, but the sixth verse of the passage suggests that the justice to be given the Gentiles through the Servant would be a blessing rather than a curse, for the Servant was to be given "for a light of the Gentiles" (42:6; see also Isaiah 60:1–5). It is helpful to understand "light" in this context as truth, knowledge, and intelligence (see D&C 93:24–37). Thus the ministry of the Messiah would serve and bless all, Israel and Gentiles alike, leading both out of darkness.

The next three verses (see Isaiah 42:2–4) tell us something about the mortal ministry of Christ. In the meridian of time, when Jesus was born, many of the descendants of Israel were looking for a Messiah who would come in great power and glory, destroy the wicked, and usher in a great theocracy of peace—they were looking for the millennial Messiah.[5] But this song speaks of a different coming of the Messiah, the coming of the mortal Messiah, whose ministry would be quiet and gentle, whose "voice" would not be "heard in the street," and whose actions would be so tender and quiet that even a delicate, bruised, or damaged reed would not be broken thereby, nor would a feeble "smoking flax" or smoldering wick of a lamp be quenched by his passing. While those close to Jesus were deeply moved and changed by his ministry, on the worldwide stage it drew little attention. The millennial Messiah's coming would shake the earth, and every knee would bow and every tongue would confess (see Isaiah 45:23; Romans 14:11; D&C 88:104), but the Servant's first coming would pass largely unnoticed by most of contemporary humankind. We see this prophecy fulfilled in Jesus's birth to a humble woman in simple surroundings and in his modest and quiet upbringing in an obscure village located in a relatively unremarkable part of the ancient world. His teachings were mostly unknown beyond his own people and land, and his death drew little notice in the Roman Empire.[6]

We further learn that though the Servant's ministry would be comparatively quiet and humble, he would indeed establish truth and justice on the earth. We are also assured that he would not fail (see Isaiah 42:3–4). Certainly we shared that conviction in the primordial councils when we accepted the Father's plan for our happiness and the Servant as our Savior. That faith is found and demonstrated in mortality as we become part of the "isles [that] shall wait for his law" (v. 4). The Book of Mormon teaches us that *isles* is the term Isaiah uses to refer to the scattered covenant people (see 1 Nephi 21:1).[7] In our dispensation it includes those who recognize Jesus of Nazareth as the mortal Messiah and who anxiously anticipate the return of the servant as the millennial Messiah. In the next two verses of this song, Jehovah reminds us of his role as the Creator and giver of life (see Isaiah 42:5) and then, again speaking in the first person as the Father, addresses the Servant directly. He assures the Servant of his divine appointment and support, explaining that he has been given in fulfillment of a covenant (see v. 6).

While scholars often do not include verse 7 in this Servant Song, it seems to be a continuation of the thought in verse 6. Here we learn that in addition to bringing "light" to the Gentiles (v. 6), he will open the eyes of the blind (see v. 7), a promise fulfilled both literally as he healed the blind during his mortal ministry and figuratively as he helps us see truth. He will set prisoners free (see v. 7), another prophecy dualistically fulfilled as he frees us from sin and death through his atoning sacrifice, and as he provided for those in spirit prison to be taught the gospel (see 1 Peter 3:18–20; 4:6; D&C 138:18–21, 30).

Thus this doctrinally rich Servant Song can give us an inspiring glimpse of the Servant Messiah as one who is chosen, loved, and supported. It assures us that though he will have a quiet and largely unnoticed mortal ministry, he will not fail as he labors to bring light, truth, vision, and freedom to all of his Father's children.

Song 2

And again: Hearken, O ye house of Israel, all ye that are broken off and are driven out because of the wickedness of the pastors of my people; yea, all ye that are broken off, that are scattered abroad, who are of my people, O house of Israel. Listen, O isles, unto me; and hearken, ye people, from far; The Lord hath called me from the womb; from the bowels of my mother hath he made mention of my name.

And he hath made my mouth like a sharp sword; in the shadow of his hand hath he hid me, and made me a polished shaft; in his quiver hath he hid me;

And said unto me, Thou art my servant, O Israel, in whom I will be glorified.[8]

Then I said, I have laboured in vain, I have spent my strength for nought, and in vain: yet surely my judgment is with the Lord, and my work with my God.

And now, saith the Lord that formed me from the womb to be his servant, to bring Jacob again to him, Though Israel be not gathered, yet shall I be glorious in the eyes of the Lord, and my God shall be my strength.

And he said, It is a light thing that thou shouldest be my servant to raise up the tribes of Jacob, and to restore the preserved of Israel: I will also give thee for a light to the Gentiles, that thou mayest be my salvation unto the end of the earth.

Thus saith the Lord, the Redeemer of Israel, and his Holy One, to him whom man despiseth, to him whom the nation abhorreth, to a servant of rulers, Kings shall see and arise, princes also shall worship, because of the Lord that is faithful, and the Holy One of Israel, and he shall choose thee.

Thus saith the Lord, In an acceptable time have I heard thee, and in a day of salvation have I helped thee: and I will preserve thee, and give thee *my servant* for a covenant of the people, to establish the earth, to cause to inherit the desolate heritages;

That thou mayest say to the prisoners, Go forth; to them that are in darkness, Shew yourselves. They shall feed in the ways, and their pastures shall be in all high places. (Isaiah 49:1–9 and 1 Nephi 21:1–9; italicized words are unique to 1 Nephi 21)[9]

As Nephi quoted this Servant Song to his brothers, he included several lines of text in the first verse not found in other current versions of the Old Testament. These unique lines are italicized in the quote above. It is not clear whether these additional lines were in the ancient text of Isaiah that Nephi knew, or if these lines are his own commentary, added to help his brothers understand that "isles," to whom this song is addressed, refers to that part of the house of Israel who had been "broken off," "driven out," and "scattered abroad" (1 Nephi 21:1)—a part of Israel that included the descendants of Lehi. As Nephi quoted the eighth verse of this passage, he also retained or added the words "my servant," thereby helping us understand that the Servant was given "for a covenant" and that this Servant Song likely extends at least through verse 9 rather than ending at verse 7 as is commonly thought.

This song begins with the Servant speaking in the first person.[10] The Servant's words add a second witness to many of the truths taught in the first song (Isaiah 42:1–7). We are taught again that the Servant was chosen and called early, even "from the womb" (49:1, 5; see also 42:1). Jesus was not, as some early Christian sects believed, simply a man that lived such a good life in mortality that God chose to put his Spirit in him.[11] Rather, he was elected in the premortal life (see John 1:1; Moses 4:2). We are also taught again that the Servant would be a "light to the Gentiles" (49:6; see also 42:1, 6), that he would be supported by the Father (see 49:8; 42:1, 6), and that he would set prisoners free (see 49:9; 42:7). It is interesting to note that the Hebrew term translated as "salvation" in 49:6 is *Yeshua*, from which the Greek name Jesus is derived, further identifying the Servant as Jesus Christ.[12]

Irony and paradox flavor much of this song. The Servant explains that though he is both well prepared and powerful, having his mouth made "like a sharp sword" and being a "polished shaft," yet he is hidden in the Father's hand and kept in the Father's quiver (49:2), reminding us again that the mortal Messiah conducted his ministry humbly and quietly, in a part of the world that many of his contemporaries would have considered obscure and unimportant (see 42:2–3).

The paradox continues in the following verses as the Servant seems to present opposing perspectives on the accomplishments of his ministry. He appears to observe that while on one hand his strength and labor seem to have been spent in vain, for "Israel hath not been gathered," on the other hand he will have accomplished God's work and is to be judged of the Lord (49:4). In response to the Servant's observation God assures him that though Jacob may not yet be "gathered," his efforts would still be pleasing and "glorious" to the Lord and God will strengthen him (49:5).

These opposing perspectives of the Savior's mortal ministry, one of failure and the other of pleasing accomplishment, can perhaps be illustrated by some of the events of the Savior's last week in mortality. On Palm Sunday, the last Sunday before his Crucifixion, Christ made his Triumphal Entry into Jerusalem for the Passover. Having endured many years of oppression and vassalage to foreign nations, the Jews at that time commonly hoped and believed that the Messiah would come at the Passover, overthrow their oppressors, and establish a theocracy of peace and prosperity.

Many at this particular Passover knew of Jesus of Nazareth and how he had recently demonstrated miraculous messianic powers by waiting until the fourth day and then raising his friend Lazarus from the tomb (see John 11:1–46). They wondered if he was indeed the hoped-for Messiah, if he would come to Jerusalem that very Passover, overthrow the Romans, and begin his messianic reign (see John 12:55–56). We can imagine the excitement that ran through the people in that climate of anxious anticipation when the word quickly spread that Jesus was indeed coming to Jerusalem. As Christ approached the city from the top of the Mount of Olives, riding on an ass in fulfillment of Zechariah's messianic prophecy (see Zechariah 9:9), the people flocked to meet him, casting clothing and palm branches to pave his way and crying out "Hosanna in the highest" (Matthew 21:9; see also Mark 11; Luke 19; John 12).

The plea "Hosanna," a contraction of two Hebrew words meaning "favor us, we implore" or "save us now, we pray," reveals what the people expected of Jesus.[13] Many likely thought he would ride into Jerusalem through the eastern gate, go to the Antonia Fortress, that hated symbol of Roman oppression and dominance built overlooking the Temple, and destroy the Romans stationed there. They wanted their Messiah to give them deliverance and freedom now. We can imagine the people's disappointment when, rather than fulfilling their messianic hopes, Christ entered the city through the gate, went to the Temple, and, after he had "looked around," left Jerusalem for Bethany (Mark 11:11). Some must have judged him a fraud and an imposter. Perhaps some were among those who only a few days later changed their cries from "Hosanna" to "Crucify him!" (Luke 23:21). Few seemed to recognize that the mortal Servant came to conquer something far greater than Romans and political oppressors. He came to conquer sin and death. How fortunate we are that at that moment, rather than doing the will of the people, Christ chose to do the will of the Father. How blessed we are that he understood that his mission was to be "glorious in the eyes of the Lord" rather than the Jews and that his "work" was with God rather than mortal man (Isaiah 49:4–5). To some it may have appeared that he spent his labor and strength "in vain," but the Father knew that his Servant's work would bring "salvation unto the end of the earth" (vv. 4, 6). Ultimately, though he would be despised of men, he would be chosen of God, and "Kings" and "Princes" would come to worship him (v. 7).

Song 3

The Lord God hath given me the tongue of the learned, that I should know how to speak a word in season to him that is weary: he wakeneth morning by morning, he wakeneth mine ear to hear as the learned.

The Lord God hath opened mine ear, and I was not rebellious, neither turned away back.

I gave my back to the smiters, and my cheeks to them that plucked off the hair: I hid not my face from shame and spitting.

For the Lord God will help me; therefore shall I not be confounded: therefore have I set my face like a flint, and I know that I shall not be ashamed.

He is near that justifieth me; who will contend with me? let us stand together: who is mine adversary? let him come near to me.

Behold, the Lord God will help me; who is he that shall condemn me? lo, they all shall wax old as a garment; the moth shall eat them up. (Isaiah 50:4–9)

The Servant again speaks in the first person in this song. He acknowledges God's hand in preparing for and supporting him in the work, giving him the "tongue of the learned," wakening and opening his ears so that he could learn (50:4–5). The testimony reminds us of the boy Jesus's remarkable ability to learn and understand his Father's will, even to the point of astonishing the "doctors" as he heard and questioned them in the Temple when he was just twelve years old (Luke 2:42–52). The Servant then speaks of the persecution he would endure as he would willingly allow himself to be smitten and spat upon (see Isaiah 50:5–6),[14] foreshadowing the cruel treatment he would receive at the hands of Pilate and the Roman soldiers commissioned to scourge and crucify him (see Matthew 26:31). The Servant closes the song by testifying of his confidence that God would sustain and support him, while his adversaries would "wax old" and be eaten up (Isaiah 50:7–9), a prophecy fulfilled as the Roman Empire and the Jewish leaders who condemned him faded in infamy, while the redeeming work of the Servant is praised and persists through eternity.

Song 4

Behold, my servant shall deal prudently, he shall be exalted and extolled, and be very high.

As many were astonied at thee; his visage was so marred more than any man, and his form more than the sons of men:

So shall he sprinkle many nations; the kings shall shut their mouths at him: for that which had not been told them shall they see; and that which they had not heard shall they consider. (Isaiah 52:13–15)

This song begins and ends with praise to the Servant, recognizing his wisdom, his exaltation, and the reverence he will receive from "kings" as they learn of him (52:13, 15). We see the prophecy fulfilled as we remember his role as Jehovah in the Old Testament, as we consider the wisdom manifested in his teachings and actions during his mortal ministry, as we recognize his place with the Father in the eternities, and as we learn of kings and rulers who have placed their faith in him.

The middle of the song speaks of the Servant's "visage" or appearance being "marred" or disfigured more than that of any other man (52:14). We can see one fulfillment of this prophecy in the Savior's agony in Gethsemane. As Elder James E. Talmage explained:

> He struggled and groaned under a burden such as no other being who has lived on earth might even conceive as possible. It was not physical pain, nor mental anguish alone, that caused Him to suffer such torture as to produce an extrusion of blood from every pore; but a spiritual agony of soul such as only God was capable of experiencing. No other man, however great his powers of physical or mental endurance, could have suffered so; for his human organism would have succumbed, and syncope would have produced unconsciousness and welcome oblivion. In that hour of anguish Christ met and overcame all the horrors that Satan, "the prince of this world" could inflict.[15]

The song then explains that the Servant would suffer and be so marred in order to "sprinkle many nations" (52:15). The Joseph Smith Translation of the Bible substitutes the word "gather" for "sprinkle" in this passage. The substitution makes excellent sense to Latter-day Saints who understand that through his atoning suffering, by being marred more than any, our Savior opened the way for us to be gathered, reunited and made "at-one" with our Heavenly Father. To the Old Testament people the Hebrew word *nazah*, translated "sprinkle" in the King James Version, would have made excellent sense as well, for this verb is typically used in the context of purification rites.[16] They would have understood, as do we today, that through his suffering, the Servant would purify and sanctify many.[17]

SUMMARY

The Servant Songs of Isaiah can be seen as a remarkable collection of prophecies about our Savior. While Isaiah 53 is perhaps the most beloved and well known by Christians, the other Servant Songs can tell us much about the mission and message of the Messiah. From them we can learn of the unity, trust, and support shared by the Father and the Son. We can be taught of the election, preparation, and determination of Christ. In them we can find a prophecy of his powerful yet humble and quiet mortal ministry, which would bless all, Israel and Gentiles alike. We can learn of his unflinching labors to do the will of the Father, even in the face of persecution and regardless of what mortal men expected of him. We are reminded that he condescended to suffer and die for us, to provide a way for us to be purified, sanctified, and gathered back to the Father.

NOTES

1. Compare for example Barry L. Bandstra, *Reading the Old Testament: An Introduction to the Old Testament* (Belmont, CA: Wadsworth/Thomson Learning, 2004), 327–28; and Stephen L. Harris and Robert L. Platzner, *The Old Testament: An Introduction to the Hebrew Bible* (Sacramento: McGraw Hill, 2008), 282–83.

2. For a sample and review of the debate, see Donald W. Parry, Jay A. Parry, and Tina M. Peterson, *Understanding Isaiah* (Salt Lake City: Deseret Book, 1998), 358; Victor L. Ludlow, *Isaiah: Prophet, Seer, and Poet* (Salt Lake City: Deseret Book, 1982), 352; Bandstra, *Reading the Old Testament*, 328–29; Harris and Platzner, *Old Testament*, 282–83.

3. In this context, Gentiles refers to nations not considered part of Israel.

4. Francis Brown, S. R. Driver, and Charles A. Briggs, *The New Brown-Driver-Briggs-Gesenius Hebrew and English Lexicon* (New York: Houghton Mifflin, 1906; reprint by Christian Copy Rights, 1983), 1047–48.

5. For a review of Jewish messianic hope in the meridian of time, see James E. Talmage, *Jesus the Christ* (Salt Lake City: Deseret Book, 1983), 40, 452; Bruce R. McConkie, *The Mortal Messiah: From Bethany to Calvary* (Salt Lake City: Deseret Book, 1979), 43, 258–59; Milton R. Hunter, *The Gospel through the Ages* (Salt Lake City: Bookcraft, 1945), 171–72.

6. The prophecies of a relatively quiet, unnoticed mortal ministry of the Messiah apply to the Old World, for in the New World of the Nephites and Lamanites, his birth was accompanied by widely recognized signs and wonders and his death by tremendous destruction and upheaval in the land, as prophesied by Samuel the Lamanite and others (see Helaman 14; 3 Nephi 1, 8–9).

7. This verse in 1 Nephi quotes from Isaiah 49 and adds several lines of clarification concerning the identity of the "isles" to whom the prophecy is directed.

8. As translated in the King James Version, this verse appears to identify Israel as the servant, though later in the song Israel is to be gathered and saved by the Servant (see Isaiah 49:5). In the Hebrew it is unclear whether Israel is the servant or the entity that is to be glorified in this verse. Regardless, even if the servant is identified as Israel, this prophecy can, and in my view should, be understood dualistically as referring to Christ as well, for only he fulfills all the Servant prophecies.

9. While most conclude the Servant Song found in chapter 49 at verse 6 (see note 1 above), the Book of Mormon addition of the phrase "my servant" in verse 8 suggests the text is still speaking of the Servant after verse 6 and that the song can be extended through verse 9, as I have chosen to do herein.

10. The Servant speaks of the future in the past tense in these verses, employing a prophetic style called the "prophetic perfect." Abinadi defined this style as "speaking of things to come as though they had already come" (Mosiah 16:6).

11. This was a belief held by some Gnostic Christians. For a discussion of the issue, see Bart D. Ehrman, *The New Testament: A Historical Introduction to the Early Christian Writings* (New York: Oxford University Press, 2004), 6–7, 191.

12. Brown, Driver, and Briggs, *Hebrew and English Lexicon*, 447.

13. Brown, Driver, and Briggs, *Hebrew and English Lexicon*, 333, 609.

14. Here again the Servant is speaking in the prophetic perfect. See note 5 above.

15. Talmage, *Jesus the Christ*, 568–69.

16. Brown, Driver, and Briggs, *Hebrew and English Lexicon*, 633.

17. The Isaiah scroll from the Qumran corpus has a verb with the same root as "Messiah," meaning "anointed," in place of the verb "marred" in this passage. The teaching that the servant would be "anointed" more than any other man likewise makes excellent sense in this passage. When teaching the descendants of Lehi, the Savior used the imagery of being marred more than any other in reference to a latter-day servant that is typically understood to be the Prophet Joseph Smith (see 3 Nephi 21:10–11).

13

"HOLINESS TO THE LORD" AND PERSONAL TEMPLE WORSHIP

Gaye Strathearn

Over twenty years ago, I embarked on a three-day excursion into the Sinai Peninsula and the traditional site of Mount Sinai. This mountain is in the middle of a mountainous desert, miles from anywhere. We arrived there in the early evening and had dinner in a Bedouin camp and then bunked down in some tents, waiting for 3:00 a.m. to arrive. That is when we were to make the 2,500-foot ascent, because our leaders said that it would be much too hot if we waited until the sun came up. Somewhere along the line, I ended up being the one who carried a huge first aid kit up the mountain. It was hard work climbing that mountain, especially with the extra weight of that pack. It took us about two hours, and toward the end I was not even sure that it was worth continuing on— after all, I was up pretty high and I had a pretty good view of things from where I stood. Why not just watch the sunrise from where I was? Besides, I was not sure that my legs would carry me another step. But somehow I kept telling myself that I had come this far, I may as well finish it out.

Gaye Strathearn is an assistant professor of ancient scripture at Brigham Young University.

At the point where I could see the end in sight and thought that there was some chance of reaching the summit, I came to the famous (or infamous) seven hundred steps, built by monks centuries ago. Now, when people have been climbing a mountain for almost two hours and their quadriceps are already like jelly, the last thing they want to see is seven hundred uneven steps! But my friends were cheering me on and encouraging me to keep going. I think those stairs were the hardest part of all, but just as I collapsed at the top, I looked up and the first rays of sunlight peeked over the horizon. What a tremendous sight! If I live to be a hundred, I will never forget that experience. Somehow, as I stood up and surveyed God's handiwork in its pristine glory, I forgot about the weight of the first aid kit, I forgot about the past two hours of torture, and I forgot about my jellified knees. Somehow those bodily inconveniences had lost their significance.

We then divided into three classes, took out our Bibles, and studied the Exodus account of Moses' ascents into this holy mountain and then had a testimony meeting. Mount Sinai was sacred space, set apart both geographically and spiritually from the rest of the world, because on that mount Moses entered the presence of God. My time on Mount Sinai was a very sacred experience for me. In a sense, on that day we also entered the presence of God, because the presence of the Holy Ghost was so strong it was almost tangible. As hard as the journey up the mountain was for me, it was worth every step. I have since contemplated the events of that day and thought about what would have happened if I had decided to stop halfway up the mountain. Certainly the sunrise would have still been magnificent, but I would have missed the supernal experience of the class discussion and the testimony meeting and the Spirit that attended both. Twenty years later, I am so glad that I kept going.

When we returned to Jerusalem, Ann Madsen gave a fireside entitled "Dare to Ascend," where she built on our experience at Sinai and taught us that, spiritually speaking, many people think that going halfway up the mountain is good enough, and so they become satisfied with the view from where they are. As a result, they keep themselves from participating in the type of supernal spiritual experiences that God wants them to have. We must resist the temptation to think that "near enough is good enough" in the journey up our spiritual mountains. We must keep pressing forward, even though the journey is difficult at times. I have thought of this experience and Sister Madsen's teaching often as I have studied the accounts of Moses in the Old Testament.

The scriptures describe Mount Sinai as a holy place. It is not just like any other mountain. Rather, according to Exodus 3:1, it is "the mountain of God." When Moses first climbed this mountain and approached the burning bush, the Lord called to him and said, "Draw not nigh hither: put off thy shoes from off thy feet, for the place whereon thou standest is holy ground" (Exodus 3:5; see also Acts 7:33).

The next time that Moses ascended Mount Sinai was just after he led the Israelites out of Egypt. While they camped at its base, Moses again climbed the mount to enter into God's presence. The Lord then informed Moses, "Now therefore, if ye will obey my voice indeed, and keep my covenant, then ye shall be a peculiar treasure unto me above all people: for all the earth is mine: and ye shall be unto me a kingdom of priests, and an holy nation. These are the words which thou shalt speak unto the children of Israel" (Exodus 19:5–6). It is noteworthy that in this visit the Lord again emphasized holiness, but this time the emphasis was not on the geographical space where Moses stood, but on the Lord's desire to make the children of Israel holy.

"GRADED HOLINESS"

Holiness is an important concept in the Old Testament. It was the determining factor in God's desire for Israel to be a peculiar people. "For thou art an holy people unto the Lord thy God, and the Lord hath chosen thee to be a peculiar people unto himself, above all the nations that are upon the earth" (Deuteronomy 14:2). Holiness was the antithesis of the profane and the unclean. In Leviticus 10:10 we read, "And that ye may put difference between holy and profane [ḥol], and between clean and unclean" (author's translation). Holiness, however, was not a one-dimensional state, where you were either in a state of holiness or you were not. Rather, there were levels of holiness.[1] Perhaps the most obvious example of this was the Tabernacle, in which the inner sanctum was called the Holy of Holies— or, in other words, the most holy (qōdeš haqodašîm)—and was separated from the holy place (haqōdeš) by a veil (see Exodus 26:33).

There is also a distinction between the Lord's command to Moses to put off his shoes because the ground was holy and his hope that Israel would be a holy people. The English translation for both of these verses does not do justice to the nuances of the original Hebrew words. Although in both instances the word translated "holy" comes from the Hebrew root *qdš*, two different forms are used. When speaking of the ground, the Lord uses the noun form *qōdeš* (accented on the first syllable, and the final consonant sounds like "sh"). In and of itself the ground was not holy, but it had been made holy by the presence of God. When he speaks of his desire for the children of Israel, however, he uses the adjectival form *qadōš* (accented on the second syllable).

E. Jan Wilson has shown that there is a significant difference in meaning between these two forms of *qdš*. In the Old Testament these two words "are not used in the same contexts: i.e. the one is *not* just the adjectival form of the other, but rather, they have linguistic ranges that do not overlap significantly. . . . While *qōdeš* simply denotes a state of belonging to the realm of the divine, those things which are *qadōš* all possess the ability to move things (or people) into, or at least toward, the realm of the divine."[2] This lexical nuance is important: *qōdeš* refers to a static state that encompasses the divine realm, whereas *qadōš* is much more dynamic, with a characteristic of enabling others to enter a state of holiness. In what follows I will discuss how an understanding of the nuances in these two words in the Old Testament can help modern temple patrons better appreciate the Lord's purposes in inviting them to enter temples where the phrase "Holiness to the LORD" is engraved above the entrance.

HOLY (QADŌŠ)

Wilson argues that God is *qadōš* because he is "the source of holiness" and "the primary agent of sanctification" (i.e., making someone or something holy).[3] Thus, in the Old Testament God is never described as *qōdeš*, only *qadōš*. Isaiah writes, "For thus saith the high and lofty One that inhabiteth eternity, whose name is Holy [*qadōš*]; I dwell in the high and holy place [*qadōš*], with him also that is of a contrite and humble spirit, to revive the spirit of the humble, and to revive the heart of the contrite ones" (Isaiah 57:15). Not only is God *qadōš*, but so is his "great and terrible name," according to the Psalmist (Psalm 99:3). A number of mortals also acknowledge that he is *qadōš*. When Joshua taught his people about the importance of choosing to serve God rather than "strange gods," he used *qadōš* to describe the holiness of God (Joshua 24:20). For Hannah and the men of Beth-shemesh, *qadōš* was intimately tied to the great power of God. When Hannah prayed in gratitude after finally giving birth to Samuel, she acknowledged, "There is none holy [*qadōš*] as the Lord" (1 Samuel 2:2). When the Israelites of Beth-shemesh were slain for looking into the ark of the covenant, the survivors declared, "Who is able to stand before this holy [*qadōš*] Lord God?" (1 Samuel 6:20). Habakkuk's concern that God would use the wicked Chaldeans to punish Israel led him to cry out, "Art thou not from everlasting, O Lord my God, mine Holy One [*qadōš*]?" (Habakkuk 1:12).

Although God is the ultimate source of the power to sanctify, at times he also uses certain people or places to sanctify, and therefore the Old Testament also describes them as *qadōš*. For example, the sacrificial court of the Tabernacle or Temple is described as a holy place (*qadōš*) (see Exodus 29:31; Leviticus 6:16, 26, 27; 7:6; 10:13; 24:9; Ezekiel 42:13) because the sacrifices bring people into the realm of holiness. Those who administer the sacrifices are also described as *qadōš*. The Lord declared of the priests, "And ye shall be holy [*qadōš*] unto me: for I the Lord am holy [*qadōš*], and have severed you from other people, that ye should be mine" (Leviticus 20:26). The account of Korah, Dathan, and Abiram, all of whom were Levites and held the priesthood, serves as an important commentary on the state of priestly *qadōš*. These three men challenged the authority of Moses and Aaron by declaring, "Ye take too much upon you, seeing all the congregation are holy [*qadōš*], every one of them, and the Lord is among them: wherefore then lift ye up yourselves above the congregation of the Lord?" (Numbers 16:3). Moses responded by falling upon his face and saying, "Even to morrow the Lord will shew who are his, and who is holy [*qadōš*]; and will cause him to come near unto him: even him whom he hath chosen will he cause to come near unto him" (Numbers 16:5). Moses and Korah seem to have a different understanding of what it means to be *qadōš*. Korah argued that the presence of the Lord qualified every member of the congregation to be *qadōš*. Moses's response, however, showed that being *qadōš* is not something that was automatic. Thus Moses instructed Korah "that the man whom the Lord doth choose, he shall be holy [*qadōš*]." This incident teaches that *qadōš* is special; even the Levites who held the priesthood were not automatically *qadōš*.

Though generally laypeople could not share in priestly holiness (i.e., *qadōš*), there were avenues available for them to become *qadōš*, even if it was for a short period of time. For example, they could participate in a Nazarite vow.[4] Those entering into the vow are also described as *qadōš* for the period of their vow (see Numbers 6:1–8). Likewise, God sometimes described Israel as being a *qadōš* people (see Deuteronomy 14:2, 21), or at least he hoped that they would become such (see Exodus 19:6; Deuteronomy 26:19; 28:9). Speaking to Israel, God said, "Ye shall not make yourselves abominable with any creeping thing that creepeth, neither shall ye make yourselves unclean with them, that ye should be defiled thereby. For I am the Lord your God: ye shall therefore sanctify yourselves, and ye shall be holy [*qadōš*]; for I am holy [*qadōš*]" (Leviticus 11:43).[5] Thus God's greatest desire for his people is that they become as he is. This was the reason that he brought his people out of the land of Egypt. "For I am the Lord that bringeth you up out of the land of Egypt, to be your God: ye shall therefore be holy [*qadōš*], for I am holy [*qadōš*]" (Leviticus 11:45).

The Lord's first attempt to have his people become *qadōš* occurred when Moses went up into Mount Sinai while the Israelites waited below. As we have noted, Moses was commanded to teach Israel that if they would obey his voice and keep his covenant they would become a peculiar people and a holy nation (see Exodus 19:5–6). Therefore, the Lord commanded Moses to sanctify his people, "for the third day the Lord will come down in the sight of all the people upon mount Sinai" (Exodus 19:11). In theory, at least, Israel would become *qadōš* because the Lord, who is *qadōš*, would be among them (see Numbers 16:3).

Unfortunately, the children of Israel were not ready for such a transformation. When "all the people saw the thunderings, and the lightnings, and the noise of the trumpet, and the mountain smoking: and when the people saw it, they removed, and stood afar off. And they said unto Moses, Speak thou with us, and we will hear, but let not God speak with us, lest we die" (Exodus 20:18–19). The Doctrine and Covenants provides some additional information about this experience. "For without this [i.e., the greater priesthood and its ordinances], no man can see the face of God, even the Father, and live. Now this Moses plainly taught to the children of Israel in the wilderness, and sought diligently to sanctify his people that they might behold the face of God; but they hardened their hearts and could not endure his presence; therefore, the Lord in his wrath, for his anger was kindled against them, swore that they should not enter into his rest while in the wilderness, which rest is the fulness of his glory" (D&C 84:22–24). Israel rejected the opportunity to enter into God's rest and receive the fulness of his glory; they rejected the opportunity to become *qadōš*. Thus we see that not only does God confer holiness upon his priests but he desires all Israel to become *qadōš*—but they have to want it.

HOLINESS (QŌDEŠ)

When Israel rejected the opportunity to have God dwell in their presence and to become *qadōš*, he introduced a temple system whereby the priests and high priests represented the people before God. Israel forfeited direct access to God. Instead the responsibility of the priests and high priests was to create on earth a realm of *qōdeš*, the static quality of belonging to the realm of the divine. The Old Testament uses *qōdeš* primarily to describe the Temple (see Exodus 28:29, 35, 43; 29:30; 35:19; 39:41; 2 Chronicles 5:11; 29:5, 7; 35:5), including priesthood garments (see Exodus 28:2, 4; 31:10), the Temple altar and the laver (see 30:28–29), and the holy mountain (see Ezekiel 28:14; Daniel 9:20; 11:45). In these instances it refers to a specific geographic area and the things contained therein that have been designated as *qōdeš*. However, at times it is also used to describe the Sabbath day (see Exodus 12:16; 16:23) and holy festivals (see Leviticus 23:2, 4, 7, 8). Less frequently it is used to describe Jerusalem (see Jeremiah 31:40; Daniel 9:24; Joel 3:17); objects devoted to God, including tithes (see Leviticus 27:28, 30, 33); the covenant (see Daniel 11:28, 30); worship (see Psalms 29:2; 96:9); and the people of Israel (see Ezra 8:28; Jeremiah 2:3; Daniel 12:7), including the holy seed (see Ezra 9:2; Isaiah 6:13).

Within the Temple, the roles of the priest and the high priest were particularly important in preparing a state of *qōdeš*. We have already noted that the priests were considered to be *qadōš* (see Leviticus 20:26), but they are also described as being *qōdeš*. As such they "stand in a special relationship with Yahweh [Jehovah] and as such belong to the divine sphere itself, a situation imposing on them the obligation to maintain cultic purity and enjoining the congregation to accord them special respect."[6] Moses was directed to "anoint Aaron and his sons, and consecrate [make holy; Piel form of *qdš*] them, that they may minister unto me in the priest's office" (Exodus 30:30). But in Leviticus 21 we see the dual nature of them being both *qadōš* and *qōdeš*. "They shall be holy [*qadōš*] unto their God, and not profane the name of their God: for the offerings of the Lord made by fire, and the bread of their God, they do offer: therefore they shall be holy [*qōdeš*]. . . . Thou shalt sanctify him therefore; for he offereth the bread of thy God: he shall be holy [*qadōš*] unto thee: for I the Lord, which sanctify you, am holy [*qadōš*]" (Leviticus 21:6, 8). As representatives of God, he declared them *qadōš* because their work helped bring others to the divine realm, and they were also *qōdeš* because they officiated within the divine realm of the Tabernacle. Thus we can understand this dual state to mean that priests are in a state of *qōdeš* except when they are actively engaged in sanctifying others, and then they are *qadōš*.

The holy garments that the priest wore are also described as *qōdeš* (see Exodus 28:2). In particular, the high priest wore a "turban-like head-band"[7] with a golden plate, on which the words "Holiness to the LORD" (*qōdeš leadonai*) were engraved (see Exodus 28:36–37). The symbolism of the phrase "Holiness to the LORD" on Aaron's headband suggests that it was not just a declaration that he had become holy so that he could offici-ate in the Tabernacle. If that was the case, it could have been embroidered on his sleeve or some other part of his clothing. Instead it was placed on his forehead, indicating that he must constantly be thinking about holiness while he officiated in the Tabernacle, particularly as he entered the presence of God. This same phrase is found five additional times in the scriptures, all of them in the Old Testament (see Exodus 39:30; Isaiah 23:18; Jeremiah 2:3; Zechariah 14:20–21; Malachi 2:11).

HOLINESS AND PERSONAL TEMPLE WORSHIP

So what does all this have to do with Temple worship today? These laws of sacrifices and rituals seem far removed from our day, but there are lessons we can learn. Our Temple experience is different from that of the Israelites because when Jesus died and "the veil of the temple was rent from the top to the bottom" (Mark 15:38), he became our High Priest. Under the law of Moses, "the way into the holiest of all was not yet made manifest, while as the first tabernacle was yet standing" (Hebrews 9:8). Through Christ's atoning sacrifice, we have the opportunity to be *qadōš*, or sanctified, and we are now encouraged to have "boldness to enter into the holiest" (Hebrews 10:19). Thus as individuals, even though we don't belong to the Levitical priestly class, we now have the opportunity, if we are worthy, to enter the Temple and enter the realm of *qōdeš*. But even more important, we have the opportunity to enter the presence of God and become *qadōš*.

When we enter the Temple today, we enter into the physical realm of *qōdeš*. While we may no longer be required to remove our shoes as we enter the Temple because it is holy ground, nevertheless there are ways that we must, like Moses and Joshua, prepare ourselves to enter the realm of *qōdeš*. In our physical preparations for the Temple, we must symbolically, physically, and spiritually prepare ourselves to leave behind the world as we enter into the divine realm. Therefore, we can begin to physically and spiritually prepare long before we enter the Temple doors. Some examples are the following. We can start by thinking more seriously about the sacrament. We partake of the sacrament so that we can petition the Lord for an endowment of his Spirit for the upcoming week. We can create opportunities in our lives where the still, small voice does not have to compete with the constant noise of our busy life. Unless we make a concerted effort, the radio, the TV, or the iPod can overwhelm his gentle promptings. Maybe it would be helpful to turn off the radio as we drive to the Temple. We can also prepare to enter the realm of *qōdeš* by participating in activities that invite the Spirit into our lives, such as actively participating in our Church membership, pondering the things of eternity by studying our scriptures and the conference talks, participating in conversations with our Father through prayer, and preparing to actively participate in our Church meetings. All of these things will help us to be worthy as we enter the realm of *qōdeš* in the Temple.

As we enter the Temple, we should consciously take note that the same phrase engraved on Aaron's headband, "Holiness to the LORD" is also engraved upon the Temple. In the dedicatory prayer of the Kirtland Temple, the Prophet Joseph Smith pled with the Lord "that all people who shall enter upon the threshold of the Lord's house may feel thy power, and feel constrained to acknowledge that . . . it is thy house, a place of thy holiness" (D&C 109:13). Just as Aaron wore the phrase on his forehead, so we must remember in everything we do and say while we are in the Temple for a short time that we have left behind the world and have entered into the realm of *qōdeš*. Modern prophets and apostles have encouraged us to increase our appreciation for the relationship between the Temple and our quest to become holy. President Howard W. Hunter declared, "The temple is a place of beauty, it is a place of revelation, it is a place of peace. It is the house of the Lord. It is holy unto the Lord. It should be holy unto us."[8] President James E. Faust directed, "We must try harder to be a holy people."[9]

But entering the realm of the divine and becoming *qōdeš* must be only the beginning, not the destination, of our Temple worship. God's hope for us, as it was for Israel, is that we not only become holy, but more importantly, become as he is. Therefore, by worthily entering the Temple and keeping our thoughts centered on holiness, we are in a position to seek to become *qadōš*. In the Temple we can receive a measure of being holy because we are surrounded by holiness, and because we make covenants that, through the Atonement, confer holiness upon us. Thus, in the Temple we seek for the same promise God gave to the Israelites as they lived their covenantal obligations: "Thou mayest be an holy [*qadōš*] people unto the Lord thy God, as he hath spoken" (Deuteronomy 26:16). Our Temple experience, therefore, should do something more to us than just becoming temporarily *qōdeš* because we enter a holy place. It is meant to transform us so that we become holy as God is holy and do the work of helping to sanctify others. I think this is what Sister Elaine S. Dalton meant when she taught, "When we are worthy, we can not only *enter* the temple, the temple can *enter* us."[10]

In a perfect, ideal setting, we would now be holy and be in the same state as our Father in Heaven. But our Temples, as beautiful as they are, are just an imitation of the celestial Temple where God and his Son reside. Hebrews 8:1–2 reads, "We have . . . an high priest [i.e., Christ], who is set on the right hand of the throne of the Majesty in the heavens; a minister of the sanctuary, and of *the true tabernacle*, which the Lord pitched, and not man" (emphasis added). Further, our ministrations in the earthly Temple are a "shadow of heavenly things, as Moses was admonished of God when he was about to make the tabernacle: for, See, saith he, that thou make all things according to the pattern shewed to thee in the mount" (Hebrews 8:5). As wonderful and as powerful as our Temples are, and in contrast to the heavenly Temple, the reality is we must leave them and return to the world. The measure of holiness we receive as the Temple enters into us can have a residual effect as we return to the world. Remember that when Moses came down from Mount Sinai, his face was shining (see Exodus 34:29–35). He had a residual effect from his Temple experience in the presence of God. It was so visibly manifest that he had to cover his face with a veil. We also can take with us a portion of that holiness as we leave the Temple, return to the world, and work to help others become sanctified.

Unfortunately, just as the shining eventually dissipated from Moses's face, so too the level of holiness we gain in the Temple can fade as we return to the world. Robert J. Matthews, the first president of the Mount Timpanogos Temple, once compared going to the Temple to lifting weights. He said that lifting weights only has the power to increase our strength if we do it regularly enough that the effect of our last workout does not wear off. Lifting weights once, twice, or even three times a year will not increase our strength. Brother Matthews's analogy reminds us that if we are to become holy we must go to the Temple often enough that the residual effects do not wear off. That does not mean that we should mandate a specific frequency with which we should attend the Temple. Instead, the Brethren encourage us to attend "as frequently as time and means and personal circumstances allow."[11] But do we understand the principle? Going to the Temple can confer holiness because we are in a holy place, but the goal of Temple worship is that we become holy beings. That is one important reason why the Lord has directed us to seek out our ancestors and do Temple work for them. Doctrine and Covenants 128:18 teaches us that the dead cannot be made perfect without the ordinance work that we perform for them. But it also teaches us that we cannot be made perfect without them. What does that mean? In part, at least, it means that doing the work for our dead ancestors provides us an opportunity we need to return often to the Temple so that we can build on the holiness received from our previous Temple experiences. It also provides us an opportunity to help them, and thus we become holy.

If we are diligent in worthily going to the Temple, having the phrase "Holiness to the LORD" indelibly imprinted upon our thoughts, we can become holy. We will achieve the Father's greatest desire for us, and we will be able to enter his presence, not just to stand and be judged (see 2 Nephi 2:10) but to dwell with him and be as he is, working to bring salvation to others. As we begin to develop a state of holiness, the changes will be manifest outside of the Temple as well. We will leave the Temple with a greater desire and a more focused resolve to help people move into the realm of the divine, not just through Temple work but with missionary work, home and visiting teaching, and magnifying our callings to an even greater extent.

I think that is what President Gordon B. Hinckley was referring to when he declared, "I make a promise to you that every time you come to the temple you will be a better man or woman when you leave than you were when you came. That's a promise. I believe it with all my heart."[12] These changes will not be externally motivated, but they will be motivated by an internal yearning to have others participate with us in holiness. Although he does not use the word qadōš, President Faust has described this state of being: "Holiness is the strength of the soul. It comes by faith and through obedience to God's laws and ordinances. God then purifies the heart by faith, and the heart becomes purged from that which is profane and unworthy. When holiness is achieved by conforming to God's will, one knows intuitively that which is wrong and that which is right before the Lord. Holiness speaks when there is silence, encouraging that which is good or reproving that which is wrong."[13]

Although Israel rejected their opportunity to become holy at Mount Sinai, it appears that the people of Enoch were able to achieve it. "The Lord came and dwelt with his people, and they dwelt in righteousness. . . . And the Lord called his people Zion. . . . And it came to pass in his days, that he built a city that was called the City of Holiness" (Moses 7:16, 18–19).

CONCLUSION

In an address on becoming a Zion people, Elder D. Todd Christofferson taught, "We are to become not only good but holy men and women."[14] Over twenty years ago, I climbed Mount Sinai. It was a difficult physical challenge for me. There were many times when I thought that "near enough was good enough" as I ascended the mountain and entered the realm of *qōdeš*. That journey required a strong measure of commitment and endurance on my part. I am so grateful that I had people surrounding me, encouraging me to continue until I completed the journey. While the memories and feelings of that physical journey and the experiences I had on top of Mount Sinai have stayed with me these twenty years, I have come to learn that they were just a foretaste of what can come from the power of Temple worship. Temple worship is much more than removing my shoes because I am standing on holy ground; it is embarking on a journey so that I can have God come and dwell with me, so that I can become as he is. This journey also requires a strong measure of commitment and endurance on my part to complete the journey rather than settle for something less. I must dare to ascend the mountain. It is not something that happens instantly, but, as I am learning, the journey is worth it. By participating in this journey I have learned that I must not settle for the view from halfway up the mountain, settle for being in the realm of holiness. Rather, I want to become holy so that I can act as an instrument in God's hands to help others become holy. The Temple can enable me to become a Mount Sinai—to help others achieve what God originally hoped for his people on Mount Sinai. That goal is the motivating power that returns me each time to the Temple.

NOTES

I am particularly grateful to Dan Belnap for introducing me to the nuances of holiness in the Old Testament, for his careful reading of a draft of this paper, and his suggestions that have helped strengthen this paper.

1. For a detailed discussion of holiness in the priestly material of the Old Testament, see Philip Peter Jenson, *Graded Holiness: A Key to the Priestly Conception of the World*, Journal for the Study of the Old Testament Supplement Series 106 (Sheffield, UK: JSOT Press, 1992).

2. E. Jan Wilson, *"Holiness" and "Purity" in Mesopotamia*, Alter Orient und Altes Testament 237 (Kevelaer: Butzon & Bercker; Neukirchen-Vluyn: Neukirchener, 1994), 87–88, emphasis added. Wilson uses a definition of holiness that was first coined by Jenson (*Graded Holiness*, 48). Wilson's distinction between *qadōš* and *qōdeš* is a refinement of Jenson's definition. He shows that this distinction is found throughout the Old Testament, and is not just confined to the priestly material. I am grateful to Dan Belnap for introducing me to Wilson's article.

3. Wilson, *"Holiness" and "Purity,"* 88.

4. David P. Wright, "Holiness (OT)," in *The Anchor Bible Dictionary*, ed. David Noel Freedman (New York: Doubleday, 1992), 3:238–39.

5. Wilson identifies other places that are also described as *qadōš*, but which are outside the scope of this paper: "the day on which Ezra reads the law (Nehemiah 8:9, 10, 11), and the water used to test the woman suspected of adultery (Numbers 5:17)" (Wilson, *"Holiness" and "Purity,"* 88).

6. Helmer Ringgren, "קדש *qdš*," in *Theological Dictionary of the Old Testament*, ed. G. Johannes Botterweck, Helmer Ringgren, and Heinz-Josef Fabry, trans. Douglas W. Stott (Grand Rapids, MI: Eerdmans, 2003), 12:533.

7. Ludwig Köhler and Walter Baumgartner, "מצנפת," in Ludwig Köhler and Walter Baumgartner, *Hebrew and Aramaic Lexicon of the Old Testament*, rev. Walter Baumgartner and Johann Jakob Stamm; trans. M. E. J. Richardson (New York: E. J. Brill, 1995), 2:624.

8. Cited by Jay M. Todd, "President Howard W. Hunter: Fourteenth President of the Church," *Ensign*, July 1994, 5.

9. James E. Faust, "Standing in Holy Places," *Ensign*, May 2005, 68.

10. Elaine S. Dalton, "Look toward Eternity!" *Ensign*, November 2006, 32.

11. Todd, "President Howard W. Hunter," 5.

12. Gordon B. Hinckley, *Discourses of President Gordon B. Hinckley* (Salt Lake City: The Church of Jesus Christ of Latter-day Saints, 2005), 2:331.

13. Faust, "Standing in Holy Places," 62.

14. D. Todd Christofferson, "Come to Zion," *Ensign*, November 2008, 39.

THE IMAGERY OF HOSEA'S FAMILY AND THE RESTORATION OF ISRAEL

Aaron Schade

Throughout the centuries, Hosea chapters 1–2 have astounded, fascinated, intrigued, and impressed both readers and scholars of the Bible alike. From the enigmatic images of Hosea's marriage to questions regarding Israel's history, punishment, restoration, and future, the content of these chapters has caused individuals either to ponder and search out the intended meaning of Hosea's message or to pass over and exclude them from any serious study because of their unusual flavor. These chapters are richly symbolic, and through symbols Hosea helps his readers understand Israel's history relevant to the past, present, and future in order to understand the overall meaning of the book.

Hosea 1–2 uses imagery to describe the Lord's covenant with Israel, relating Israel's covenant to that of the patriarch Abraham; the text unfolds several phases of the covenant relationship between God and his people with past and future generations. While Hosea's message carries with it proclamations of destruction and hardship, it also includes words of hope and reconciliation for Israel and its descendants. In fact,

---

Aaron Schade is an assistant professor of religion at Brigham Young University–Hawaii.

as Ehud Ben Zvi, a prominent scholar on the book of Hosea, has written, "It is precisely the element of hope—hope against a background of apparent hopelessness—that has led to the book's wide use in Jewish liturgy."[1] When the metaphors in the book of Hosea are viewed beyond their literal application, the word of the Lord through Hosea becomes a vivid description of the scattering and gathering of Israel and offers glimmers of hope of restoration and the fulfillment of covenants with the Lord.

This paper will address a few major issues in Hosea 1–2, including how the imagery of the names of Hosea's family members are used, what they really mean in context, how the history and condition of Israel is presented, and what clues the text gives us about the nature of Israel's reconciliation and restoration. I will show how Hosea intersperses teachings on the scattering and gathering of Israel, how he references the Abrahamic covenant to intertwine dispensations, and how he draws upon images of the Creation, the Fall, and the earth receiving its paradisiacal glory. I will show that the family imagery is used to portray Israel's then-present situation in relation to its near and distant future. This demonstration will contribute to the text's rich language in defining Israel's separation from and eventual reconciliation with God.

INTRODUCTION

The book of Hosea begins by stating that it contains "the word of the Lord that came unto Hosea, the son of Beeri, in the days of Uzziah, Jotham, Ahaz, and Hezekiah, kings of Judah, and in the days of Jeroboam the son of Joash, king of Israel" (Hosea 1:1). We do not know the details of how or where Hosea received this word, and the ordering and numbers of the kings listed in verse 1 has raised many questions concerning the audience and the time in which the oracle was given. Although Judah is referenced in verse 7, Hosea's message appears to be primarily directed toward the Northern Kingdom of Israel prior to its destruction. The listing of Judahite kings first has led some to believe that Hosea was meant to be read and reread by diverse audiences (including Judah) over the years.[2] We do not know many details about the historical person of Hosea; based on the content of the book, his prophetic activity is usually dated from near the end of Jeroboam II's reign (circa 750 BC) to around the fall of Samaria (circa 722 BC).[3]

The book of Hosea applies to different dispensations and shows us glimpses of the past, present, and future of Israel through a divine lens. Because of the ambiguity of the text and the lack of specific historical detail, readers from various generations have assigned a multifarious range of applications to the book.[4] Hosea's message was timely not only to ancient Israel and Judah but also to his audiences in future days. Especially in chapters 1–2, Hosea addresses issues pertaining to the scattering and gathering of Israel as well as to the time of millennial peace. Thus the book's content has meaning for our day as we witness the fulfillment of the Lord's words to Hosea over two thousand seven hundred years ago.

HOSEA 1

The most notable question arising from Hosea 1 has centered on the meaning of Hosea's marriage. Hosea 1:2–3 states, "The beginning of the word of the Lord by Hosea. And the Lord said to Hosea, Go, take unto thee a wife of whoredoms and children of whoredoms: for the land hath committed great whoredom, departing from the Lord. So he went and took Gomer the daughter of Diblaim; which conceived, and bare him a son."[5] These verses have long perplexed readers, and debates have run rampant as to whether or not this marriage was symbolic, literal, or a combination of both. The fact of the matter remains that even if the marriage is indeed historical, we do not possess sufficient information to interpret with any accuracy the details surrounding the circumstances of the marriage. Many accept the marriage as literal, but because no one can verify the speculative details surrounding it, most cautiously make comments such as the following, which concentrates on the image the marriage represents in Hosea's prophecy:

> The text is written so as to strongly communicate to its intended readers that its main concern is *not* with the reported sexual sins and marital life of Gomer (or of the unnamed woman in chapter 3 [see . . . the final clause of v. 2]) or even the fate and actions of Hosea, but rather that which they symbolized. These descriptions point on the one hand to the 'harlotry of the land and its inhabitants'—that is, the worship of gods other than YHWH—and on the other, to the construction of a literary and ideological image of a prophetic personage who on the one hand represents YHWH, but with whom

Israel is also supposed to identify.... The main intention of the text
was not to provide the readers with a kind of (personal life) biography of a particular man, Hosea, nor to elicit thoughts about his
supposed prophetic growth through his difficult family or marital
experiences. Instead, it was to instill a hope for the future based on
the theme of obeying YHWH and following YHWH's lordship
and on an explanation of Israel's (hi)storical disasters in terms of a
just retribution for Israel's rejection of YHWH.[6]

Though we may wonder whether the marriage is literal or metaphorical, the message is clear: The necessity of fidelity to the Lord and covenants.[7] I agree with Sidney B. Sperry's conclusion that "the Lord's call
to Hosea to take a harlotrous woman to wife represents the prophet's
call to the ministry—a ministry to an apostate and covenant-breaking
people. The evil children of this apparent union represent the coming
of the judgments of the Lord upon Israel, warning of which was to be
carried to the people by the prophet. The figure of the harlotrous wife
and children would, I believe, be readily understood at the time by the
Hebrew people without reflecting on Hosea's own wife, or, if he was unmarried, on himself."[8]

I believe there is ample evidence in the scriptures to demonstrate that
Hosea's marriage is a metaphor of his message to the people.[9] The syn-
tactic and pragmatic features of the command for Hosea to take a wife
also seem to support this. "Go, take unto thee a wife of whoredoms and
children of whoredoms: *for* the land hath committed great whoredom,
departing from the Lord" (Hosea 1:2; emphasis added). Here, the word
for introduces a causal clause[10] (it is because the land—which includes
its leaders and its inhabitants—is committing great whoredom and departing from the Lord that Hosea is told to take a wife and children of
whoredoms).[11] This detail brings our understanding of Israel and all her
people into focus and explains that it is she who is going to whore away
from following the Lord. The language is metaphoric, and the wife and
children Hosea refers to represent the kingdom of Israel and its inhabitants.[12] What seems to bolster this interpretation is that the usual formula
"to take for yourself a wife" is not employed here, and referring to Israel
as a woman forsaking the Lord is a common motif in Hosea, Jeremiah,
and the Old Testament in general.[13] The symbolism here may be along

the lines of Ezekiel or John eating a book at the beginning of their min-istries, which action represents internalizing and proclaiming the bitter and sweet message of the Lord to the people.[14] Similarly, Hosea's mes-sage is both bitter and sweet, as will be seen in the names of the children conceived from this union.[15] The image of the marriage thus provides a powerful description of the message Hosea bears in his ministry to Israel.

The name Gomer may have originally meant "perfection" or "com-plete" but has here become a pejorative "complete," as in "done."[16] Because of disobedience to God's commandments, Israel's political existence was literally almost finished. If the chapter can be situated during the reign of Jeroboam II (circa 788–747 BC), then within a few decades, Israel would be overrun by the Assyrians and cease to be a political entity. The name Gomer is thus appropriate in the Lord's message through Hosea.[17] The name Diblaim is from an unused root, but it probably means something like "two cakes." It is interesting that, using a different but synonymous word, Hosea 7:8 describes Ephraim as "a cake not turned." According to 7:9–10, this term refers to the leaders of Israel entering foreign alli-ances rather than trusting in the Lord for protection. The image is that Ephraim has not risen to its full potential; it is burning on one side but is spiritually doughy or undeveloped on the other, resulting in the kingdom coming to an end as it forsakes its covenants with the Lord. Though this connection is not certain, it may offer some insight into the symbolic im-age of the end of the kingdom of Israel.

The names of the children coming from the marriage in chapter 1 represent Hosea's oracles and the various stages of Israel's scattering, gathering, and restoration with the Lord.[18] The first child mentioned (Jezreel—"God will scatter") seems to represent the message Hosea is proclaiming as the word of the Lord: "And the Lord said unto him, Call his name Jezreel; for yet a little while, and I will avenge the blood of Jezreel upon the house of Jehu, and will cause to cease the kingdom of the house of Israel" (Hosea 1:4). Kent P. Jackson summarizes one of the reasons leading up to this pronouncement as follows:

> Conveyed in this symbolic name is a forewarning of the Lord's
> vengeance on Jehu's dynasty and the destruction of the kingdom
> of Israel. Jehu was the king who had come to power in Israel by
> overthrowing the previous king in the city of Jezreel, beginning

his massacre of the descendants of King Ahab. Jehu's descendants still ruled Israel in Hosea's day. The use of the name Jezreel is a prophetic pronouncement that the blood shed by Jehu at that place would now be avenged upon his dynasty, whose kings were wicked like their ancestor.[19]

At this time the literal scattering of Israel was about to begin, and Hosea forewarns them of this with a prophecy couched in the name of the child Jezreel.

Hosea 1:6 then seems to pass into the next phase or portion of the word of the Lord through Hosea: "And she conceived again, and bare a daughter. And God said unto him, Call her name Lo-ruhamah: for I will no more have mercy upon the house of Israel; but I will utterly take them away." Lo-ruhamah ("not pitied," "not having obtained mercy") comes after the warning that God will scatter Israel. For hundreds of years since the Exodus, God had protected, prolonged, and extended mercy to the people of Israel. Hosea declares through the name of this child that this mercy had run out.[20]

Hosea 1:9 then describes another son, representing another phase of Hosea's prophetic teaching, who is named Lo-ammi ("not my people"), "for ye are not my people, and I will not be your God." The language here is often described in terms of divorce, especially in relation to the following verses. However, it is more of a declaration by the Lord that the people have disqualified themselves from the blessings that come from his mercy through disobedience to the covenant. Rather than a divorce, it is more of a temporary separation, as the Lord clearly wants Israel back, and in a future day this reuniting will happen.[21]

Hosea 1:10 marks a shift in Hosea's prophesying—from Israel's separation from God to their eventual restoration with him. "Yet the number of the children of Israel shall be as the sand of the sea, which cannot be measured nor numbered; and it shall come to pass, that in the place where it was said unto them, Ye are not my people, there it shall be said unto them, Ye are the sons of the living God." The language of the children being as "the sands of the sea" is a reference back to the covenant between the Lord and Abraham.[22] This reference to Abraham signals an important feature of salvation in Hosea's message. Hosea's words point the reader forward to the day when that covenant will continue amongst the house of Israel and when they shall be called "sons of the living God."[23]

Verse 11 then describes the fulfillment of the promises made to Abraham, the reunification of the tribes of Israel, and the coming of the Lord to rule over the house of Israel forever more. "Then shall the children of Judah and the children of Israel be gathered together, and appoint themselves one head, and they shall come up out of the land: for great shall be the day of Jezreel." Hosea plays on the name Jezreel, meaning both "God shall scatter" (v. 4; emphasizing the dissemination of Israel) and "God shall sow" (emphasizing the Lord's preservation of Israel and the preparations necessary to disperse, grow, and gather her). That this day was still in the future to Hosea's audience is clear from verse 11. Under Rehoboam, Israel was split into the Northern Kingdom of Israel (ten tribes) and the Southern Kingdom of Judah (Judah, Simeon, and parts of Benjamin).[24] This gathering will ultimately be fulfilled in both religious and political realms when all the tribes are gathered under "one head," or the Messiah.[25] Zechariah says of the coming of the Lord in the latter days, "And the Lord shall be king over all the earth: in that day shall there be one Lord, and his name one" (Zechariah 14:9), and Nephi states, "And he gathereth his children from the four quarters of the earth; and he numbereth his sheep, and they know him; and there shall be one fold and one shepherd; and he shall feed his sheep, and in him they shall find pasture" (1 Nephi 22:25; see also Mosiah 5:7–8). That shepherd will be the God of Israel, even Jehovah, who will gather his people and fulfill the promises made to Abraham and the fathers (see Abraham 1:2). As described, the Lord's harvest will be sown and eventually gathered into his protective care through the covenant. Hosea's message here is clear: the gathering will include a fulfillment in the latter days of the promises God made to Abraham.

Hosea 2

Hosea 2 brings the covenant marriage metaphor between the Lord and Israel into focus. "Say ye unto your brethren, Ammi; and to your sisters, Ruhamah. Plead with your mother, plead: for she is not my wife, neither am I her husband: let her therefore put away her whoredoms out of her sight, and her adulteries from between her breasts" (vv. 1–2).

The plural command "say ye" speaks to all Israel and all readers in a powerful manner. Thus the "mother" is the nation; her children are the people of Israel.[26] Concerning this message, Farres Nyman states:

It also carries the same message as another prophecy of Isaiah (49:3, 6). The people of Israel, as the gathered servant, are to raise up the tribes of Jacob and restore the preserved of Israel (among the Gentiles). As they are gathering the preserved of Israel, they will also give the Gentiles an opportunity to be numbered with Israel and further fulfill the Lord's covenant to Abraham that his seed would bless the nations of the Gentiles (Genesis 12:3). Thus, in the context of Hosea, Ammi and Ruhamah represent the small gathered remnant children who are to plead with the mother of Israel, representing the vast number of the body of Israel.[27]

It is possible that Ammi and Ruhamah here represent those "gathered" children of Israel who are to plead with their brothers and sisters to return to the covenant with the Lord. When we stay in alignment with the apparent interpretation of the ancient context, the "mother" in a latter-day context may represent religious and political entities that govern scattered Israel throughout the world. Thus the plea is to establish an environment where the gathering of Israel might be facilitated.[28] This gathering process may be witnessed in Daniel's visions (see Daniel 2 and 7), which describe the historical circumstances surrounding the establishment of the kingdom of God in the latter days.

It is sometimes argued that the language in Hosea 2:2 ("for she is not my wife") represents a divorce, but the Lord is not trying to divorce Israel, he is trying to reclaim her.[29] The designations of Ammi ("my people") and Ruhamah ("pitied" or "receiving mercy") mark a reversal of Hosea's message in chapter 1, verses 6 and 9. Israel is to be shown mercy, be gathered, and become the Lord's people once again.[30] In chapter 1, Hosea uses the image of a husband-and-wife relationship to describe judgments or aspects of his teaching that will come to pass. In Hosea 2, the Lord becomes the husband who faithfully endures those prophecies, working to recover unfaithful Israel and encouraging her to return and reestablish her covenant relationship with him.

Hosea then challenges his readers to remember Israel's past, where they have come from, how the Lord has blessed them, and how they have forsaken the Lord in order to comprehend the judgment that is coming upon them for forsaking their covenants.[31] "Lest I strip her naked, and set her as in the day that she was born, and make her as a wilderness, and set her like a dry land, and slay her with thirst. And I will not have mercy upon her children; for they be the children of whoredoms. For their mother hath played the harlot: she that conceived them hath done shamefully: for she said, I will go after my lovers, that give me my bread and my water, my wool and my flax, mine oil and my drink" (Hosea 2:3–5).

Here the Lord's warning against whoredoms and adulteries refers not only to idolatry but also to political alliances not sanctioned by the Lord and to Israel's lack of trust in him. The symbolism in 2:3 takes us back to the birth of Israel during the Exodus, when she struggled for physical and spiritual survival and was literally sustained by the Lord with manna and living water.[32] It was a time when Israel had nothing and needed to rely on the Lord or perish. Because Israel would not repent, the Lord would withdraw his mercy, leaving Israel in a state of lack and nothingness. In 722 BC the Assyrians would destroy the kingdom of Israel and begin to fulfill this prophecy.

The images of mother and children in Hosea 2:4–5 seem to parallel the image of Gomer representing Israel as an entity in Hosea 1:3. In verse 5 the mother has played the harlot, going after political alliances that have led all Israel down paths of destruction (see Hosea 5:13, 7:11, 8:4). The children seem to represent the general populace of Israel and parallel the image in 1:2.

Hosea 2:3–13 contains an image in which the prosperous and productive land of Israel sins and is punished, drying up and losing its fertility. We read of the loss of opportunity to participate in sacred acts of worship (v. 11) and Israel's eventual desire to repent and return to her husband. We read of thorns hedging up the way and of Israel's shame and nakedness being uncovered—specifically of items that were given to "cover her nakedness" (vv. 6–9). These items may relate to some of the images of the Fall in the book of Genesis.[33] The creation motif is used later in the chapter, but here the images depict Israel's fall and destruction before she says, "I will go and return to my first husband; for then was it better with me than now" (v. 7). In verse 9 the Lord says, "I . . . will recover my wool and my flax given to cover her nakedness." Ultimately, Israel had created an environment in which she was destroying herself, and though the Lord had had mercy on her for several hundred years by calling prophets and warning of this destruction, Israel was then Lo-ruhamah ("not obtaining mercy"); the children of Israel had "sown the wind, and they shall reap the whirlwind" (Hosea 8:7). Israel had essentially undone creation by forsaking the covenant and all the blessings God had desired for her.

Hosea 2:14–16 marks a turning point in restoring Israel from her fallen state. It draws upon images of Israel's deliverance from Egypt, when Moses gathers the Lord's people and leads them successfully into their land of promise: "Therefore, behold, I will allure her, and bring her into the wilderness, and speak comfortably unto her. And I will give her her vineyards from thence, and the valley of Achor for a door of hope: and she shall sing there, as in the days of her youth, and as in the day when she came up out of the land of Egypt. And it shall be at that day, saith the Lord, that thou shalt call me Ishi; and shalt call me no more Baali." Just as in the days of the Exodus, Israel will be led to safety and back into the covenant with the Lord, after which Israel will call the Lord "Ishi" (my husband). The covenant relationship will be restored, preparing for the day referenced in 1:11 when all Israel will be gathered and appoint "one head." What follows in Hosea 2:18 draws upon the imagery of the Creation and points to the millennial reign of the Lord and the earth's paradisiacal glory. "And in that day will I make a covenant for them with the beasts of the field, and with the fowls of heaven, and with the creeping things of the ground: and I will break the bow and the sword and the battle out of the earth, and will make them to lie down safely." Mark E. Rooker writes, "The reference to the animals from Gen. 1:30 in the restoration passage of Hos. 2:18 is thus a re-creation accomplished by God under the provisions He promised to Israel in the new covenant. The reference to the series of animals in Hos. 2:18, following the creation order, is a return to the harmony that existed in creation as the animal kingdom is to be maintained."[34]

The restoration of Israel will precede this millennial reign of peace when the Lord fulfills the marriage described in Hosea: "And I will betroth thee unto me for ever; yea, I will betroth thee unto me in righteousness, and in judgment, and in lovingkindness, and in mercies. I will even betroth thee unto me in faithfulness: and thou shalt know the Lord. . . . And I will sow her unto me in the earth; and I will have mercy upon her that had not obtained mercy; and I will say to them which were not my people, Thou art my people; and they shall say, Thou art my God" (Hosea 2:19–20, 23). The restoration of the covenant described in the marriage between the Lord and Israel thus marks a reversal in the meaning of the names of the children described in chapter 1 and highlights the message of the Lord. Israel will be sown with the intent to be gathered, obtain mercy, and become the Lord's people once again through the covenant. Another millennial passage that discusses the gathering of Israel describes this process and the marriage metaphor of the covenant: "For the Lord hath comforted his people, and will have mercy upon his afflicted. . . . And as I live, saith the Lord, thou shalt surely clothe thee with them all, as with an ornament, and bind them on even as a bride" (1 Nephi 21:13, 18; compare Isaiah 49:13, 18). The purposes of the Lord will then be fulfilled as the covenant is fulfilled and as he extends mercy by reclaiming his bride.

SUMMARY

The covenant of Abraham referenced in Hosea 1:10 lies at the heart of the promised restoration, and Hosea's message is a multigenerational call to repentance, hope, and responsibility in entering into and keeping covenants with the Lord.[35] Hosea 1–2 demonstrates the concept from Amos 3:7 that the Lord always sends prophets to declare his word. Hosea is sent to a kingdom that is nearly finished. As the Lord's representative and prophet, he attempts to nurture its people and bring them back into the covenant. Hosea's prophetic ministry produces oracles of the scattering of Israel, the withdrawal of the Lord's mercy until she repents, and Israel's separation from the Lord (as is depicted in the names of the children Jezreel, Lo-ruhamah, and Lo-ammi). The Lord's covenant relationship with Israel is defined in chapter 2, showing that the Husband is not about to give up on his love. The promises find their fulfillment in a future day—our day—when the gospel has been restored in its fullness and Israel has "come to the knowledge of the true Messiah, their Lord and their Redeemer" (1 Nephi 10:14).

The appeal of the book of Hosea for Latter-day Saints is that we live in a day when the Restoration has begun and when latter-day Israel is under solemn obligation and responsibility to carry forth the work of the Restoration and fulfill the Abrahamic covenant.[36] Thanks to the words of the Lord given to his prophets, we get a better understanding that "the gathering of Israel following the scattering is thus foretold through

Hosea" and that "this interpretation is strengthened through Paul's quoting of Hosea 2:23 as a promise to be fulfilled to the Gentiles."[37] Indeed we have an opportunity to participate in the events leading up to the millennial reign of Christ and to participate in the fulfillment of Hosea's great prophecies of the Restoration when the Lord will say, "Thou art my people; and they shall say, Thou art my God" (Hosea 2:23).

NOTES

1. Ehud Ben Zvi, "Hosea," in *The Jewish Study Bible*, ed. Adele Berlin and Marc Zvi Brettler (New York: Oxford University, 2004), 1143. He continues, "Thus Hosea 14.2–10 is read in the afternoon service of Tish'ah be'av (Sephardic and Yemenite traditions; others read Isa. 55.6–56.8) and on Shabbat Shuvah, the Sabbath between Rosh Ha-Shanah (the New Year) and Yom Kippur (the Day of Atonement). Hosea 2.1–22 is read as the haftarah for the parashah of Be-midbar (Num. 1.1–4.20). Hosea 2.21–22 are recited as part of the ritual for donning tefillin (phylacteries)."

2. Ehud Ben Zvi, *Hosea*, vol. 1, The Forms of the Old Testament Literature 21A (Grand Rapids, MI: Eerdmans, 2005), 20.

3. Brad E. Kelle, *Hosea 2: Metaphor and Rhetoric in Historical Perspective*, Academia Biblica (Atlanta: Society of Biblical Literature, 2005), 4. This is not unanimously agreed upon but offers an approximate time for Hosea's ministry.

4. Ben Zvi writes, "The text requires from the readers only to accept the sequential, internal logic of the narration. But there are no temporal markers beyond that, nor is any social or historical precise background given. This openness is not accidental. This narrative is not presented to its intended readers as one about historical or biographical events, dependent on a particular *Sitz im Leben*, or meaningful only against a precise set of socio-historical circumstances. The readership is asked to go above and beyond these concerns, and particularly so as the narrative turns into a basic meta-narrative: a mythical reconstruction of a terrible past that will be transformed into a great future, and that serves to encapsulate and shape an authoritative understanding of Israel's understanding of its (own terrible) past as well as its hopes and certitude for the future" (*Hosea*, 56; see also Kelle, *Hosea 2*, 7–8).

5. F. C. Fensham describes "whoredom" here as an "abstract conception which points to an attribute" and says that this verbal form is used figuratively for idolatry and is regarded as Israel's infidelity to the Lord ("The Marriage Metaphor in Hosea for the Covenant Relationship Between the Lord and His People," *Journal of Northwest Semitic Languages* 12 [1984], 72). It does not represent a profession. Elder Bruce R. McConkie remarks, "In a spiritual sense, to emphasize how serious it is, the damning sin of idolatry is called *adultery*. When the Lord's people forsake him and worship false gods, their infidelity to Jehovah is described as whoredoms and adultery. (Jer. 3:8–9; Hos. 1:2; 3:1.) By forsaking the Lord, his people are unfaithful

to their covenant vows, vows made to him who symbolically is their Husband" (*Mormon Doctrine*, 2nd ed. [Salt Lake City: Bookcraft, 1966], 25).

6. Ben Zvi, *Hosea*, 40, 60.

7. I don't think it is safe for us to assume that the people of Israel would have had extensive knowledge about Hosea's wife or children, as we do not possess many details of his life or his origin other than that he came from the Northern Kingdom. Douglas Stuart notes, "The personal details Hosea gives us are so few, and those details are so inextricably linked to the message Yahweh intended—rather than having any useful interest of their own—that any attempt to write Hosea's biography on the basis of such scanty information is doomed to failure. . . . While these questions are not irrelevant to the understanding and appreciation of the book's message, they are definitely peripheral to it. For as the early chapters are structured, no details exist for the satisfaction of our curiosity about the people involved: all details serve the interest of the divine message of wrath and redemption and are inextricably woven into that message" (*Hosea–Jonah*, Word Biblical Commentary 31 [Waco, TX: Words Books, 1987], 11).

8. Sidney B. Sperry, *The Voice of Israel's Prophets* (Salt Lake City: Bookcraft, 1952), 281. In justifying the cited conclusion, Sperry rejects the literal union of Hosea to a wife of whoredoms because it "would be imputing to God a command inconsistent with His holy character." Brent L. Top cautions against such reasoning, stating, "Rejecting the literal nature of this or any other scriptural episode that we find disturbing, illogical, or at odds with our own finite view of God and his dealings with man opens a Pandora's box of issues surrounding the historicity of the scriptures" ("The Marriage of Hosea and Gomer: A Symbolic Testament of Messianic Love and Mercy," in *A Witness of Jesus Christ: The 1989 Sperry Symposium on the Old Testament*, ed. Richard D. Draper [Salt Lake City: Deseret Book, 1989], 227). I agree with Top.

9. The Targum states that these opening verses represent a prophecy that Hosea was to speak to Israel: "Go (and) speak a prophecy against the inhabitants of the idolatrous city, who continue to sin. For the inhabitants of the land surely go astray from the worship of the Lord. So he went and prophesied concerning them that, if they repented, they would be forgiven; but if not, they would fall" (Tg. Hosea 1:2–3).

10. On this construction, see Bruce K. Waltke and Michael O'Connor, *An Introduction to Biblical Hebrew Syntax* (Winona Lake, IN: Eisenbrauns, 1990), 640.

11. The King James Version translates this portion of the text in the past tense ("for the land hath committed"), but the Hebrew reflects a condition that is certain in regards to the future ("for the land will surely"), and this is why the Lord sent Hosea to call Israel to repentance: to help them avoid what was coming. Francis Andersen and David Freedman interpret "land" as including kings, priests, and the people (*Hosea: A New Translation with Introduction and Commentary*, Anchor Bible 24 [Garden City, NY: Doubleday, 1980], 169).

12. Kelle sees the wife in chapter 2 as Samaria, the capital and governing city of Israel, thus marking a distinction between the wife and children (*Hosea 2*, 93). Gale A. Yee comments, "Hosea's accusations are targeted primarily at a male audience: the king and his political and cultic élite. The marriage metaphor effectively

feminizes this male ruling hierarchy, by depicting its members collectively in a graphic image of a promiscuous wife" ("'She Is Not My Wife and I Am Not Her Husband': A Materialist Analysis of Hosea 1–2," *Biblical Interpretation* 9, no. 4 [2001], 368).

13. "Another matter to take into account, despite the high use of sexual metaphors: the text consistently avoids the expected formulas 'X knew/came to/approached his wife/Y and she conceived and bore . . .' or some variant of them (e.g., Gen 4:1, 17; 16:4; 30:4–5; 38:18; 1 Sam 1:19–20; Isa 8:3; Ruth 4:13; 1 Chron 7:23). Although an explicit reference to Hosea's intercourse with Gomer may seem unnecessary in 1:3 (see Exodus 2:1–2), the consistent avoidance of such references is noticeable" (Ben Zvi, *Hosea*, 52). For a few examples of Israel or its cities personified as a woman or wife, see Jeremiah 3:8–9, 14, 20; 5:7; Ezekiel 16:30–35; 23:7; Nahum 3:4; Hosea 5:3–4; 6:10; 9:1.

14. See Ezekiel 2:7–3:4 (and comments in Ben Zvi, "Ezekiel," in *The Jewish Study Bible*, 1049); Revelation 10:9–10; and Bruce R. McConkie, *Doctrinal New Testament Commentary* (Salt Lake City: Bookcraft, 1973), 3:507. Contrast 1 Nephi 1:10–15, where Lehi reads a book containing the Lord's message to his people.

15. What also may be relevant in discussing the metaphors in Hosea's "marriage" are the parallels we find in 1 Nephi. In 1 Nephi 1:13–15, Lehi describes seeing the destruction of Jerusalem but is able to rejoice and declare God's mercy. At first glance this seems out of place, but verses 18–19 seem to clarify why Lehi rejoices; he speaks of "the coming of a Messiah, and also the redemption of the world." As we read chapters like 1 Nephi 11–15, we see how the Nephites glory in the prospect of a restoration of their people in a future day. Lehi and Hosea may have thus seen similar visions of the destruction and restoration of their people.

16. Ben Zvi, *Hosea*, 54.

17. Andersen and Freedman say of Gomer, "The name does not seem to be symbolic; there is no wordplay on it as there is on the names of the children" (*Hosea: New Translation*, 171). However, I see a logical sequence depicted in the names of his wife and children, representing Hosea's going to a kingdom that is about to end, preaching of its scattering, and so forth.

18. Ben Zvi writes, "Martin Buss once wrote, 'A paradoxical union of attitudes occurs in Hosea's naming of Gomer's children, at divine command. . . . Hosea, by giving them names, accepts them into his family. Yet the names themselves say the opposite' (Buss, 'Tragedy and Comedy,' 75). The above observations show that although, for obvious rhetorical purposes, the names defamiliarize the situation, they in fact do tell the readers of the book that YHWH (as represented by Hosea) has accepted Israel (the children) as his children, for the names carry the seed of their reversal and certainly draw the attention of the [readers] and evoke among them the memory of their reversal" (*Hosea*, 46).

19. Kent P. Jackson, "The Marriage of Hosea and Jehovah's Covenant with Israel," in *Isaiah and the Prophets*, ed. Monte Nyman (Provo, UT: Religious Studies Center, Brigham Young University, 1984), 61.

20. Jarom 1:3 and Mosiah 1:13 also describe the process of the Lord's mercy being extended to a people and eventually being withdrawn due to their disobedience. The implication is that the prophets taught their people that mercy would not rob

justice and that the word of the Lord would come to pass against them if they did not repent; see also 2 Kings 13:23.

21. See, for example, Hosea 2:19–23; 6:1–3; 14:1. For a discussion on the arguments against the interpretation of divorce, see Kelle, *Hosea 2*, 54. In the Hebrew text, chapter 1 ends with verse 9.

22. Others also recognize the importance of the Abrahamic covenant at this juncture. Mark E. Rooker comments, "The language and the comparison represent a dependency on God's promise to Abraham in Gen. 15:5 and 22:17. The expression provides a clear example of the borrowing of a prominent phrase drawn from the promise to the nation via the Patriarch which is now applied to the future reinstalling of Israel" ("The Use of the Old Testament in the Book of Hosea," *Criswell Theological Review* 7, no. 1 [1993]: 53).

23. Becoming sons and daughters of God denotes entering into covenants with him. For more on this process, see Moses 6:62, 64; 7:1. Genesis 6:2 and Moses 8:13–15, 21 also seem to contain episodes where sons and daughters of God factor importantly into the story. Elder Bruce R. McConkie defines becoming sons of God as follows: "Those who receive the gospel and join The Church of Jesus Christ of Latter-day Saints have power given them to become the sons of God (D&C 11:30; 35:2; 39:1–6; 45:8; John 1:12). Sonship does not come from Church membership alone, but admission into the Church opens the door to such high status, if it is followed by continued faith and devotion (Rom. 8:14–18; Gal. 3:26–29; 4:1–7). The sons of God are members of his family and, hence, are joint-heirs with Christ, inheriting with him the fullness of the Father (D&C 93:17–23). . . . Those who become the sons of God in this life (1 John 3:1–3) are the ones who by enduring in continued righteousness will be gods in eternity" (*Mormon Doctrine*, 745).

24. Though attempts have been made to describe how this unification had already taken place during the time of the Persian empire, none have been able to fully justify such claims, and future days still lie in the interpretations. The *Jewish Study Bible*, 1146, states, "The motif of a future reunification of (northern) Israel and Judah appears elsewhere in prophetic literature (cf. Ezekiel 37.15–28), though it was never fulfilled."

25. Concerning this "head," Ben Zvi writes, "A similar rhetorical approach led to the choice of 'one head' in the same verse, over the alternative 'king.' The use of the former allows an allusion to Moses (cf. Num 14:4, where the 'Anti-Moses' is referred to as 'head'), whereas the term 'king' would have not. Yet, the readers of this set of prophetic readings know also that this 'head' of the ideal future will be like Moses, but also a Davidic king. . . . It goes without saying that in periods later than the Persian era, the image of a future Messiah who will combine features of a David with those of Moses fulfilled important roles and influenced among others the characterization of Jesus" (*Hosea*, 51). President Joseph Fielding Smith gave the following explanation of Isaiah 2:3 and described the future reign of Christ: "Jerusalem of old . . . shall become a holy city where the Lord shall dwell and from whence he shall send forth his word unto all people. Likewise, on this continent, the city of Zion, New Jerusalem, shall be built, and from it the law of God shall also go forth. There will be no conflict, for each city shall be headquarters for the

Redeemer of the world, and from each he shall send forth his proclamations as occasion may require. Jerusalem shall be the gathering place of Judah and his fellows of the house of Israel, and Zion shall be the gathering place of Ephraim and his fellows. . . . These two cities, one in the land of Zion and one in Palestine, are to become capitals for the kingdom of God during the Millennium" ("Zion and Jerusalem," *Improvement Era*, July 1919, 815–16). This emphasizes the coming together of Israel under "one head."

26. See *Jewish Study Bible*, 1146. Stuart also makes a distinction "between corporate Israel as the prostituting wife, and at least certain of her children, or citizens" (*Hosea–Jonah*, 47). Kelle discusses the "close relationship between the children and their mother, which produces a sense of urgency for the children" (*Hosea 2*, 231).

27. Farres H. Nyman, in *The Words of the Twelve Prophets: Messages to the Latter-day Saints* (Salt Lake City: Deseret Book, 1990), 26–27.

28. See 1 Nephi 21:22–23 and Isaiah 49:22–23, which describe kings and queens nursing Israel in the gathering process. Victor L. Ludlow writes, "Verses 22 and 23 answer Israel's question as to how she will grow so quickly. Her growth will come from the Gentile nations who will assist both temporally and spiritually to gather Israel. (D&C 77:11; 1 Ne. 22:3). . . . This gathering of Israel through the aid of foreign nations is taking place today" (*Isaiah: Prophet, Seer, and Poet* [Salt Lake City: Deseret Book, 1982], 414).

29. Kelle concludes, "A majority of interpreters now proposes that, while Hos 2:4 does depend upon the image-base of the legal stipulations for marriage and divorce, it is not an actual Israelite divorce formula. This position seems to rest on the most secure evidence. The words, 'She is not my wife, and I am not her husband' are not attested anywhere else in the Hebrew Bible as a formula of divorce, and they are essentially dissimilar from those formulas found in Babylonian and Elephantine texts. Also, as Buss observes, 2:4 has no parallel in Jewish texts, and the rest of Hos 2 is dedicated to convincing the wife to return. Verse 4 is more of a 'negated marriage formula' that describes the current situation" (*Hosea 2*, 54).

30. For a description of this mercy in relation to the gathering of Israel, see 1 Nephi 13:33–42.

31. Thomas B. Dozeman writes, "The book of Hosea provides a window on election traditions in the northern kingdom during the eighth century BCE. '[It] is quite remarkable how thoroughly Israel's history is embedded in Hosea's proclamation'" ("Hosea and the Wilderness Wandering Tradition," in *Rethinking the Foundations: Historiography in the Ancient World and in the Bible*, ed. Steven L. McKenzie, Thomas Römer, and Hans Heinrich Schmid [Berlin: Walter de Gruyter, 2000], 55).

32. For a message addressed to Jerusalem along these lines, see Ezekiel 16:4–15.

33. For a brief comment on the "thorns" in Hosea 2:6, see Andersen and Freedman, *Hosea: New Translation*, 237, where they discuss thorns as part of the scenery in Sheol and they note that in Hosea 9:6 "the reversion of farmland to waste is sufficient to explain the reference to thorns." See also Rooker, "Use of the Old Testament," 52–53, which makes a possible connection with the Genesis account.

34. Rooker, "Use of the Old Testament," 52.

35. Rooker comments, "It perhaps should be mentioned that the Hoseanic eschatological texts have as their background covenantal promises made to Israel by the Patriarchs. The promises made to Israel in Israel's covenants were the basis for the confidence of future blessings" ("Use of the Old Testament," 66).

36. President Ezra Taft Benson taught, "The responsibility of the seed of Abraham, which we are, is to be missionaries to 'bear this ministry and Priesthood unto all nations' (Abr. 2:9)" ("The Book of Mormon and the Doctrine and Covenants," *Ensign*, May 1987, 85).

37. Nyman and Nyman, "Hosea," 27.

15

THE HOLY SPIRIT: CREATING, ANOINTING, AND EMPOWERING

Lynne Hilton Wilson

We sound the depths of the Old Testament for many wonderful teachings. One doctrine we do not often think about in the context of the Old Testament is the Holy Spirit. In fact, American theologians caught up in the Second Great Awakening omitted everything before Christ's ascension in their definition of the "Dispensation of the Holy Spirit."[1] Closer to the twenty-first century, the *Encyclopedia Judaica* and *Dictionary of the Old Testament* lack sections on the Spirit.[2]

This study challenges these limited views of the Holy Spirit and explores what ancient Israelite records share about the Holy Spirit.[3] We argue that the workings of the Spirit extend to God's people in the Old Testament. Further, by understanding the Spirit in the Old Testament, we see the continuity of the gospel of Jesus Christ over time. To set the stage, the first half of this study compares the treatment of the Spirit in the Old Testament and other Latter-day Saint scripture. Especially relevant is the way pre-Christian passages of the Book of Mormon and the books of Moses and Abraham discuss the Spirit. After we establish

---

Lynne Hilton Wilson is a PhD candidate in theology at Marquette University and an institute instructor at Stanford Institute of Religion.

this baseline, the second half of the paper focuses on the Old Testament workings of the Spirit. Even though the Old Testament mentions the Spirit less frequently, the citations illustrate the Spirit's influence to create, anoint, and empower.

OLD TESTAMENT COMPARED WITH OTHER SCRIPTURE

To start, we should evaluate the words used as well as the frequency of that usage across the scriptural canon. This study is limited to the Old Testament use of the word *spirit* from the Hebrew word *rûah* (also transcribed *ruach, ruakh, ru'ah,* and *ruwach*); in addition, *rûah* is sometimes translated wind, breath, mind, or the spirit in each human.[4] *Rûah* appears 389 times in the Old Testament, but only one-fifth of those citations allude to a spirit from God (they are listed in the appendix).[5] Narrowing the references of *rûah* to the Holy Spirit is not a clear science, and separating the premortal Lord's spirit from the Holy Spirit is not the purpose of this study.[6] I separated references by context, content, and how other scripture used the same titles for the Spirit. The reader is invited to do the same by going through each of the scriptures in the appendix. During my analysis, the Book of Mormon clarified which titles referred to the Holy Spirit. As a case in point, the name "Spirit of the Lord" is used by the editors Mormon and Moroni for the Holy Ghost in their pre- and postresurrection commentary.[7] However, the purpose of this study is not to identify which verse points to which member of the Godhead; it is to argue that the workings and gifts of the Spirit were functioning at some level in the Old Testament. Within these bounds, we find similarities between the operations of the Spirit throughout scripture and across dispensations.

First we'll take a quantitative look at how many times the scriptures refer to the Spirit. The Old Testament mentions *rûah* as a spirit from God in nearly half of its books (twenty of thirty-nine) with Isaiah as the most prolific.[8] By comparison, nearly all of the New Testament books (twenty-three of twenty-seven) refer to the Spirit (*pneuma, parakletos, theopneustos* in Greek). Some of those New Testament references allude to the Spirit's consistent work among ancient Israel (e.g., Acts 28:25, "Well spake the Holy Ghost by Esaias the prophet unto our fathers"). The following table outlines each biblical reference by book.

BIBLICAL REFERENCES TO THE HOLY SPIRIT

Old Testament (610,303 words)	*rûah*	New Testament (180,565 words)	*pneuma*	*parakletos*	*theopneustos*
Genesis	3	Matthew	11		
Exodus	2	Mark	2		
Numbers	6	Luke	16		
Judges	7	John	16	4	
1 Samuel	7	Acts	54		
2 Samuel	1	Romans	26		
1 Kings	2	1 Corinthians	21		
2 Kings	1	2 Corinthians	9		
2 Chronicles	4	Galatians	16		
Nehemiah	2	Ephesians	12		
Job	3	Philippians	4		
Psalms	5	Colossians	1		
Proverbs	1	1 Thessalonians	4		
Isaiah	15	2 Thessalonians	1		
Ezekiel	7	1 Timothy	1		
Joel	2	2 Timothy	1		1
Micah	2	Titus	1		
Haggai	1	Hebrews	7		
Zechariah	2	1 Peter	6		
Malachi	1	2 Peter	1		
		1 John	6		
		Jude	2		
		Revelation	11		
Total: 20/39 books, 74 citations		Total: 23/27 books, 234 citations			

Given the Old Testament's reduced references to the Holy Ghost, it is easy to understand why some theologians have not appreciated the Spirit's involvement in ancient Israel. These figures are more striking when we compute the size of each book of scripture in a word-ratio analysis. Word ratios help us see how often the Spirit is named but not how long the subject is discussed; nevertheless, it still provides a basis to compare the relative depth of the scriptural pneumatology (or study of the Holy Spirit) in each of the standard works. We must also add the other vocabulary the scriptures use to describe the Spirit. While the King James Version (KJV) of the Old Testament translates *rûah* as "spirit," the KJV New Testament and modern revelation also use the terms *pneuma*, *parakletos*, *theopneustos*, *Holy Ghost*, *Comforter*, and *baptism of fire*.[9] The following table compares each of these four titles in the four standard works.

Portions of the Book of Mormon and the Pearl of Great Price claim to share similar origins with the Old Testament, but they are very different in the frequency that they mention the Spirit. This is especially

Word ratio of *Spirit, Holy Ghost, Comforter,* and *Baptism by Fire*

Text:	Spirit	Holy Ghost	Comforter	Baptism by fire	Total	Word ratio
Doctrine & Covenants[10] 107,289 total words	148	49	23	4	224	0.209%
Pearl of Great Price: Moses 12,544 total words	12	10	1	1	24	0.191%
New Testament 179,011 total words	144	90	4		238	0.133%
Book of Mormon 266,944 total words	200	92	1	6	299	0.112%
Old Testament 609,269 total words	73				73	0.012%
Total:	577	241	29	11	858	

evident in contrasting the book of Genesis to the book of Moses (Joseph Smith's revision of Genesis).[11] A simple counting of the first eight chapters of Genesis and Moses identifies an enormous difference in the number of times the Spirit is mentioned (see appendix). In fact, the book of Genesis mentions the Spirit only twice, while in the same sampling from the book of Moses we find twenty-four references extended to the lives of Adam, Enoch, and Noah—closer to the New Testament than the Old Testament. Not only does the book of Moses exceed the Old Testament's word ratio by ten times, but the previous table also shows a richer tradition of spiritual outpouring in the three other standard works.[12]

FEWER REFERENCES IN THE OLD TESTAMENT TO THE SPIRIT

One plausible reason why the Old Testament does not refer to the Holy Spirit as often as other scripture does is the fact that most of the text deals with people living under the Mosaic law. The children of Israel at large did not receive the gift of the Holy Ghost under the Aaronic order. Furthermore, perhaps passages on the Spirit were some of the "plain and precious things taken away" (1 Nephi 13:28) from the Old Testament, as Nephi noted. One of those lost details is the need for special priesthood authority to confirm the gift of the Holy Ghost. While Genesis is silent, the book of Abraham teaches that Adam, Seth, Noah, Melchizedek, and Abraham all received the higher priesthood (see Abraham facsimile 2, figs. 3 and 7; see also D&C 107:41–53). With God's authority in place, the book of Moses explains "the Gospel began to be preached, from the beginning ... by the gift of the Holy Ghost" (Moses 5:58; see also 6:52; 7:27). This important point is absent in the Old Testament as it now stands.

Another detail that the Prophet Joseph Smith restored was an emphasis on the Spirit. This is seen easily by looking at word ratios in the book of Moses and the Doctrine and Covenants. Not only does the Doctrine and Covenants have the highest word ratio (Holy Ghost references of any kind divided by the total number of words) among the standard works, but it is 63 percent higher than the New Testament. Both the book of Moses and the Doctrine and Covenants mention the Spirit 500 percent more often than the Old Testament. This comparison suggests that an emphasis on the Spirit was similarly important to the beginning of the dispensations of Adam, Moses, and Joseph Smith, although no longer seen in the Old Testament.[13]

OLD TESTAMENT DESCRIPTIONS OF THE SPIRIT

References to the Spirit/*rûah* in the Old Testament usually connect the Spirit to God or the Lord. Phrases like the "Spirit of God" or the "Spirit of the Lord" stand out in over half of the citations. The table below organizes the most likely seventy-three references of *rûah* as the Spirit in the KJV Old Testament.[14]

USAGE OF *RÛAH* IN THE OLD TESTAMENT	
Filled him with the Spirit	2
His Holy Spirit	2
His Spirit	5
My Spirit	13
Spirit	7
Spirit of God	14
Spirit of the Lord	26
Thy Spirit	4
Total	73

The Old Testament emphasizes seven titles of the Spirit/*rûah* that are found across several different books. When we add the Book of Mormon into the comparison, we find, not surprisingly, a predominance of the same favorite two titles used in the Old Testament: "Spirit of God" and "Spirit of the Lord." This is expected because the Book of Mormon originated out of Old Testament historic and linguistic tradition. As a second witness of the Spirit's work in ancient Israel, the Book of Mormon acts as a clarifying text with forty references to the "Spirit of the Lord" and twenty to the "Spirit of God." Significantly, the majority of those Book of Mormon citations occur before Christ's birth (thirty-five references to the "Spirit of the Lord" and eighteen references to the "Spirit of God").

We now turn to explore what the Old Testament teaches about the Spirit. Each of the references to the Spirit/*rûah* falls into roles of creating, anointing, and empowering. Its references to empowerment include the gifts of the Spirit and specifically highlight the gift of prophesy.

Creating. The Spirit oversees everything in the scriptural creation accounts (see Genesis 1:2; Job 26:13; 33:4; Psalm 104:30; Moses 2:2; Abraham 4:2). The first chapter of Genesis describes the world developing through the Holy Spirit from chaos and darkness to life and light. The text implies that the Spirit protected and watched over the process. As "the Spirit of God *moved* upon the face of the waters," it "hovered [*rachaph*]" (Genesis 1:2; emphasis added). The same verb is found in Deuteronomy 32:11 for "flutter" when "an eagle stirreth up her nest, fluttereth over her young, spreadeth abroad her wings, taketh them, beareth them on her wings." The beautiful biblical image of a maternal eagle hovering over her young is in harmony with God's nurturing Spirit hovering over the Creation.

The Old Testament also reveals the Spirit as a source of life.[15] "And the Lord God formed man of the dust of the ground, and breathed into his nostrils the breath of life; and man became a living soul" (Genesis 2:7). Job reiterates the crucial role of the Spirit in creation: "The Spirit of God hath made me, and the breath of the Almighty hath given me life" (Job 33:4; see also Job 27:3; 34:14; Psalm 33:6). For Job, life is a gift from God by the handiwork of his Spirit. With an intimacy as close as breath, the Psalmist teaches that the Spirit will speak to, sustain, and renew humanity. "Thou sendest forth thy spirit, they are created: and thou renewest the face of the earth" (Psalm 104:30).

Beyond the physical creation, the Spirit also has a role in creating the spiritual man: "Thou gavest also thy good spirit to instruct them" (Nehemiah 9:20; see also Isaiah 59:21).[16] The Spirit's purpose in giving instructions was to renew God's people to "do good" and "walketh uprightly" (Micah 2:7; see also Ezekiel 36:27). The Spirit directed the process of generating a *new heart*—not merely circumcised—but a full transplant for whole-hearted obedience.[17] "And the Lord thy God will circumcise thine heart" (Deuteronomy 30:6). "A new heart also will I give you, and a new spirit will I put within you: and I will take away the stony heart out of your flesh, and I will give you an heart of flesh and I will put my spirit within you" (Ezekiel 36:26–27). The Old Testament describes the process of creating a new man through obedience to the instructions of the Spirit (see Ezekiel 37:14; 1 Samuel 10:6). Creating a new man includes the Spirit-driven process of sanctification and then sealing. The Lord covenants with humanity that his Spirit will seal the righteous "from henceforth and for ever" (Isaiah 59:21; see also 34:16–17; Ephesians 1:13; D&C 124:124; 132:7, 18–19; Moses 6:59–60).

The Spirit helps create life and seals one for the life hereafter (see Ezekiel 11:19; 18:31; 36:26). According to Ezekiel's vision of the dry bones taking flesh and life, the Holy Spirit is involved in the re-creation of the body and spirit in the Resurrection (see Ezekiel 37:1–14). The Holy Spirit came into the valley of dry bones as "wind" (*rûah*, Ezekiel 37:9) and blew the "breath" (*rûah*, Ezekiel 37:5, 6, 8, 9, 10) of life, infusing the bones with life.[18] "Thus saith the Lord God; Let the Spirit come from every quarter and breathe into these slain, that they may live" (Ezekiel 37:9; author's translation). Ten times in the account of Ezekiel's vision he uses the word *rûah*. The whole revelation is permeated with *wind, spirit,* and the *breath of life*. Especially at the beginning and end of the section, Ezekiel unambiguously references the Spirit of God (see Ezekiel 37:1, 14). This Old Testament account demonstrates the Spirit breathing life-giving power at the Creation and Resurrection.

Anointing. The Old Testament associated the Spirit's anointing with making something sacred. Consecrated structures, clothing, people, and offerings affiliated with the Tabernacle or Temple were all anointed (see Exodus 29:29, 36; 30:26; 40:10–15; Leviticus 2:4; 8:10). Whether the anointed one was a person, place, or thing, if the Spirit was involved in its anointing, it became something holy (see 1 Samuel 16:13; Isaiah 61:1). An "anointed one" or "messiah/*mashiach*" meant chosen and commissioned by God to do his work. Beginning with Aaron, we read of priests being anointed to function in the Tabernacle or Temple (see Exodus 29:7). A king's anointing set him apart for special leadership callings (see 1 Kings 1:39, 45; 2 Kings 9:3, 6; 11:12; 23:30). Beginning with King Saul, prophetic anointing became the sign that the call was divine: "Then Samuel took a vial of oil, and poured it upon his head, and kissed him, and said, Is it not because the Lord hath anointed thee to be captain over his inheritance?" (1 Samuel 10:1; see also 1 Kings 1:39, 45; 5:1;

2 Kings 9:6; 11:12). Even after Saul squandered his position, young David honored the king as the "Lord's anointed" (1 Samuel 24:10).

The Old Testament mentions the Spirit in conjunction with anointing many times (see Exodus 28:41; 2 Kings 9:6; Psalm 45:7; 84:9; Ezekiel 28:14).[19] The text highlights the connection with the Spirit, first at David's anointing: "Then Samuel took the horn of oil, and anointed him in the midst of his brethren: and the Spirit of the Lord came upon David from that day forward" (1 Samuel 16:13). The anointing is described as David's initial bond with the Spirit. Another verse that links the Spirit with anointing is a messianic promise in Isaiah. The Spirit appears to enable this special Anointed One to fill his special mission: "The Spirit of the Lord God is upon me; because the Lord hath anointed me to preach good tidings unto the meek; he hath sent me to bind up the brokenhearted, to proclaim liberty to the captives, and the opening of the prison to them that are bound" (Isaiah 61:1; see also D&C 138:18, 31, 42). In the Davidic and Isaianic references, a spiritual protection and blessing work together with the Spirit's anointing.

Of all the *m'shiachi*—or anointed ones—in the Old Testament, none is as honored as the "rod out of the stem of Jesse" (Isaiah 11:1) who became known as Messiah ben David.[20] All anointings throughout the Old Testament typify, at least to a degree, the Anointed One or Promised Messiah. God endows the Messiah ben David with an extraordinary anointing of the Spirit. This divine anointing includes a perfect nature, a unique birth, and a crucial calling: "And the spirit of the Lord shall rest upon him, the spirit of wisdom and understanding, the spirit of counsel and might, the spirit of knowledge and of the fear of the Lord" (Isaiah 11:2; see also 42:1–7).[21] The tie between this Anointed One and the Spirit carries on when Christ announces in the New Testament that John will baptize with the Spirit (see John 1:33). As the Anointed One, Jesus shares a special relationship with the Holy Spirit in the Godhead, and the two work in harmony "to bring to pass the immortality and eternal life of man" (Moses 1:39).

Empowerment. The Old Testament shows the Holy Spirit empowering humanity with divine attributes and callings. The Old Testament describes the Spirit as giving discernment, wisdom, understanding, knowledge, and instruction. The first man described as filled or empowered with the Spirit's attributes is Hur's grandson Bezaleel. He was chosen to work on the Tabernacle because God "filled him with the spirit of God, in wisdom, and in understanding, and in knowledge, and in all manner of workmanship" (Exodus 31:3). Likewise, the youthful Elihu acknowledged the Spirit's empowerment, or that which "giveth them understanding" (Job 32:8; see also Isaiah 11:2). Ezekiel records the Lord's empowerment: "And I will put my spirit within you, and cause you to walk in my statutes, and ye shall keep my judgments, and do them" (Ezekiel 36:27). Each of these three men felt the Spirit blessing humanity with gifts of the Spirit.

The Old Testament regularly ascribes power as a characteristic of the Spirit.[22] Micah depicts the Spirit as nearly synonymous with power: "Truly I am full of power by the spirit of the Lord" (Micah 3:8; see also Zechariah 4:6). In Hebrew, power (*koach*) relates to man's or God's strength, power, and might. Different books of the Old Testament attribute the work of the Spirit to the power of protection, power in battles, power in judgment, and power over generations (see Judges 3:10; Isaiah 59:19; Zechariah 4:6). Sometimes the power of the Spirit is demonstrated "mightily" as with Samson (Judges 14:6), and sometimes as "a still small voice" as with Elijah (1 Kings 19:12). In all cases, the Spirit's power works best when God's servants realize their personal powerlessness without it. Moses exemplified that level of meekness. The Bible explains that he did not rely on his own gifts but turned to God and was strengthened by his Spirit (see Numbers 11:10–17; 12:3). The Spirit's empowerment to Moses became a model for all Israelites—especially the prophet-leaders (see Psalm 77:20; 1 Corinthians 10:1–5; 1 Nephi 4:2; 17:29; 2 Nephi 25:20; Helaman 8:11, 13). The Old Testament punctuates Israelite history with the Spirit giving power to God's special servants.

The Spirit accompanies divine callings and energizes the prophets, servants, and judges from Genesis to Zechariah.[23] The authority of the Spirit inspired prophets to speak in the Lord's name, as Ezekiel exemplifies: "And the Spirit of the Lord fell upon me, and said unto me Speak; Thus saith the Lord" (11:5). As another impressive example, the Spirit of God empowered Elijah to stop the heavens and then miraculously provide food for himself and a widow and her son, raise that son from the dead, call down fire from heaven to devour the drenched stone altar in front of the priests of Baal, and later kill hundreds of servants of King

Ahab (see I Kings 17:1, 15–23; 18:36–40; 2 Kings 1:10–13). Yet the Old Testament does not specifically mention the Spirit in conjunction with Elijah's work until the impressive story of his fiery chariot and horses when he was magnificently translated "by a whirlwind into heaven" (2 Kings 2:11). Elijah's dutiful disciple, Elisha, asked for a double portion of Elijah's spirit—most likely meaning the Spirit of God (see 2 Kings 2:9, 15). The law of Moses dictated that the firstborn receive a double portion. Elisha took that role as the head of the "sons of the prophets" (Deuteronomy 21:17).[24] However, Elijah could not grant a double portion of the Spirit—the gift was utterly dependent upon God. Of all the "sons of the prophets" that followed Elijah, God chose Elisha as Elijah's successor (2 Kings 2:3). The Old Testament symbolically portrays the transfer of the prophetic call by Elijah's falling mantle (see 2 Kings 2:3, 5, 7, 13–15). The cloak was not the source of spiritual power though—the Spirit supplied God's power. And the Spirit often became the identification of authority in the Old Testament.[25]

In addition to prophets, the Spirit empowered other servants of God, like the Seventy. The story of Moses's lesson in delegation teaches that whoever the Spirit endows is empowered to work for God: "And the Lord came down in a cloud, and spake unto him, and took of the spirit that was upon him, and gave it unto the seventy elders: and it came to pass, that, when the spirit rested upon them, they prophesied, and did not cease" (Numbers 11:17, 25; a similar experience happened in I Samuel 19:20 when Saul's servants prophesied). The Spirit's presence identified those whom God called: "Can we find such a one as this is, a man in whom the Spirit of God is?" (Genesis 41:38). Even non-Israelites recognized the empowerment of the Spirit as a sign that God had chosen another servant.

The Spirit's empowerment became a signal for action to Israelite judges and military leaders (see Judges 11:29; 13:25; 15:14). The book of Judges explains that after Joshua's death, Caleb's younger brother, Othniel, was raised up by God's Spirit to lead Israel. "And the Spirit of the Lord came upon him, and he judged Israel, and went out to war: and the Lord delivered" (Judges 3:10). Then a few chapters later, the account of Gideon describes: "the Spirit of the Lord came upon Gideon, and he blew a trumpet" (Judges 6:34). Literally, when the Spirit came/*labash* upon Gideon, God's Spirit "clothed" him with power. Hosea describes the Spirit communicating through the lives or ministry of righteous servants: "I have also spoken by the prophets, and I have multiplied visions, and used similitudes, by the ministry of the prophets" (12:10). The Spirit directed these leaders to put things right.

Empowerment through the gifts of the Spirit. While all of the standard works speak of the gifts of the Spirit, the Old Testament alone does not systematically catalog the gifts of the Spirit. The closest list we find is in Isaiah 11:2: "The spirit of the Lord shall rest upon him, the spirit of wisdom and understanding, the spirit of counsel and might, the spirit of knowledge and of the fear of the Lord." Doctrine and Covenants 46 and 1 Corinthians 12 both list the gifts of wisdom and knowledge. Isaiah's reference to the spirit of understanding can be compared with the gift of discernment, and the fear of the Lord to "the beginnings of faith."[26] In addition to this verse, we find several examples of the gifts of the Spirit when we peruse the Old Testament. The same Spirit-filled manifestations that follow those who believe the gospel of Jesus Christ in the New Testament are found in the Old. The following table organizes the gifts of the Spirit from Corinthians, Moroni, and the Doctrine and Covenants and then fills in examples of each gift from the Old Testament.

GIFTS OF THE SPIRIT

1 Corinthians 12:1–11	Moroni 10:7–18	D&C 46:8–31	Old Testament
Testify of Jesus		Know Jesus the Son	Job 19:25; Proverbs 1:23; Isaiah 7:14; 49; 53; 59:21
		Believe others' testimony	Exodus 4:5; 19:9; 2 Chronicles 20:20; Isaiah 28:16; 43:10
Administrations		Administrations	Judges 3:10; 2 Samuel 23:2; Isaiah 42:1; Micah 3:8
Operations		Operations	Exodus 26–28; Judges 6:34, Isaiah 11:2; Ezekiel 36:27
Wisdom	Teach wisdom	Wisdom	Exodus 31:3; Ezra 7:25; Psalm 90:12; Isaiah 11:2; Daniel 1:4

GIFTS OF THE SPIRIT (CONTINUED)

Knowledge	Teach knowledge	Knowledge	Exodus 31:3; 35:31; Numbers 24:16; Psalm 119:66; Isaiah 11:2
Faith	Faith	Faith to be healed	Numbers 21:7–9; 1 Kings 17:24; Habakkuk 2:4; Hosea 6:3; 8:2
Healing	Healing	Faith to heal	Genesis 20:17; 2 Kings 20:5–8; 2 Chronicles 30:20
Miracles	Miracles	Miracles	Exodus 4–15; 1 Kings 18:12; 2 Kings 2:16, 21–22; Nehemiah 9:19–21; Ezekiel 37:14
Prophecy	Prophecy	Prophecy	Numbers 1:17; 1 Samuel 10:6, 10; 19:20–23; Proverbs 31:1; Joel 2:28; Daniel 9:24
Tongues	Tongues	Tongues	Numbers 22:28; 2 Samuel 23:2
Interpretation of tongues	Interpretation of tongues	Interpretation of tongues	Interpret dreams: Genesis 40:8; 41:15; Judges 7:15; Daniel 2:45; 4:19, 24; 5:12
Hope	Hope		Psalms 31:24; 33:18, 22; 38:15; 39:7; 43:5; 71:5, 14; 119; Isaiah 61:1
Charity	Charity		Leviticus 19:18, 34; Deuteronomy 7:9, 13; Hosea 3:1
Discerning of spirits	Ministering spirit	Discerning of spirits	Understanding: Exodus 31:3; 35:32; 2 Samuel 14:17; 1 Kings 3:9; Job 20:3; 32:8; Isaiah 11:2
	Beholding angels (Visions, Articles of Faith 1:7)		Genesis 15:1; Numbers 24:2; 1 Samuel 3:15–17; Isaiah 1:1; Ezekiel 11:24; Daniel 8–9:24

Except for the gift of tongues (the talking donkey in Numbers 22:28–29 may be too much of a stretch), every other gift of the Spirit tallied above is manifest in the Old Testament. Sometimes the text uses different words to describe the spiritual empowerment but the gifts are comparable. Paul, Moroni, and Joseph Smith emphasize that the gifts of the Spirit are given to all who ask in faith (see 1 Corinthians 12:11; Moroni 10:7; D&C 46:7, 30). The same is true in the Old Testament, where Moses's plea rings through the entire testament: "I wish that all the Lord's people were prophets and that the Lord would put his Spirit on them!" (New International Version, Numbers 11:29).

The spirit of prophecy.[27] Of all the gifts of the Spirit in the Old Testament, the gift of prophecy is linked most closely to the Spirit. The Spirit authorized certain servants to speak for God "in the name of the Lord" (Deuteronomy 18:22; see also Numbers 11:25–26; 1 Samuel 10:6, 10, 20–21, 24; Ezekiel 11:24; 37:1).[28] Prophecy usually came through the Lord's prophets, but not exclusively. King David acknowledged the Spirit as the source of his prophecy in his last words: "The Spirit of the Lord spake by me, and his word was in my tongue" (2 Samuel 23:2; see also 24:11; 1 Samuel 10:1–13; 1 Chronicles 17:3; 1 Kings 12:22). Elsewhere in the Old Testament, the Spirit prophesies as direction from God against the wicked (see Isaiah 30:1; Nehemiah 9:20, 30), promises justice for the poor (see Micah 3:8; Jeremiah 9:23–24; 22:15–16), foretells blessings for the righteous (see Numbers 23:11–12, 25–26), and predicts conditions for the Millennium (see Zechariah 12:10; 14:5–9; Isaiah 11).

The Old Testament teaches that the Spirit prophesied to different cultures, generations, and peoples. Joseph of old received revelation for Egypt (see Genesis 41:25), Daniel for Babylon (see Daniel 2:47), and Malachi for the Latter-day Saints (see Malachi 3:1; 4:5–6; D&C 110:14; 128:17). Isaiah encouraged all his readers to study the prophecies: "Seek ye out of the book of the Lord, and read: no one of these shall fail" (Isaiah 34:16; similarly, Zechariah 7:12). Amos admonishes us to study prophecy in order to know God's plan of action: "Surely, the Lord God will do nothing, but he revealeth his secret unto his servants the prophets" (Amos 3:7; see also Ezekiel 24:14). Sincere seekers received prophecy throughout the Old Testament for themselves and their posterity: "Those things which are revealed belong unto us and to our children for ever, that we may do all the words of this law" (Deuteronomy 29:29).

Through the whisperings of the Spirit, the same scriptural prophecy can have multiple meanings. For example, Joel's prophecy of a future deluge of the Spirit, "I will pour out my spirit upon all flesh" (Joel 2:28) applied to more than one period of history. Peter claimed Joel's fulfillment on the day of Pentecost (see Acts 2:14–18), and the angel Moroni for the Restoration (see Joseph Smith—History 1:41). The continuity of prophecy is provided by the Spirit: "For I will pour water upon him that is thirsty, and floods upon the dry ground: I will pour my spirit upon thy seed, and my blessing upon thine offspring" (Isaiah 44:3). The Spirit can personalize prophecy as well and provide a variety of levels of relevancy, understanding, and interpretation.

According to the Old Testament, sin silences the spirit of prophecy and revelation. "Woe to the rebellious children, saith the Lord, that take counsel, but not of me; and that cover with a covering, but not of my spirit, that they may add sin to sin" (Isaiah 30:1; see also Proverbs 1:23). God warned, "My spirit shall not always strive with man" (Genesis 6:3). When the children of Israel rebelled, they grieved the Spirit (see Isaiah 63:10; Zechariah 7:12). The Psalmist implored, "Hide thy face from my sins, and blot out all mine iniquities. . . . Cast me not away from thy presence; and take not thy holy spirit from me" (Psalm 51:9, 11; see also 1 Samuel 16:14). A century later the Spirit inspired Zechariah the priest to explain why the people could not prosper: "Because ye have forsaken the Lord, he hath also forsaken you" (2 Chronicles 24:20).[29] But even the estrangement of sin can be overcome through our Redeemer's gift of repentance: Proverbs teaches that God's wrath is assuaged through repentance and the cleansing of the Spirit. If Israel will "turn . . . at my reproof: behold, I will pour out my spirit unto you, I will make known my words unto you" (Proverbs 1:23; see also Ecclesiastes 12:7; Isaiah 28:6; 30:1; 54:8). Isaiah further promised Israel "that if they repent, "the Spirit of the Lord" will cause "him to rest" and become "a glorious name" (Isaiah 63:14). Repentance was a regular cry from prophets like Micah, who was moved by the Spirit "to declare unto Jacob his transgression, and to Israel his sin" (3:8; see also 2 Chronicles 7:14; Ezekiel 14:6; 18:30).[30] The prophet Isaiah linked an awareness of the covenant with an awareness of the Spirit. After a discussion on repentance, he prophesies the return of the Spirit for those who return to the covenant: "As for me, this is my covenant with them, saith the Lord; my spirit that is upon thee, and my words which I have put in thy mouth, shall not depart out of thy mouth, nor out of the mouth of thy seed" (Isaiah 59:21).[31] When the Spirit of prophecy directs Israel, the covenant is intact.

Conclusion

The Old Testament witnesses to the workings of God's Spirit. The Apostle Peter defended the Spirit's role in inspiring ancient prophets: "For the prophecy came not in old time by the will of man: but holy men of God spake as they were moved by the Holy Ghost" (2 Peter 1:21). Evidence of the Spirit's promptings extends across scripture and time. The Spirit's work is consistent as it reveals the gospel of Jesus Christ in the Old Testament as an "abundance of peace and truth" (Jeremiah 33:6). Even though the Old Testament has fewer statements dealing with the Spirit, its examples stand along with other holy writ as a witness that God's Spirit breathes life into the physical and spiritual world.

The Old Testament shows the Spirit's influence creating, energizing, instructing, encouraging, prophesying, blessing, and anointing the obedient chosen people. Moses yearned for the day when "all the Lord's people were prophets and that the Lord would put his Spirit on them!" (Numbers 11:29). Joel answered that plea with the Lord's promise, "I will pour out my spirit upon all flesh; and your sons and your daughters shall prophesy, your old men shall dream dreams, your young men shall see visions: and also upon the servants and upon the handmaids in those days will I pour out my spirit" (Joel 2:28–29). Joel foretold of a time when the Spirit would communicate to a greater degree than in his day—a time when the Spirit's work of dreams, visions, and prophecy would have no distinctions for gender, age, rank, intelligence, or birthright. He prophesied of a time when the Spirit would bless people who have a broken heart to seek their salvation through the Messiah whom the Spirit fully anointed.

Joel's prophecy validates the work of Joseph Smith and the Restoration of the gospel of Jesus Christ. Old Testament prophets looked forward to this day "with anxious expectation to be revealed in the last times, which their minds were pointed to by the angels" when "God shall give unto you knowledge by his holy Spirit, yea, by the unspeakable gift of the Holy Ghost, that has not been revealed since the world was until now" (D&C 121:26–27). The Prophet Joseph Smith acknowledged that the gift of the Holy Ghost differentiated his work from all other denominations. The gifts of the Spirit functioned in the Old Testament among a select few, but now the gift of the Holy Ghost offers sanctification to all who "walk in the meekness of my Spirit" (D&C 19:23).

APPENDIX: REFERENCES TO THE SPIRIT

PROBABLE OLD TESTAMENT REFERENCES TO *RŬAH* AS THE HOLY GHOST

Genesis 1:2. "And the earth was without form, and void; and darkness was upon the face of the deep. And the Spirit of God moved upon the face of the waters."

Genesis 6:3. "And the Lord said, My spirit shall not always strive with man, for that he also is flesh: yet his days shall be an hundred and twenty years."

Genesis 41:38. "And Pharaoh said unto his servants, Can we find such a one as this is, a man in whom the Spirit of God is?"

Exodus 31:3. "And I have filled him with the spirit of God, in wisdom, and in understanding, and in knowledge, and in all manner of workmanship."

Exodus 35:31. "And he hath filled him with the spirit of God, in wisdom, in understanding, and in knowledge, and in all manner of workmanship."

Numbers 11:17. "And I will come down and talk with thee there: and I will take of the spirit which is upon thee, and will put it upon them; and they shall bear the burden of the people with thee, that thou bear it not thyself alone."

Numbers 11:25. "And the Lord came down in a cloud, and spake unto him, and took of the spirit that was upon him, and gave it unto the seventy elders: and it came to pass, that, when the spirit rested upon them, they prophesied, and did not cease."

Numbers 11:26. "But there remained two of the men in the camp, the name of the one was Eldad, and the name of the other Medad: and the spirit rested upon them; and they were of them that were written, but went not out unto the tabernacle: and they prophesied in the camp."

Numbers 11:29. "And Moses said unto him, Enviest thou for my sake? would God that all the Lord's people were prophets, and that the Lord would put his spirit upon them!"

Numbers 24:2. "And Balaam lifted up his eyes, and he saw Israel abiding in his tents according to their tribes; and the spirit of God came upon him."

Numbers 27:18. "And the Lord said unto Moses, Take thee Joshua the son of Nun, a man in whom is the spirit, and lay thine hand upon him."

Judges 3:10. "And the Spirit of the Lord came upon him, and he judged Israel, and went out to war: and the Lord delivered Chushanrishathaim king of Mesopotamia into his hand."

Judges 6:34. "But the Spirit of the Lord came upon Gideon, and he blew a trumpet."

Judges 11:29. "Then the Spirit of the Lord came upon Jephthah, and he passed over Gilead, and Manasseh, and passed over Mizpeh of Gilead."

Judges 13:25. "And the Spirit of the Lord began to move him at times in the camp of Dan between Zorah and Eshtaol."

Judges 14:6. "And the Spirit of the Lord came mightily upon him, and he rent him as he would have rent a kid, and he had nothing in his hand: but he told not his father or his mother what he had done."

Judges 14:19. "And the Spirit of the Lord came upon him, and he went down to Ashkelon, and slew thirty men of them, and took their spoil."

Judges 15:14. "And when he came unto Lehi, the Philistines shouted against him: and the Spirit of the Lord came mightily upon him, and the cords that were upon his arms became as flax that was burnt with fire, and his bands loosed from off his hands."

1 Samuel 10:6. "And the Spirit of the Lord will come upon thee, and thou shalt prophesy with them, and shalt be turned into another man."

1 Samuel 10:10. "And when they came thither to the hill, behold, a company of prophets met him; and the Spirit of God came upon him, and he prophesied among them."

1 Samuel 11:6. "And the Spirit of God came upon Saul when he heard those tidings, and his anger was kindled greatly."

1 Samuel 16:13. "Then Samuel took the horn of oil, and anointed him in the midst of his brethren: and the Spirit of the Lord came upon David from that day forward. So Samuel rose up, and went to Ramah."

1 Samuel 16:14. "But the Spirit of the Lord departed from Saul, and an evil spirit from the Lord troubled him."

1 Samuel 19:20. "And Saul sent messengers to take David: and when they saw the company of the prophets prophesying, and Samuel standing as appointed over them, the Spirit of God was upon the messengers of Saul, and they also prophesied."

1 Samuel 19:23. "And he went thither to Naioth in Ramah: and the Spirit of God was upon him also, and he went on, and prophesied, until he came to Naioth in Ramah."

2 Samuel 23:2. "The Spirit of the Lord spake by me, and his word was in my tongue."

1 Kings 18:12. "And it shall come to pass, as soon as I am gone from thee, that the Spirit of the Lord shall carry thee whither I know not."

1 Kings 22:24. "But Zedekiah the son of Chenaanah went near, and smote Micaiah on the cheek, and said, Which way went the Spirit of the Lord from me to speak unto thee?"

2 Kings 2:16. "Behold now, there be with thy servants fifty strong men; let them go, we pray thee, and seek thy master: lest peradventure the Spirit of the Lord hath taken him up, and cast him upon some mountain, or into some valley. And he said, Ye shall not send."

2 Chronicles 15:1. "And the Spirit of God came upon Azariah the son of Oded."

2 Chronicles 18:23. "Then Zedekiah the son of Chenaanah came near, and smote Micaiah upon the cheek, and said, Which way went the Spirit of the Lord from me to speak unto thee?"

2 Chronicles 20:14. "Then upon Jahaziel the son of Zechariah, the son of Benaiah, the son of Jeiel, the son of Mattaniah, a Levite of the sons of Asaph, came the Spirit of the Lord in the midst of the congregation."

2 Chronicles 24:20. "And the Spirit of God came upon Zechariah the son of Jehoiada the priest, which stood above the people, and said unto them, Thus saith God, Why transgress ye the commandments of the Lord, that ye cannot prosper? because ye have forsaken the Lord, he hath also forsaken you."

Nehemiah 9:20. "Thou gavest also thy good spirit to instruct them, and withheldest not thy manna from their mouth, and gavest them water for their thirst."

Nehemiah 9:30. "Yet many years didst thou forbear them, and testifiedst against them by thy spirit in thy prophets: yet would they not give ear: therefore gavest thou them into the hand of the people of the lands."

Job 26:13. "By his spirit he hath garnished the heavens; his hand hath formed the crooked serpent."

Job 27:3. "All the while my breath is in me, and the spirit of God is in my nostrils."

Job 33:4. "The Spirit of God hath made me, and the breath of the Almighty hath given me life."

Psalm 51:11. "Cast me not away from thy presence; and take not thy holy spirit from me."

Psalm 104:30. "Thou sendest forth thy spirit, they are created: and thou renewest the face of the earth."

Psalm 139:7. "Whither shall I go from thy spirit? or whither shall I flee from thy presence?"

Psalm 143:10. "Teach me to do thy will; for thou art my God: thy spirit is good; lead me into the land of uprightness."

Proverbs 1:23. "Turn you at my reproof: behold, I will pour out my spirit unto you, I will make known my words unto you."

Isaiah 11:2. "The spirit of the Lord shall rest upon him, the spirit of wisdom and understanding, the spirit of counsel and might, the spirit of knowledge and of the fear of the Lord."

Isaiah 30:1. "Woe to the rebellious children, saith the Lord, that take counsel, but not of me; and that cover with a covering, but not of my spirit, that they may add sin to sin."

Isaiah 32:15. "Until the spirit be poured upon us from on high, and the wilderness be a fruitful field, and the fruitful field be counted for a forest."

Isaiah 34:16. "Seek ye out of the book of the Lord, and read: no one of these shall fail, none shall want her mate: for my mouth it hath commanded, and his spirit it hath gathered them."

Isaiah 40:7. "The grass withereth, the flower fadeth: because the spirit of the Lord bloweth upon it: surely the people is grass."

Isaiah 40:13. "Who hath directed the Spirit of the Lord, or being his counsellor hath taught him?"

Isaiah 42:1. "Behold my servant, whom I uphold; mine elect, in whom my soul delighteth; I have put my spirit upon him: he shall bring forth judgment to the Gentiles."

Isaiah 44:3. "For I will pour water upon him that is thirsty, and floods upon the dry ground: I will pour my spirit upon thy seed, and my blessing upon thine offspring."

Isaiah 48:16. "Come ye near unto me, hear ye this; I have not spoken in secret from the beginning; from the time that it was, there am I: and now the Lord God, and his Spirit, hath sent me."

Isaiah 59:19. "So shall they fear the name of the Lord from the west, and his glory from the rising of the sun. When the enemy shall come in like a flood, the Spirit of the Lord shall lift up a standard against him."

Isaiah 59:21. "As for me, this is my covenant with them, saith the Lord; My spirit that is upon thee, and my words which I have put in thy mouth, shall not depart out of thy mouth, nor out of the mouth of thy seed, nor out of the mouth of thy seed's seed, saith the Lord, from henceforth and for ever."

Isaiah 61:1. "The Spirit of the Lord God is upon me; because the Lord hath anointed me to preach good tidings unto the meek; he hath sent me to bind up the brokenhearted, to proclaim liberty to the captives, and the opening of the prison to them that are bound."

Isaiah 63:10. "But they rebelled, and vexed his holy Spirit: therefore he was turned to be their enemy, and he fought against them."

Isaiah 63:11. "Then he remembered the days of old, Moses, and his people, saying, Where is he that brought them up out of the sea with the shepherd of his flock? where is he that put his holy Spirit within him?"

Isaiah 63:14. "As a beast goeth down into the valley, the Spirit of the Lord caused him to rest: so didst thou lead thy people, to make thyself a glorious name."

Ezekiel 3:24. "Then the spirit entered into me, and set me upon my feet, and spake with me, and said unto me, Go, shut thyself within thine house."

Ezekiel 11:5. "And the Spirit of the Lord fell upon me, and said unto me, Speak; Thus saith the Lord; Thus have ye said, O house of Israel: for I know the things that come into your mind, every one of them."

Ezekiel 11:24. "Afterwards the spirit took me up, and brought me in a vision by the Spirit of God into Chaldea, to them of the captivity. So the vision that I had seen went up from me."

Ezekiel 36:27. "And I will put my spirit within you, and cause you to walk in my statutes, and ye shall keep my judgments, and do them."

Ezekiel 37:1. "The hand of the Lord was upon me, and carried me out in the spirit of the Lord, and set me down in the midst of the valley which was full of bones."

Ezekiel 37:14. "Put my spirit in you, and ye shall live, and I shall place you in your own land: then shall ye know that I the Lord have spoken it, and performed it, saith the Lord."

Ezekiel 39:29. "Neither will I hide my face any more from them: for I have poured out my spirit upon the house of Israel, saith the Lord God."

Joel 2:28. "And it shall come to pass afterward, that I will pour out my spirit upon all flesh; and your sons and your daughters shall prophesy, your old men shall dream dreams, your young men shall see visions."

Joel 2:29. "And also upon the servants and upon the handmaids in those days will I pour out my spirit."

Micah 2:7. "O thou that art named the house of Jacob, is the spirit of the Lord straitened? are these his doings? do not my words do good to him that walketh uprightly?"

Micah 3:8. "But truly I am full of power by the spirit of the Lord, and of judgment, and of might, to declare unto Jacob his transgression, and to Israel his sin."

Haggai 2:5. "According to the word that I covenanted with you when ye came out of Egypt, so my spirit remaineth among you: fear ye not."

Zechariah 4:6. "Then he answered and spake unto me, saying, This is the word of the Lord unto Zerubbabel, saying, Not by might, nor by power, but by my spirit, saith the Lord of hosts."

Zechariah 7:12. "The words which the Lord of hosts hath sent in his spirit by the former prophets: therefore came a great wrath from the Lord of hosts."

Malachi 2:15. "And did not he make one? Yet had he the residue of the spirit."

272 LYNNE HILTON WILSON

POSSIBLE OLD TESTAMENT REFERENCES TO *RÛAH* AS THE HOLY GHOST

Numbers 14:24. "But my servant Caleb, because he had another spirit with him, and hath followed me fully, him will I bring into the land whereinto he went."

2 Samuel 22:16. "And the channels of the sea appeared, the foundations of the world were discovered, at the rebuking of the Lord, at the blast of the breath [*rûah*] of his nostrils."

2 Kings 2:9. "And Elisha said, I pray thee, let a double portion of thy spirit be upon me."

2 Kings 2:15. "The spirit of Elijah doth rest on Elisha. And they came to meet him, and bowed themselves to the ground before him."

Job 4:9. "By the blast of God they perish, and by the breath [*rûah*] of his nostrils are they consumed."

Job 34:14. "If he set his heart upon man, if he gather unto himself his spirit and his breath."

Psalm 18:15. "Then the channels of waters were seen, and the foundations of the world were discovered at thy rebuke, O Lord, at the blast of the breath [*rûah*] of thy nostrils."

Isaiah 4:4. "When the Lord shall have washed away the filth of the daughters of Zion, and shall have purged the blood of Jerusalem from the midst thereof by the spirit of judgment, and by the spirit of burning."

Isaiah 42:5. "Thus saith God the Lord, he that created the heavens, and stretched them out; he that spread forth the earth, and that which cometh out of it; he that giveth breath unto the people upon it, and spirit to them that walk therein."

Ezekiel 2:2. "And the spirit entered into me when he spake unto me, and set me upon my feet, that I heard him that spake unto me."

Ezekiel 3:12. "Then the spirit took me up, and I heard behind me a voice of a great rushing, saying, Blessed be the glory of the Lord from his place."

Ezekiel 3:14. "So the spirit lifted me up, and took me away, and I went in bitterness, in the heat of my spirit; but the hand of the Lord was strong upon me."

Ezekiel 8:3. "And he put forth the form of an hand, and took me by a lock of mine head; and the spirit lifted me up between the earth and the heaven, and brought me in the visions of God to Jerusalem."

Ezekiel 11:1. "Moreover the spirit lifted me up, and brought me unto the east gate of the Lord's house, which looketh eastward."

Ezekiel 43:5. "So the spirit took me up, and brought me into the inner court; and, behold, the glory of the Lord filled the house."

Daniel 4:8. "But at the last Daniel came in before me, whose name was Belteshazzar, according to the name of my god, and in whom is the spirit of the holy gods."

Daniel 4:9. "O Belteshazzar, master of the magicians, because I know that the spirit of the holy gods is in thee, and no secret troubleth thee, tell me the visions of my dream that I have seen, and the interpretation thereof."

Daniel 4:18. "O Belteshazzar, declare the interpretation thereof, forasmuch as all the wise men of my kingdom are not able to make known unto me the interpretation: but thou art able; for the spirit of the holy gods is in thee."

Daniel 5:11. "There is a man in thy kingdom, in whom is the spirit of the holy gods; and in the days of thy father light and understanding and wisdom, like the wisdom of the gods, was found in him."

Daniel 5:14. "I have even heard of thee, that the spirit of the gods is in thee, and that light and understanding and excellent wisdom is found in thee."

Zechariah 12:10. "And I will pour upon the house of David, and upon the inhabitants of Jerusalem, the spirit of grace and of supplications: and they shall look upon me whom they have pierced, and they shall mourn for him, as one mourneth for his only son, and shall be in bitterness for him, as one that is in bitterness for his firstborn."

(There are several references to the work of the Spirit without the word *rûah*. For example in Exodus 13:21, "And the Lord went before them by day in a pillar of a cloud, to lead them the way; and by night in a pillar of fire, to give them light; to go by day and night." These are not included because this study has limited its scope to references of *rûah* that point to the third member of the Godhead.)

PROBABLE PEARL OF GREAT PRICE REFERENCES TO THE SPIRIT

Moses 1:15. "Blessed be the name of my God, for his Spirit hath not altogether withdrawn from me, or else where is thy glory, for it is darkness unto me? And I can judge between thee and God; for God said unto me: Worship God, for him only shalt thou serve."

Moses 1:24. "And it came to pass that when Satan had departed from the presence of Moses, that Moses lifted up his eyes unto heaven, being filled with the Holy Ghost, which beareth record of the Father and the Son."

Moses 1:27. "And it came to pass, as the voice was still speaking, Moses cast his eyes and beheld the earth, yea, even all of it; and there was not a particle of it which he did not behold, discerning it by the spirit of God."

Moses 1:28. "And he beheld also the inhabitants thereof, and there was not a soul which he beheld not; and he discerned them by the Spirit of God; and their numbers were great, even numberless as the sand upon the sea shore."

Moses 2:2. "And the earth was without form, and void; and I caused darkness to come up upon the face of the deep; and my Spirit moved upon the face of the water; for I am God."

Moses 5:9. "And in that day the Holy Ghost fell upon Adam, which beareth record of the Father and the Son, saying: I am the Only Begotten of the Father from the beginning, henceforth and forever, that as thou hast fallen thou mayest be redeemed, and all mankind, even as many as will."

Moses 5:14. "And the Lord God called upon men by the Holy Ghost everywhere and commanded them that they should repent."

Moses 5:58. "And thus the Gospel began to be preached, from the beginning, being declared by holy angels sent forth from the presence of God, and by his own voice, and by the gift of the Holy Ghost."

Moses 6:5. "And a book of remembrance was kept, in the which was recorded, in the language of Adam, for it was given unto as many as called upon God to write by the spirit of inspiration."

Moses 6:8. "Now this prophecy Adam spake, as he was moved upon by the Holy Ghost, and a genealogy was kept of the children of God."

Moses 6:26. "And it came to pass that Enoch journeyed in the land, among the people; and as he journeyed, the Spirit of God descended out of heaven, and abode upon him."

Moses 6:34. "Behold my Spirit is upon you, wherefore all thy words will I justify; and the mountains shall flee before you, and the rivers shall turn from their course; and thou shalt abide in me, and I in you; therefore walk with me."

Moses 6:52. "And he also said unto him: If thou wilt turn unto me, and hearken unto my voice, and believe, and repent of all thy transgressions, and be baptized, even in water, in the name of mine Only Begotten Son, who is full of grace and truth, which is Jesus Christ, the only name which shall be given under heaven, whereby salvation shall come unto the children of men, ye shall receive the gift of the Holy Ghost, asking all things in his name, and whatsoever ye shall ask, it shall be given you."

Moses 6:59. "That by reason of transgression cometh the fall, which fall bringeth death, and inasmuch as ye were born into the world by water, and blood, and the spirit, which I have made, and so became of dust a living soul, even so ye must be born again into the kingdom of heaven, of water, and of the Spirit, and be cleansed by blood, even the blood of mine Only Begotten; that ye might be sanctified from all sin, and enjoy the words of eternal life in this world, and eternal life in the world to come, even immortal glory."

Moses 6:60. "For by the water ye keep the commandment; by the Spirit ye are justified, and by the blood ye are sanctified."

Moses 6:61. "Therefore it is given to abide in you; the record of heaven; the Comforter; the peaceable things of immortal glory; the truth of all things; that which quickeneth all things, which maketh alive all things; that which knoweth all things, and hath all power according to wisdom, mercy, truth, justice, and judgment."

Moses 6:64. "And it came to pass, when the Lord had spoken with Adam, our father, that Adam cried unto the Lord, and he was caught away by the Spirit of the Lord, and was carried down into the water, and was laid under the water, and was brought forth out of the water."

Moses 6:65. "And thus he was baptized, and the Spirit of God descended upon him."

Moses 6:65. "And thus he was born of the Spirit, and became quickened in the inner man."

Moses 6:66. "Thou art baptized with fire, and with the Holy Ghost. This is the record of the Father, and the Son, from henceforth and forever."

Moses 7:11. "And he gave unto me a commandment that I should baptize in the name of the Father, and of the Son, which is full of grace and truth, and of the Holy Ghost, which beareth record of the Father and the Son."

Moses 7:27. "And Enoch beheld angels descending out of heaven, bearing testimony of the Father and Son; and the Holy Ghost fell on many, and they were caught up by the powers of heaven into Zion."

Moses 8:17. "And the Lord said unto Noah: My Spirit shall not always strive with man, for he shall know that all flesh shall die."

Moses 8:24. "Believe and repent of your sins and be baptized in the name of Jesus Christ, the Son of God, even as our fathers, and ye shall receive the Holy Ghost, that ye may have all things made manifest; and if ye do not this, the floods will come in upon you."

Abraham 4:2. "And the earth, after it was formed, was empty and desolate, because they had not formed anything but the earth; and darkness reigned upon the face of the deep, and the Spirit of the Gods was brooding upon the face of the waters."

NOTES

1. John Owen, *Pneumatologia; or, a Discourse Concerning the Holy Spirit* (Philadelphia: Towar and Hogan, 1827), 60; Samuel Macauley Jackson, ed., *The New Schaff-Herzog Encyclopedia of Religious Knowledge* (New York: Funk and Wagnalls, 1911), 193; Clarence Larkin, *Dispensational Truth or God's Plan and Purpose in the Ages* (circa 1918, digitalized: Kessinger, 2005), 54.

2. Michael Berenbaum and Fred Skolnik, eds. *Encyclopedia Judaica,* 2nd ed. (Detroit: Macmillan, 2007); and Bill T. Arnold and H. G. M. Williamson, eds., *Dictionary of the Old Testament* (Downers Grove, IL: InterVarsity Press, 2005). Even though some modern Old Testament and Jewish reference books do not mention the Spirit, as one looks back in time to older editions, listings of the Spirit tend to increase with age, for example, *Encyclopedia of Judaica.* Jerusalem: Encyclopedia Judaica (New York: Macmillan, 1972) has a section on *"rûah hakodesh"* that begins, "Although the phrase *Ru'ah ha-Kodesh* occurs in the Bible . . . its specific connotation

as divine inspiration is wholly post-biblical" (14.364). Similarly, the *Universal Jewish Encyclopedia* has a section on *rûah hakodesh* that reads, "The term 'spirit' (*ruah*) occurs frequently in the Bible in the sense of the divine inspiration which enters the body of the prophets and causes them to enounce the will of God. There is no indication, however, that the 'holy spirit' was regarded as a separate entity. Christian theology developed from the term its doctrine of the Holy Ghost as a member of the Trinity" (Isaac Landman, ed. [New York: Ktav, 1969], 9:268). Only in much older works like *The Jewish Encyclopedia* do we find a section titled "Holy Spirit" (Joseph Jacobs, ed. [New York: Funk and Wagnalls, 1904], 6:450). It appears that the association between the Old Testament and the Spirit became less and less popular in some groups of academia during the twentieth century.

3. When referring to the third member of the Godhead, this study follows the scriptural pattern of using the names "Holy Ghost," "Spirit," and "Holy Spirit" interchangeably.

4. Following the writing of the Old Testament, rabbis used the word "*shekhinah*" to describe the presence of the Lord that filled the Tabernacle or Solomon's Temple. This is not included in our study as it is not used this way in the Old Testament. (*Shikkên* is found in Psalm 78:60 and Jeremiah 7:3 and 7, for dwelling, but these instances do not share the rabbinic definition.) The "glory of the Lord" is mentioned thirty-four times in the KJV Old Testament and can arguably reference the presence or influence of the Lord. When the KJV has both "glory of the Lord" and "Spirit" in the same phrase, they appear to be two distinct thoughts. This study will only examine the Hebrew *rûah* for the Spirit.

5. William A. Dyrness, *Themes in Old Testament Theology* (Exeter, Australia: Paternoster Press, 1979), 86, enumerates 389 appearances of "spirit/*rûah*" in the Old Testament, but I have tried to distinguish which references directly referred to the Holy Spirit from the Godhead (see the appendix).

6. The most difficult question in making this judgment in the Old Testament is separating out the "Spirit of God" or the "Spirit of the Lord." In this study all such references are attributed to the Holy Ghost, although they may refer literally to the eternal spirit of Jehovah. The context of most usage of "the Spirit of the Lord" points to the Holy Ghost. For the sake of continuity, all references to God's *rûah* are defined as the third member of the Godhead to see the working of the Spirit in the Old Testament.

7. As fifth-century editors, Mormon and Moroni recorded the names "Spirit of God" and "Spirit of the Lord" just as they were found in the brass plates (see Alma 5:46–47; 1 Nephi 11:1; 13:13; 15:12; Words of Mormon 1:7; Mosiah 2:36; Mormon 2:26; Ether 15:19). Because some of their references clearly point to the Holy Ghost, it is probable that they constantly used those titles for the Holy Spirit. The prophet Zenos, whose writings were recorded, at least in part, on the brass plates, used the phrase "Spirit of God" in 1 Nephi 19:12 just as Mormon does centuries after Christ's Resurrection (Moroni 10:8–9). The phrase "Spirit of the Lord" is used by the Old Testament prophet Isaiah (Isaiah 11:2), just as Mormon and Moroni's postresurrection writings include the same title of the Holy Ghost (see Mormon 2:26; 5:16; Moroni 9:4). If these two prophet-editors knew the Lord as a

resurrected being and consistently identified the Holy Ghost as "the Spirit of God" or "the Spirit of the Lord," we can likely identify these titles as the third member of the Godhead in the Old Testament. Similarly, the New Testament uses these same titles for the Holy Ghost.

8. The Triple Combination cites the "Spirit" more often than does the Bible. In the Book of Mormon, thirteen of the fifteen books reference the Spirit. The Doctrine and Covenants mentions the Holy Spirit at least once in 68 of the 138 sections.

9. This category includes minor derivations as well—for example "baptized with fire," "baptize with fire," "baptism by fire," and "baptism of fire." It does not include every discussion of baptism by the Spirit (see Matthew 3:11; Mark 1:8; Luke 3:16; John 1:33; Acts 1:5; 1 Corinthians 12:13) as those figures are included in the heading of "Spirit."

10. These numbers represent the sections Joseph Smith received, D&C 1–133, 137.

11. Two months after the organization of the Church and three months after the Book of Mormon was published, Joseph Smith was commanded to begin a revision of the Bible (see D&C 35:20; 45:60–61). Joseph Fielding Smith summarized, "From June, 1830, until March 7, 1831, the Brethren labored with the revision of the early chapters of Genesis. . . . The work continued through both the Old and New Testaments until July 2, 1833" (Joseph Smith, *Teachings of the Prophet Joseph Smith*, comp. Joseph Fielding Smith [Salt Lake City: Deseret Book, 1976], 45).

12. Interestingly, when we compare the book of Abraham with the book of Moses, we find very different uses of the Spirit in their retelling of the same creation story. The translation of the Abraham papyri has only one reference to the Spirit, making it closer to Genesis, which also references the Spirit once in its creation story. On the other hand, Joseph Smith's inspired revision of Moses refers to the Holy Spirit twenty-four times, a similar word ratio to that of the Doctrine and Covenants. These two examples suggest that Joseph Smith's prophetic voice has a special interest in the role of the Holy Spirit.

13. Even though the book of Moses speaks of the time of Adam, the emphasis on the Spirit is from the writer's perspective (traditionally presumed as Moses) centuries after Adam.

14. Only seventy-three examples of Spirit/*rûah* in the Old Testament are cited later in this text, but other possibilities are found in the appendix. The appendix only includes *rûah*, even though the Old Testament has a few references that may refer to the Holy Ghost that use a different Hebrew word, *nshamah,* which is usually translated breath (for example, Job 32:8, "But there is a spirit in man: and the inspiration [*nshamah*] of the Almighty giveth them understanding").

15. The idea of the breath of life initiating from the breath of God was also taught by the Egyptians, Babylonians, Assyrians, Canaanites, and Phoenicians. These similar doctrines could have stemmed from two possibilities—either they all initiated from the same doctrine, or, as biblical scholar Edmond Jacob suggests, "It must have offered itself spontaneously to different peoples through the simple observation that life and breath ceased together, and because of the anthropomorphic picture of the deity the origin of this breath was attributed to his breath"

THE HOLY SPIRIT 279

(Ben C. Ollenburger, Elmer A. Martens, and Gerhard F. Hasel, eds., *The Flowering of Old Testament Theology: A Reader in Twentieth-Century Old Testament Theology, 1930–1990* [Winomalk, IN: Eisenbrauns, 1992], 158). I disagree with Edmond Jacob and see logic in the first option.

16. When the context of Nehemiah 9:20 is taken into account, "good spirit" appears to refer to the Holy Spirit. For continuity, "good spirit" in Alma 3:26 is included in table 2.

17. Dyrness, *Themes in Old Testament Theology*, 207–8.

18. Richard Averbeck of Trinity Evangelical School sees Ezekiel's vision as also prophesying the Spirit's return to Israel after their Babylonian captivity. He sees the vision foretelling Jesus's baptism by the Spirit: "Jesus continues the pattern of reference to Ezekiel in John 3:8 when he uses the same play on words between 'wind/breath' and 'Spirit' for the life giving Spirit of God as the one that appears in the valley of dry bones vision in Ezekiel 37. Jesus said, 'The *wind (pneuma)* blows wherever it pleases. You hear its sound, but you cannot tell where it comes from or where it is going. So it is with everyone born of the *Spirit (pneuma)*' (John 3:8). In the valley of dry bones the 'wind' (*rûah* v. 9) blew 'breath' (*rûah* vv. 5, 6, 8, 9, 10) into the dry bones as they came together and flesh grew on the skeletons. Thus the bodies of Israelites would come alive, referring to their restoration from captivity, because the Lord would give them his Spirit." Oral reading at the Society of Biblical Literature lecture of an unpublished paper by Richard Averbeck, "Patterns of Presence and Cleansing in the Old and New Testaments," Boston, November 2008, 17.

19. The Spirit is associated with anointing three times in the Doctrine and Covenants: 132:7, 18–19; and twice in the New Testament: Luke 4:18; Acts 10:38.

20. There are Judaic traditions that separate the anointing of a Messiah ben David from a Messiah ben Aaron or a Messiah ben Joseph. The latter came initially in the Babylonian Talmud, but as publicized in *Biblical Archaeology Review*, a three-foot stone dating from around the first century BC records the Messiah, son of Joseph, giving signs to David (Israel Knohl, "The Messiah Son of Joseph: 'Gabriel's Revelation' and the Birth of a New Messianic Model," *Biblical Archaeology Review* 34, no. 5 [September/October 2008]: 59).

21. Tragically, in order to fulfill his mission, the greatest Anointed One was rejected and abused (see Isaiah 53). As the "righteous servant," he was required to offer himself as a sacrifice to "justify many; for he shall bear their iniquities" (Isaiah 53:11).

22. In Hebrew, power is often associated with the Spirit—especially in modern scripture. The phrase, the "power of the Holy Ghost" is mentioned once in the New Testament, twenty-five times in the Book of Mormon, and five times in the Doctrine and Covenants. The phrase "Spirit and power" is used three more times in the Book of Mormon. Even though these distinct expressions are not stated in the Bible, the word "Spirit" (or Holy Ghost) is associated with "power" ten times throughout the Bible. Looking for the same pattern in the Book of Mormon again demonstrates its theological emphasis. Even though the Book of Mormon is one-third the length of the Bible, the word "power" is linked to God's Spirit fifty-seven times (sixteen times more than in the Bible). The Doctrine and Covenants

continues with an even greater ratio, connecting the Holy Ghost or Spirit to power. Because Joseph Smith's portion of the Doctrine and Covenants is less than half the size of the Book of Mormon (107,289 words to 266,944 words), the Doctrine and Covenants' thirty-four citations demonstrate nearly one-and-a-half times greater concentration of connections between Spirit and power than the Book of Mormon. Theologically, this was important to the Prophet Joseph Smith and the Restoration.

23. The association of the Spirit's role in calling God's servants is even more pronounced in the Book of Mormon (see Alma 8:24; 13:4; 18:34; 22:4; 43:2).

24. Kent P. Jackson and Robert L. Millet, eds., *Studies in Scripture* (Salt Lake City: Deseret Book, 1989), 3:79: "The birthright inheritance included a double portion of the land and possessions left by the father. With this inheritance came the responsibility to care for the needs of the mother, the sisters until they were married, to be a resource for the other brothers, and to serve as the family leader."

25. The Old Testament features God's Spirit empowering other leaders and prophets to speak for the Lord: Joshua (see Numbers 27:18), Azariah (see 2 Chronicles 15:1), Jahaziel (see 2 Chronicles 20:14), Zechariah (see 2 Chronicles 24:20), Ezekiel (see Ezekiel 3:24), Isaiah (see Isaiah 48:16), and Elisha (see 2 Kings 2:16). For a clearer correlation, see also Mosiah 18:13, 26; Alma 17:3.

26. Victor L. Ludlow, *Isaiah: Prophet, Seer, and Poet* (Salt Lake City: Deseret Book, 1982), 296. In a discussion of Isaiah 6, Ludlow explains: "Fear of the Lord . . . goes beyond a sense of awe and the beginnings of faith to include entire devotion to God." Also President Kimball: "Teach them faith in the living God and in his Only Begotten Son—not a superficial, intellectual kind of acceptance, but a deep spiritual inner feeling of dependence and closeness; not a fear composed of panic and terror, but a fear of the Lord composed mostly of intense love and admiration" (*The Teachings of Spencer W. Kimball*, ed. Edward L. Kimball [Salt Lake City: Bookcraft, 1982], 73). Bishop Thorpe B. Isaacson suggested in his April 1952 conference talk, "The fear of the Lord is the beginning of great wisdom" (17).

27. The phrase "spirit of prophecy" is actually not mentioned in the Old Testament but is found once in Revelation 19:10, eighteen times in the Book of Mormon, twice in the Doctrine and Covenants, and twenty-three times in the *History of the Church*. This is obviously an important doctrine of the Restoration. Joseph Smith believed the spirit of prophecy was not only his gift and the foundation of his title as prophet, but also the doorway for Church members and proselytes to learn truth and to receive their own witness of the Spirit.

28. Twenty-seven times the Book of Mormon connects the Holy Ghost with prophecy before Jesus's visitation (see 2 Nephi 25:4, 7; Jacob 1:6; Alma 3:27; 4:13, 20; 9:21; 3 Nephi 3:19). In contrast, the Old Testament has only two.

29. Seven priests named Zechariah or Zachariah are mentioned in the books of Chronicles. The most famous was a sixth-century prophet and has a book of the Old Testament named after him, "Zechariah, the son of Berechiah" (Zechariah 1:1). The one quoted here is "Zechariah the son of Jehoiada," who lived at the end of the ninth century BC and was stoned to death in the courtyard of the Temple (2 Chronicles 24:20). These two Zechariahs were confused in Matthew 23:35, "the blood of Zacharias *son of Barachias*, whom ye slew between the temple and the

altar" (emphasis added). This mixup is further entangled in the apocryphal account *Protevangelium of James*, where these two Old Testament Zechariahs are further befuddled with the New Testament priest Zacharias, the father of John the Baptist (see Luke 1). The apocryphal account has the man from the ninth century BC, the man from the sixth century BC, and the man from the turn of the millennium, all joined together as one person. A whole yarn was developed around this perplexity, claiming that Herod killed Zacharias, John the Baptist's father. This tale is false but has worked its way into Christian circles and found its way into the *Times and Seasons* newspaper and from there is quoted in several Latter-day Saint publications. My translation from *Bibliotheca Bodmeriana; "Protevangil de Jacques"* (Geneva, Switzerland: Papyrus Bodmer V–VI, 1958); or in English, Wihlelm Schneemelcher, ed. *Edgar Hennecke New Testament Apocrypha* (Philadelphia: Westminster Press, reprint 1963), 1.387–88.

30. One of the purposes of the Book of Mormon according to Lehi's prophecy to his son Joseph is for the prophecies of his people to join the Old Testament prophets in crying repentance in this battle against sin. He prophesies that the Book of Mormon will "cry from the dust; yea, even repentance unto their brethren, even after many generations have gone by them. And it shall come to pass that their cry shall go, even according to the simpleness of their words" (2 Nephi 3:20; see also Alma 29:1; Mormon 3:3).

31. The Spirit also confirms the promises of the gospel covenant in the New Testament and modern revelation (see Mosiah 18:10; D&C 29:30; 132:19).

16

TYPES, SHADOWS, AND SYMBOLS OF CHRIST SEEN BY THE CHURCH FATHERS

Alonzo L. Gaskill

After the close of the New Testament, the exegetical torch laid down by the Apostles at their deaths was first taken up by the apostolic fathers, then by the apologists, and eventually by other bishops, priests, and doctors of theology. These men, commonly known as the church fathers, were the authors of the most important Christian writings after the New Testament. Some, like the apostolic fathers, had been disciples of actual Apostles. Others were simply high-ranking clergymen or renowned theologians in the post–New Testament era. While Latter-day Saints traditionally do not place heavy emphasis on the writings of these men, Roman Catholic and Eastern Orthodox traditions, along with some Protestant denominations, have elevated these writings to nearly canonical status.

Like Latter-day Saints, the Christian church of the second through eighth centuries was prone to see references to, images of, and prophecies about Christ in the Old Testament. A Christocentric reading of the Hebrew Bible certainly finds support in the Book of Mormon. For example, Nephi wrote, "Behold, . . . *all things* which have been given of

Alonzo L. Gaskill is an assistant professor of Church history and doctrine at Brigham Young University.

God from the beginning of the world, unto man, are the typifying of him" (2 Nephi 11:4; emphasis added).[1] Nephi's brother Jacob recorded, "Behold, I say unto you that *none* of the prophets have written, nor prophesied, save they have spoken concerning this Christ" (Jacob 7:11; emphasis added; see also Mosiah 13:33–34). And in the book of Moses the Lord himself stated, "And behold, *all* things have their likeness, and *all* things are created and made to bear record of me" (Moses 6:63; emphasis added). From these prophetic utterances it appears that (1) *all* things given by God symbolize or typify Christ; (2) *all* prophets have prophesied and testified of Christ; and (3) potentially *all* things can remind us of Christ. Indeed, one modern typologist remarked, "The red line of [Christ's] blood runs all through the Old Testament, and . . . thus we are constantly reminded of the shed blood, without which there is not remission."[2]

Speaking in general terms, many of the church fathers from both Greek and Latin traditions would have resonated with the aforementioned scriptural declarations about the Christocentric nature of the scriptures. Indeed, most of the fathers tended to read the Hebrew Bible through Christian lenses, seeing references to, types and shadows of, and symbols for Christ in literally thousands of verses and stories scattered throughout the entirety of the Old Testament. Indicative of how the church fathers read the Hebrew Bible is the following comment from John of Damascus (circa AD 650–750):

> The tree of life which was planted by God in Paradise pre-figured this precious Cross. For since death was by a tree, it was fitting that life and resurrection should be bestowed by a tree. Jacob, when He worshipped the top of Joseph's staff, was the first to image the Cross, and when he blessed his sons with crossed hands he made most clearly the sign of the cross. Likewise also did Moses' rod, when it smote the sea in the figure of the cross and saved Israel, while it overwhelmed Pharaoh in the depths; likewise also the hands stretched out crosswise and routing Amalek; and the bitter water made sweet by a tree, and the rock rent and pouring forth streams of water and the rod that meant for Aaron the dignity of the high priesthood: and the serpent lifted in triumph on a tree as though it were dead, the tree bringing salvation to those who in faith saw their enemy dead, just as Christ was nailed to the

tree in the flesh of sin which yet knew no sin. The mighty Moses cried, *You will see your life hanging on the tree before your eyes*, and Isaiah likewise, *I have spread out my hands all the day unto a faithless and rebellious people*. But may we who worship this obtain a part in Christ the crucified. Amen.[3]

John of Damascus's comment well represents how thoroughly, in the mind of the church fathers, Jesus is present in the Old Testament. Indeed, Irenaeus (circa AD 115–202) wrote, "If any one . . . reads the Scriptures with attention, he will find in them an account of Christ. . . . For Christ is the treasure which was hid in the field, that is . . . the treasure hid in the Scriptures, since He was pointed out by means of types and parables."[4] Gracing the stage between the ministries of Irenaeus and John of Damascus, Augustine (AD 354–430) too saw the Hebrew Bible as thoroughly symbolic of Christ. He held that within the Old Testament, the New is concealed; in the New Testament, the Old is revealed.[5]

Of course, it should be understood that though many church fathers saw the stories, rites, people, and events of the Old Testament as types, shadows, or symbols of Christ, some went far beyond what a reasonable interpretation of the Bible would allow. Because of this, some fathers of the church either rejected a symbolic Christocentric reading of the Old Testament or, at the very least, expressed caution about how far such exegesis should be taken.[6] Having said that, fathers from both traditions—East and West—and from both schools—Antiochene and Alexandrian—have provided us with literally thousands of examples of the patristic tendency to see nearly everything in the Old Testament as testifying of Christ.[7] People, possessions, prophetic events, animals, and even actions were all seen by these early Christians as somehow symbolizing or foreshadowing Jesus and his divine mission and ministry. Quite literally, many of the fathers of the church would have borne witness as did Nephi that "*all things* which have been given of God from the beginning of the world, unto man, are the typifying of him" (2 Nephi 11:4; emphasis added).

It seems best to allow the words of the original authors to speak for themselves; thus what follows is a sampling of how patristic sources interpret the Old Testament as being a typological foreshadowing of Christ. The length of this paper will not allow for an exhaustive treatment of the many categories and examples of Christocentric symbolism believed by the early Christians to be present in the Hebrew Bible. However, the following examples should be a sufficient sampling of how extensive those early Christian writers believed this Christ-centered biblical symbolism was.[8]

While Latter-day Saints may find the exegesis of these fathers curious, more valuable than their interpretations is their example of the dangers of ignoring context and authorial intent. Though various fathers at times offer interpretations or applications of passages that may be illuminating and insightful, as some of our examples will show, various church fathers were so set upon finding Christ in the Old Testament that they were prone to misinterpret passages simply for the sake of finding Jesus hidden within the pages of the Bible—a practice of which no Latter-day Saint should be found guilty.

PEOPLE DEEMED CHRISTOCENTRIC BY PATRISTIC SOURCES

The church fathers saw nearly every faithful figure in the Hebrew Bible as a type of the Savior. Indeed, the number of examples that could be cited here to establish this fact is voluminous. One singular illustration is a fourth-century Syriac-speaking monk by the name of Aphrahat (flourished circa AD 340), who in one treatise offered a dozen detailed examples of biblical figures whose lives typified Christ's in some detail.[9] Extensive lists like this one were commonplace in the writings of the early church.

For the sake of brevity, I have selected one example of a biblical figure commonly seen in patristic sources as a typological foreshadowing of Christ—namely the man Adam. Of him, one early twentieth-century expert on biblical typology wrote, "The earliest foreshadowing of the Lord's death seems to be given in *the deep sleep* that God caused to fall upon Adam when He formed [or organized] Eve."[10] This statement well summarizes how the majority of early Christian authors read the Genesis account of God causing a "deep sleep" (Genesis 2:21) to come upon the man Adam.

For example, Augustine wrote, "The woman was made of a rib taken from the side of the man while he slept," and so "that sleep of the man was [symbolic of] the death of Christ, whose side, as He hung lifeless upon the cross, was pierced with a spear."[11] Elsewhere, Augustine added, "Adam's sleep was a mystical foreshadowing of Christ's death, and when his dead body hanging from the cross was pierced by the lance [in] his side."[12]

Augustine's contemporary, Quodvultdeus (flourished circa AD 430)—a man who strove at length to establish that the New Testament fulfilled the Old Testament—penned, "Since Eve had been created from the side of the sleeping Adam, . . . from the side of Christ hanging on the cross the church . . . must be created. In fact the church is 'the woman.'"[3]

Drawing on the teachings of the Apostle Paul (see 1 Corinthians 15:45), Jerome (circa AD 347–420) stated, "We have heard about the first Adam [and how he was injured in his side in order to produce Eve]; let us come now to the second Adam and see how the church is made from his side. The side of the Lord Savior as he hung on the cross is pierced with a lance."[14]

Similarly, Tertullian of Carthage (circa AD 155–225) taught, "For as Adam was a figure of Christ, Adam's sleep shadowed out the death of Christ, who was to sleep a mortal slumber, that from the wound inflicted on His side might, in like manner (as Eve was formed), be typified the church, the true mother of the living."[15]

Each of these fathers argued that the symbolic message in the "deep sleep" that came upon Adam and the creation of Eve through that sleep is that Christ's death on the cross is the event that gave birth to his Church. In other words, in the eyes of the early Church, had Jesus not died, Christianity would not exist. Indeed, its teachings and rites would be purposeless and powerless aside from Christ's sacrifice. Thus his death gave life to the Church. Or, as one Latter-day Saint scholar noted, "The taking of Eve from Adam's side also bears a resemblance to the relationship between the church and the Son of God, who permitted himself to become weak that others of his body (the Church) might have strength."[16]

WATER FROM THE ROCK

Some years after the Exodus from Egypt, the children of Israel found themselves in Kadesh, in the desert of Zin in the extreme south of Canaan. During their time there, the people began to complain against Moses and Aaron because "there was no water for the people to drink" (Exodus 17:1; see also Numbers 20:2). In response to the developing rebellion, Moses and Aaron entered the Tabernacle to pray for guidance. In answer to their pleadings, the Lord appeared to them (see

Numbers 20:6). He commanded Moses to perform a miracle on behalf of the people by causing water to flow from a rock, thereby quenching Israel's thirst and increasing their faith in him. Thus, in Numbers 20:11, we read: "And Moses lifted up his hand, and with his rod he smote the rock twice: and the water came out abundantly, and the congregation drank, and their beasts also."

Millennia later, the Apostle Paul referred to this event with Christological application. He wrote, "Moreover, brethren, I would not that ye should be ignorant, how that all our fathers . . . did . . . drink the same spiritual drink: for they drank of that spiritual Rock that followed them: and that Rock was Christ" (1 Corinthians 10:1, 4). While Paul clearly supports a Christocentric reading of the passage, the church fathers took the symbolism one step further than Paul did and offered a twist that may be surprising to many readers. Of this verse Augustine wrote, "The rock was Christ in sign. . . . The rock was smitten twice with a rod; the double smiting signified the two wooden beams of the cross."[17] Elsewhere Augustine penned this about the miracle recorded in Numbers 20:11: "'Blessed are they that hunger and thirst after righteousness, for they shall be filled.' And our thirst is quenched from the rock in the wilderness: for 'the Rock was Christ,' and it was smitten with a rod that the water might flow. But that it might flow, the rock was smitten twice: because there are two beams of the cross. All these things, then, which were done in a figure, are made manifest to us."[18]

Like Augustine, Caesarius of Arles (circa AD 470–542) also saw a foreshadowing of Jesus's crucifixion in Moses's double smiting of the rock. He wrote: "'Therefore Moses struck the rock twice with his staff.' What does this mean, brethren? . . . The rock was struck a second time because two trees were lifted up for the gibbet of the cross: the one stretched out Christ's sacred hands, the other spread out his sinless body from head to foot."[19]

Though less specific, John of Damascus (circa AD 650–750) clearly saw the same symbolic message in the Mosaic miracle. He wrote that the "precious Cross" of Christ was symbolized by "the rock [rent] and pouring forth streams of water."[20]

Around the same time that Augustine began serving as bishop of Hippo, John Chrysostom (circa AD 347–407) wrote, "Instead of water from a rock, [we have received the] blood from His side; instead of Moses' or Aaron's rod, the Cross."[21]

Thus, for early Christians, this miracle of Moses served to remind readers of the staff that pierced Christ's side and the blood and water that flowed therefrom (see John 19:34). To the fathers of the church, the rock was more than just Christ, as Paul explained it. Rather, it was "Jesus Christ, *and* him crucified" (1 Corinthians 2:2; emphasis added).[22] Though the water flowing from the rock quenched Israel's physical thirst, it foreshadowed the reality that Jesus's atoning sacrifice would quench covenant Israel's spiritual thirst. As one modern typologist noted, "The smitten rock was the source of the rivers of water; just as the death of Christ must precede the descent of the Holy Spirit."[23]

THE GATHERING OF ISRAEL

In the thirty-third chapter of Deuteronomy, we find a secondary account of Jacob's blessings pronounced upon the twelve tribes of Israel (see also Genesis 48–49). In Moses's Deuteronomic version of Jacob's blessing on Joseph, we read, "His glory is like the firstling of his bullock, and his horns are like the horns of unicorns: with them he shall push the people together to the ends of the earth" (Deuteronomy 33:17).

At face value, this passage appears to be speaking of the promised glory and power that will come to Joseph and his descendants (Ephraim and Manasseh). Though this passage is traditionally seen by commentators as highlighting the military strength of Ephraim and Manasseh,[24] the church fathers saw this as a promise of spiritual strength rather than temporal power. According to patristic sources, the glory of Joseph and his descendants was to be as the glory of Christ, and because Christ was in their glory or countenance, they would (on behalf of Christ) be capable of moving thousands toward Zion and eventually toward the Savior.

Tertullian of Carthage saw a clear reference to Jesus's Crucifixion in the blessing Jacob pronounced upon Joseph. Tertullian wrote:

> For Joseph is withal blest by his father after this form: "His glory (is that) of a bull; his horns, the horns of an unicorn; on them shall he toss nations alike unto the very extremity of the earth." Of course no one-horned rhinoceros was there pointed to, nor any two-horned minotaur. But Christ was therein signified:

"bull," by reason of each of His two characters,—to some fierce, as Judge; to others gentle, as Saviour; whose "horns" were to be the extremities of the *cross*. For even in a ship's yard—which is part of a *cross*—this is the name by which the extremities are called; while the central pole of the mast is a "unicorn." By this power, in fact, of the cross, and in this manner horned, He does now, on the one hand, "toss" universal nations through *faith*, wafting them away from earth to heaven; and will one day, on the other, "toss" them through *judgment*, casting them down from heaven to earth.[25]

Tertullian saw Jacob's choice of words to his chosen son, Joseph, as prophetic rather than coincidental. It was his belief that Jacob was conveying to Joseph—either knowingly or under the influence of the Holy Spirit—the promise that he and his descendants would serve the world as powerful reminders and examples of Christ. Their lives of sacrifice and service would provoke conversion and change in the lives of those to whom they bore witness.

DANIEL'S PROPHECY

Latter-day Saints are wont to quote a passage from the second chapter of Daniel as a foreshadowing of the Restoration of the fullness of the gospel of Jesus Christ.[26] The germane verse reads, "Thou sawest till that a stone was cut out without hands, which smote the image upon his feet that were of iron and clay, and brake them to pieces" (Daniel 2:34).[27]

While early Christian interpretations of this verse are not necessarily contradictory with Latter-day Saint views, patristic sources do tend to put a more Christocentric spin on the passage than do most Latter-day Saint exegetes. For example, Augustine interpreted Daniel's prophecy as follows:

The prophet [Daniel] wishes that by the mountain should be understood the Jewish kingdom. But the kingdom of the Jews had not filled the whole face of the earth. The stone was cut out from thence, because from thence was the Lord born on His advent among men. And wherefore without hands? Because without the cooperation of [a mortal] man did the Virgin [Mary] bear Christ. Now then was that stone cut out without hands before the eyes of the Jews; but it was humble. Not without reason; because not yet had the stone increased and filled the whole earth: that He showed in His kingdom, which is the Church, with which He has filled the whole face of the earth. Because then it had not yet increased, they stumbled at Him as at a stone. . . . At first they fell upon Him lowly: as the lofty One He shall come upon them; but that He may grind them to powder when He comes in His exaltation, He first broke them in His lowliness. They stumbled at Him, and were broken; they were not ground, but broken: He will come exalted and will grind them.[28]

Augustine's fourth-century interpretation of Daniel is curious, though not unique when compared with the writings of other church fathers.

Like Augustine, Irenaeus saw Daniel's prophecy as pertaining to Christ and his manner of birth. He wrote: "Daniel, foreseeing His advent, said that a stone, cut out without hands, came into this world. For this is what 'without hands' means, that His coming into this world was not by the operation of human hands, that is, of those men who are accustomed to stone-cutting; that is, Joseph taking no part with regard to it, but Mary alone co-operating with the pre-arranged 'plan.' For this stone from the earth derives existence from . . . God. . . . So, then, we understand that His advent in human nature was not by the will of a man, but by the will of God."[29]

Similarly, Jerome wrote, "He [Christ] is foretold to be 'a stone cut out of the mountain without hands,' a figure by which the prophet [Daniel] signifies that He is to be born . . . of a virgin."[30] Thus the fathers of the church commonly saw Daniel's prophecy as a reference to the virgin birth rather than the Restoration of the gospel.[31]

Moses's Outstretched Arms

In the seventeenth chapter of the book of Exodus is recorded the famed story of Joshua's fight against the Amalekites. The salient portion of the account reads as follows:

The Amalekites came and attacked the Israelites at Rephidim. Moses said to Joshua, "Choose some of our men and go out to fight the Amalekites. Tomorrow I will stand on top of the hill with the staff of God in my hands."

So Joshua fought the Amalekites as Moses had ordered, and Moses, Aaron and Hur went to the top of the hill. As long as Moses held up his hands, the Israelites were winning, but whenever he lowered his hands, the Amalekites were winning. When Moses' hands grew tired, they took a stone and put it under him and he sat on it. Aaron and Hur held his hands up—one on one side, one on the other—so that his hands remained steady till sunset. So Joshua overcame the Amalekite army with the sword. (New International Version, Exodus 17:8–13)

Moses's outstretched or upraised arms—traditionally implying his communion with God on behalf of Joshua and his soldiers—appears to have given Israel's army confidence to fight against her enemies. Yet patristic sources see more in this episode than simple manifest faith in the power of prayer or, as Latter-day Saints traditionally read the passage, an obligation on the part of the Saints to uphold and sustain their prophets.[32] For example, Cyprian of Carthage (circa AD 200–258) interpreted this passage as follows: "In Exodus, when Moses, for the overthrow of Amalek, who bore the type of the devil, raised up his open hands in the sign . . . of the cross, and could not conquer his adversary unless when he had stedfastly persevered in the sign with hands continually lifted up."[33]

Archelaus (flourished circa AD 278), bishop of Carchar in Mesopotamia, drew a typological parallel between Moses and Christ. He wrote: "Moses . . . stretched forth his hands and fought against Amalek; and . . . the Lord Jesus, when we were assailed and were perishing by the violence of that erring spirit who works now in the just, stretched forth His hands upon the cross, and gave us salvation."[34]

In passing, Augustine noted the Christological typology:

There are, however, some who think themselves capable of being cleansed by their own righteousness, so as to contemplate God, and to dwell in God; whom their very pride itself stains above all others. For there is no sin to which the divine law is more opposed, and over which that proudest of spirits, who is a mediator to things below, but a barrier against things above, receives a greater right of mastery: unless either his secret snares be avoided by going another way, or if he rage openly by means of a sinful people (which Amalek, being interpreted, means), and forbid by fighting the passage to the land of promise, he be overcome by the cross of the Lord, which is prefigured by the holding out of the hands of Moses.[35]

Elsewhere, Augustine was more to the point when he penned, "Amalek's resistance [was] subdued by the sign of the Cross."[36]

John Chrysostom wrote the following regarding the symbolic message of this Exodus passage: "See how the type was 'given by Moses,' but the 'Truth came by Jesus Christ' (Exodus 17:12). Again, when the Amalekites warred in Mount Sinai, the hands of Moses were supported, being stayed up by Aaron and Hur standing on either side of him (Exodus 17:12); but when Christ came, He of Himself stretched forth His Hands upon the Cross. Hast thou observed how the type 'was given,' but 'the Truth came'?"[37]

Finally, one of the Cappadocian fathers, Gregory of Nazianzus (circa AD 329–90), noted, "Moses is to conquer him by stretching out his hands upon the mount, in order that the cross, thus typified and prefigured, may prevail."[38]

Though the common message in the episode is traditionally interpreted by Latter-day Saints to be our obligation to sustain the Lord's prophets as they align themselves with God's will, for early Christians the message was more Christocentric. They saw this narrative as teaching the importance of faith in the atoning sacrifice of the Lord Jesus Christ. For them, faith centered in that act—and in Christ's mediating role—made it possible to successfully conquer all of our enemies and overcome all of our trials.

CONCLUSION

President Boyd K. Packer is known to consistently ask a question at the conclusion of a talk, lesson, or presentation: "Therefore, what?"[39]—or, in the vernacular of our day, "So what?" In other words, what should the impact of what I have learned be on my life, mission, ministry, or stewardship? Elder Jeffrey R. Holland noted, "Sermons and exhortations [are of] no avail if the actual lives of [Christ's] disciples [do] not change."[40]

A number of questions might be asked regarding the way the early church read the Old Testament. Chief among those questions is this: *Is their reading of the Hebrew Bible a legitimate approach to scripture?* Not all will agree on how to answer this question. For example, one colleague of mine conveyed to me his feelings about how the church fathers read the Old Testament in these words: "Symbolism as a genre of biblical studies is not typically recognized as a genuine academic enterprise. Therefore, early Christian writers . . . have nothing of value to tell us about the Old Testament as a witness for Christ." While I do not agree with this colleague that the fathers of the church "have nothing of value to tell us about the Old Testament as a witness for Christ," I must nevertheless admit that I find some of their symbolic readings of certain passages to be fanciful at best. Thus, it is the opinion of this author that they sometimes have helpful insights, but their exegesis is, at other times, quite forced. Of course, we must remember that they did not have the advantage we enjoy of contemporary prophetic guidance. Thus, we acknowledge that they did their best with what they had. However, as already noted, Latter-day Saints must be cautious that they do not force a symbolic reading of scriptural passages when the original author did not intend such a reading.

I suppose it is somewhat ironic that while one of my colleagues indicated that he wholesale rejected the symbolic approach of the fathers, another colleague described his feelings to me in these words: "I was quite touched and humbled, when I first began to read the fathers of the church, to realize how Justin Martyr, as an example, was able to see and interpret types of Christ in even the most obscure references. I use the word 'humbled' because I, for one, don't think I read the scriptures with such a propensity to seek out the Savior in every word, and yet I would so like to learn to read scripture with an attitude akin to that of Justin."

Which of these two approaches is legitimate? The reader may form his or her own opinion. Perhaps neither is wrong, as each may have different needs from, or even agendas for, their reading of scripture. One commentary advised: "In reading any of the standard works of the Church it is well to ascertain the literal meaning of the passage read first, and the lesson it was intended to convey to those to whom it was first communicated. And then it might be well to ask, What lesson does it convey to my time and age? To my nation? My community? My family? Or to myself?"[41]

In the end, we cannot say (on behalf of God) whether the innately Christocentric reading of the Old Testament by those of the early church was correct or flawed. Some have argued strongly that it was eisegetical rather than exegetical. Yet in light of Nephi's declaration—"I did liken *all* scriptures unto us, that it might be for our profit and learning" (1 Nephi 19:23; emphasis added)—who is to say that the fathers were wrong in their approach, though unquestionably some were overzealous in their practice? As we noted at the beginning of this article, Nephi claimed that "*all things* . . . are the typifying" of Christ (2 Nephi 11:4; emphasis added), and Moses recorded that "*all* things are created and made to bear record" of the Messiah (Moses 6:63; emphasis added). One certainly must acknowledge that a Christocentric approach to the Old Testament, as attempted by many of the church fathers, finds strong support in such prophetic utterances. And, I suppose, one would be hard-pressed to make an argument that these scriptural declarations do not mean exactly what they say.

NOTES

1. Of this verse, Elder Jeffrey R. Holland noted, "Nephi testified that 'all things . . . are the typifying of [Christ].' The literary evidence of that is seen throughout the holy scriptures" (*Christ and the New Covenant: The Messianic Message of the Book of Mormon* [Salt Lake City: Deseret Book, 1997], 159).

2. Ada R. Habershon, *Study of the Types* (Grand Rapids, MI: Kregel Publications, 1974), 35.

3. John of Damascus, "Exposition of the Orthodox Faith," book IV, chapter XI, in *Nicene and Post-Nicene Fathers—Second Series*, ed. Philip Schaff and Henry Wace (Peabody, MA: Hendrickson Publishers, 2004), volume 9, part 2, 80–81; emphasis in the original.

4. Irenaeus, "Against Heresies," book 4, chapter 26, paragraph 1, in Alexander Roberts and James Donaldson, eds., *Ante-Nicene Fathers* (Peabody, MA: Hendrickson Publishers, 1994), 1:496.

5. See Augustine, "On the Spirit and the Letter," chapter 27, in Philip Schaff, ed., *Nicene and Post-Nicene Fathers—First Series* (Peabody, MA: Hendrickson Publishers, 2004), 5:95; see also Sidney Greidanus, *Preaching Christ from the Old Testament: A Contemporary Hermeneutical Method* (Grand Rapids, MI: Eerdmans, 1999), 100.

6. *Eisegesis* is reading into a scriptural text what one believes, regardless of context or the intent of the original author who penned the passage being interpreted. *Exegesis* is seeking to understand what the author who penned the scriptural text being interpreted intended, aside from the modern reader's particular preconceived

notions or beliefs. It is the attempt to let the text speak for itself rather than reading into the scriptural text what one already believes. Thanks to Alexander the Great's fourth-century BC conquering of the Persian Empire, the Egyptian "Alexandrian School," as it would become known, interpreted scripture allegorically. Following the Jewish thinker Philo, Christian Alexandrians (like Clement) held that scripture traditionally had a minimum of two levels of meaning: the literal meaning and the allegorical or symbolic meaning. Origin, Clement's successor, believed that scripture had three levels—the literal, the moral, and the spiritual. In the opinion of the Alexandrian School, only through the allegorical method could one ascertain the true hidden meaning that God had imbedded in the scriptures. In the eyes of its critics, one of the weaknesses of the approach of the Alexandrian School was that it tended to be arbitrary and subjective. What principle of exegesis guided or governed the Alexandrian interpretation of scripture? "Faith in Christ, in his person and in his work, is the key to scripture" (Robert M. Grant with David Tracy, *A Short History of the Interpretation of the Bible*, second ed., rev. and enlarged [Philadelphia: Fortress Press, 1984], 56). As would be expected, some criticized the Alexandrians for reading into the Bible Christian beliefs, thereby practicing eisegesis rather than exegesis. But Origin of Alexandria responded to the critics by arguing that the Alexandrian School was not reading these things into the Bible. Rather, God inspired the original writers of each biblical passage to include the higher or symbolic meaning in the texts they wrote (William Klein, Craig Blomberg, and Robert Hubbard, *Introduction to Biblical Interpretation* [Waco, TX: Word Publishing, 1993], 35; Grant with Tracy, *A Short History*, 66).

In response to the Alexandrian School and its approach, a new school of biblical exegesis developed, known as the Antiochene School (originating in Antioch, Syria). Initially it generally rejected the symbolic or allegorical approach to scripture, preferring instead to teach that scripture had one meaning—that which was conveyed by the grammar and words. Nothing was hidden behind the obvious literal meaning of the words. The Antiochene School's greatest interpreter, Theodore of Mopsuestia, argued that Christians were inappropriately reading the Old Testament through Christian lenses, per se. Thus, the Antiochene School rejected the allegorical approach to scripture, insisting that a passage's historical sense was what one should seek to understand. Having said that, over time the Antiochenes began to accept typology as a legitimately present form of scriptural symbolism, though they remained uncomfortable with an allegorical approach. So the Antiochene School was not *entirely* antisymbolism.

Today the Antiochene School's influence is more evident in contemporary Christian exegesis than is the Alexandrian School's. However, not all commentators feel that the triumph of the Antiochene approach was necessarily a victory for Christianity.

7. As to the overarching consistency among the fathers of the early church in interpreting the Old Testament in a Christological manner, one source notes, "While there were definite differences among the fathers regarding their understanding of the literal-historical sense of Scripture, as well as the typological and allegorical, there existed a general consensus that Scripture should be interpreted

christologically" (David S. Dockery, *Biblical Interpretation Then and Now: Contemporary Hermeneutics in the Light of the Early Church* [Grand Rapids, MI: Baker Book House, 1992], 157). One scholar noted that from the third through the sixteenth centuries, the symbolic (i.e., allegorical and typological) reading of the Old Testament was the primary approach used in Christianity (Greidanus, *Preaching Christ*, 70).

8. I have intentionally avoided some of the more common symbols Latter-day Saints would likely see as Christocentric, such as Abraham's sacrifice of Isaac or the Passover meal of Exodus chapter 12. Like Latter-day Saints, most early Christian fathers also saw these as symbolic of Jesus's Atonement. However, the focus of this paper will be on passages of scripture which many Christians would not recognize as having a Christocentric message.

9. See Aphrahat, "Select Demonstrations: Demonstration XXI—Of Persecution," vv. 9–20, in Schaff and Wace, *Nicene and Post-Nicene Fathers—Second Series*, 13:395–400. Aphrahat's list of typologically significant figures includes Joseph of Egypt, Moses, Joshua, Jephthah, David, Elijah, Elisha, Hezekiah, Josiah, Daniel, Hananiah, and Mordecai.

10. Habershon, *Study of the Types*, 43–44.

11. Augustine, *City of God*, book 22, chapter 17, in Schaff, ed., *Nicene and Post-Nicene Fathers—First Series*, 2:496.

12. Augustine, *City of God*, 22:17, in Andrew Louth, ed., *Ancient Christian Commentary on Scripture: Old Testament I—Genesis 1–11* (Downers Grove, IL: InterVarsity Press, 2001), 70.

13. Quodvultdeus, "Book of Promises and Predictions of God" 1:3, in Louth, ed., *Ancient Christian Commentary*, 71.

14. Jerome, "Homilies," 66, in Louth, ed., *Ancient Christian Commentary*, 70. One fifth century bishop wrote: "Since Eve had been created from the side of the sleeping Adam, . . . from the side of Christ hanging on the cross the church . . . must be created. In fact the church is 'the woman.'" See Quodvultdeus, "Book of Promises and Predictions of God" 1:3, in Louth, ed., *Ancient Christian Commentary*, 71.

15. Tertullian, "A Treatise on the Soul," in Roberts and Donaldson, eds., *Ante-Nicene Fathers*, 3:222.

16. Roger R. Keller, "Adam: As Understood by Four Men Who Shaped Western Christianity," in Joseph Fielding McConkie and Robert L. Millet, eds., *The Man Adam* (Salt Lake City: Bookcraft, 1990), 177.

17. Augustine, "On the Gospel of St. John," tractate 26:12, in Schaff, ed., *Nicene and Post-Nicene Fathers—First Series*, 7:172.

18. Augustine, "On the Gospel of St. John," tractate 28:9, in Schaff, ed., *Nicene and Post-Nicene Fathers—First Series*, 7:182.

19. Caesarius of Arles, "Sermon" 103:3, cited in Joseph T. Lienhard, ed., *Ancient Christian Commentary on Scripture: Exodus, Leviticus, Numbers, Deuteronomy* (Downers Grove, IL: InterVarsity Press, 2001), 239.

20. See John of Damascus, "Exposition of the Orthodox Faith," book IV, chapter XI, in Philip Schaff and Henry Wace, eds., *Nicene and Post-Nicene Fathers—Second Series*, 9:80–81.

21. John Chrysostom, "Homilies on Second Corinthians," Homily 11:18, in Schaff, ed., *Nicene and Post-Nicene Fathers—First Series*, 12:333.

22. This is not to say that Paul missed the point of the type or its relationship to the cross. The only point I wish to make here is that Paul did not highlight the cross-Atonement symbolism, whereas the church fathers traditionally did.

23. Habershon, *Study of the Types*, 43.

24. See, for example, J. A. Thompson, *Tyndale Old Testament Commentaries: Deuteronomy* (Downers Grove, IL: InterVarsity Press, 1974), 314; Ian Cairns, *International Theological Commentary: Deuteronomy—Word and Presence* (Grand Rapids, MI: Eerdmans, 1992), 298.

25. Tertullian, "An Answer to the Jews," in Roberts and Donaldson, *Ante-Nicene Fathers*, 3:165. Elsewhere, Tertullian made a similar comment, noting that "Joseph [of Egypt] . . . was a type of Christ. . . . He is blessed by his father in these words: 'His glory is that of a bullock; his horns are the horns of a unicorn; with them shall he push the nations to the very ends of the earth,'—he was not, of course, designated as a mere unicorn with its one horn, or a minotaur with two; but Christ was indicated in him—a bullock . . . whose horns were the extremities of His cross. For of the antenna, which is a part of a cross, the ends are called *horns*; while the midway stake of the whole frame is the *unicorn*. By this virtue, then, of His cross, and in this manner 'horned,' He is both now pushing all nations through faith, bearing them away from earth to heaven; and will then push them through judgment, casting them down from heaven to earth" ("Against Marcion," in Roberts and Donaldson, *Ante-Nicene Fathers*, 3:336). Justin Martyr's reading of this verse is almost identical to Tertullian's ("Dialogue with Trypho," in Roberts and Donaldson, *Ante-Nicene Fathers*, 1:245). Justin and Tertullian's symbolic approach to this Deuteronomic passage is somewhat challenged by the fact that the Hebrew does not read "unicorn," as the King James translates it. Rather, "wild ox" would be a more accurate rendering. Thus, the image of a singular unicorn horn rising up as the vertical sake of a cross is lost when the passage is accurately translated, and Justin and Tertullian's suggested meaning of the passage appears to be without support. On the other hand, the overarching message they draw from the imagery is that Joseph's descendants will act as representatives of Christ, pushing thousands towards Zion and her God. In this regard, though the symbolism of the cross is weak, the metaphor of an ox and a bullock using their horns (i.e., power) to move an object along a desired path (as a representation of what Joseph's descendants were called to do as representatives of their God) seems harmonious with the general intention of the passage.

26. While Latter-day Saints are not necessarily unique in their interpretation of most of the passages examined in this paper, this particular verse is an exception. Non-Latter-day Saint exegetes are far from united on the meaning of Daniel's words cited here. Latter-day Saints, on the other hand, consistently interpret Daniel 2:34 as having prophetic reference to the Restoration of the fulness of the gospel of Jesus Christ. For that reason I have chosen to highlight the seeming distinction between Latter-day Saint and early Christian readings of this verse.

27. Verse 45 of this same chapter reads, "Forasmuch as thou sawest that the stone was cut out of the mountain without hands, and that it brake in pieces the iron, the

brass, the clay, the silver, and the gold; the great God hath made known to the king what shall come to pass hereafter: and the dream is certain, and the interpretation thereof sure."

28. Augustine, "On The Gospel of St. John," tractate 4:4, in Schaff, *Nicene and Post-Nicene—First Series*, 7:26.

29. Irenaeus, "Against Heresies," book 3, chapter 21:7, in Roberts and Donaldson, *Ante-Nicene Fathers*, 1:453.

30. Jerome, "Letter 22:19," in Schaff and Wace, eds., *Nicene and Post-Nicene Fathers—Second Series*, 6:29.

31. The reader may wonder how these early Christian interpretations square with the traditional Latter-day Saint view that the "stone" is the restored gospel of Jesus Christ "rolling forth" to "consume" or convert the earth. See, for example, Bruce R. McConkie, *The Millennial Messiah* (Salt Lake City: Deseret Book, 1982), 130–31; Spencer W. Kimball, *Faith Precedes the Miracle* (Salt Lake City: Deseret Book, 1979), 293–94; Ezra Taft Benson, *Teachings of Ezra Taft Benson* (Salt Lake City: Bookcraft, 1998), 168; Neal A. Maxwell, *Things As They Really Are* (Salt Lake City: Deseret Book, 1978), 46. These two alternate interpretations are not as much at odds as one might think. First of all, note that though the early Christian church *did* fall into apostasy, the message that Jesus is the Christ *has* rolled forth consuming much of the earth—and continues to do so. Additionally, we must remember that the word "gospel" means literally "good news." The gospel of Jesus Christ is not only founded upon Christ, but Christ is himself the "good news" or "gospel" of which we testify to the world. And he is, after all, the "Stone of Israel." Thus, the two interpretations of Daniel's words are hardly contradictory. Though the emphasis may appear to be slightly different, the meaning is basically the same—particularly since the restored gospel is only the vehicle which brings us to Christ. Ultimately, however, Christ is the message, and it is Christ that must consume the world, entering into the hearts of all mankind (see Proverbs 2:10), causing every knee to bow and every tongue to confess that Jesus is the Christ (see Philippians 2:10–11).

32. See, for example, M. Russell Ballard, *Counseling with Our Councils: Learning to Minister Together in the Church and in the Family* (Salt Lake City: Deseret Book, 1997), 123; Harold B. Lee, *The Teachings of Harold B. Lee*, ed. Clyde J. Williams (Salt Lake City: Bookcraft, 1998), 536; Roy W. Doxey, *The Doctrine and Covenants Speaks* (Salt Lake City: Deseret Book, 1964), 2: 312–13; Brett P. Thomas, "The Weak Things of the World," in *The Heavens Are Open: The 1992 Sperry Symposium on the Doctrine and Covenants and Church History*, ed. Byron R. Merrill and others (Salt Lake City: Deseret Book, 1993), 310–11.

33. Cyprian, "The Treatises of Cyprian," treatise 11:8, in Roberts and Donaldson, eds., *Ante-Nicene Fathers*, 5:501.

34. Archelaus, "Disputation with Manes," in Roberts and Donaldson, eds., *Ante-Nicene Fathers*, 6:220.

35. Augustine, "On the Trinity," in Schaff, ed., *Nicene and Post-Nicene Fathers—First Series*, 3:79–80.

36. Augustine, "On the Psalms," Psalm 44:8, in Schaff, ed., *Nicene and Post-Nicene Fathers—First Series*, 8:142.

37. John Chrysostom, "Homilies on St. John," Homily 14:4, in Schaff, ed., *Nicene and Post-Nicene Fathers—First Series*, 14:50.

38. Gregory of Nazianzus, "In Defense of His Flight to Pontus," Oration 2:88, in Schaff and Wace, eds., *Nicene and Post-Nicene Fathers—Second Series*, 7:222.

39. See Jeffrey R. Holland, "'Therefore, What?'" Twenty-fourth annual Church Educational System religious educators conference—CES conference on the New Testament, Provo, Utah, August 8, 2000, 4–5.

40. Holland, "'Therefore, What?'" 4–5.

41. George Reynolds and Janne M. Sjodahl, *Commentary on the Book of Mormon* (Salt Lake City: Deseret Book, 1955–61), 1:206.

INDEX

Boaz
  as redeemer, 200–203
  hesed and, 174–75, 201
  relationship with Ruth, 196–97
Brazen serpent, 91

Caesarius of Arles, 287
Cain, 21, 99, 133
Caph, 142, 147–48, 150 n. 14
Church fathers, 282–85, 293–94
Circumcision, 119, 193
Covenants
  curses and, 111–13, 131–37
  cutting, 110, 120
  extrabiblical, 111–12
  importance of, 109
  modern, 123
  new gospel, 122–23
  reverse effects of curses, 132–37, 150 n. 17
Cowdery, Oliver, 91
Creation, the, 4, 48, 96, 256–57
Cyprian of Carthage, 291

Dalton, Elaine S., 228
Daniel, 289–90
Dathan, 223
David, 40, 173–74, 263
Day of Atonement, 74, 78, 102
Debts, 191–92
DeFiguierido, Bryce, 14
Delilah, 25
Dew, Sheri L., 35
Diblaim, 235, 237

Edwards, Jeroldeen, 32
Egypt, 53–60
Egyptian mummies, 7
Eisegesis, 52, 294–95 n. 6
Eisodus, the, 53
Eli, 39
Elias, 28
Elihu, 259
Elijah, 26, 259–60
Elimelech, 194, 202
Elisha, 41, 260
Elkanah, 38–39
Endowment, 103
Enoch, 5–7, 230
Esarhaddon, 112
Esau, 24
Eve, 4–5, 20, 35, 102, 132

Exegesis, 52, 285, 293–94, 294–95 n. 6
Exodus, the, 53, 62, 160–61
Eyring, Henry B., 20
Ezekiel, 90, 259
Ezra, 25

Fall, the, 4, 21, 48, 132–33
Famine, 149 n. 6, 194
Faust, James E., 228, 230
Flood, the, 23
Foreigners, caring for, 192–93

Garment, 103
Gehazi, 41
Gethsemane, 216
Gideon, 260
Gleaning, 189
God
  man's potential to become like, 132, 228, 230–31
  performs hesed, 171, 176–78, 193–94
  role of, in motherhood, 38
Gō'el, 192, 196
Gold plates, 3
Gomer, 235, 237, 241
Gospel of Abraham, 28
Gregory of Nazianzus, 292

Hagar, 155–59
Handel, Georg Frideric, 12
Hands, 141–43
Hannah, 38, 223
Haqqah, 147
Hart, Charles H., 41
Hesed
  meaning of, 170, 181–82, 183 n. 2
  remembering as, 179–81
  truth and, 178–80
Hezekiah, 95, 97, 161, 174
Hinckley, Gordon B., 46 n. 16, 230
Holiness, 221–22
Holiness (*qōdeš*), 225–26
Holiness to the Lord, 226, 230
Holland, Jeffrey R., 292
Holy (*qadōš*), 222–25
Holy Ghost. See Spirit, the
Hosea
  as prophet, 234
  children of, 237–38
  marriage of, 235–37

on knowledge, 89
on ordinances, 89, 130–31, 148
on sacrifice, 100
on Temples, 124, 227–28
on the New Testament, 3–4
on the Old Testament, viii, 3–4, 15
priesthood and, 26–28
Restoration and, 12, 15, 22
Smith, Joseph Fielding, 18, 20, 23
Sodom and Gomorrah, 157
Solomon, 25, 174
Soul, 89
Southern Kingdom (Judah), 95, 234, 239
Sperry, Sidney B., 236
Spirit, the (Holy Ghost)
anointing role of, 257–58
creating role of, 256–57
empowering role of, 89, 258–61
gifts of, 261–63
references to, in the scriptures, 59–60,
250–55, 266–76
Spirit of prophecy, 263–64

Tabernacle-Temple, 116
Talmage, James E., 51, 216

Taylor, John, 18
Temple, 93, 139, 227–30
qualifications to enter, 103–5
Terah, 9
Tertullian of Carthage, 286, 288–89
Threshing, 198
Trespass offering, 77, 84 n. 21
Truth, 178–80

Urim and Thummim, 3

Washings and anointings, 100
Wenham, Gordon J., 70, 73, 75
Woodruff, Wilford, 21

Yom Kippur. *See* Day of Atonement
Young, Brigham, viii, 15, 18–19

Zedekiah, 117–19
Zenock, book of, 48
Zenos, book of, 48
Zilpah, 22
Zimri-Lim, 111
Zion, 6–7, 230, 247 n. 25